ISBN 978-1-331-25770-7
PIBN 10165312

1 MONTH OF
FREE
READING

at

www.ForgottenBooks.com

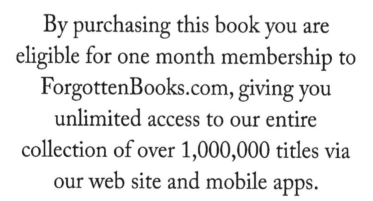

By purchasing this book you are eligible for one month membership to ForgottenBooks.com, giving you unlimited access to our entire collection of over 1,000,000 titles via our web site and mobile apps.

To claim your free month visit:

www.forgottenbooks.com/free165312

English
Français
Deutsche
Italiano
Español
Português

www.forgottenbooks.com

Mythology Photography **Fiction**
Fishing Christianity **Art** Cooking
Essays Buddhism Freemasonry
Medicine **Biology** Music **Ancient**
Egypt Evolution Carpentry Physics
Dance Geology **Mathematics** Fitness
Shakespeare **Folklore** Yoga Marketing
Confidence Immortality Biographies
Poetry **Psychology** Witchcraft
Electronics Chemistry History **Law**
Accounting **Philosophy** Anthropology
Alchemy Drama Quantum Mechanics
Atheism Sexual Health **Ancient History**
Entrepreneurship Languages Sport
Paleontology Needlework Islam
Metaphysics Investment Archaeology
Parenting Statistics Criminology
Motivational

NEW YORK
ANNOTATED CASES

SELECTED FROM THE

CURRENT DECISIONS OF THE NEW YORK COURTS.

WITH NOTES

By WAYLAND E. BENJAMIN.

CASES OF GENERAL INTEREST AND USEFULNESS WITH SPECIAL
REFERENCE TO POINTS OF

PLEADING, PRACTICE, EVIDENCE, ETC.,

AND A

TABLE OF CODE CITATIONS

IN OFFICIAL SERIES OF NEW YORK REPORTS ISSUED DURING THE
PERIOD COVERED BY THIS VOLUME.

VOL. IV.

NEW YORK:
THE DIOSSY LAW BOOK COMPANY,
Publishers.
1898.

INDEX TO SPECIAL NOTES

VOLUMES I TO IV (INCLUSIVE)

NEW YORK ANNOTATED CA

WAYLAND E. BENJAMIN, Editor.

[Each volume of these reports will contain a complete index to the Special Notes in all the
preceding volumes. See also, Table of Special Notes in each volume.]

Abatement and Revival, abatement by death after verdict, vol. iii, p. 310.

Abuse of Process, action for, vol. iv, p. 178.

Account Stated, action on, vol. ii, p. 42.

Actions, without precedent, vol. iv, p. 15.
for abuse of process, vol iv, p. 178.
consolidation of actions, vol. iv, p. 235.
separate actions for injuries to person and property from the same tort, vol. iv, p. 212.
suspension of right to sue by acceptance of note, vol. iv, p. 262.

Affidavits, on information and belief, vol. ii, p. 58.

Alimony, allowance to defend action, vol. i, p. 256.

Amendment, of summons as to designation of parties, vol. i, p. 84.
of complaint, on motion before trial, vol. i, p. 45.

Appeal, waiver of, vol. ii, p. 165.
What is appealable to the Court of Appeals under the new constitution, vol. iii, p. 370.
introduction of evidence on, vol. iv, p. 127.

Arrest, affidavit on information and belief, vol. ii, p. 58.
motion to vacate order of, on merits, vol. iii, p. 43.

Attachment, affidavit on information and belief, vol. ii, p. 58.
proof of cause of action to sustain, vol. ii, p. 200.
action in aid of, vol. iii, p. 50.
levy, on chose in action, vol. iv, p. 245.

Attorney and Client, substitution of attorneys, vol. i, p. 352.

Bailment, duty of pledgee to defend title and possession, vol. ii, p. 119.

Bills, Notes and Checks, suspension of right to sue by acceptance of note, etc., vol. iv, p. 262.

Blasting, trespass by, vol. iii, p. 308.

Calendar, preference of, vol. iv, p. 253.

Causes of Action, actions without precedent, vol. iv, p. 15.
separate actions for injuries to person and property from same tort, vol. iv, p. 212.
suspension of right to sue by acceptance of note, vol. iv, p. 262.

dismissal for neglect to prosecute, p. 316.
dismissal on the merits, vol. ii.

Constitutional Law, modern police power, vol. i, p. 604.

Contracts, remedy for fraud, vol. iv, p. 92.
time, when of the essence, vol.
term of employment under contract, p. 390.

Conversion, substitution of securities, vol. iv, p. 62.

Corporations, primary liability and stockholders, vol. iii, p.
protection of minority, vol. iii, p. 308.
statutory provision for the enforcement of claims for wages, iii, p. 7.

Costs on demurrer, vol. i, p. 272.
double, vol. ii, p. 102.
charging third persons, vol. i,
protection of attorney's lien, on vol. i, p. 352.

Creditor's Suit, to reach surplus iii, p. 16.

Death, proximate cause of death act, vol ii, p. 404.
abatement by death after verdict, 310.

Debtor and Creditor, creditor's surplus income, vol. iii, p. 16.

Defence, of former action p. iii, p. 215.

Deposition, physical examination before trial, vol. i, p. 171.

Dismissal of Complaint, for neglect prosecute, vol. i, p. 316.
on the merits, vol. ii, p. 240.

Divorce, allowance of alimony to i, p. 256.

Election of Remedies, suit for suit on contract, vol. iv, p. 93

Equity, relief against judgments fraud, vol. ii, p. 382.

Evidence, physical exhibits at trial, iv, p. 25.
introduction of evidence on ap

foreign corporations, jurisdiction of non-residents, vol. iv, p. 343.
service of summons on vol. ii, p. 73.

Former Action Pending, defense of, vol. iii, p. 215.

Former Adjudication, separate actions for injuries to person and property from the same tort, vol. iv, p. 212.

Fraud, annulment of marriage for, vol. i, p. 382.
equitable relief against judgments obtained by, vol. ii, p. 362.
following proceeds of personal property unlawfully acquired, vol. ii, p. 10.
remedy for, after suit on contract, vol. iv, p. 93.

Frauds, pleading statute of, vol. iv, p. 325.

Husband and Wife, tenancy by the entirety, vol. i, p. 130.

Insurance, fire, actions on Lloyds' policies, vol. iv, p. 367.

Interpleader, by order, vol. ii, p. 236.

Joinder of Actions, vol. iv, p. 205.

Judgment, equitable relief against judgment obtained by fraud, vol. ii, p. 362.

Jurisdiction, of non-residents, vol. iv, p. 343.

Jury, communications between judge and jury after retirement of jury, vol. i, p. 3.

Landlord and Tenant, summary proceeding by assignee, lessee, and grantee of lessor, vol. ii, p. 345.
constructive eviction, vol. iii, p. 75.

Limitations, suspension of statute by absence from State, vol. i, p. 212.
supplementary proceedings, vol. i, p. 34.

Marriage, annulment for fraud, vol. i, p. 382.

Master and Servant, servant's remedy for wrongful discharge, vol. i, p. 378.
term of employment under contract, vol. ii, p. 390.
statutory provisions for the protection and enforcement of claims for wages, etc., vol. iii, p. 7.

Motions and Orders, renewal of motion, vol. iv, p. 35.
reference of issues arising on motion, vol. iv, p. 140.

Municipal Corporations, liability for tortious acts of officers, agents, etc., vol. i, p. 366.

Names, statutes regulating business names, vol. i, p. 376.

Negligence, separate actions for injuries to person and property, vol. iv, p. 212.
proximate cause of death by wrongful act, vol. ii, p. 404.
trespass by blasting, vol. iii, p. 322.

Parent and Child, parent's liability for support of minor children, vol. i, p. 396.

Parties, substitution of sheriff's indemnitors, vol. iv, p. 62.
actions on Lloyds' policies, vol. iv, p. 367.
bringing in new defendants, vol. i, p. 217.
designation in summons; amendment, vol. i, p. 34.

Partnership, statutes regulating business names, vol. i, p. 376.

prosecution, vol. i, p. 116.

Police Power, modern doctrine

Preference, on the calendar, vo

Principal and Agent, munici tortious acts of officers, ag p. 366.

Reference, compulsory, in act for services, vol. ii, p. 272 of issues arising on motions,

Service, of summons on foreign vol. ii, p. 73.
statutes for the protection an of claims for wages, etc., vo

Sheriff, substitution of sheriff' vol. iv, p. 62.

Statute of Frauds, pleading p. 325.

Stipulations, parol, in pending p. 36.
affecting subsequent trials o vol. iii, p. 54.
limiting liability of telegra vol. iii, p. 135.

Summary Proceedings, by ass and grantee of lessor, vol.

Summons, amendment as to parties, vol. i, p. 34.
service on foreign corporation

Supplementary Proceedings, i, p. 34.
procedure where property i i, p. 152.

Taxes, taxable interest under t vol. iii, p. 105.
succession, against estate of vol. iii, p. 179.

Telegraph Companies, stipula liability, vol. iii, p. 135.

Tenancies, by the entirety, vol

Time, when of the essence of iv, p. 104.

Trespass, by blasting, vol. iii,

Trial, preference on the calen 203.
communications between ju after retirement of jury, vo
examination to frame compl 181.
physical examination of plai 171.
stipulation affecting subsequ proceedings, vol. iii, p. 54.
presumption from omission t ness, vol. iii, p. 32.
necessity of exception to arr vol. iii, p. 204.
physical exhibits at the trial,

Trusts, following proceeds of erty wrongfully acquired, v creditor's suit to reach su vol. iii, p. 152.

CONTENTS.

	Page
TABLE OF CASES REPORTED	v
TABLE OF CASES CITED	xiii
TABLE OF SPECIAL NOTES	xlvii
TABLE OF CODE CITATIONS	xlix
CASES REPORTED	1
INDEX OF CASES AND NOTES	403

[iii]

TABLE OF CASES REPORTED.

[References to Official Reports in Parentheses.]

A.

Page

Albany Hardware & Iron Co. v. Day (11 App. Div.
230).. 90
Allentown Foundry & M. Works v. Loretz (16 App.
Div. 172)... 294
Armstrong v. Coombs (15 App. Div. 246)............ 155

B.

Balaban, Sorensen v................................... 7.
Ballard, Hewitt v..................................... 228
Beinecke, Hartford Nat. Bank v........................ 219
Bidwell v. Sullivan (17 App. Div. 629)................ 161
Blackmer v. Greene (20 Misc. 532).................... 395
Bliven v. Robinson (152 N. Y. 333)................... 151
Boice, Drennan v...................................... 141
Bowman v. McClenahan (20 App. Div. 346).......... 388
Brainard, Lupean v.................................... 322
Brooklyn Heights R. R. Co., Rost v................... 19
Bryer v. Foerster (14 App. Div. 315)................. 120
Buchner, Lehmaier v................................... 82
Burton v. Linn (21 Misc. 266)........................ 275
Butler, Sewell v...................................... 305
Buttling, Leonard v................................... 59

C.

Page

Canary, Gillin v................................... 200
Cantoni, Forster v 375
Carr, Wessels v.. 223
Carvalho, Sheehan v............................... 32
Clapp. Sharp v.................................... 190
Clason v. Nassau Ferry Co. (20 Misc. 315)............ 166
Climax Cycle Co., Cohen v....... 332
Cohen v. Climax Cycle Co. (19 App. Div. 158)........ 332
Colwell, Williams v............................... 96
Coombs, Armstrong v.. 155
Cremore v. Huber (18 App. Div. 231)............... 317
Crocker, Smith v.................................. 77

D.

Day, Albany Hardware & Iron Co. v................. 90
Dewey, Stevens v.................................. 40
Dishaw v. Wadleigh (15 App. Div. 205) 170
Donnelly v. Pancoast (15 App. Div. 323)............. 237
Drennan v. Boice (19 Misc. 641).................... 141
Dubroff, Knox v................................... 251
Duhrkop v. White (13 App. Div. 293)............... 47
Durante, People v................................. 384
Dutton v. Smith (10 App. Div. 566)................. 25

E.

E. L. Goodsell Co., Tucker v...................... 86
Etienne, Manda v.................................. 65

F.

Foerster, Bryer v................................. 120
Forster v. Cantoni (19 App. Div. 306).............. 375

Page

Flandrow *v.* Hammond (13 App. Div. 325)............ 56
Furbush *v.* Nye (17 App. Div. 325)................. 241

G.

Gibbs, Halbert *v.*.................................. 232
Gillin *v.* Canary (19 Misc. 594)..................... 200
Goldman, Kujek *v.*................................. 11
Graham *v.* Lawyers' Title Ins. Co. (20 App. Div. 440) 379
Greene, Blackmar *v.*.......................... 395

H.

Halbert *v.* Gibbs (16 App. Div. 126)............... 232
Hammond, Flandrow *v.*........................... 56
Hartford Nat. Bank *v.* Beinecke (15 App. Div. 474)... 219
Heerdegen *v.* Loreck (17 App. Div. 515)........... 297
Hewitt *v.* Ballard (16 App. Div. 466).............. 228
Hill *v.* Schneider (13 App. Div. 299) 70
Hoefler *v.* Hoefler (12 App. Div. 84)............... 1
Huber, Cremore *v.*................................ 317
Humfreyville, Matter of (19 App. Div. 381 ; rev'd 154
    N. Y. 115)... 265

I.

Ivoroyd Mfg. Co., Welling *v.*.................... 145

J.

Jencks, Seventy-Third St. Building Co. *v.*........... 398

K.

Kellogg *v.* Mayor, etc., of New York (15 App. Div. 326) 182
Knapp *v.* Murphy (20 App. Div. 83)................. 313

Page

Knox *v*. Dubroff (17 App. Div. 290) 251
Kratzenstein *v*. Lehman (19 App. Div. 228)......... 335
Kujek *v*. Goldman (150 N. Y. 176)................... 11

L.

Lauer, Purcell *v*.. 129
Lawyers' Title Ins. Co., Graham *v*.................... 379
Lehmaier *v*. Buchner (14 App. Div. 263)............. 82
Lehman, Kratzenstein *v*............................... 335
Leonard *v*. Buttling (13 App. Div. 179)............. 59
Linn, Burton *v*....................................... 275
Livingston, Pollmann *v*............................... 214
Loreck, Heerdegen *v*................................... 297
Loretz, Allentown Foundry & M. Works *v*............ 294
Lupean *v*. Brainard (20 App. Div. 213)............. 322

M.

Maas *v*. McEntegart.................................... 370
McClenahan, Bowman *v*.................................. 388
McEntegart, Maas *v*................................... 370
Mackintosh, Martens-Turner Co. *v*.................... 279
Malone *v*. Third Avenue R. R. Co. (12 App. Div. 508).. 43
Manda *v*. Etienne (13 App. Div. 237).............. 65
Martens-Turner Co. *v*. Mackintosh (17 App. Div. 419). 279
Mayor, etc., of N. Y., Kellogg *v*.................... 182
Mayor, etc., of N. Y., Missano *v*................... 186
Merrill, Tillinghast *v*............................... 50
Metropolitan Telephone Co., Sterne *v*............... 328
Missano *v*. Mayor, etc., of N. Y. (17 App. Div. 536).... 186
Murphy, Knapp *v*...................................... 313
Musgrave, Woodward *v*................................ 136

N.

Nassau Ferry Co., Clason *v*........................... 166
National Mutual Ins. Co., People *v*.................. 340

Page

N. Y. Central, etc., R. R. Co., Peri v............... 288
Nye, Furbush v.. 241

P.

Palmer v. Van Santvoord (17 App. Div. 194 ; aff'd 153
    N. Y. 612)...................................... 249
Pancoast, Donnelly v.................................. 237
People v. Durante (19 App. Div. 292)............... 384
People v. National Mutual Ins. Co. (19 App. Div. 247). 340
Peri v. N. Y. Central, etc., R. R. Co. (152 N. Y. 521).. 288
Pollmann v. Livingston (17 App. Div. 528)........... 214
Purcell v. Lauer (14 App. Div. 33)................... 129

R.

Ralli v. White (21 Misc. 285)...................... 357
Raymond & Campbell Mfg. Co., Schreiber v.......... 270
Reilly v. Sicilian Asphalt Paving Co. (14 App. Div. 242) 209
Robinson, Bliven v................................... 151
Rose, Trepagnier & Bros. v.......................... 300
Rost v. Brooklyn Heights R. R. Co. (10 App. Div. 477) 19

S.

Schneider, Hill v.................................... 70
Schreiber v. Raymond & Campbell Mfg. Co. (18 App.
    Div. 158)...................................... 270
Seventy-third St. Building Co. v. Jencks (19 App. Div.
    314)... 398
Sewell v. Butler (16 App. Div. 77).................. 305
Sharp v. Clapp (15 App. Div. 445)................... 190
Sheehan v. Carvalho (12 App. Div. 430)............. 32
Sicilian Asphalt Paving Co., Reilly v........ 209
Smith v. Crocker (14 App. Div. 245)................. 77
Smith, Dutton v...................................... 25

Page

Sorensen v. Balaban (11 App. Div. 164)............. 7
Stafford, Walton v................................ 114
Sterne v. Metropolitan Telephone Co. (19 App. Div.
    316).. 328
Stevens v. Dewey (13 App. Div. 312)............;.... 40
Sullivan, Bidwell v............................... 161
Supervisors of Oneida County, Toole v............. 124

T.

Tamsen, Uhlfelder v.............................. 194
Taylor, Wyckoff v......... 102
Third Avenue R. R. Co., Malone v............ ... 43
Tillinghast v. Merrill (151 N. Y. 135).......... ...: 50
Toole v. Supervisors of Oneida County (13 App. Div.
    471).. 124
Trepagnier & Bros. v. Rose (18 App. Div. 393) 300
Tucker v. E. L. Goodsell Co. (14 App. Div. 89)........ 86

U.

Uhlfelder v. Tamsen (15 App. Div. 436)...... 194
U. S. Pipe Line Co., Matter of (16 App. Div. 188)..... 308

V.

Van Santvoord, Palmer v........................... 249

W.

Wadleigh, Dishaw v........ :..................... 170
Walton v. Stafford (14 App. Div. 310) 114
Welling v. Ivoroyd Mfg. Co. (15 App. Div. 116)...... 145
Wessels v. Carr (15 App. Div. 360)................. 223

                                              Page
White, Duhrkop v................................... 47
White, Ralli v................................ ... 357
Whitney, Matter of (153 N. Y. 259)................ 259
Williams v. Colwell (14 App. Div. 26)............... 96
Wise v. Wise Co.................................. 352
Woodward v. Musgrave (14 App. Div. 291).......... 136
Wyckoff v. Taylor (13 App. Div. 241)............... 102

TABLE OF CASES CITED.

A.

Page

Abram French Co. *v.* Shapiro, 11 Misc. 633 ; s. c., 33 Supp. 9 ;
66 St. R. 510..215, *n.*

Adams *v.* Arkenburgh, 106 N. Y. 615 ; rev'g 42 Hun, 278..... 191

—— *v.* Brown, 16 Ohio St. 75.............................. 362

—— *v.* Pennsylvania Bank, 35 Hun, 393................... .. 247

—— *v.* Roberts, 1 Civ. Pro. R. 204 ; s. c., 62 How. Pr. 253..219, *n.*

—— *v.* Sage, 28 N. Y. 103.................................223, *n.*

Albany City Bank *v.* Schermerhorn, 9 Paige, 372.............40, *n.*

Alberti *v.* N. Y. Lake Erie & W. R. R. Co., 118 N. Y. 77.... . 24

Aldinger *v.* Pugh, 57 Hun, 181 ; s. c., 19 Civ. Pro. R. 91....... 141

Alexander *v.* Bennett, 38 Super Ct. 505 ; 60 N. Y. 204......... 203

Alger *v.* Weston, 14 Johns. 231,...........................384, *n.*

Allen *v.* Crofoot, 5 Wend. 505.............................. 181

—— *v.* Gibbs, 12 Wend. 202............... 36

American Exchange Nat. Bank *v.* Voisin, 44 Hun, 85......... 283

Ames *v.* Dwoning, 1 Bradf. Supp. 326...................... 221

Andrews *v.* Appel, 22 Hun, 429...................398, *n.*, 399, *n.*

—— *v.* Davis, 5 St. R. 859................................ 112

—— *v.* Rowan, 28 How. Pr. 126...........................125, *n.*

Angle *v.* Kaufman, 4 Civ. Pro. R. 201....................... 256

Anonymous, 6 Cow. 41......................................

Antcliff *v.* June, 81 Mich. 477 ; s. c., 45 N. W. Rep. 1019...... 175

Anthony *v.* Wood, 96 N. Y. 180 ; s. c., Civ. Pro. R. 164....346, 348

Apsley *v.* Wood, 67 How. Pr. 406.......................... 39

Archer *v.* Sixth Ave. R. R. Co., 20 Super Ct. (J. & S.) 378..... 24

Armour *v.* Michigan Central R. R. Co., 65 N. Y. 111........... 362

Armstrong *v.* Percy, 5 Wend. 535............. ....127, *n.*, 374

Arrex *v.* Brodhead, 19 Hun, 269............. 179

Arthur *v.* Griswold, 55 N. Y. 400...........................225, *n.*

Ashley *v.* Dixon, 48 N. Y. 430............................. 16

Ashton *v.* City of Rochester, 133 N. Y. 187 ; s. c., 44 St. R. 526. 198

Page

Atkin v. Saxton, 77 N. Y. 195.................... 347
Attorney General v. Bradbury, 7 Ex. (W. H. & G.) 97...... 100, n.
Averell v. Barber, 44 St. R. 542 ; s. c., 18 Supp. 81........... 38
Avery v. N. Y. Central, etc., R. R. Co., 6 Supp. 547 ; s. c., 24
    St. R. 918.... ....220, n.

B.

Babcock v. Emerick, 64 How. Pr. 435...................... 112
—— v. Mayor, 56 Hun, 196; s. c., 24 Abb. N. C. 276 ; 31 St. R.
    110 ; 9 Supp. 368.................... 188
——v. Smith, 19 Supp. 817................................. 315
Bach v. Tuch, 126 N. Y. 53 .... 96, n.
Backus v. Kimball, 27 Abb. N. C. 361 ; s. c., 62 Hun, 122 ; 16
    Supp. 619 ; 41 St. R. 446. 347
Baham v. Bach, 13 La. Ann. 287......... 393
Bailey v. Burton, 8 Wend. 339.... 349
—— v. Murphy, 136 N. Y. 50; s. c., 49 St. R. 82.............. 293
Baird v. Mayor, 74 N. Y. 382................... 374
Baker v. Spencer, 47 N. Y. 562........................... 224, n.
Baldwin v. Weed, 17 Wend. 224........................ 180
Baltimore, etc., R. R. Co. v. Kemp, 61 Md. 74................ 135
Balter v. Ripp, 1 Abb. Ct. App. Div. 78 ; s. c., 3 Keyes, 210... 349
Bamberger v. Duden, 9 St. R. 686. .... 66, n.
Bangs v. Mosher, 23 Barb. 478.............................. 286
Bank v. Dakin, 51 N. Y. 519.............................. 346
Bank of Albion v. Burns, 46 N. Y. 170, 177.. 285
Bank of Attica v. Metropolitan Nat. Bank, 91 N. Y. 239....... 259
Bank of Batavia v. N. Y., Lake Erie & W. R. R. Co., 106 N. Y.
    199....... 362
Bank of Benson v. Hove, 45 Minn. 40 159
Bank of Charleston v. Emerich, 2 Sandf. 718.............. 127, n.
Bank of Havana v. Moore, 5 Hun, 624...................... 36
Bank of the Metropolis v. Lissner, 6 App. Div. 378........ 214, n.
Bank of Rondout v. Hamilton, 50 How. Pr. 116.............. 36
Bank of U. S. v. Strong, 9 Wend. 451............... .. 201, 208
Banks v. Potter, 21 How. Pr. 473............. 382
Barber v. Case, 12 How. Pr. 351............................ 141
Barrett v. Johnson, 77 Hun, 527.......................... 324
—— v. Third Ave. R. R. Co., 45 N. Y. 628................. 20
Bartlett v. Mudgett, 75 Hun, 297........................... 204
—— v. Musliner, 92 N. Y. 646............................ 259
Bates v. Plansky, 28 Hun, 112............................. 347

Page

Bancus *v.* Stover, 14 W. Dig. 313.......................... 267, *n.*

Bannatyne *v.* Florence Milling Co., 77 Hun, 289............. 324

Beamish *v.* Hoyt, 2 Robt. 307,............................. 40. *n.*

Beards *v.* Wheeler, 76 N. Y. 213........................... 29

Bebinger *v.* Sweet, 1 Abb. N. C. 263...................... 180

Beebe *v.* Dowd, 22 Barb. 255. 112

Beecher *v.* Stephens, 25 Minn. 146.................... 97, *n*, 101

Beers *v.* Shannon, 73 N. Y. 297........................... 383

Bellinger *v.* Ford, 14 Barb. 250.......................... 203

—— *v.* Martindale, 8 How. Pr. 113........................ 39

Belmont *v.* Erie Ry. Co., 52 Barb. 637.................... 36

Bendernagle *v.* Cocks, 19 Wend. 207...................... 213

Benedict *v.* Lynch, 1 Johns Ch. 370................ 106, *n.*, 111

Benkendorf *v.* Vincenz, 52 Mo. 441................. 98, *n.*, 101

Bennard *v.* Leo, 7 N. Y. Daily Reg. 1069, 1213............ 271 *n.*

Bennett *v.* Bennett, 116 N. Y. 584........................ 14

Benson *v.* Tilton, 41 N. Y. 619; aff'g 24 How. Pr. 494.... 112

Berg *v.* Parsons, 90 Hun, 267 ; s. c., 35 Supp. 780 ; .70 St, R.
    284... 71, *n.*

Berrien *v.* Southack, 7 Supp. 324.......................... 325

—— *v.* Westervelt, 12 Wend. 194.....................156. *n,*

Betz *v.* Buckel, 30 Abb. N. C. 278 ; s. c., 54 St. R. 324 ; 24
    Supp. 487..276, *n.*

Bevans *v.* United States, 13 Wall. 56... 55

Boardman *v.* Lake Shore & M. R. R. Co., 84 N. Y. 157........ 362

Board of Supervisors of Ulster Co. *v.* Brodhead, 44 How Pr.
    411..232. *n.*

Bode *v.* Maiberger, 12 Civ. Pro. R. 53...................... 39

Boecha *v.* Brown, 9 App. Div. 369.......................... 203

Bogert *v.* Perry, 17 Johns. 351.......................... 351

Bohnet *v.* Mayor, etc., of N. Y., 3 N. Y., Ann. Cas. 249 ; s. c.,
    150 N. Y. 279. ....196, *n.*

Bonnell *v.* Griswold, 80 N. Y. 128.......................237, *n.*

—— *v.* Henry, 13 How. Pr. 142............................395, *n.*

Booth *v.* Rome, W. & O. R. R. Co., 140 N. Y. 267............ 74

Boots *v.* Ferguson, 46 Hun, 129........ 95

Borst *v.* Corey, 15 N. Y. 509..... 203

Bovee *v.* King, 11 Hun, 250................................ 179

Bowden *v.* Parrish, 86 Va. 68............................. 158

Bowe *v.* Wilkins, 105 N. Y. 322 ; s. c., 7 St. R. 539.........226, *n.*

Bowery Savings Bank *v.* Richards, 3 Hun, 366..............271, *n.*

Bowling Green Sav. Bank *v.* Todd, 52 N. Y. 489.............. 236

Bowman *v.* Purtell, 1 Monthly L. Bull. 29................... 208

—— *v.* Sheldon, 5 Sandf. 657.............................. 39

Page

Boyd v. Schlesinger, 59 N. Y. 301...................... 112
Boyden v. United States, 13 Wall. 17...................... 55
Boyle v. Staten Island & S. B. L. Co., 87 Hun, 233 ; s. c., 33
    Supp. 836 ; 67 St. R. 424.............................. 208
Biggert v. Hicks, 18 Misc. 593 367
Bishop v. Agricultural Ins. Co., 130 N. Y. 488............... 362
—— v. Hendrick, 82 Hun, 323 ; aff'd 146 N. Y. 398........... 168
Bissell v. Saxton, 66 N. Y. 55............................51, n.
Blair, Matter of, 84 N. Y. 581 ; aff'd 152 N. Y. 645............ 260
Blair v. Wait, 69 N. Y. 113................................ 362
Blake v. Bolte, 1 N. Y. Ann. Cas. 78.......................41, n.
—— v. Wheeler, 18 Hun, 406 ; rev'd 80 N. Y. 128..........237, n.
Blank v. Blank, 107 N. Y. 91............................. 29
Bliss v. Molter, 58 How. Pr. 112...................... 156, n.
Bloom v. National, etc., Loan Co., 1 N. Y. Ann. Cas. 26....297, n.
Brackett v. Griswold, 112 N. Y. 454 ; s. c., 4 St. R. 219......225, n.
Bradley v. Glass, 20 App. Div. 200........................ 397
Brady v. McCrosson, 5 Redf. 431.......................... 264
Brand v. Hinchman, 68 Mich. 590 ; s. c., 36 N. W. 664........ 175
Brasher v. Cortlandt, 2 Johns. Ch. 505................ 275, n.
Brashier v. Gratz, 6 Wheat. 533........................ 110
Brewster v. Carnes, 103 N. Y. 556 ; s. c., 4 St. R. 264....156, n., 160
—— v. Stewart, 3 Wend. 44 ; 9 Id. 441...................... 208
Bridenbecker v. Lowell, 32 Barb. 9.................... 362
Briggs v. Gaunt, 4 Duer, 664........................ 208
Brinkerhoff v. Brinkerhoff, 8 Abb. N. C. 207...............220, n.
Bristor v. McBean, 1 App. Div. 217 ; s. c., 72 St. R. 658 ; 37
    Supp. 181...400, n.
Broisted v. Breslin, 5 St. R. 67 ; aff'd 105 N. Y. 682.......... 397
Bromley v. Williams, 32 Beav. 177 ; 32 L. J. Ch. 176.......... 365
Bronson v. Woolsey, 15 Johns. 46........................51, n.
Brooks v. Higby, 11 Hun, 235.........................127, n.
Brown v. A. B. C. Fence Co., 52 Hun, 151 ; s. c., 23 St. R. 415 ;
    5 Supp. 95... 250
—— v. Brockett, 55 How. Pr. 32........................314, n.
—— v. Brown, 1 Barb. Ch. 189.........................56, n.
—— v. Clark, 77 N. Y. 377................................ 261
—— v. Cook, 3 E. D. Smith, 123........................ 349
—— v. Feeter, 7 Wend. 301...........................179, 180
Browne v. Ritter, 26 N. F. 458.......................276, n.
Brownell v. Flagler, 5 Hill. 582........................ 17
Bruce v. Davenport, 1 Abb. Ct. App. Dec. 235............... 299
—— v. Platt, 80 N. Y. 379..........................237, n.
Brunsden v. Humphrey, 14 Q. B. Div. 141.................209, n.

Page

Brush *v.* Vandenberg, 1 Edw. Ch. 21...................... 110
Bryan *v.* Smith, 13 Daly, 331.......................... 350
Buess *v.* Koch, 10 Hun, 299............................ 112
Buffalo L. Oil Co. *v.* Everest, 30 Hun, 586................... 16
Buffum *v.* Forster, 77 Hun, 27......................125, *n.*
Bullymore *v.* Cooper, 46 N. Y. 236.................... 179
Bumpus *v.* Bumpus, 79 Hun, 526. ....380, *n.*
Burdick *v.* Freeman, 120 N. Y. 420..........78, *n.*, 244, 246
—— *v.* McVauner, 2 Denio, 170...................... 351
Burdin *v.* Williamson, 5 Hun, 560...................142, *n.*
Burgett *v.* Fancher, 35 Hun, 647............124, *n.*, 125, *n.*
Burnett *v.* Snyder, 41 Super Ct. (J. & S.) 342........... 141
Burns *v.* Delaware, L. & W. R. R. Co., 135 N. Y. 268 ; s. c., 48
    St. R. 106.. 150
Burt *v.* Place, 4 Wend. 591...................127, *n.*
Bush *v.* Abrahams, 2 Supp. 391 ; 4 Supp. 833.......... 206
Bushnell, Matter of, 19 Misc. 307.....................309, *n.*
Butler *v.* Kelsey, 15 Johns. 177.....................333, *n.*

C.

Camman *v.* N. Y. Ins. Co., Col. & Cai. 188................ 207
Camp Mfg. Co. *v.* Reamer. 14 App. Div. 408.............. 240
Campbell Printing Press & Mfg. Co. *v.* Lyddy, 1 Civ. Pro. R.
    364.. 208
Cantine *v.* Clark, 41 Barb. 629........................ 181
Cantor *v.* Grant, 23 Abb. N. C. 424 ; s. c., 10 Supp. 223...... 65
Carnrick *v.* Myers, 14 Barb. 9........................ 181
Caro *v.* Metropolitan El. R. R. Co., 2 Civ. Pro. R. 371......229, *n.*
Carpenter *v.* Stilwell, 11 N. Y. 73.................... 362
Carrigan *v.* Washburn, 14 Civ. Pro. R. 350............. 315
Carroll *v.* Cone, 40 Barb. 220 ; aff'd 41 N. Y. 216.......... 349
Carter *v.* Beckwith, 128 N. Y. 312.....................27, *n.*
—— *v.* Bowe, 47 Hun, 628............................ 64
—— *v.* Sulley, 28 Abb. N. C. 130 ; s. c., 19 Supp. 244...205, 207, 208
Carter, Rice & Co. *v.* Howard, 17 Misc. 381............ 144
Cary *v.* Western Union Telegraph Co., 20 Abb. N. C. 336..... 325
—— *v.* White, 52 N. Y. 138, 139.......282, 283, 285, 286, 287
Case *v.* Phoenix Bridge Co., 134 N. Y. 78............ 113
Cassidy *v.* Boyland, 15 Civ. Pro. R. 520 ; s. c., 3 Supp. 258. 190, *n.*
Catlin *v.* Adirondack Co., 20 Hun, 19.................314, *n.*
—— *v.* Grissler, 57 N. Y. 363........................ 128
Cavanagh *v.* Oceanic S. S. Co., 9 Supp. 198 ; s. c., 30 St. R.
    532...................................... 220, *n.*

Page

Caylus v. N. Y., Kingston & S. R. R. Co., 76 N. Y. 609...... 92,94

Cazet v. Hubbell, 36 N. Y. 680............................. 277

Central West. Co. v. N. Y. City & N. R. R. Co., 110 N. Y. 250
     s. c., 18 St. R. 30 ; rev'g 47 Hun, 587 ; s. c., 15 St. R. 17
                                                      354,355

Chamberlain v. Dumville, 21 Supp. 827 ; s. c., 50 St. R. 356... 38

—— v. Lindsay, 1 Hun, 236... 20

Champlin v. Johnson, 39 Barb. 606.......................... 349

Chanler v. Hoag, 2 Hun, 613 ; aff'd 63 N. Y. 624... ....537, n.

Chapman v. Forbes, 123 N. Y. 532 ; s. c., 34 St. R. 351........ 198

—— v. McCormick, 86 N. Y. 479.................43, n., 44, n., 46

Chappel v. Chappel, 12 N. Y. 215..........................395 n.

Chautauqua County Bank v. Risley, 19 N. Y. 369......120, n., 122

Cheever v. Schall, 87 Hun, 32 324

Chemung Canal Bank v. Judson, 8 N. Y. 254...............371, n.

Christman v. Thatcher, 48 Hun, 446.......................195, n.

City Bank of Boone v. Radtke, 87 Iowa, 363...... 158

City National Bank v. National Park Bank, 62 How. Pr. 495... 258

Claffin v. Ostrom, 54 N. Y. 581.. 285

Claflin & Co. v. Hamlin, 62 How. Pr. 284................... 296

Clark v. Dillon, 97 N. Y. 370..............................226, n.

Clay v. Clay, 21 Hun, 609..................................196, n.

Clearwater v. Brill, 4 Hun, 728............................. 179

Clements v. Gerow, 1 Keyes, 297..........................395, n.

Closson v. Staples, 42 Vt. 217............................. 177

Clute v. Jones, 28 N. Y. 280............................... 110

Cobb v. Knapp, 71 N. Y. 348............................... 145

Coffin v. Tracy, Col. & Cai. 470 ; s. c., 3 Cai. 129........204, 370, n.

Cohen, Matter of, 1 Tuck. 286.............................. 265

Coit v. Campbell, 82 N. Y. 509 ; aff'g 20 Hun, 50............376, n.

Colby v. Osgood, 29 Barb. 339.............................400, n.

Cole v. Sackett, 1 Hill, 516................................ 284

—— v. Tyler, 65 N. Y. 73..................................120, n.

Collier v. Whipple, 13 Wend. 232..........................276, n.

Collins v. Hydorn, 135 N. Y. 320..........................380, n.

Colt v. Davis, 50 Hun, 366; s. c., 3 Supp. 354 ; 16 Civ. Pro. R.
     180 ; 20 St. R. 309.................................208, 209

Columbian Ins Co., Matter of, 3 Abb. Ct. App. Dec. 239...352, 354,
                                                  355

Columbus, H. V. & T. R. R. Co. v. Ellis, 25 Abb. N. C. 150
                                          220, n.

Comboy v. Jennings, 16 s. c., 622........................ 264

Commonwealth v. Comly, 3 Penn. 372........................ 55

Concklin v. Taylor, 68 N. Y. 221...........................48, n.

Pag:

Conner *v.* Webber, 12 Hun, 580............................ 346
Conrow *v.* Little, 115 N. Y. 387 ; rev'g 41 Hun, 395........... 95
Continental Steamship Co. *v.* Clark, 7 Civ. Pro. R. 183....... 141
Converse *v.* Sickles, 2 N. Y. Ann. Cas. 16..................26, *n.*
Conway, Matter of, 124 N. Y. 455 ; s. c., 36 St. R. 486 ; rev'g 58
 Hun, 16.. ....260, 262
Cook *v.* Metropolitan Bank, 5 Sandf. 665.................... 207
Cooper *v.* Weed, 2 How. Pr. 40............................ 207
Corbit *v.* Nicoll, 12 Civ. Pro. R. 235 ; s. c., 9 St. R. 525.......66, *n.*
Corley *v.* N. Y. & Harlem R. R. Co., 12 App. Div. 409........ 25
Cormier *v.* Hawkins, 69 N. Y. 188.........................93, *n.*
Corn *v.* Tamsen, 16 Misc. 670 ; s. c., 25 Civ. Pro. R. 129 ; 39
 Supp. 129..63, 64
Cornell *v.* Roach, 101 N. Y. 373.........................237, *n.*
Corrigan *v.* Coney Island Jockey Club, 27 Abb. N. C. 294 ;
 rev'd 48 St. R. 582 ; s. c., 20 Supp. 437.............. ... 17
Coster *v.* Greenpoint Ferry Co., 5 Civ. Pro. R. 146 ; 98 N. Y.
 660.. 292
Cox *v.* Mitchell, 7 C. B. (N. S.) 55...........................77, *n.*
Coxe *v.* State, 144 N. Y. 396 ; s. c,, 63 St. R. 642............. 202
Countryman *v.* Norton, 21 Hun, 17......................... 299
County Commrs. *v.* Duckett, 20 Md. 468.................... 6
Cousinery *v.* Pearsall, 8 J. & S., 113...................... 129
Craig *v.* Town of Andes, 93 N. Y. 405...................... 204
Crane, Matter of, 1 N. Y. Ann. Cas. 148....................41, *n.*
—— *v.* Kolhler, 6 Abb. Pr. 328, *n*............................ 208
—— *v.* Powell, 19 Supp. 220 ; aff'd 139 N. Y. 379...324,325,326. 327
Crawford *v.* Colliers, 45 Barb. 269................ 361
Crippen *v.* Heermance, 9 Paige Ch. 211....................106, *n.*
Critten *v.* Vredenburgh, 4 App. Div. 216 ; aff'd 151 N. Y. 536.. 396
Crocker *v.* Crocker, 1 Sheld. 274. :...... 39
Crossman *v.* Universal Rubber Co., 127 N. Y. 35 ; 131 N. Y.
 636.. 95
Cunard Co. *v.* Voorhis, 104 N. Y. 525...................... 204
Cunningham *v.* Hatch, 3 Misc. 101 ; s. c., 30 Abb. N. C. 31 ; 22
 Supp. 707..271, *n.*
Curry *v.* City of Buffalo, 135 N. Y. 366; s. c., 48 St. R. 482
 182, *n.*, 183, *n.*, 185,188
Curry *v.* Wiborn, 12 App. Div. 1.......... ....190, *n.*, 192
Curtin *v.* Western Union Tel. Co., 3 N. Y. Ann. Cas. 286...... 15
Curtis *v.* Aspinwall, 114 Mass. 187........................ 393
Cythe *v.* La Fontain, 51 Barb. 192......................... 111

D.

Page

Dampton *v.* Sympson, Cro. Eliz. 520......................... 18
David Mayer Brewing Co. *v.* Rizzo, 13 Misc. 336............ 384
Davidsburgh *v.* Knickerbocker Life Ins. Co., 90 N. Y. 526
               81, 204, 247
Davidson *v.* Associates of the Jersey Co., 71 N. Y. 333........ 111
Day *v.* Hunt, 112 N. Y. 191.............................110, 112
—— *v.* Town of New Lots, 107 N. Y. 148.. 128
De Bost *v.* Albert Palmer Co., 35 Hun, 386.................44, *n.*
Decker *v.* Decker, 108 N. Y. 128......................... 230
De Groot *v.* Jay, 30 Barb. 483.........................294 *n.*
Delaney *v.* Miller, 1 N. Y. Ann. Cas. 266.................233, *n.*
Delaware *v.* Ensign, 21 Barb. 85.........................395, *n.*
Delevan *v.* Duncan, 4 Hun, 29......................... 112
Delie *v.* Chicago, etc., R. R. Co., 51 Wis. 400................ 135
Demarest *v.* Darg, 32 N. Y. 281........................ 28
Demelt *v.* Leonard, 19 How. Pr. 140 ; s. c., 11 Abb. Pr. 252.... 141
Dempsey *v.* Baldwin, 15 Misc. 455 ; s. c., 37 Supp. 28.......215, *n.*
Dennett *v.* Taylor, 5 Redf. 561........................... 264
Dennerlein *v.* Dennerlein, 111 N. Y. 578...................389, *n.*
Denton *v.* Livingston, 9 Johns. 96... 349
—— *v.* Noyes, 6 Johns. 297.............................25, *n.*
De Witt *v.* Buchanan, 54 Barb. 31...............78, *n.*, 245, 247
De Wolfe *v.* Abraham, 3 N. Y. Ann. Cas. 301 ; rev'g 6 App. Div.
  172.......................................206, 214
Dieter *v.* Fallon, 34 St. R. 680........................... 112
Dillon *v.* Masterson, 42 Super. Ct. (J. & S.) 176.............. 113
Dissosway, Matter of, 91 N. Y. 235......................... 268
Doe *v.* Roe, 1 Johns. Cas. 402...... 159
Doelfus *v.* Frosch, 5 Hill, 493............. 38
Dolbier *v.* Stout, 139 N. Y. 486; s. c., 54 St. R. 801 ; rev'g 61
  Super. Ct. 172..............................294, *n.*, 295
Doolin *v.* Ward, 6 Johns. 194.... ....389, *n.*
Doolittle *v.* Lewis, 7 Johns. Ch. 45.................. 58
Doubleday *v.* Kress, 60 Barb. 181.......................
Dougherty *v.* Metropolitan Life Ins. Co., 3 App. Div. 317..... 150
Douglass *v.* Ireland, 37 N. Y. 100.....................380, *n.*
Douglass *v.* Phenix Ins. Co., 138 N. Y. 209...................347
Dovale *v.* Ackerman, 7 Supp. 833 ; s. c., 27 St. R. 895........ 141
Dreher *v.* Connolly, 16 Daly, 106 ; s. c., 30 St. R. 674......... 363
Dresser *v.* Brooks, 3 Barb. 429.........................127, *n.*
Dudley *v.* Mayhew, 3 N. Y. 9............................. 312

Page

Duffy v. Dawson, 2 Misc. 401.......................... 348

—— v. O'Donovan, 46 N. Y. 223........................... 112

Dumond v. Sharts, 2 Paige, 182........................... 111

Dunford v. Weaver, 84 N. Y. 445 128

Dunham v. Townshend, 118 N. Y. 281 ; aff'g 43 Hun, 580..... 129

—— v. Waterman, 17 N. Y. 9..............................395, n.

Dunn v. Mason, 7 Hill, 154................................ 208

—— v. Meserole, 5 Daly, 434 ··· 39

—— v. Steubing, 120 N. Y. 232............................ 362

Dunning v. Bank of Auburn, 19 Wend. 23................... 208

Dupignac v. Van Buskirk, 44 Hun, 45...................... 209

Dusseldorf v. Redlich, 16 Hun, 624........................66, n.

Durkee v. National Bank of Fort Edward, 36 Hun, 566....... 283

Dwight v. St. John, 25 N. Y. 203.............28, 29, 30, 140, 141

Dyer v. Tilton, 25 Vt. 315................................ 93

Dyett v. Hyman, 129 N. Y. 351......................... . 61, 63

E.

Eagan v. Lynch, 49 Super Ct. (J. & S.)...................271, n.

Earl v. Hart, 20 Hun, 75......................... ......195, n., 197

East River Gaslight Co. v. Donnelly, 93 N. Y. 557............ 18

Easterly v. Barber, 65 N. Y. 252...........................237, n.

Easton v. Pickersgill, 75 N. Y. 599............. ....27, n.

Ebenreiter v. Dahlman, 19 Misc. 9......................... 63

Eckerson v. Archer, 10 App. Div. 344.....................298, n.

Eden v. Rathbone, 3 Cow. 296.............................333, n.

Edgerton v. Peckham, 11 Paige Ch. 352..............107, 111, 112

Ehrgott v. Mayor, etc., of N. Y., 96 N. Y. 264................ 134

Einstein v. Climax Cycle Co., 3 N. Y. Ann. Cas. 203........83, n.

Eldridge v. Chapman, 13 Abb. Pr. 68, n...................310, n.

Eleventh Ward Sav. Bank v. Hay, 8 Daly, 328 ; aff'd 73 N. Y.
  609... 208

Elfers v. Wooley, 110 N. Y. 294............................ 24

Elliott v. Brown, 2 Wend. 497............................. 321

Eppens v. McGrath, 3 Supp. 213........................... 283

Epstin v. Levenson, 79 Ga. 718........................... 201

Equitable Co-operative Foundry Co. v. Hersee, 103 N.Y. 25,.91, 94.

Erie Ry. Co. v. Ramsay, 57 Barb. 449.... 36

Ervin v. Oregon R. R. & N. Co., 28 Hun, 269.... 247

Esmond v. Kingsley, 3 Supp. 696 ; s. c., 19 St. R. 665........45, n.

Evangelical Lutheran St. John's O. H. v. Buffalo Hydraulic
  Assn., 64 N. Y. 561.................................. 351

Page

Everitt *v.* Park, 2 N. Y. Ann. Cas. 205.....................83, *n.*
Excelsior Steam Power Co. *v.* Cosmopolitan Pub. Co., 80 Hun,
    592......... 347

F.

Fairbanks *v.* Bloomfield, 5 Duer, 434....................... 349
Fake *v.* Whipple, 39 N. Y. 397...........................51, *n.*
Falconer *v.* Freeman, 4 Sandf. Ch. 565....................... 347
Farjeon *v.* Fogg, 16 Misc. 219..........................359, 367
Farmers' & M'fr's. Bank *v.* Tracy, 19 Wend. 23...........206, 208
Farnham *v.* Campbell, 10 Paige, 598.. ....40, *n.*
Farrell *v.* Hildreth, 38 Barb. 178...... :.............. 350
Farrelly *v.* Hubbard, 148 N. Y. 592........................ 315
Fellows *v.* Prentiss, 3 Denio, 512, 518....................285, 286
Fenlon *v.* Dempsey, 50 Hun, 131...........................167, *n.*
Ferguson *v.* Crawford, 70 N. Y. 253.................26, *n.*, 28, 30
—— *v.* Hubbell, 97 N. Y. 507............................71, *n.*
—— *v.* Neilson, 33 St. R. 814............................. 81.
Field *v.* Gibson, 20 Hun, 274...........................56, *n.*, 58
—— *v.* Parker, 4 Hun, 342................................ 179
Fielden *v.* Lahens, 2 Abb. Ct. App. Dec. 111................ 374
First Nat. Bank of Cooperstown *v.* Tamajo, 77 N. Y. 476...... 49
First Nat. Bank of Oxford *v.* Turner, 24 Supp. 793..........142, *n.*
First National Bank of Salem *v.* Davis, 88 Hun, 169 ; s. c., 35
    Supp. 532.. 346
Fischer *v.* Blank, 138 N. Y. 671, s. c., 53 St. R. 293........... 230
Fisher *v.* Hersey, 17 Hun, 370 ; 78 N. Y. 387..........388, *n.*, 394
—— *v.* Marvin, 47 Barb. 159................................ 284
Fleischmann *v.* Bennett, 79 N. Y. 579....................215, *n.*
Flushing Ave., Matter of, 98 N. Y. 445....................27, *n.*
Foerster *v.* Gallinger, 262 Hun, 439........................ 283
Foley *v.* Mayor, 1 App. Div. 586 ; s. c., 73 St. R. 187 ; 37 Supp.
    465...................................... :............... 188
—— *v.* Stone, 30 St. Rep. 834 ; s. c., 18 Civ. Pro. R. 190 ; aff'g
    15 Civ. Pro. R. 224, s. c., 3 Supp. 288.................211, *n.*
Foote *v.* Lathrop, 41 N. Y. 358.............................. 28
Fortman *v.* Rottier, 8 Ohio St. 548......................... 175
Foster *v.* Oldham, 4 Misc. 201. s. c., 53 St. R. 488 ; 23 Supp.
    1024.. 117
—— *v.* Persch, 68 N. Y. 400................................142, *n.*
Fowler *v.* Huber, 7 Robt. 52................................ 39
Fox *v.* Quinn, 12 Supp. 725................................. 258

Page

Frank *v.* Batten, 49 Hun, 91..................................... 348

Frear *v.* Sweet, 118 N. Y. 454................................... 374

Freligh *v.* Brink, 22 N. Y. 418.............................395, *n.*

Frisbie *v.* Averell, 87 Hun, 217............................216, *n.*

—— *v.* Larned, 21 Wend. 450, 452.............................. 284

Fromme *v.* Gray, 14 Misc. 592, 595 ; s. c., 2 N. Y. Ann. Cas.
    266 ; aff'd 148 N. Y. 695, 698....................274, 471, *n.*

Fullerton *v.* McLaughlin, 70 Hun, 568....................... 107

G.

Gale *v.* Archer, 42 Barb. 320.................................. 108

Galen *v.* Brown, 22 N. Y. 37.................................. 349

Gallagher *v.* McMullin, 7 App. Div. 321 ....44, *n.*

Galt *v.* Provident Sav. Bank, 18 Abb. N. C. 431.............. 247

Garbaczewski *v.* Third Ave. R. R. Co., 5 App. Div. 186....... 47

Gardner *v.* Clark, 21 N. Y. 399..............................190, *n.*

—— *v.* Thomas, 14 Johns. 134 ....78, *n.*, 244, 246

Garwood *v.* N. Y. Cent. R. R. Co., 19 W. Dig. 416 ; aff'd 116
    N. Y. 649..298, *n.*

Gedney, Matter of, 17 Misc. 500............................... 263

Gelhaar *v.* Ross, 1 Hilt. 117........................... 349

Gelstone *v.* Codwise, 1 Johns. Ch. 189....................... 230

Genet *v.* Davenport, 66 Barb. 412............................ 128

Gerding *v.* Anderson, 64 Ga. 304................. 201

German Exchange Bank *v.* Kroder, 14 Misc. 179 ; s. c., 35 Supp.
    380.. .. 36

Gerstein *v.* Fisher, 12 Misc. 211 ; s. c., 33 Supp. 1120 ; 67 St.
    R. 824..215, *n.*

Gilbs *v.* Nash, 4 Barb. 449.................................... 325

Giles *v.* Grover, 9 Bing. 130... 354

Gillespie *v.* Mulholland, 12 Misc. 44.. 141

Gillies *v.* Kruder, 1 Dem. 349..............................266, *n.*

Gillin *v.* Canary, 4 N. Y. Ann. Cas. 200 ; s. c., 19 Misc. 594..370, *n.*

Gilman, Matter of, 38 Barb. 364 ; s. c., Redf. 354...... 264

Ginna *v.* Second Ave. R. R. Co., 8 Hun, 494 ; aff'd 67 N. Y.
    596..130, *n.*

Gwalter *v.* N. Y. Seal Plush, etc., Co., 46 St. R. 137...........283

Gloucester Iron Works *v.* Board of Water Commrs., 10 Supp.
    168... 206

Goddard *v.* Stiles, 99 N. Y. 640.............................. 36

Goodhue *v.* Berrian, 2 Sandf. Ch. 630...................... 158

Goodsell *v.* Western Union Tel. Co., 109 N. Y. 151........... 230

Page

Goodwin *v.* Massachusetts Mut. Life Ins. Co., 73 N. Y. 480.... 113
Gould *v.* Cayuga Co. Nat. Bank, 86 N. Y. 81, 99 Id. 338 ....226, 228
Goulet *v.* Asseler, 22 N. Y. 225.............................. 349
Grace *v.* Mitchell, 31 Wis. 545.............................. 178
Graham *v.* Meyer, 99 N. Y. 611.....................,........224, *n.*
—— *v.* Negus, 8 Supp. 679; s. c., 55 Hun, 440; 29 St. R. 114.. 280
Grainger *v.* Hill, 4 Bing. N. C. 212......................... 175
Grannis & Hurd L. Co. *v.* Deeves, 72 Hun. 171; s. c., 55 St. R.
    674; 25 Supp. 375.. 113
Greathead *v.* Bromley, 7 T. R. 455........................... 36
Green *v.* Hudson River R. R. Co., 2 Abb. Ct. App. Dec. 277... 8
Greenby *v.* Wilcocks, 2 Johns 1........................... 399, *n.*
Greenleaf *v.* Brooklyn, Flatbush & C. I. R. R. Co., 102 N. Y.
.   96...333, *n.*
Gregory *v.* Thomas, 20 Wend. 17............................ 284
Griffin *v.* Borst, 4 Wend. 195..............................155, *n.*
—— *v.* Spencer, 6 Hill, 525................................ 351
Griswold *v.* Haven, 25 N. Y. 395........................... 362
Grocers' Bank *v.* Penfield, 7 Hun, 279; aff'd 69 N. Y. 504...... 283
Groesbeck *v.* Seeley, 13 Mich. 330 158
Grosvenor *v.* N. Y. Central R. R. Co., 39 N. Y. 34............ 362
Grow *v.* Gleason, 20 Supp. 590; s. c., St. R. 912............298, *n.*
Grunberg *v.* Grant, 3 Misc. 230 181
Guerineau *v.* Weil, 8 Misc. 94; s. c., 60 St. R. 158; 28 Supp.
    775 257
Guliano *v.* Whitenack, 1 N. Y. Ann. Cas. 75................233, *n.*
—— *v.* —— 1 N. Y. Ann. Cas. 75........................289, *n.*
Gulick *v.* Gulick, 33 Barb. 92............................56, *n.*
Gumb *v.* Twenty-third St. Ry. Co., 114 N. Y. 411............ 106
Gurney *v.* Atlantic & G. W. R. R. Co., 58 N. Y. 358........249, *n.*
Gutta Percha & R. M'fg. Co. *v.* Mayor, etc., of Houston, 108
    N. Y. 276... 244

H.

H——, Matter of, 93 N. Y. 381............................ 235
Haas *v.* Colton, 12 Misc. 308 ; s. c., 34 Supp. 35; 67 St. R. 836
    215, *n.*
—— *v.* Craighead, 19 Hun, 396...............194, *n.*, 196, *n.*, 197
Haebler *v.* Bernharth, 115 N. Y. 459........................ 89
Hagaman *v.* Jackson, 1 Wend. 502.......................... 351
Halbert *v.* Gibbs, 16 App. Div. 126; s. c., 45 Supp..113......289, *n.*
—— *v.* State, 22 Ind. 125................................. 55

Page

Hale *v.* Sweet, 40 N. Y. 97, 103.......................... 350

Hall *v.* Dean, 13 Johns. 105........................ ....399, *n.*

—— *v.* Emmons, 39 How. Pr. 187......................... 38

—— *v.* Fisher, 9 Barb. 17................................ 362

—— *v.* Richardson, 22 Hun, 444......................380, *n.*

—— *v.* Sampson, 35 N. Y. 274........................349, 350

—— *v.* U. S. Reflector Co., 21 W. Dig. 37.................. 128

Hallenbeck *v.* Whitaker, 17 Johns. 2.................... ..156, *n.*

Hamburger *v.* Baker, 35 Hun, 455......................... 346

Hamer *v.* Sidway, 124 N. Y. 538, 548....................324, 327

Hamill *v.* Gillespie, 48 N. Y. 556... 349

Hammers *v.* Dole, 61, 111, 307 158

Hammond *v.* Baker, 3 Sandf. 704.......................,. 296

Hankinson *v.* Page, 12 Civ. Pro. R. 279 ; s. c., 19 Abb. N. C.

274......................................303, 339

Hanley *v.* Crowe. 19 St. R. 828...........................229, *n.*

—— *v.* Foot, 19 Wend. 516............................ 284

Happy *v.* Mosher, 48 N. Y. 313.......................280, 285

Harding *v.* Elliott, 12 Misc. 521......................... 346

Harris *v.* Knickerbacker, 5 Wend. 638...................... 325

—— *v.* Treu, 2 N. Y. Ann. Cas. 380......................26, *n.*

—— *v.* Troup, 8 Paige, 423................................ 112

Harrison *v.* Gibbons, 77 N. Y. 58.........................395, *n.*

—— *v.* Miller, 2 Esp. 513 ; 7 T. R. 340, *n.*................... 365

—— *v.* Neher, 9 Hun, 127................................ 39

Hart *v.* Dubois, 20 Wend. 236............................ 179

Hartwell *v.* Gurney, 16 R. I. 78........................... 393

Hatch *v.* Cobb, 4 Johns. Ch. 559..........................106, *n.*

Hathaway *v.* Brayman, 42 N. Y. 322.....................349, 350

Haux *v.* Dry Dock Savings Inst., 150 N. Y. 581.............. 257

Hayden *v.* National Bank of State of N. Y., 130 N. Y. 146

301, *n.*, 348

Hayes *v.* Davidson, 98 N. Y. 19 ; rev'g 34 Hun, 243.......... 63

Hays *v.* Consolidated Gas Co., 60 St. R. 480................ 257

—— *v,* Midas, 104 N. Y. 602...............................91, 94

Hazard *v.* Harding, 63 How. Pr. 326....................... 179

Hazel *v.* Dunham, 1 Hall, 655. 393

Hebrew Free School Assn. *v.* Mayor, etc., of N. Y., 99 N. Y. 488. 128

Hein *v.* Davidson, 96 N. Y. 175.........................61, 62, *n.*

Hendrickson *v.* Winne, 3 How. Pr. 127..................... 122

Herbage *v.* City of Utica, 109 N. Y. 81 ; s. c., 14 St. R. 845 ; 14

Civ. Pro. R. 79...... 307

Herbst *v.* Vacuum Oil Co., 68 Hun, 222 ; s. c., 22 Supp. 807.298, *n.*

Hergman *v.* Dettleback, 11 How. Pr. 46.................... 181

Page

Herman v. Brookerhoff, 8 Watts, 240........................ 175
Hermance v. James, 32 How. Pr. 142...,................... 14
Hernandez v. Drake, 81, 111, 34 101
Hero Fruit Jar Co. v. Grant, 11 Supp. 28 ; s. c., 32 St. R. 209.. 65
Herring v. N. Y., Lake Erie & W. R. R. Co., 105 N. Y. 340...26, n.
Hesse v. Mackaye, 55 Hun, 365........................... 303
Hevenor, Matter of, 1 N. Y. Ann. Cas. 144 ; aff'g 70 Hun, 56
                                                    114, n.
Hewitt, Matter of, 91 N. Y. 261.................... .....260, 263
Hexamer v. Webb, 101 N. Y. 377........................ 75
Heyer v. Barger, Hoff. Ch. 1......................... 370, n.
Hickey v. Morrell, 102 N. Y. 454...................... 225, n.
Hicks v. Foster, 13 Barb. 663......................... 168
Higgins v. Delaware, L. & W. R. R. Co., 60 N. Y. 553......... 108
—— v. McConnell, 130 N. Y. 482; s. c., 42 St. R. 363...... 347, 751
Hill v. Beebe, 13 N. Y. 556........................... 284
—— v. Fowler, 6 Hill, 630............................ 203
Hiller v. Village of Sharon Springs, 28 Hun, 344............. 23
Hiscox v. N. Y. Staats Zeitung, 23 Civ. Pro. R. 87........... 208
Hitchcock v. Thompson, 6 Hun, 279 ; rev'g1 5 Abb. Pr. (N. S.)
    211 264
Hoag v. Weston, 10 Civ. Pro. R. 92.....................190, n.
Hobart v. Hobart, 86 N. Y. 636....................... .48, n.
Hoes v. Edison General E. Co., 150 N. Y. 87 ; s. c., 3 N. Y. Ann.
    Cas. 247.......................................371, n.
Hoffman v. Livingston, 1 Johns. Ch. 211.................. 39
—— v. Union Ferry Co., 68 N. Y. 386.................... 169
—— v. Van Nostrand, 14 Abb. Pr. 336..................232, n.
Hogans v. Carruth, 18 Fla. 587......................... 158
Holsman v. St John, 90 N. Y. 464..................... 378
Holyoke v. Adams, 59 N. Y. 233....................... 218
Homer v. Guardian Mut. Life Ins. Co., 67 N. Y. 478.. 113
Hoorman v. Climax Cycle Co., 3 N. Y. Ann. Cas. 201........83, n.
—— v. —— 9 App. Div. 579 ; aff'g 3 N. Y. Ann. Cas. 201,
                                                86, n., 88
Hoover v. Rochester Printing Co., 2 App. Div. 11 ; s. c., 37
    Supp. 419 ; 72 St. R. 717... 39
Hopkins v. Ensign, 122 N. Y. 144...................390, n.
Hopper, Matter of, 9 Misc. 171 ; s. c., 60 St. R. 638 ; 29 Supp.
    715 ; aff'd 145 N. Y. 605... ....271, n.
—— v. Ersler, 1 N. Y. Ann. Cas. 192..................289, n.
—— v. ——, 1 N. Y. Ann. Cas. 192..................233, n.
—— v. Hopper, 125 N. Y. 400 ; aff'g 53 Hun, 394 ; s. c., 25 St.
    R. 132 ; 6 Supp. 271 ; which rev'd 3 Supp. 640.......56, n., 58

Page

Hornby *v*. Gordon, 9 Bosw. 659 ....196, *n*.
Howell *v*. Mills, 53 N. Y. 332......................27 *n*., 389, *n*.
Howland *v*. Willett, 3 Sandf. 607............................ 349
Hoyt, Estate of, 12 Civ. Pro. R. 208.............. ....232, *n*.
Hubbard *v*. Copcutt, 9 Abb. Pr. (N. S.) 289.............. ... 230
—— *v*. Gurney, 64 N. Y. 547.. ....280, 283
Hubbel *v*. Von Schoening, 49 N. Y. 331.................... 112
—— *v*. Fowler, 1 Abb. Pr. (N. S.) 207..... ....219, *n*.
Hubble *v*. Wright, 23 Ind. 322............................. 158
Hugh *v*. Wilson, 2 Johns. 46.............................127, *n*.
Hughes *v*. Wheeler, 8 Cow. 77.........................284, 285
Hull *v*. Carnby, 17 N. Y. 202, 501 ; rev'g 2 Duer, 99.......349, 350
—— *v*. ——, 11 N. Y. 503 350
—— *v*. King, 38 Minn. 349.........................97, *n*., 101
—— *v*. L'Eplatinier, 5 Daly, 534 ; s. c., 49 How. Pr. 500....271, *n*.
Hunnewell *v*. Shaffer, 9 Supp. 540..................... 256
Hunt *v*. Hunt, 72 N. Y. 228................................ 203
Hunter *v*. N. Y., Ontario & W. R. R. Co., 116 N. Y. 615 ; s. c..
    27 St. R. 729........ ....114, *n*., 119
Hurwitz *v*. Hurwitz, 9 Misc. 201 ; s. c., 30 Supp. 208.......... 6
Hutcheson *v*. Peck, 5 Johns. 196.......................... 14
Hyde *v*. Paige, 9 Barb, 150..............................142, *n*.

I.

Importers' & T. Nat. Bank *v*. Quackenbush, 1 N. Y. Ann. Cas.
    20...41, *n*.
Ingalls *v*. Lord, 1 Cow. 240.... ....343, 349
Inhabitants of Hancock *v*. Hazzard, 12 Cush. 112............ 55
Inhabitants of New Providence *v*. McEachron, 33 N. J. L. 339. 55
Irving Nat Bank *v*. Adams, 28 Hun, 108, ...127, *n*.
Isaacs *v*. Cohen, 2 N. Y. Ann. Cas. 99 ; s. c., 86 Hun, 119...... 64
Isear *v*. Daynes, 1 App. Div. 557.......... 205

J.

Jackson *v*. Parker, 9 Cow. 73......................... 351
—— *v*. Scott, 18 Johns. 94................................. 351
—— *v*. Willard, 4 Johns. 41,............................... 351
Jacobi *v*. Gorman, 1 Misc. 222.............................. 63
Jacobson, Matter of, 19 St. R. 262 ; s. c., 6 Dem. 298.......... 263
Jefferson County Nat. Bank *v*. Townley, 92 Hun, 172...... 146, *n*.

Page

Jencks *v.* Kearney, 42 St. R. 826 ; s. c., 17 Supp. 143 ; aff'd 138
    N. Y. 634... 112
Jewelers' Agency *v.* Rothschild, 6 App. Div. 499 169
Jones *v.* City of Albany, 151 N. Y. 223.....................183, *n.*
Johnson *v.* Dalton, 1 Cow. 543........... ....78, *n.*, 246
——— *v.* Girdwood, 7 Misc. 651; aff'd 143 N. Y. 660...........226, *n.*
——— *v.* Hardwood Door & T. Co., 79 Hun, 407; s. c., 61 St. R.
    502; 29 Supp. 797 242
——— *v.* Hitchcock, 15 Johns. 185............................ 16
——— *v.* Reed, 136 Mass. 421................................. 175
——— *v.* Wallis, 112 N. Y. 230......................... 56, *n.*, 58
Johnston *v.* Donvan, 106 N. Y. 269; s. c., 8 St. R. 676; 12 Civ.
    Pro. R. 315 ; rev'g 6 St. R. 861.....................195, *n.*, 198
Joliet *v.* Harwood, 86, Ill., 110............... 76
Jordan *v.* Bowen, 46 Super. Ct. (J. & S.) 355................. 24
Journeay *v.* Brackley, 1 Hilt. 447 117
Jucker *v.* Chicago, etc., R. R. Co., 52 Wis. 150.............. 135

K.

Kafka *v.* Levensohn, 18 Misc. 205.......................... 375
Kamp *v.* Kamp, 59 N. Y. 212................................ 204
Keck *v.* Werder, 86 N. Y. 264.............................. 29
Keeler *v.* Keeler, 102 N. Y. 30, 36........................ 328
Keiley *v.* Dusenbury, 77 N. Y. 597.......................27, *n.*
Keller *v.* Payne, 22 Abb. N. C. 352........................ 347
Kellogg *v.* Carrico, 47 Mo. 157.......................98, *n.*, 101
——— *v.* Cowing, 33 N. Y. 408...........................395, *n.*
Kelly *v.* Mayor, etc., of N. Y., 19 Misc. 257.............183, *n.*
Kelsey *v.* Pfandler, P. F. Co., 20 St. R. 533.............167, *n.*
Kennedy *v.* Carrick, 18 Misc. 38; s. c., 40 Supp. 1127..... .288, *n.*
——— *v.* McKone, 10 App. Div. 88 ; s. c., 41 Supp. 782......... 106
Kenner *v.* Morrison, 12 Hun, 204........................... 18
Kenney *v.* Apgar, 93 N. Y. 539 ....229, *n.*, 230
Kerner *v.* Boardman, 14 Supp. 787......................... 63
Kerr *v.* Hitt, 75 Ill. 51..............................97, *n.*, 101
——— *v.* Mount, 28 N. Y. 659.............................. 180
Kiersted *v.* Orange & A. R. R. Co., 69 N. Y. 343............ 117
King *v.* Barnes, 113 N. Y. 476.... 5
Kingsley *v.* First Nat. Bank, 31 Hun, 329........... 149
Kittle *v.* Kittle, 8 Daly, 72.............................. 296
Klumpp *v.* Gardner, 44 Hun, 515 ; s. c., 9 St. R. 355.........34, 38

Page

Koehler *v.* Farmer's & D. Bank, 14 Civ. Pro. R. 71 ; aff'd 6
Supp. 470.... 38
—— *v.* Olsen, 68 Hun, 63.............................384, *n.*
Koke *v.* Balkew, 15 App. Div. 415........................ 96, *n.*
Koy *v.* Clough, Col. & Caines, 425....................333. *n.*
Knapp, Matter of, 85 N. Y. 284............................ 236
—— *v.* Simon, 96 N. Y. 290...................142, *n.*, 145
Knight *v.* Alexander, 38 Minn. 384........................98, *n.*
Knock *v.* Funke, 28 Abb. N. C. 240........................ 376
Know *v.* Bates, 11 Misc. 501 ; 12 Id. 395.............259, 367
Kratzenstein *v.* Lehman, 4 N. Y. Ann. Cas. 335 ; s. c., 19 App.
Div. 228.................................303, 340
Krekeler *v.* Ritter, 62 N. Y. 372....................215, *n.*, 217
Krone *v.* Klatz, 3 N. Y. Ann. Cas. 36 ; s. c., 3 App. Div. 587
289, *n.*, 374
Krumm *v.* Beach, 96 N. Y. 398.........................226, *n.*
Kuh *v.* Barnett, 6 Supp. 881...........................156, *n.*
Kurtzman, Matter of, 2 St. Rep. 655...................... 268

L.

Ladd *v.* Stevenson, 112 N. Y. 325 ....195, *n.*
Ladenburg *v.* Commercial Bank, 2 N. Y. Ann. Cas. 397; s. c., 5
App. Div. 220.................................83, *n.*, 89
Ladew *v.* Hart, 8 App. Div. 150 327
LaFlamme *v.* City of Albany, 91 Hun, 65; s. c., 36 Supp. 686.183, *n.*
Laird *v.* Fisk, 44 N. Y. 618 113
Lamb *v.* Stone, 11 Pick. 527 4
Landon *v.* Townshend, 112 N. Y. 93; s. c., 20 St. R. 223; 16
Civ. Pro. R. 161 ; rev'g 44 Hun, 561.................... 382
Lane *v.* Cotton, 1 Ld. Raym. 646.......................... 53
Lange, *Ex parte*, 18 Wall. 163............................ 203
—— *v.* Benedict, 73 N. Y. 12............................. 17
Lapolt *v.* Maltby, 10 Misc. 330............................125, *n.*
Laprad *v.* Sherwood, 79 Mich. 520........................ 158
Larned *v.* Donovan, 31 Abb. N. C. 308 ; s. c., 29 Supp. 825..156, *n.*
Latourette *v.* Clark, 30 How. Pr. 242....................78 *n.*, 244
Lawrence *v.* Harrington, 63 Hun, 195 ; s. c., 43 St. R. 413 ; 17
Supp. 649 ; aff'd 133 N. Y. 690...................472, *n.*, 274
—— *v.* Lawrence, 3 Barb. Ch. 74........................ 58
—— *v.* Samuels, 20 Misc. 15 ; s, c., 44 Supp. 602..........305, *n.*
—— *v.* Schaefer, 20 App. Div. 80 ; s. c., 46 Supp. 719.....359, 368

Page

Lawson v. Hogan, 93 N. Y. 39............................109, 113
Lawton v. Lawton, 54 Hun, 415 ; s. c., 27 St. R. 302 ; 7 Supp.
556 ....195, *n.*, 197
Leachman v. Dougherty, 81 Ill. 324........................ 178
Lee v. Thompson, 24 Wend. 337 374
—— v. Vacuum Oil Co., 126 N. Y. at page 587 ; s. c., 38 St. R.
662.. 293
Lees v. Smith, 7 T. R. 338............................... 365
Lefler v. Field, 50 Barb. 407............................. 362
Lehmaier v. Buchner, 4 N. Y. Ann. Cas. 82.................. 86
Leiter v. Beecher, 2 App. Div. 577.....................359, 368
Leland v. Maning, 4 Hun, 7............................... 287
Lemmer v. Morison, 89 Hun, 277.......................... 159
Leonard v. N. Y., etc., Tel. Co., 41 N. Y. 544.............. 135
Le Roy v. Bedell, 1 Code R. (N. S.) 201................... 208
Levy v. Cohn, 45 St. R. 278.........................167, *n.*
Lewis v. City of Syracuse, 13 App. Div. 587..............183, *n.*
Livingston, Matter of, 34 N. Y. 555...................... 38
Livingston v. Livingston, 6 Johns. Ch. 497................. 74
Lister v. Wright, 2 Hill, 320............................. 247
Loftus, Matter of, 41 St. R. 537 ; s. c., 16 Supp. 323......... 37
Longyear v. Carter, 2 N. Y. Ann. Cas. 192.........233, *n.*, 288, *n.*
Longuemare v. Nichols, 7 Supp. 672...................... 316
Lorrillard v. Clyde, 102 N. Y. 59 ; 122 Id. 41, 498.......... 129
Louisville & N. R. R. Co. v. Kelly, 24 U. S. App. 103........ 46
Lovell v. Martin, 21 How. Pr. 238........................ 34
Lowry v. Inman, 46 N. Y. 129............................ 374
—— v. Polk Co., 51 Iowa, 50.............................. 55
Lynch v. Dowling, 1 Robt. C. C. 163....................384, *n.*
—— v. Durfee, 24 L. R. A. 793......................97, *n.*, 101
—— v. Livingston, 6 N. Y. 422.....................155, *n.*, 158
Lyon v. Manhattan Ry. Co., 142 N. Y. 303 ; s. c., 31 Abb. N. C.
356 ; 58 St. R. 860 ; aff'g 7 Misc. 401................. 202
—— v. Park, 111 N. Y. 350 ....376, *n.*
—— v. Second Ave. R. R. Co., 2 N. Y. Ann. Cas. 402.......130, *n.*
Ludlum v. Couch, 42 Supp. 370 ; s. c., 10 App. Div. 603...... 230

M.

McAndrew v. Lake Shore & M. S. Ry. Co., 70 Hun, 46 ; 146 N.
Y. 377... 212
McArthur v. Commercial Fire Ins. Co., 67 How. Pr. 510...... 257
McAveney v. Brush, 1 N. Y. Ann. Cas. 414 ; 3 Id. 143, 66, *n.*, 211, *n.*

Page

McBride *v.* Tappen, 10 Supp. 137 ; s. c., 31 St. R. 477........ 63

McCafferty *v.* Spuyten Duyvil & P. M. R. R. Co., 61 N. Y. 178.71, *n.*

McCartee *v.* Orphan Asylum, 9 Cow. 507................... 202

McClaskey *v.* Mayor, etc., of Albany, 64 Barb. 310........... 112

McCormick *v.* Pennsylvania R. R. Co., 49 N. Y. 303.......247, 370

McCotter *v.* Lawrence, 4 Hun, 107........................ 112

McCrea *v.* Marsh, 12 Gray, 211...........................317, *n*

McDonald *v.* Neilson, 2 Cow. 139.......................... 181

McDuffie *v.* Beddoe, 7 Hill, 578..........................314, *n.*

M'Farlane *v.* Moore, 1 Overton (Tenn.) 174.................. 6

MacGowan *v.* Duff, 14 Daly, 315 ; s. c., 12 St. R. 680....... 317, *n.*

McGuckin *v.* Milbank, 152 N. Y. 302...................... 402

McGuire *v.* Kerr, 2 Bradf, 244....................... 264

McHugh *v.* Astrophe, 2 Misc. 478........................ 256

McIvor *v.* McCabe, 26 How. Pr. 257 ....78, *n.*

McKay *v.* Reed, 12 Abb. N. C. 58, *n.*..................... 205

McKee *v.* Metropolitan Life Ins. Co., 25 Hun, 583........... 339

McKenna *v.* Edmondstone, 91 N. Y. 231................... 202

McKinnon *v.* Bliss, 21 N. Y. 206........................115, *n.*

McMahon *v.* Rauhr, 47 N. Y. 67............ ..204, 370, *n.*, 371, *n.*

McMaster *v.* State of N. Y., 108 N. Y. 542................. 113

McNaier *v.* Manhattan Ry. Co., 4 Supp. 310................ 24

McNally *v.* Phoenix Ins. Co., 137 N. Y. 398................. 366

McNamara *v.* Dwyer, 7 Paige, 239........................56, *n.*

McNaughton *v.* Osgood, 114 N. Y. 574...................151, *n.*

McQuigan *v.* Delaware, L. & W. R. R. Co., 129 N. Y. 50 ; s. c.,
    41 St. R. 382 ; 21 Civ. Pro. R. 396................... 307

McSorley *v.* Hughes, 58 Hun, 360........................ 112

McSwyny *v.* Broadway & S. A. R. R. Co., 27 St. R. 363; s. c., 7
    Supp. 456.. 24

Mandelick, Matter of, 6 Misc. 71.......................... 264

Mandeville *v.* Reynolds, 68 N. Y. 528...................... 328

Manhattan Co. *v.* Dunn, 13 Civ. Pro. R. 166................. 256

Mankleton *v.* Lilly, 3 St. R. 421..........................333, *n.*

Manning *v.* Monaghan, 28 N. Y. 585 ; rev'g 10 Bosw. 231..... 349

Manufacturers' Bank *v.* Goolsby, 35 Ga. 82.................. 201

Manufacturers' & Traders' Bank *v.* Hazard, 30 N. Y. 226...... 362

Maretzek *v.* Cauldwell, 4 Robt. 666....................... 256

Marie *v.* Garrison, 83 N. Y. 14...........................225, *n.*

Marsh *v.* Lawrence, 4 Cow. 461........................ . 351

Marshall *v.* Boyer, 23 St. R. 302.............. 230

—— *v.* Meech, 51 N. Y. 140................................. 140

—— *v.* Sherman, 148 N. Y. 42...........................237, *n.*

Marston *v.* Swett, 66 N. Y. 209...........................324, 325

Page

Martin *v.* Hodges, 45 Hun, 38............................... 140

—— *v.* W. J. Johnston Co., 62 Hun, 557 ; aff'd 133 N. Y. 692.167, *n.*

Marvin *v.* Brewster Iron Mining Co., 55 N. Y. 538.,...........71, *n.*

Mason *v.* Henry, 152 N. Y. 529. aff'g 83 Hun, 546 ; s. c., 31
Supp. 1063 ; 65 St. R. 45................................ 328

Mass *v.* Hess, 41 Ill. App. 282........................96, *n.*, 101

Mather *v.* Parsons, 32 Hun, 338.........................26, *n.*

Matter of Application for Charter, 11 Phila. 200.. ......97, *n.*, 101

Matthews *v.* Matthews, 154 N. Y. 228..... 326

Mattison *v.* Bancus, Lalor's Supp. to Hill & D. R. 321 ; 1 N. Y.
295........... ...... : 203. 349

Mattlage *v.* N. Y. Elevated R. R. Co., 17 Supp. 537 ; s. c., 44
St. R. 289..........................\.................... 168

Mayor *v.* Coffin, 90 N. Y. 312.......................... 207

—— *v.* Mayor, 11 Abb. N. C. 367.............. 206

Maxson *v.* Delaware & L. R. R. Co., 112 N. Y. 561 ; s. c., 21
St. R. 767 ; rev'g 48 Hun, 172............................ 184

Mechanies' & Traders' Bank *v.* Loucheim, 55 Hun, 396 ; s. c., 8
Supp. 520.. 88

Meeker *v.* Claghorn, 44 N. Y. 351.......................... 145

Melville *v.* Matthewson, 17 Super. Ct. (J. & S.) 388........... 39

Mercantile Nat. Bank *v.* Corn Exchange Bank, 25 Supp. 1068
220, *n.*

Merchants' Bank *v.* Thomson, 55 N. Y. 7.. 112

Meriden Nat. Bank *v.* Gallaudet, 120 N. Y. 298.............. 361

Metropolitan El. R. R. Co. *v.* Manhattan Ry. Co., 14 Abb. N.
C. 103, 215..27, *n.*

Meyer *v.* Lathrop, 73 N. Y. 315............................ 328

Michalson *v.* All, 21 S. E. Rep. (S. C.) 323.................. 6

Middlebrook *v.* Merchants' Bank, 41 Barb. 481.. ....56, *n.*

Millard *v.* Holmes, Booth & Hayden, 142 N. Y. 492... 177

Miller *v.* Bear, 3 Paige, 466................................. 112

—— *v.* Collyer, 36 Barb. 250............................... 277

—— *v.* Taylor, 4 Burr. 2345.... 6

—— *v.* Woodhead, 52 Hun, 127 ; s. c., 23 St. R. 412........314, *n.*

Millicant *v.* People, 14 W. Dig. 252. .. ..384, *n.*

Milliken *v.* Western Union Tel. Co., 110 N. Y. 403; s. c., 18
St. R. 328 ; rev'g 53 Super. Ct. 111....................225, *n.*

Mills *v.* Brown, 16 Pet. (U. S.) 525.......................371, *n.*

—— *v.* Thursby, 11 How. Pr. 114............................ 39

Milwaukee & St. P. R. R. Co. *v.* Kellogg, 94 (U. S.) 469....... 134

Mitchell *v.* Allen, 12 Wend. 290....................... 37

—— *v.* Rochester Ry. Co., 4 Misc. 575.................15, 135

Page

Mitchell *v.* Rochester Ry. Co., 3 N. Y. Ann. Cas. 283; rev'g 4
Misc. 575.. 15
—— *v.* Smith, 1 Paige, 287.. 311
—— *v.* Van Buren, 27 N. Y. 300................................396, *n.*
—— *v.* Wilson, 4 Edw. Ch. 695.................................... 107
Molony *v.* Dowes, 8 Abb. Pr. 316 ....78, *n.*, 244, 247
Moncrieff *v.* Goldsborough, 4 H. & McH., 281................ 393
Montgomery *v.* Chapin, 5 Cow. 485......................... 351
—— *v.* Phillips, 53 N. J. Eq. 203............................. 148
Montifiori, *v.* Montifiori 1 Wm. Bl. 363.................... 13
Moore *v.* Duffy, 74 Hun, 78 ; s. c., 57 St. R. 746 ; 26 Supp. 340. 381
—— *v.* Taylor, 42 Hun, 45................................ 107
—— *v.* Williams, 23 Super. Ct. (J. & S.) 116 ; aff'd 115 N. Y.
586.. 128
More *v.* Smedburgh, 8 Paige Ch. 600..............106, n., 112
Morgan *v.* Bowes, 62 Hun, 623 ; s, c., 17 Supp. 22............ 74
Moriarty *v.* City of Albany, 8 App. Div. 118...........183, *n.*
Morris *v.* Knox, 6 Abb. Pr. 628, *n.*...................... 208
Moosbrugger *v.* Kaufman, 7 App. Div. 380 ; s. c., 40 Supp.
213 150
Moser *v.* Mayor, etc., of N. Y., 21 Hun, 163................ 128
Mostyn *v.* Fabrigas, 2 Smith's L. C. (9 Am. Ed.) 916....78, *n.*, 246
Mulford *v.* Gibbs, 9 App. Div. 490.......................... 42
Munoz *v.* Wilson, 111 N. Y. 295............................ 128
Munzinger *v.* Courier Co. 1 N. Y., Ann. Cas. 32...........380, *n.*
Murdock *v.* Jones, 3 App. Div. 221......................... 109
Murphy, Matter of, 9 Misc. 647............................125, *n.*
—— *v.* Stickley Simonds Co., 82 Hun, 158 ; s. c., 31 Supp. 295 ;
63 St. R. 744... 108
Murray *v.* Judson, 9 N. Y. 73.............................395, *n.*
Muzzy *v.* Shattuck, 1 Den. 233............................ 53
Myer *v.* Abbett, 20 App. Div. 390.......................288, *n.*
Myers *v.* Becker, 95 N. Y. 486............................ 277
—— *v.* De Mier, 4 Daly, 350; 52 N. Y. 647................ 112
—— *v.* Welles, 5 Hill 463................................285, 286

N.

Nason *v.* Directors of the Poor, 126 Penn St. 445............ 55
Nathans *v.* Hope, 77 N. Y. 420............................ 211
National Bank *v.* Sprague, 20 N. Y. Eq. 159................ 393
National Bank of Port Jervis *v.* Hansee, 15 Abb. N. C. 488...27, *n.*
National Park Bank *v.* Salomon, 17 Civ. Pro. R. 8.........396, *n.*

Page

Neligh *v.* Michenor, 3 Stvekt. Ch. 542...................... 386
Neuberger *v.* Keim, 134 N. Y. 35 ; s. c., 45 St. R. 394........ 154
Neville *v.* Wilkinson, 1 Brown's Ch. Cas. 543................ 14
Newberry *v.* Lee, 3 Hill, 523............................... 180
New Jersey & Penn. C. W. *v.* Ackermann, 6 App. Div. 540.... 359
New Jersey & Penn. C. W. *v.* Ackermann... 368
Newman *v.* Goddard, 3 Hun, 70..... ....78, *n.*, 246
N. Y. Lackawanna & W. R. R. Co., Matter of, 26 Hun, 194..196, *n.*
——, Matter of, 98 N. Y. 447.........................370, *n.*, 374
N. Y. Life Ins. Co. *v.* Universal Life Ins. Co., 88 N. Y. 424, 428
257, 304, 339
N. Y. & New Haven R. R. Co. *v.* Schuyler, 34 N. Y. 30....... 362
Nichols *v.* Mead, 2 Lans, 222 ; aff'd 47 N. Y. 653............ 349
—— *v.* Nichols, 12 Hun, 428............. 296
—— *v.* Scranton Steel Co., 135 N. Y. 634. 258
Nies, Matter of, 13 St. R. 756............................... 264
Noble *v.* Holmes, 5 Hill, 194............................... 179
Noonan *v.* N. Y., Lake Erie & W. R. R. Co., 68 Hun, 387...... 36
North River Bank *v.* Aymar, 3 Hill, 262.................... 362

O.

O'Connor *v.* Felix, 87 Hun, 179........................... 30
O'Gorman *v.* Arnoux, 63 How. Pr. 159.....................219, *n.*
Oliver *v.* French, 41 Supp. 106.......... 39
Olney *v.* Baird, 7 App. Div. 95............................146, *n.*
—— *v.* ——, 15 Misc. 385 ; aff'g 7 App. Div. 95............147, *n.*
Onderdonk *v.* Voorhis, 2 Robt. 623........................ 128
Oneida County Bank *v.* Bonney, 101 N. Y. 173.......77, *n.*, 294, *n.*
O'Neil, Matter of, 91 N. Y. 516............................. 260
—— *v.* Dry Dock, E. B. & B. R. R. Co., 129 N. Y. 125.,....44, *n.*
O'Shaughnessy *v.* Baxter, 121 Mass. 515.................... 178
Owen *v.* Evans, 31 N. E. Rep. 999......................... 113

P.

Page *v.* McDonnell, 55 N. Y. 299....................... 112
—— *v.* Waring, 76 N. Y. 463............................. 160
Palmer *v.* Darby, 2 Ohio N. P. 410....................... 169
—— *v.* Mutual Life Ins. Co., 55 Supr. Ct. (J. & S.) 352 ; s. c.,
14 St. R. 759.......................................196, *n.*
—— *v.* Phoenix Mutual Life Ins. Co., 84 N. Y. 63............57, *n.*

Page

Pardel *v.* Leith, 6 Lans. 303.................................. 349
Parker *v.* Selye. 3 N. Y. Ann. Cas. 210......................77, *n.*
—— *v.* Spear, 62 How. Pr. 394........................314, *n.*, 316
Parrot *v.* Green, 1 McCord, 521............................ 201
Patten *v.* Bullard, 3 St. R. 735............................ 141
Pattison *v.* Bacon, 12 Abb. Pr. 142 ; s. c., 21 How. Pr. 478 .34, 39
Pearson *v.* Fiske, 2 Hilt. 146................................. 374
Peck *v.* List, 23 W. Va. 338................................. 393
Pendleton *v.* Weed, 17 N. Y. 72...................... 141
Pennock's Appeal, 14 Penn. St. 446....................... 393
People *v.* Albany & V. R. R. Co., 77 N. Y. 232.........195, *n.*, 197
—— (*ex rel.* Alexander) *v.* Alexander, 3 Hun, 211............. 141
—— (*ex rel.* Day) *v.* Bergen, 53 N. Y. 504.................48, *n.*
—— *v.* Beveridge Brewing Co., 91 Hun, 313 ; s. c., 3 N. Y.
　　Ann. Cas. 4 ....249, *n.*, 250
—— *v.* Board of Commissioners, 18 St. R. 797.............195, *n.*
—— *v.* Conroy, 153 N. Y. 174........................298, *n.*
—— (*ex rel.* Musell) *v.* Court of Oyer & Terminer, 101 N. Y.
　　245... 274
—— (*ex rel.* Wilbur) *v.* Eddy, 3 Lans. 80.... 37
—— (*ex rel.* Nash) *v.* Faulkner, 107 N. Y. 486.............. 53
—— *v.* Grant, 11 St. R. 558.............................48, *n.*
—— *v.* King, 110 N. Y. 418..............................317, *n.*
—— *v.* Liscomb, 60 N. Y. 559........................... 203
—— *v.* Loew, 19 Misc. 248.......................364, 369
—— (*ex rel.* Goetchius) *v.* McGoldrick, 1 N. Y. Ann. Cas. 401
　　　　　　　　　　　　　　　　　　　　　　　40, *n.*
—— *v.* Mercein, 3 Hill, 416................................. 36
—— (*ex rel.* Einsfeld) *v.* Murray, 149 N. Y. 367.............. 387
—— (*ex rel.* Clason) *v.* Nassau Ferry Co., 86 Hun, 128......166, *n.*
—— *v.* National Trust Co., 31 Hun, 20...................... 38
—— *v.* Remington, 45 Hun, 329; s. c., 10 St. R. 310; aff'd 109
　　N. Y. 631.................................250, 251
—— (*ex rel.* Stokes) *v.* Riseley, 38 Hun, 280 ....384, *n.*
—— *v.* Schooley, 89 Hun, 391...........................162, *n.*
—— *v.* Spalding, 2 Paige, 326.... ....156, *n.*
—— *v.* Stephens, 71 N. Y. 527...........................390, *n.*
—— (*ex rel.* Delmar) *v.* St. Louis & S. F. R. R. Co., 44 Hun,
　　552.....................................140, 141
—— *v.* Sullivan, 2 Edm. 294................... 129
—— (*ex rel.* Wise) *v.* Tamsen, 17 Misc. 212 ; s. c., 40 Supp.
　　1047....................................271, n.
—— *v.* Utica Ins. Co., 15 Johns. 358...................... 159
—— (*ex rel.* Cauffman) *v.* Van Buren, 136 N. Y. 252 347

Page

—— *v.* Warren, 5 Hill, 440........ 178
—— *v.* Wasson, 64 Id. 167.................................294, *n.*
—— (*ex rel.* Canaday) *v.* Williams, 90 Hun, 501 ; s. c., 71 St. R.
  401 ; 36 Supp. 65.... ....125, *n.*,
—— (*ex rel.* Scott) *v.* Williams, 6 Misc. 185.................125, *n.*
Percy *v.* Seward, 6 Abb. Pr. 326.......................... 207
Perley *v.* County of Muskegon, 32 Mich. 132................. 55
—— *v.* Eastern R. R. Co., 98 Mass. 414.................... 135
Perls *v.* Metropolitan Ins. Co., 29 St. R. 409 ; s. c., 8 Supp. 532
  219, *n.*
Perry *v.* Dickerson, 85 N. Y. 345.......................... 210
Petersen *v.* Chemical Bank, 32 N. Y. 21.................56, *n.*, 58
Petrie *v.* Trustees of Hamilton College, 92 Hun, 81 ; s. c., 71
  St. R. 804 ; 36 Supp. 1009................................ 230
Peyser *v.* Wendt, 84 N. Y. 642............................ 257
Pfeffele *v.* Second Ave. R. R. Co., 34 Hun, 479............ 44, *n.*
Phelps *v.* Gee, 29 Hun, 202.............................190, *n.*
—— *v.* Nowlen, 72 N. Y. 39............................... 18
Philadelphia Steamship Dock Co. *v.* Lorillard Steamship Co.,
  54 How. Pr. 508......... : 257
Philbrook *v.* Kellogg, 21 Hun, 238...................314, *n.*, 316
Pierce *v.* Lyon, 3 Hill, 450........... 208
—— *v.* Waters, 10 W. Dig. 432........................232, *n.*
—— *v.* Wood, 3 Fost. (N. H.) 519......................... 227
Pinckney *v.* Hagadorn, 1 Duer, 98....................... 112
Piper *v.* Hoard, 107 N. Y. 73 ; s. c., 11 St. R. 371...........12, 13
Pitchie *v.* Seaboard Nat. Bank, 12 Misc. 146................. 258
Place *v.* Hayward, 117 N. Y. 487 ; s. c., 27 St. R. 710 ; rev'g
  55 Super. Ct. 208........................27, *n.*, 151, *n.*, 153
—— *v.* McIlvain, 38 N. Y. 96......... 286
Platt *v.* Munroe, 34 Barb. 291........................... 20
Poillon *v.* Lawrence, 43 Super. Ct. (J. & S.) 385 ; rev'g 77 N. Y.
  207...,.220, *n.*
Polhemus *v.* Fitchburg R. R. Co., 113 N. Y. 617 ; 123 N. Y.
  502... 257
Pollett *v.* Long, 56 N. Y. 200............................ 135
Pool *v.* Ellison, 30 St. R. 135.......................... 63
Poole *v.* Belcha, 131 N. Y. 200 ; s. c., 42 St. R. 856 ; 22 Civ.
  Pro. R. 67...... 293
Porous Plaster Co. *v.* Seabury, 43 Hun, 611................ 5
Porter *v.* Swann, 44 St. R. 375.......................... 362
—— *v.* Williams, 9 N. Y. 150...... 382
—— *v.* Waring, 69 N. Y. 250...........................127, *n.*
—— *v.* Wormser, 94 N. Y. 431......... 325

Page

Post & Co. *v.* Toledo, etc., R. R. Co.. 144 Mass. 341 311
Pratt *v.* Coman, 37 N. Y. 440 286
Prentiss *v.* Knickerbocker Life Ins. Co., 77 N. Y. 483 112
Presbrey *v.* Public.Opinion Co., 6 App. Div. 600 ; s. c., 39 Supp.
    957 331
Price *v.* McGown, 10 N. Y. 465 .... 106, *n.*
Priestly *v.* Fernie, 3 H. & C. Exch. 982 144
Prospect Auenue, Matter of, 1 N. Y. Ann. Cas. 347 .... 232, *n.*
Proweeder *v.* Lewis, 11 Misc. 109 ; s. c., 31 Supp. 996 ; 24 Civ.
    Pro. R. 299 .... 380, *n.*
Purcell *v.* Daly, 19 Abb. N. C., 301 .... 317, *n.*
Purdy *v.* Huntington, 42 N. Y. 334 351
—— *v.* Manhattan Ry. Co., 11 Misc. 394 .... 215, *n.*
Putman *v.* Lewis, 8 Johns. 389 .... 285, 286

Q.

Quigley *v.* Quigley, 45 Hun, 23 .... 196, *n*

R.

Raabe *v.* Squier, 148 N. Y. 81 .... 151, *n.*, 153
Rabenstein *v.* Kahn, 5 Misc. 408 .... 384, *n.*
Raht *v.* Attrill, 106 N. Y. 423 .... 27, *n.*
Railton *v.* Lauder, 26 Ill. App. 655 ; aff'd 126 Ill. 219 .... 97, *n.*, 101
Ralli *v.* Hillyer, 15 Misc. 692 367
Ramsey *v.* Robinson, 86 Hun, 511 203
Ranson *v.* Miner, 3 Sandf. 692 349
Rathbone *v.* Hooney, 58 N. Y. 463 .... 380, *n.*
—— *v.* Tucker, 15 Wend. 498 .... 142, *n.*
Ray *v.* Conner, 3 Edw. Ch. 478 39
Raymond *v.* Merchant, 3 Cow. 147 .... 284, 285
Read *v.* French, 28 N. Y. 285 .... 395, *n.*
Redman *v.* Redman, 1 Vern. 348 14
Redwood County *v.* Tower, 28 Minn. 45 55
Reed *v.* Chilson, 142 N. Y. 152 ; aff'g 16 Supp, 744 ; s. c., 40
    St. R. 960 .... 77, *n.*, 243
Reich *v.* Colwell Lead Co., 21 Supp. 495 109
Reilley *v.* Sabater, 26 Civ. Pro. R. 34 ; s. c., 43 Supp. 383 328
—— *v.* Byrne, Civ. Pro. R, 201 258
—— *v.* Sicilian Asphalt P. Co., 4 N. Y. Ann. Cas. 209, ... 214, *n.*
Reinmiller *v.* Skidmore, 7 Lans. 161 349

Page

Reliance Marine Ins. Co. *v.* Herbert, 87 Hun, 285..........298, *n.*

Remington Paper Co. *v.* O'Dougherty, 81 N. Y. 474.... 155, *n.*, 158

Renwick *v.* Renwick, 1 Bradf. 237......................... 112

Requa *v.* Rea, 2 Paige, 339.............................. 277

Reynolds *v.* City, 81 Hun, 353; s. c., 63 St. R. 118; 30 Supp.
    954.. 202

Rexford *v.* Rexford, 7 Lans. 6.....................161, *n.*

Rice *v.* Dewey, 54 Barb. 455.......................... 284

Richmond *v.* Foote, 3 Lans. 244.. ....112, 351

—— *v.* Hamilton, 9 Abb. Pr. 71, *n*.....................47, *n.*

Ridgway *v.* Symons, 4 App. Div. 98...................147, *n.*

Riendeau *v.* Bullock, 20 Supp. 976.................... 108

Riggs *v.* Cleveland R. R. Co., 21 W. Dig. 45.............66, *n.*

—— *v.* Palmer, 115 N. Y. 506 ; s. c., 23 Abb. N. C. 452 ; 26 St.
    R. 198.. 159

—— *v.* Purcell, 74 N. Y. 370....................27, *n.*, 29, 30

Rinchey *v.* Stryker, 28 N. Y. 45 ; s. c., 26 How. Pr. 75......... 346

Risley, Matter of, 10 Daly, 44..........................114, *n.*

Ritchie *v.* Putnam, 13 Wend. 524.....................127, *n.*

Robbins *v.* Ferris, 5 Hun, 286.......................... 39

Roberge *v.* Winne, 144 N. Y. 709.....................96, *n.*

Roberts *v.* Ogdensburg & L. C. R. R. Co., 29 Hun, 154........ 24

—— *v.* Thomas, *Term. Rep.* (6 Durnf. & East.) 88............ 335

—— *v.* White, 5 Super. Ct. (J. & S.) 168.................... 112

—— *v.* White, 73 N. Y. 375............................ 299

Robertson *v.* Lawton, 91 Hun, 67..................... 343

Rbinson o*v.* Oceanic Steam Nav. Co., 112 N. Y. 315..........
                  78, *n.*, 81, 204, 247, 248

—— *v.* Schellhaas, 62 Hun, Pr. 489...................... 258

Rochester Distilling Co. *v.* Devendorf, 72 Hun, 428......91, 92, 94

Rochester & K. F. L. Co. *v.* Raymond, 4 App. Div. 600......237, *n.*

Rodman *v.* Henry, 17 N. Y. 484....................... 373

Roeber *v.* Dawson, 14 Civ. Pro. R. 354.................. 316

Rogers *v.* Brewster, 5 Johns. 523....................... 180

—— *v.* Handfield, 14 Daly, 399 ; s. c., 12 St. R. 671..........70, *n.*

—— *v.* Hosack, 5 Hill, 521............................. 259

—— *v.* Mutual R. F. Assn., 1 How. Pr. (N. S.) 194........220, *n.*

Romain *v.* Chauncey, 129 N. Y. 566 ; aff'g 60 Hun, 477......40, *n.*

Roraback *v.* Stebbins, 4 Abb. Ct. at App. Dec. 100........352, 355

Rose *v.* Chadwick, 3 N. Y. Ann. Cas. 389.................240, *n.*

Rosenberg *v.* Flack, 10 Supp. 759......................194, *n.*

—— *v.* Salomon, 1 N. Y. Ann. Cas. 11 ; s. c., 144 N. Y.92.194, *n.*, 198

—— *v.* Staten Island R. R. Co., 14 Supp. 476 ; s. c., 38 St. R.
    106..206, 213

Page

Ruff *v.* Rinaldo, 55 N. Y. 664........................ 113

Rugg, Matter of, 3 St. R. 224 ; s. c., 4 Dem. 105.........12, 67, *n.*

S.

Sage *v.* Cartwright, 9 N. Y. 49............................. 351

Salomon *v.* Belden, 12 Abb. N. C. 58 205

Sampson *v.* Welsh, 24 How. (U. S.) 207....................371. *n.*

Sanders *v.* Soutter, 126 N. Y. 193 ; s. c., 37 St. R. 1 ; rev'g 36 Id.
824. ....225, *n.*

Sanderson, Matter of, 9 Misc. 574......................... 263

Sands *v.* St. John, 36 Barb. 628........ 327

Sauter *v.* N. Y. Central, etc., R. R. Co., 66 N. Y. 50....130, *n.*, 135

Savall *v.* Wauful, 21 Civ. Pro. R. 18......................... 348

Savill *v.* Savill, 1 P. Mins. 745.............................275, *n.*

Savin, Matter of, 9 Civ. Pro. R. 175....... ....309, *n.*

Schaettler *v.* Gardiner, 47 N. Y. 404.....................26, *n.*

Scheffler *v.* R. R. Co., 105 U. S. 249......................... 133

—— *v.* Minneapolis & St. L. Ry. Co., 32 Minn. 521........... 119

Schlachter *v.* Hopkins, 84 Hun, 402........................ 109

Schlichting *v.* Wintgen, 25 Hun, 626........................ 133

Schmidt *v.* Reed, 132 N. Y. 108............................. 110

Schoonmaker *v.* Bonnie, 16 Civ. Pro. R. 66; s. c., 51 Hun, 34 ;
20 St. R. 428 ; 3 Supp. 492......................... 230

Schultz *v.* Cohen, 34 Supp. 927....................... 324

—— *v.* Rodewald, 1 Abb. N. C. 365......................... 39

Schuyler *v.* Curtis, 147 N. Y. 434........................... 15

Schwan *v.* Mutual Trust F. L. Assn., 9 Civ. Pro. R. 82......220, *n.*

Scofield *v.* Demorest, 55 Hun, 254.......................220, *n.*

Scott *v.* Scott, 1 Cox, 378................................. 14

Scribner *v.* Beach, 4 Den. 448............................. 321

—— *v.* Jacobs, 9 Supp. 856................................ 109

—— *v.* Williams, 1 Paige, 550.............................. 128

Seaman *v.* Reynolds, 20 Super. Ct. (J. & S.) 543....... 39

—— *v.* Van Renselaer, 10 Barb. 86. 112

Secor *v.* Sturgis, 16 N. Y., 548.........................211, 212

Seiser Bros. Co. *v.* Potter Produce Co., 23 Civ. Pro. R. 348.... 248

Seligman *v.* Falk, 13 Civ. R. 77............................. 347

Selkirk v. Wood, 9 Civ. Pro. R. 141......................... 207

Seller *v.* Seixas, 4 Abb. Pr. 103 285

Sessions *v.* Palmeter, 75 Hun, 268 ; s. c., 58 St. R. 289 ; 26 Supp.
1076...... ....,................ 236

Shand *v.* Hanley, 71 N. Y. 319...................120, *n.*, 121, *n.*

Page

Shankland *v.* Washington, 5 Pet. 390................... 371, *n.*

Sheldon v. Williams, 52 Barb. 183..................... 230

Sheridan *v.* Andrews, 80 N. Y. 648................... 230

Shottenkerk *v.* Wheeler. 3 Johns. Ch. 275............ 351

Shultz *v.* Whitney, 17 How. Pr. 471; s. c., 9 Abb. Pr. 71..... 47, *n.*

Sias *v.* Rochester R. R. Co., 92 Hun, 140.............. 133

Sickles v. Richardson, 23 Hun, 559................... 350

Simis v. Wissel, 1 App. Div. 323.................... 324

Simpson   Hart, 14 Johns. 63................... 36

Sinclair *v.* Dwight, 9 App. Div. 297 ; **s. c.,** 41 Supp. 193......237, *n.*

Sire *v.* Kneuper, 22 Abb. N. C. 62 ; s. c., 15 Daly, 40 ; 15 Civ.

     Pro. R. 434 ; 19 St. R. 43 ; 3 Supp. 533...............205, 206

Sisters of Charity *v.* Kelly, 67 N. Y. 409; rev'g 7 Hun,

     290.. 260, 262, 264

Smith *v.* Applegate, 1 Daly, 91..................... 286

—— *v.* Crocker, 3 App. Div. 473.................. 80

—— *v.* Crocker, 4 N. Y. Ann. Cas. 77 ; s. c., 14 App. Div.

     245..242, 294, *n.*

—— *v.* Greenlee, 2 Dev. 126...................... 393

—— *v.* Keepers, 5 Civ. Pro. R. 66.................256, 258

—— *v.* Lewis, 3 Johns. 157....................... 18

—— *v.* Longuiere, 247 Hun, 257................... 346

—— *v.* Second Nat. Bank, 70 Hun, 357............56, n.

—— *v.* Slosson, 89 Hun, 568 ; 35 Supp. 548.......... 324

—— *v.* Smith, 7 Misc. 37........................ 113

—— *v.* Smith, 20 Hun, 555; 26 Id. 573.............. 179

—— *v.* Spalding, 3 Robt. 615..................... 39

—— *v.* Union Milk Co., 70 Hun, 348................ 248

—— *v.* Wagner, 9 Misc. 122 ; s. c., 59 St. R. 710 ; 29 Supp. 284 ;

     aff'g 7 Misc. 739............................... 117

—— *v.* Warden, 4 Hun, 787...................... 179

—— *v.* Zalinski, 94 N. Y. 519.................... 36

Sneeden *v.* Harris, 109 N. C. 349 ; 13 S. E. 920........ 174, 175

Snyder *v.* White, 6 How Pr. 321................... 38

Soldiers' Orphan Home *v* Sage, 1 N. Y. Ann. Cas. 106...... 379

Solomon *v.* Belden, 12 Abb. N. C. 58............... 208

—— *v.* Metropolitan Ins. Co., 42 Super. Ct. (J. & S.) 24...... 363

Spaulding *v.* Village of Waverly, 12 App. Div. 594, s. c., 44

     Supp. 112...............................183, *n.,* 186, *n.*

Spears *v.* Mayor, 72 N. Y. 442.................... 217

Stafford *v.* Van Zandt, 2 Johns. Cas. 66..............229, *n.*

Staines *v.* Shone, 16 Penn. St. 200................. 393

Standard *v.* Williams, 10 Wend. 599................ 37

Stanton *v.* Embrey, 93 U. S. 548...................77, *n.*

	Page
State *v.* Harper, 6 Ohio, 607	55
—— *v.* Powell, 67 Mo. 395	55
Steele *v.* Ellmaker, 11 S & R. 86	393
Steinway *v.* Steinway, 68 Hun, 430	221, *n.*
Stelle *v.* Palmer, 7 Abb. Pr. 181	141
Stephens *v.* Perrine, 1 N. Y. Ann. Cas. 81	41, *n.*
Steuben County Bank *v.* Alberger, 83 N. Y. 274	27, *n.*, 37
Stevenson *v.* Stevenson, 34 Hun, 157	40, *n.*
Stewart *v.* Long Island R. R. Co., 102 N. Y. 601	117
—— *v.* Slater, 6 Duer, 83	350
—— *v.* Sonneborn, 98 U. S. 187	168
Stieglitz *v.* Belding, 20 Misc. 297	359
Stillwell *v.* Carpenter, 59 N. Y. 423	26, *n.*
—— *v.* ——, 2 Abb. N. C, 238 ; s. c., 62 N. Y. 639	127, *n.*
—— *v.* Stilwell, 1 N, Y. Ann. Cas. 31	229, *n.*
St. Lawrence State Hospital *v.* Fowler, 15 Misc. 159	125, *n.*
Stockwell *v.* Bank of Malone, 36 Hun, 583	124, *n.*, 125, *n.*
Storm *v.* Waddell, 2 Sandf. Ch. 494	122
Stout *v.* Jones, 9 St. R. 570 ; aff'd 120 N. Y. 638	362
Strong *v.* Harvey, 3 Bing. 104; 11 Moore, 72	365
Strowbridge Litho. Co. *v.* Crane, 20 Civ. Pro. R. 15; s. c., 12 Supp. 834	195, *n.*
Stryker, Matter of, 73 Hun, 327 ; s. c., 55 St. R. 903; 26 Supp. 209	251
Stubbs *v.* Ripley, 39 Hun, 620	141
Studwell *v.* Charter Oak Ins. Co., 19 Hun, 127	304
Sullivan *v.* Dunham, 3 N. Y. Ann. Cas. 324	71, *n.*
—— *v.* N. Y. Elevated R. R. Co., 14 Misc. 426	215, *n.*
—— *v.* Tioga R. R. Co., 112 N. Y. 643	130, *n.*
Sulzbacher *v.* Cawthra, 14 Misc. 544	66, *n.*
Sumner *v.* Beeler, 50 Ind. 341	178
Supervisors of Albany Co. *v.* Dorr, 25 Wend. 440 ; 7 Hill, 584, 52	53
Supervisors of Omro *v.* Kaime, 39 Wis. 468	55
Suyder, Matter of, 103 N. Y. 178 ; aff'g 34 Hun, 302	266, *n.*

T.

Talbot *v.* Chamberlain, 3 Paige, 219	351
Talcott *v.* Burnstein, 13 St. R. 552	38
Talmadge *v.* Nevins, 32 N. Y. Super. Ct. (J. & S.) 38	362
Tannenbaum *v.* Rossenog, 22 Abb. N. C. 346	347
Taylor *v.* Hatch, 12 Johns. 340	156, *n.*

Page

—— v. Wing, 83 N. Y. 527...................................258
Teller v. Randall, 26 How. Pr. 155.........................373
Tenny v. Beger, 93 N. Y. 524...............................236
Terry v. Munger, 121 N. Y. 161. 95
Thelberg v. National Starch Mfg. Co., 12 App. Div. 173.......324
Third Ave. R. R. Co. v. Mayor, etc., of N. Y., Id. 159.......294, *n.*
Thompson v. Quimby 2 Bradf, 449...........................264
—— v. Shepard, 9 Johns. 262...............................208
Thorne v. French, 4 Misc. 436 ; aff'd 143 N. Y. 679........112, 113
Throop v. Hatch Litho. Co., 125 N. Y. 530 ; s. c., 35 St, R. 816.

148

Throop Grain Cleaner Co. v. Smith, 110 N. Y. 83.............346
Thurber v. Blanck, 50 N. Y. 80...... 346
Tilby v. Hayes, 27 Hun, 253................................196, *n.*
Tilden, Estate of, 5 Civ. Pro. R. 449.....................196, *n.*
Tillotson v. Wolcott, 48 N. Y. 188........................125, *n.*
Titus v. Glen Falls Ins. Co., 81 N. Y. 410................113
Tompkins v. Hyatt, 28 N. Y. 347...........................112
Tonnelle v. Hail, 4 N. Y. 140.............................264
Towle v. Leavitt, 23 N. H. 360............................393
Townsend v. Coon, 7 Civ. Pro. R. 56.......................213
—— v. Whitney, 75 N. Y. 425...............................267, *n.*
Travis v. Myers, 67 N. Y. 542.............................294, *n.*
Trepagener & Bros. v. Rose, 4 N. Y. Ann. Cas. 300.336, *n.*, 340, *n.*
Trimm v. Marsh, 54 N. Y. 599..............................351
True, Matter of, 4 Abb. N. C. 90..........................346
Trust v. Delaplaine, 3 E. D. Smith, 219..... ....389, *n.*
—— v. Repoor, 15 How. Pr. 570............................232, *n.*
Tuck v. Manning, 53 Hun, 455 ; s. c., 25 St. R. 130 ; 6 Supp.
    140 ; 17 Civ. Pro. R. 175.............................236
Tucker v. E. L. Goodsell Co., 4 N. Y. Ann. Cas. 86.........82, *n.*
—— v. Ely, 37 Hun, 565...................................45, *n.*
Tuttle v. Hills, 6 Wend. 213..............................351
Tyler v. Aetna Fire Ins. Co., 2 Wend, 280.................304

U.

Underhill v. Ramsay, 2 Supp. 451 ; aff'd without opinion, 125
    N. Y. 681... 95
Union Bank of Sullivan Co. v. Bush, 36 N. Y. 631..........396, *n.*
Union Nat. Bank v. Warner, 12 Hun, 306...............120, *n.*, 122
United States v. Dashiel, 4 Wall. 182..................... 55
—— v. Hoge, 6 How. (U. S.) 297...........................287

Page

United States v. Keeler, 9 Wall. 83.......................... 55
—— v. Morgan, 11 How. (U. S.) 154........................ 55
—— v. Prescott, 3 How. (U. S.) 578..................51, n., 55
——·v. State Bank of N. C., 6 Pet. 29...................... 354
—— v. Thomas, 15 Wall. 337....................51, n., 54
U. S. Trust Co. v. R. R. Co., 117 U. S. 434......... 354
Utica C. & S. C. R. R. Co. v. Gates, 3 N. Y. Ann. Cas. 242..398, n.

V.

Vail v. Knapp, 49 Barb. 299............. 296
—— v. Reynolds, 118 N. Y. 297.........................226, n.
Van Alfen v. Farmers' Joint Stock Ins. Co., 10 Hun, 397; aff'd
    72 N. Y. 604... 363
Van Amburgh v. Baker, 81 N. Y. 46....... ....237, n.
Van Cortlandt v. Tozer, 17 Wend. 338.................158, 159, n.
Van Etten v. Van Etten, 69 Hun, 499...................... 203
Van Ingen v. Whitman, 62 N. Y. 523....................... 222
Van Nuys v. Titsworth, 57 Hun, 5........................224, n.
Vans v. Middlebrook, 3 St. R. 277.. ....384, n.
Vary v. Godfrey, 6 Cow. 587.............................156, n.
Veazie v. Williams, 8 How. (U. S.) 134............. 392
Vermilya v. Beatty, 6 Barb. 429............. 58
Victor v. Henlein, 34 Id. 562; s. c., reported fully, 1 How. Pr.
    (N. S.) 160... 283
Vilas v. Plattsburgh & M. R. R. Co., 123 N. Y. 440......26 n., 141
Village of Oneida v. Thompson, 92 Hun, 16............... 50, n.
Vitto v. Farley, 3 N. Y. Ann, Cas. 308......................57, n.
Von Compton v. Knight, 65 N. Y. 580................... 112
Voorhees v. De Meyer, 2 Barb. 37........................... 112

W.

Walker, Matter of, 136 N. Y. 20........... ....204, 370, n.
Walker v. Beecher, 15 Misc. 149............................. 361
Wallace v. Baring, 3 N. Y. Ann. Cas. 16...................328, n.
Wallman v. Society of Concord, 45 N. Y. 485....... 113
Walsh v. City of Buffalo, 92 Hun, 438................182, n., 183, n.
Walton v. Meeks, 41 Hun, 311.......... 112
—— n. Ogden, Col. and Cai.. 419......................... 256
Wamsley v. H. L. Horton Co., 87 Hun, 347 ; s. c., 34 Supp.
    306 ; 68 St. R. 458.................................215, n.

Page

Ward v. Height, 3 Johns. Cas. 80..........................333, n.
—— v. School District, 10 Neb. 293......................... 55
—— v. Town of Southfield, 102 N. Y. 287.................26, n.
Warner v. Fourth National Bank, 12 Civ. Pro. R. 186... 349
—— v. Perry, 14 Hun, 337................................... 18
Washbon v. Cope, 144 N. Y. 287.....................25, n.
Wasson v. Connor, 54 Miss. 351............................158
Waters v. Stewart, 1 Caines' Cas. 47.... 351
—— v. Travis, 9 Johns. 450...........................111, 112
Watson v. Nelson, 69 N. Y. 537............................ 269
Waydell v. Luer, 5 Hill, 448............................... 284
Webb, Matter of, 11 Hun, 124........................... 57
—— v Buckelew, 82 N. Y. 555.......................27, n.
Webber v. Gay, 24 Wend. 485.......................... 179
Webster v. Bainbridge, 13 Hun, 180.................283, 284
Wehle v. U. S. Mutual Accident Assoc. 11 Misc. 36; aff'd 153
    N. Y. 116.. 367
Weinhaer v. Morrison, 49 Hun, 498. 325
Weiss v. Ashman, 1 N. Y. Ann. Cas. 314...................40, n.
—— v. Morrell, 7 Misc. 539..............................255
Weller v. J. B. Pace Tobacco Co,, 2 Supp. 292.............. 346
Wells v. Monihan, 129 N. Y. 161.......................324, 326
—— v. Smith, 2 Edw. Ch. 78 ; aff'd 7 Paige, 22............106, n.
Wells, Fargo & Co.. v. Wellsville, C. & P. R. R. Co., 12 App.
    Div. 47.. 39
Wentworth v. Wentworth, 51 How. Pr. 289................. 36
West v. Bacon, 13 App. Div. 371 ; s. c., 43 Supp. 206.......289, n.
Westfall v. Preston, 49 N. Y. 349......................... 180
Westfield Bank v. Cornen, 37 N. Y. 320.................... 362
Weston v. Turner, 8 St. R. 296..........................380, n.
West Side Bank v. Pugsley, 47 N. Y. 368........ 373
Wharton v. Winch, 140 N. Y. 287......................... 107
Wheeler v. Brady, 2 Hun, 347............................. 39
—— v. Jones, 42 Hun, 374............................. 287
—— v. McGuire, 2 L. R. A. 812............................. 144
White v. Merritt, 7 N. Y. 352..........................26, n.
—— v. Monroe, 12 Abb. Pr. 357 ; s. c., 33 Barb. 650.......... 39
—— v. Summer, 16 App. Div. 70 ; s. c., 44 Supp. 692........289, n.
Whitfield v. Le Despencer, Cowp. 754..................... 53
Whiting v. Barrett, 7 Lans. 106..........................125, n.
—— v. Edmonds, 94 N. Y. 309. ....298, n.
Whitlock, Matter of, 51 Hun, 351.................308, n., 309, n.
Whitney v. Davis, 3 N. Y. Ann. Cas. 88.. 346
—— v. Deniston, 2 Supm. Ct. (T. & C.) 471................. 67

Page

Whittenbrock *v.* Mabins, 57 Hun, 146....................309, *n.*

Wigand *v.* Sichel, 3 Keyes, 120............................ 283

Wiggant *v.* Smith, 2 Lans. 185.......................124, *n.*

Wildner *v.* Lane, 34 Barb. 54 ; s. c., 12 Abb. Pr. 351.......... 259

Wildrick *v.* De Vinney, 18 W. Dig. 355...................125, *n.*

Wilkes *v.* Ferris, 5 Johns. 335........................ 349

Wilkinson *v.* Johnson, 4 Hill, 46........................... 208

Willard *v.* Judd, 15 Johns. 531...........................156, *n.*

Willett *v.* Fayerweather, 1 Barb. 72....................... 39

Williams *v.* Huber, 5 Misc. 488.................. ..,........35, *n.*

—— *v.* Lindblom, 90 Hun, 370............................215, *n.*

—— *v.* Vanderbilt, 28 N. Y. 217........................ 135

—— *v.* Wilson, 18 Misc. 42 ; s. c., 40 Supp. 1132 ; rev'g 17 Misc.
317 ; s. c., 40 Supp. 350.......................... ....288, *n.*

Willis *v.* Dawson, 34 Hun, 492............................ 110

—— *v.* Webster, 1 App. Div. 301 ; s. c., 37 Supp. 354 ; 72 St. R.
743.. 109

Williston *v.* Williston, 41 Barb. 635..................... 112

Wilmore *v.* Flack, 96 N. Y. 512.. 204

Wilson *v.* Barney, 5 Hun, 257................................ 38

—— *v.* Brentwood Hotel Co., 16 Misc. 48 ; s. c., 37 Supp. 655 ;
73 St. R. 274.......................................237, *n.*

—— *v.* Goit, 17 N. Y. 442................................. 10

—— *v.* How, 8 Johns. 444..... ....389, *n.*

—— *v.* Traer & Co., 20 Iowa, 231............................ 158

Winchester *v.* Brown, 26 Abb. N. C. 387...................220, *n.*

Winsmore *v.* Greenback, Willes, 577, 580.................... 12

Winterson *v.* Hitchings, 1 N. Y. Ann. Cas. 193.....233, *n.*, 289, *n.*

Withy *v.* Mumford, 5 Cow. 137............................399, *n.*

Wonzer *v.* De Baun, 1 E. D. Sm. 261......................93, *n.*

Wood *v.* Amory, 105 N. Y. 278........ ....26, *n.*

—— *v.* Bach, 54 Barb. 134.............................161, *n.*

—— *v.* Baker, 60 Hun, 337.........................228, *n.*

—— *v.* Furtick, 17 Misc. 561............................. 347

—— *v.* Leadbitter, 13 M & W. 838.....:..................317, *n.*

—— *v.* Mitchell, 117 N. Y. 439 ; s. c., 27 St. R. 704 ; rev'g 53
Hun, 451 ; s. c., 25 St. R. 147 ; 6 Supp. 232 ; 17 Civ. Pro.
R. 346..... 396

—— *v.* Northwestern Ins. Co., 46 N. Y. 421........ ....115, *n.*

—— *v.* Swift, 81 N. Y. 31............................197, 297, *n.*

Woods *v.* Hart, Col. & Caines, 447.......................333, *n.*

Woodward *v.* Frost, 19 W. Dig. 125....................... 208

Woolsey *v.* Morris, 96 N. Y. 312. 179

Page

Wooster *v.* Case, 12 Supp. 769 ; s. c., 34 St. R. 577......... . 206
Wright *v.* Hooker, 10 N. Y. 51............................. 361

Y.

Yates *v.* Stiles, 15 W. Dig. 113............................. 258
Yates County Nat. Bank *v.* Carpenter, 119 N. Y. 550........124, *n.*
Yeamans *v.* Tannehill, 15 Supp. 958; s. c., 40 St. R. 548...... 107
York *v.* Texas, 137 U. S. 15............................. .. 31
Younger *v.* Duffie, 94 N. Y. 535........................... 264

TABLE OF SPECIAL NOTES

IN THIS VOLUME.

	Page
Actions without Precedent	15
Physical Exhibits at the Trial	23
Renewal of Motion	35
Substitution of Sheriff's Indemnitors	62
Remedy for Fraud after Suit on Contract	93
When Time is of the Essence of a Contract	106
Introduction of Evidence on Appeal	127
Reference of Issues Arising on Motions	140
Actions for Abuse of Process	176
Consolidation of Actions	205
Separate Actions for Injuries to Person and Property from the Same Tort	212
Jurisdiction of Non-Residents	243
Preference on the Calendar	253
Testator's Subscription at End of Will	261
Suspension of Right to Sue by Acceptance of Note, etc	282
Pleading Statute of Frauds	325
Levy of Attachment and Execution on Choses in Action	345
Actions on Lloyds' Policies	367

TABLE OF CODE CITATIONS.

IN

VOL. IV. N. Y. ANNOTATED CASES,

AND IN

The following volumes of the Official Reports, viz:

151, 152 NEW YORK REPORTS, 10 to 20 APPELLATE DIVISION
REPORTS, and 18 to 20 MISCELLANEOUS REPORTS.

[Each volume of the N. Y. ANNOTATED CASES contains a Table
of Code Citations in the volume, and in the current Official Series
of New York Reports.]

CODE OF CIVIL PROCE-
DURE.

c. 8, tit. 6, art. 4, 18 App. Div. 585.
c. 9, tit. 3, art. 1, 18 App. Div. 588.
c. 12, tit. 1, 3, 16 App. Div. 472.
c. 14, tit. 1, 10 App. Div. 608.
c. 14, tit. 1, art. 5, 15 App. Div. 24.
c. 16, tit. 2, 15 App. Div. 294.
c. 18, 10 App. Div. 129.
c. 18, tit. 4, art. 2, 12 App. Div. 138
c. 18, tit. 6, 12 App. Div. 138.
c. 19, 12 App. Div. 95.
§ 3 (subd. 8), 18 Misc. 192.
§ 7, 19 Misc. 134.
§ 8 (subd. 3), 10 App. Div. 28.
§§ 8-10, 20 Misc. 694.
§ 14, 18 App. Div. 159, 160; (subd. 4), 12 App. Div. 90; 18 Id. 158; 4 N. Y. Ann. Cas. 270.
§ 15, 19 App. Div 381.
§ 22, 19 Misc. 503.
§ 46, 10 App. Div. 349.

§ 65, 13 App. Div. 605.
§ 66, 152 N. Y. 521; 11 App. Div. 288; 13 Id. 373; 16 Id. 71, 129; 18 Misc. 40; 4 N. Y. Ann. Cas, 232, 288.
§ 67, 152 N. Y. 596; 10 App. Div. 513; 20 Id. 320.
§§ 68, 69 20 App. Div. 320.
§ 70, 20 Misc. 167.
§ 86, 20 Misc. 234.
§ 119, 19 Misc. 359.
§§ 162, 165, 18 App. Div. 129.
§ 190, 151 N. Y. 172, 557; 152 Id. 521; (subd. 1), 4 N. Y. Ann. Cas. 288.
§ 191, 151 N. Y. 50, 171, 549; 14 App. Div. 19; (subd. 2), 152 N. Y. 212, 630; 18 Misc. 196.
§ 192, 13 App. Div. 225.
§§ 215, 216, 218, 19 Misc. 281.
§ 232, 151 N. Y. 210.
§ 234, 18 App. Div. 163, 165, 167, 169.
§§ 249, 250, 20 App. Div. 504, 506.
§ 256, 20 Misc. 213.
§ 340 (subd. 1), 20 App. Div. 4.

§ 315, 4 N. Y. Ann. Cas. 201 ; 19 Misc. 101.

§ 316, 18 Misc. 196 ; 19 Id. 595 ; 4 N. Y. Ann. Cas. 200.

§ 325, 4 N. Y. Ann. Cas. 48, *n.*

§ 338, 16 App. Div. 186.

§ 340, 16 App. Div. 619.

§ 340, subd. 3, 16 App. Div. 618.

§ 341. 20 App. Div. 157.

§ 342, 10 App. Div. 348.

§ 348, 16 App. Div. 618.

§ 353, 17 App. Div. 578.

§ 365, 12 App. Div. 109.

§ 368, 12 App. Div. 115 ; 17 Id. 255.

§ 369. 12 App. Div. 113 ; 19 Misc. 290.

§ 370, 18 Misc. 321.

§ 371, 12 App. Div. 115.

§ 372, 12 App. Div. 10, 115,

§ 376, 17 App. Div. 597.

§ 382, 152 N. Y. 529 ; 17 App. Div. 184.

§ 383, subd. 5, 15 App. Div. 328 ; 4 N. Y. Ann. Cas. 185.

§ 390, 17 App. Div. 518.

§ 394, 18 App. Div. 593.

§ 395, 14 App. Div. 267 ; 19 Misc. 217.

§ 398, 11 App. Div. 479 ; 15 Id. 104.

§ 399, 18 Misc. 215.

§ 401, 19 Misc. 261 ; 19 App. Div. 435, 436.

§ 410 (subd. 1), 10 App. Div. 450.

§ 414, 10 App. Div. 138.

§ 417, 15 App. Div. 496.

§§ 418, 419, 15 App. Div. 446 ; 4 N. Y. Ann. Cas. 192.

§ 420, 14 App. Div. 462 ; 15 Id. 447 ; 4 N. Y. Ann. Cas. 192.

§ 421, 15 App. Div. 496.

§ 422, 15 App. Div. 497.

§ 423, 4 N. Y. Ann. Cas. 164 ; 17 App. Div. 630.

§ 432, 4 N. Y. Ann. Cas. 248.

§ 434, 18 App. Div. 409.

§ 440, 14 App. Div. 398.

§ 443, 14 App. Div. 398.

§ 446, 17 App. Div. 619.

§ 448, 14 App. Div. 262.

§ 449, 17 App. Div. 619 ; 20 Id. 87 ; 19 Misc. 243, 616 ; 4 N. Y. Ann. Cas. 369.

§ 452, 13 App. Div. 337 ; 15 Id. 437 ; 20 Id. 480, 481 ; 4 N. Y. Ann. Cas. 194 ; 19 Misc. 567.

§§ 454, 455, 20 Misc. 37.

§ 456, 16 App. Div. 618.

§§ 458, 460, 18 Misc. 354, 568.

§ 461, 18 Misc. 599 ; 19 Id. 592.

§ 481, 13 App. Div. 557 ; 20 Misc. 202 ; (subd. 2), 20 App Div. 226.

§ 484, 151 N. Y. 186 ; 10 App. Div. 269, 517 ; 13 Id. 277 ; 18 Misc. 648 ; (subd. 9), 13 App. Div. 278.

§ 487, 20 App. Div. 215.

§ 488, 12 App. Div. 168 ; 13 Id. 9 ; 14 Id. 261 ; 15 Id. 490 ; 20 Id. 116, 215 ; 20 Misc. 49 ; (subd. 3), 18 Misc. 427 ; (subd. 4), 17 App. Div. 248.

§ 490, 18 Misc. 427 ; 20 Id. 49.

§ 493, 19 Misc. 216.

§ 494, 18 Misc. 648.

§ 495, 20 Misc. 49.

§ 496, 20 Misc. 49.

§ 498, 13 App. Div. 9 ; 14 Id. 261 ; 20 Id. 116, 215.

§ 499, 12 App. Div. 168 ; 13 Id. 9, 337 ; 16 Id. 452, 625 ; 20. Id. 116, 215 ; 18 Misc. 113, 175 ; 20 Id. 195.

§ 500, 11 App. Div. 99 ; 13 Id. 183 ; 17 Id. 329 ; 20 Id. 12, 621 ; 19 Misc. 400, 426 ; 20 Misc. 50.

§ 501, 12 App. Div. 81 ; 15 Id. 104, 499 ; 17 Id. 248 ; 18 Id. 566 ; 20 Misc. 49, 300, 504.

§ 502 (subd. 1), 10 App. Div. 194; 15 Id. 601 ; 20 Misc. 504.

§ 506, 14 App. Div. 433.

§§ 507, 508, 19 Misc. 3, 16, 400 426.

§ 516, 15 App. Div. 476 ; 4 N. Y. Ann. Cas. 219.

§ 519, 11 App. Div. 98.

§ 522, 16 App. Div. 205 ; 20 Id. 167 ; 19 Misc. 426.

§ 525 (subd. 3), 18 Misc. 628.

§ 532, 16 App. Div. 187 ; 20 Id. 5,

§ 533 15 App. Div. 384.

§ 534, 20 Misc. 242, 679.

§ 535, 16 App. Div. 82, 271.

§ 536, 16 App. Div. 82 ; 18 Id. 148.

§ 537, 20 Misc. 142.

§ 541, 12 App. Div. 198.

§ 542, 11 App. Div. 522 ; 20 Id. 325.

§ 543, 13 App. Div. 94.

§ 544, 152 N. Y. 201 ; 11 App. Div. 100; 16 Id. 75, 17 Id. 530 ; 20 Misc. 382.

§ 546, 13 App. Div. 124 ; 20 Misc. 282, 300.

§ 549, 19 Misc. 130, 356; (subd. 1), 18 Misc. 99, 364; (subds. 1, 2), 16, App. Div. 479; (subd. 4), 19 Misc. 512 ; 20 Id. 404.

§ 557, 19 Misc. 669.

§§ 567, 568, 16 App. Div. 480.

§ 572, 4 N. Y. Ann. Cas. 316.

§ 603, 20 Misc. 193.

§ 613, 20 App. Div. 355.

§ 627, 12 App. Div. 433.

§ 635, 13 App. Div. 225 ; 14 Id. 467 ; 4 N. Y. Ann, Cas. 244, 248.

§ 636, 13 App. Div. 225; 19 Misc. 670; (subd. 2), 13 App. Div. 13; 16 Id. 523.

§ 641, 18 Misc. 429.

§ 644, 16 App. Div. 353 ; 19 Id. 234.

§ 648, 16 App. Div. 353; 19 Id. 230, 231, 234; 4 N. Y. Ann. Cas. 337.

§ 649, 16 App. Div. 353 ; 18 Misc. 591 ; 4 N. Y. Ann. Cas. 335, 337, 345, 347, 348; (subd. 2), 19 Misc, 601 ; 4 N. Y. Ann. Cas. 300 ; 18 App. Div. 394, 396 ; 19 Id. 229, 231, 235.

§ 655, 18 Misc. 592 ; 4 N. Y. Ann. Cas. 546.

§ 658, 18 Misc. 37.

§ 674, 12 App. Div. 323.

§ 682, 12 App. Div. 442 ; 13 Id. 237 ; 4 N. Y. Ann. Cas. 65.

§ 683, 20 Misc. 96.

§§ 687–690, 4 N. Y. Ann. Cas. 66, n.

§ 708, 12 App. Div. 323.

§ 714, 11 App. Div. 64.

§ 717, 4 N. Y. Ann. Cas. 384.

§ 721, 10 App. Div. 289.

§ 723, 10 App. Div. 326, 394 ; 18 Id. 323; 20 Id. 624 ; 18 Misc. 581, 662; 19 Id. 498.

§ 724, 14 App. Div. 227 ; 18 Id. 266, 323.

§ 727, 13 App. Div. 95.

§ 728, 18 App. Div. 323.

§ 731, 18 Misc. 688.

§ 738, 10 App. Div. 95, 522 ; 19 Id. 582 ; 18 Misc. 688.

§ 755, 19 App. Div. 307 ; 4 N. Y. Ann. Cas. 375, n., 377.

§ 756, 19 Misc. 422 ; 20 Id. 319 ; 18 App. Div. 203 ; 19 Id. 246.

§ 757, 11 App. Div. 48 ; 12 Id. 313; 17 Id. 227 ; 19 Id. 306, 308 ; 19 Misc. 226; 4 N. Y. Ann. Cas. 375, 376, n., 377, 378.

§ 759, 20 App. Div. 525, 526.

§ 764, 4 N. Y. Ann. Cas, 56, n.

§ 765, 20 App. Div. 525.

§ 769, 151 N. Y. 556.

§ 772, 20 Misc. 206.

§ 779, 17 App. Div. 227 ; 18 Id. 409.

§ 780, 20 Misc. 207.

§ 784, 10 App. Div. 289 ; 14 Id. 232.

§ 790, *et seq.*, 4 N. Y. Ann. Cas. 253.

§ 791, 152 N. Y. 642 ; (subd. 4), 151 N. Y. 266, 647 ; (subd. 5) 16 App. Div. 214 ; (subd. 7), 151 N. Y. 669.

§ 812, 4 N. Y. Ann. Cas. 66, *n.*

§ 817, 4 N. Y. Ann. Cas. 200, 205 ; 19 Misc. 595 ; 20 Id. 508.

§ 818, 4 N. Y. Ann. Cas. 205.

§ 820, 10 App. Div. 234 ; 12 Id. 80 ; 19 Id. 610.

§ 823, 152 N. Y. 584.

§ 825, 19 Misc. 420 ; 20 Id. 693.

§ 827, 11 App. Div. 602.

§ 829, 13 App. Div. 67, 493, 535, 622 ; 14 Id. 201 ; 15. Id. 215 ; 16 Id. 547 ; 17 Id, 268 ; 18 Id. 491, 492 ; 19 Id. 354, 355, 453 ; 19 Misc. 385,

§ 831, 14 App. Div. 81.

§ 832, 14 App. Div. 192 ; 20 Id. 517.

§ 833, 11 App. Div. 430.

§ 834, 151 N. Y. 201 ; 11 App. Div. 429.

§ 835, 11 App. Div. 430 ; 13 Id. 569 ; 17 Id. 245.

§ 836, 151 N. Y. 196 ; 11 App. Div. 430.

§ 840, 20 App. Div. 186.

§ 841, 12 App. Div. 109 ; 20 Misc. 250.

§§ 854, 855, 856, 16 App. Div. 192.

§ 855 *et seq.* 4 N. Y. Ann. Cas. 308.

§ 859, 16 App. Div. 193.

§ 868, 18 App. Div. 589,

§§ 870-873, 16 App. Div. 77 ; 4 N. Y. Ann. Cas. 306.

§ 871, 18 App. Div. 586, 589.

§ 872, 18 Misc. 562 ; 4 N. Y. Ann. Cas. 167, *n ;* (subd. 4), 20 Misc. 421 ; 15 App. Div. 398 ; 16 Id. 79, 318 ; 18 Id. 586 ; (subd. 7), 18 Id. 586, 588, 589 ; 19 Id. 317.

§ 873, 16 App. Div. 79 ; 4 N. Y. Ann. Cas. 24, 167, *n ;* 20 Misc. 16, 279.

§ 887-913, 20 Misc. 510.

§§ 914-920, 19 Misc. 307.

§§ 914-917, 16 App. Div. 191.

§ 915, 16 App. Div. 189 ; 4 N. Y. Ann. Cas. 308.

§ 920, 16 App. Div. 190.

§ 933, 152 N. Y. 433 ; 10 App. Div. 389.

§§ 935, 936, 4 N. Y. Ann. Cas. 163 ; 17 App. Div. 629.

§ 942, 20 Misc. 305, 333.

§ 964, 19 Misc. 426.

§ 977, 18 Misc. 296.

§ 984, 18 App. Div. 398, 399.

§ 970, 20 Misc. 77.

§ 977, 19 App. Div. 237.

§ 992, 13 App. Div. 467 ; 20 Misc. 512, 558.

§ 993, 13 App. Div. 467.

§ 994, 11 App. Div. 319 ; 13 Id. 467 ; 20 Misc. 512, 558.

§ 997, 11 App. Div. 318.

§ 998, 11 App. Div. 318.

§ 999, 14 App. Div. 162 ; 19 Id. 269, 563 ; 18 Misc. 193 ; 19 Id. 270, 414 ; 20 Id. 303, 351. 601.

§ 1000, 151 N. Y. 551 ; 4 N. Y. Ann. Cas. 183.

§ 1002, 18 App. Div. 7 ; 19 Id. 625.

§ 1003, 14 App. Div. 162 ; 19 Misc. 200.

§ 1005, 19 App. Div. 625.

§ 1010, 16 App. Div. 265.

§ 1013, 20 Misc. 155.

§ 1015, 11 App. Div. 602 ; 17 Id. 610 ; 4 N. Y. Ann. Cas. 140, *n.*

§ 1019, 18 App. Div. 314, 315.

§ 1021, 19 Misc. 411.

§ 1022, 151 N. Y. 282 ; 152 N. Y. 435 ; 10 App. Div. 172; 11 Id. 562 ; 12 Id. 110, 266 ; 13 Id. 117, 443 ; 15 Id. 280 ; 16 Id. 592 ; 18 Id. 431 ; 20 Id. 305, 306.

§ 1023, 20 App. Div. 305.

§ 1027, 151 N. Y. 82.

§ 1200, 19 Misc. 596 ; 18 App. Div. 408.

§ 1204, 16 App. Div. 618.

§ 1205, 16 App. Div. 618.

§ 1207, 18 Misc. 552.

§ 1209, 13 App. Div. 602.

§ 1211, 14 App. Div. 155.

§ 1217, 12 App. Div. 477 ; 14 Id. 370; 4 N. Y. Ann. Cas. 248.

§ 1219 (subd. 2), 14 App. Div. 369.

§ 1221 (subd. 3), 14 App. Div. 629.

§ 1228, 15 App. Div. 281.

§ 1230, 1231, 15 App. Div. 281.

§ 1240, 4 N. Y. Ann. Cas. 313.

§ 1241, 20 App. Div. 529.

§ 1252, 20 Misc. 499.

§ 1253, 4 N. Y. Ann. Cas. 351.

§ 1260, 13 App. Div. 607.

§ 1279, 10 App. Div. 506.

§ 1280, 10 App. Div. 508.

§ 1282, 1283, 14 App. Div. 227 ; 16 Id. 475.

§ 1294, 151 N. Y. 520 ; 13 App. Div. 603.

§ 1300, 13 App. Div. 607.

§ 1301, 14 App. Div. 368.

§ 1303, 16 App. Div. 103.

§ 1304, 11 App. Div. 196.

§ 1317, 152 N. Y. 505 ; 16 App. Div. 469 ; 20 Id. 28 ; 4 N. Y. Ann. Cas. 228.

§ 1323, 151 N. Y. 552 ; 15 App. Div. 295 ; 20 Misc. 336.

§ 1326, 18 App. Div. 564.

§ 1327, 15 App. Div. 337 ; 18 Id. 564.

§ 1274, 4 N. Y. Ann. Cas. 395; 20 App. Div. 583 ; (subd. 2), 151 N. Y. 536 ; 20 App. Div. 201.

§ 1337, 152 N. Y. 433 ; 13 App. Div. 127.

§ 1340, 16 App. Div. 472.

§ 1347 (subd. 2), 14 App. Div. 163.

§ 1351, 20 Misc. 512.

§ 1353, 13 App. Div. 550.

§ 1356, 15 App. Div. 294.

§§ 1356–1361, 14 App. Div. 57.

§ 1375, 17 App. Div. 597.

§ 1377, 17 App. Div. 184.

§ 1380, 14 App. Div. 317 ; 4 N. Y. Ann. Cas. 122.

§ 1393, 4 N. Y. Ann. Cas. 124 n. ; 20 App. Div. 244.

§ 1404, 20 Misc. 496.

§ 1405, 12 App. Div. 493 ; 15 Id. 341.

§§ 1405 et seq., 4 Ann. Cas. 348.

§ 1406, 18 App. Div. 436.

§ 1411, 19 App. Div. 251 ; 20 Id. 567; 4 N. Y. Ann. Cas. 344, 348.

§ 1412, 4 N. Y. Ann. Cas. 348.

§§ 1413, 1414, 19 App. Div. 344.

§ 1418, 4 N. Y. Ann. Cas. 333, n., 334 ; 19 App. Div. 159.

§ 1419, 18 Misc. 37 ; 4 N. Y. Ann. Cas. 333, n., 334.

§ 1420, 19 App. Div. 159.

§ 1421, 13 App. Div. 182 ; 18 Misc. 37 ; 4 N. Y. Ann. Cas. 62, n., 64 ; 19 Misc. 220.

§ 1427, 4 N. Y. Ann. Cas. 62, n., 64.

§ 1434, 14 App. Div. 32 ; 18 Misc. 405 ; 4 N. Y. Ann. Cas. 96.

§ 1440, 19 App. Div. 387.

§§ 1449, 1450, 19 App. Div. 387.

§ 1487, 4 N. Y. Ann. Cas. 313.

§ ; 502, 151 N. Y. 496 ; 15 App. Div. 579.

§ 1503, 152 N. Y. 182.

§ 1504, 20 App. Div. 227.

§ 1505, 20 App, Div. 228.

§ 1507, 20 App. Div. 229.

§ 1524, 12 App. Div. 114.

§ 1532, 18 App. Div. 173. 312 ; 20 Misc. 246.

§ 1533, 20 Misc. 246.

§ 1538, 18 App. Div. 312.

§ 1546, 18 App. Div. 173, 174.

§ 1554, 18 App. Div. 174.

§ 1572, 19 App. Div. 223.

§ 1577, 17 App. Div. 322.

§ 1582, 19 App. Div. 222, 223.

§ 1587, 18 App. Div. 173.

§ 1625, 18 App. Div. 313.

§ 1628, 18 Misc. 55 ; 19 Id. 56.

§ 1632, 15 App. Div. 315 ; 17 Id. 151.

§§ 1638, 1639, 15 App. Div. 24.

§ 1641, 15 App. Div. 24.

§ 1642, 15 App. Div. 26.

§ 1659, 4 N. Y. Ann. Cas. 23.

§ 1667, 12 App. Div. 616.

§ 1670, 15 App. Div. 414.

§ 1671, 17 App. Div. 150.

§ 1674, 10 App. Div. 37.

§ 1678, 14 App. Div. 32 ; 18 Misc. 136, 175, 405 ; 4 N. Y. Ann. Cas. 98.

§ 1679, 10 App. Div. 608 ; 13 Id. 216.

§ 1680, 152 N. Y. 174.

§ 1690, 16 App. Div. 631.

§ 1690 (subd. 3), 16 App. Div. 631.

§ 1695, 18 Misc. 661.

§§ 1709, 1710, 1711, 13 App. Div. 180 ; 4 N. Y. Ann. Cas. 60; 19 Misc. 220.

§ 1712, 18 Misc. 661.

§ 1717, 12 App. Div. 174.

§ 1718, 12 App. Div. 175.

§ 1721, 20 Misc. 4, 323.

§ 1723, 19 App. Div. 296.

§§ 1726, 1727, 20 Misc. 431.

§ 1744, 18 App. Div. 316.

§ 1748, 152 N. Y. 126.

§ 1758, 19 Misc, 237.

§ 1759, 20 App. Div. 396 ; 18 Id. 35 ; 18 Misc. 335.

§ 1762, 20 Misc. 643.

§ 1766, 14 App. Div. 544.

§ 1769, 11 App. Div. 200 ; 19 Misc. 655.

§ 1770, 4 N. Y. Ann. Cas. 247.

§ 1771, 14 App. Div. 544 ; 20 Id. 396. 18 Misc. 335.

§ 1772, 19 Misc. 653.

§ 1774, 4 N. Y. Ann. Cas. 248.

§ 1766, 19 Misc 657 ; 20 App. Div. 167.

§ 1778, 19 Misc. 686 ; 4 N. Y. Ann. Cas. 338.

§ 1778, 18 App. Div. 130, 396 ; 19 Id. 232.

§ 1779, 13 App. Div. 15 ; 18 Misc. 425.

§ 1780, 13 App. Div. 15 ; 17 Id. 393; 20 Id. 632 ; 18 Misc. 379 ; 20 Id. 685 ; 4 N. Y. Ann. Cas. 78, n.

§ 1781, 20 App. Div. 259, 554, 586.

§ 1782, 20 App. Div. 259, 584.

§ 1784, 11 App. Div. 518 ; 15 Id. 341 ; 18 Misc. 390, 422, 552.

§ 1785, 10 App. Div. 333 ; 11 Id. 518.

§ 1788, 11 App. Div. 393 ; 16 Id. 151 ; 18 Misc. 390, 422, 552.

§ 1789, 18 Misc. 390, 422, 552.

§ 1793, 151 N. Y. 597 ; 14 App. Div, 328 ; 15 Id. 341.

§ 1798, 11 App. Div. 518.

§ 1808, 10 App. Div. 333.

§ 1812, 18 Misc. 553 ; 20 Id. 14 290.

§ 1815, 20 Misc. 507.

§ 1822, 18 Misc. 140.

§ 1835, 15 App. Div. 217; 19 Misc. 555.

§ 1836, 15 App. Div. 217.

§ 1843, 18 Misc. 146.

§ 1865, 19 Misc. 337.

§ 1873–1875, 4 N. Y. Ann. Cas. 351, 352.

§ 1879, 15 App. Div. 341.

§ 1899, 19 Misc. 134.

§ 1900, 15 App. Div. 209; 4 N. Y. Ann. Cas. 174.

§ 1902, 11 App. Div. 165; 12 Id. 31, 156, 524; 13 Id. 170; 14 Id. 51; 4 N. Y. Ann. Cas. 9; 20 Misc. 66.

§ 1903, 12 App. Div. 32.

§ 1904, 12 App. Div. 31.

§ 1907, 17 App. Div. 617.

§ 1909, 19 Misc. 16; 20 Id. 504.

§ 1910, 18 Misc. 502.

§ 1913, 152 N. Y. 71; 18 Misc. 506; 17 App. Div. 247.

§ 1917, 20 Misc. 657.

§§ 1819–1924, 13 App. Div. 225; 20 Misc. 182, 216.

§ 1921, 13 App. Div. 224.

§ 1922, 20 Misc. 17

§ 1925, 10 App. Div. 549; 19 Id. 394.

§ 1932, 15 App. Div. 162.

§§ 1932–1936, 19 Misc. 171.

§§ 1937, 1938, 20 Misc. 413.

§§ 1934, 1935, 15 App. Div. 162.

§ 1942, 19 Misc. 626,

§ 1948, 19 Misc. 249, 673.

§ 1948, et seq., 4 N. Y. Ann. Cas. 369.

§ 1983, 19 Misc. 673.

§ 1997, 10 App. Div. 394.

§§ 2015, 2017, 2020, 2027, 2028, 2031, 19 Misc. 678

§ 2050, 11 App. Div. 329.

§ 2068, 20 App. Div. 27.

§ 2070, 12 App. Div. 537, 20 Id. 50, 342; 19 Misc. 673.

§ 2076, 20 App. Div. 9.

§ 2077, 20 App. Div. 12.

§§ 2082, 2083, 20 Misc. 29.

§ 2088, 20 App. Div. 11; 20 Misc. 28; 151 N. Y. 386.

§ 2120, 20 App. Div. 3.

§§ 2121, 2122, 152 N. Y. 214.

§ 2127, 152 N. Y. 51; 17 App. Div. 203.

§ 2129, 17 App. Div. 202.

§ 2136, 17 App. Div. 562.

§ 2231, 19 Misc. 521, 540; (subd. 2) 20 Misc. 349; 11 App. Div. 264; (subd. 3), 18 Misc. 418.

§ 2235, 18 Misc. 241; 20 Misc. 193, 350.

§ 2237, 18 Misc. 242.

§ 2240, 11 App. Div. 265.

§ 2244, 18 Misc. 421; 20 Id. 614.

§ 2251, 14 App. Div. 549.

§ 2253, 18 Misc. 475; 19 Id. 604; 20 Id. 47.

§ 2254 (subd. 3), 18 Misc. 242.

§ 2259, 18 Misc. 417.

§ 2259, 18 Misc. 419.

§ 2260, 14 App. Div. 584.

§ 2266, 19 App. Div 296.

§ 2268, 19 App. Div. 296.

§ 2281, 18 App. Div. 368.

§ 2284, 11 App. Div. 401; 17 Id. 431; 18 Id. 309.

§ 2321, 18 Misc. 407; 19 Id. 689.

§ 2322, 18 Misc. 407.

§ 2337, 18 App. Div. 497.

§ 2339, 18 Misc. 407; 19 Id. 689; 18 App. Div. 498.

§ 2343, 19 Misc. 689.

§ 2348, 20 Misc. 235.

§ 2351, 18 App. Div. 500.

§ 2365, et seq., 12 App. Div. 427.

§ 2380, 12 App. Div. 427.

§ 2408, 20 App. Div. 441.

§ 2419, 10 App. Div. 331.

§ 2420, 151 N. Y. 511.

§ 2423, 11 App. Div. 393; 14 Id. 390.

§ 2428, 151 N. Y. 511.

§ 2429, 14 App. Div. 320, 629.

§ 2430. 12 App. Div, 494.

§ 2433, 17 App. Div. 582.

§ 2433, (subd. 1), 18 Misc. 388.

§ 2433, (subd. 2), 12 App. Div. 125.

§ 2441, 19 Misc. 668.

§ 2446, 18 Misc. 40.

§ 2447, 4 N. Y. Ann. Cas. 289.

§ 2451, 19 Misc. 670.

§ 2458, 18 Misc. 388.

§ 2463, 19 Misc. 484; 20 Id. 14.

§ 2465, 20 Misc. 519.

§ 2468, 4 N. Y. Ann. Cas. 381.

§ 2471a, 15 App. Div. 572.

§§ 2472-2474, 19 Misc. 325 ; 20 Id. 537 ; 152 N. Y. 508 ; 13 App. Div. 99; (subd. 3), 11 Id. 347.

§ 2476, 19 Misc. 80.

§ 2481, 152 N. Y. 508 ; 19 Misc. 325 ; 18 App. Div. 308 ; (subds. 6, 11), 11 App. Div. 347 ; 18 Id. 308 ; 20 Id. 383 ; (subd. 11), 20 App. Div. 383.

§ 2514, (subd. 6), 12 App. Div. 135.

§ 2537, 20 App. Div. 66.

§ 2545, 10 App. Div. 374; 17 Id. 268, 271 ; 19 Id. 489.

§ 2546, 18 App. Div. 114.

§ 2548, 14 App. Div. 162.

§ 2550, 18 App. Div. 303.

§ 2554, 4 N. Y. Ann. Cas. 269.

§ 2555, 19 App. Div. 382, 383.; (subd. 4), 18 Id. 308.

§ 2555, 4 N. Y. Ann. Cas. 265.

§ 2556, 18 App. Div. 303.

§ 2557, 10 App. Div. 129; 20 Misc. 307.

§ 2558, 10 App. Div. 129 ; 15 Id. 547.

§ 2562, 20 Misc. 307.

§ 2568, 11 App. Div. 354.

§ 2570, 12 App. Div. 17 ; 18 Id. 303.

§ 2576, 10 App. Div. 594 ; 17 Id. 6.

§ 2577, 11 App. Div. 45.

§ 2580. 11 App. Div. 45.

§ 2586, 10 App. Div. 401 ; 17 Id. 6.

§ 2588, 14 App. Div. 162.

§ 2596, 10 App. Div. 359.

§ 2603, 10 App. Div. 129.

§ 2606, 13 App. Div. 23.

§ 2613, 18 App. Div. 61.

§ 2620, 16 App. Div. 139; 19 Id. 267.

§ 2621, 19 Misc. 337.

§ 2627, 14 App. Div. 446.

§ 2638, 19 Misc. 85.

§ 2653a, 14 App. Div. 599; 16 Id. 457.

§§ 2662, 2663, 15 App. Div. 547.

§ 2685, 15 App. Div. 545.

§ 2685, (subd. 3), 11 App. Div. 195.

§§ 2686, 2687, 15 App. Div. 546.

§ 2693, 15 App. Div. 547.

§ 2695, 4 N. Y. Ann. Cas. 56, n. ; 17 App. Div. 519.

§ 2707-2709, 11 App. Div. 290.

§ 2712, 19 App. Div. 450.

§ 2713, 19 Misc. 86.

§ 2718, 13 App. Div. 23 ; 15 Id. 217 ; 17 Id. 5.

§ 2719, 19 Misc. 222.

§ 2721, 19 Misc. 255.

§ 2722, 16 App. Div. 36.

§ 2727, 16 App. Div. 36.

§§ 2727, 2728, 16 App. Div. 38.

§ 2728, 20 Misc. 307.

§ 2729, 16 App. Div. 38; 18 Id. 113.

§ 2730, 12 App. Div. 135; 13 Id. 97 ; 19 Misc. 376.

§ 2731, 152 N. Y. 515.

§ 2732 (subd. 7), 20 Misc. 65.

§ 2739, 152 N. Y. 515.

§ 2742, 152 N. Y. 498.

§ 2743, 152 N. Y. 320, 508 ; 20 Misc. 307.

§ 2749, *et seq.*, 151 N. Y. 208.

§ 2750, 20 App. Div. 68.

§ 2759, (subd. 4), 18 App. Div. 373.

§ 2775, 12 App. Div. 17.

§ 2798, 20 App. Div. 65, 66.

§ 2799, 20 App. Div. 66.

§ 2802, 12 App. Div. 136.

§ 2805, 20 Misc. 159.

§ 2807, 17 App. Div. 311.

§ 2814, 19 Misc. 325.

§ 2818, 10 App. Div. 510; 19 Misc. 325.

§ 2821, 20 Misc. 538.

§ 2830, 18 App. Div. 497.

§§ 2832–2834, 10 App. Div. 129.

§ 2938, 20 Misc. 332.

§§ 2861, 2863, 18 Misc. 241.

§ 2869, 20 App. Div. 167 ; (subd. 2), 19 App. Div. 452.

§ 2870, 16 App. Div. 192 ; 4 N. Y. Ann. Cas. 312.

§ 2871, 19 Misc. 308.

§ 2878, 20 Misc. 74.

§ 2895, (subd. 2), 4 N. Y. Ann. Cas. 315 ; 20 App. Div. 87, 88.

§ 2896, 4 N. Y. Ann. Cas. 315.

§ 2910, 15 App. Div. 228.

§ 2940, 20 Misc. 108.

§ 2943, 18 Misc. 205 ; 19 Id. 39, 180.

§ 2944, 14 App. Div. 10.

§ 2951, 2952, 18 Misc. 241.

§ 2954, 18 Misc. 241.

§ 2959, 16 App. Div. 64.

§ 2960, 14 App. Div. 10.

§§ 2974–2977, 16 App. Div. 192 ; 4 N. Y. Ann. Cas. 312.

§ 2983, 14 App. Div. 10.

§ 2990, 13 App. Div. 47 ; 18 Misc. 192.

§ 2991, 151 N. Y. 82.

§ 2995, 18 Misc. 192.

§ 3006, 18 Misc. 192.

§ 3015, 14 App. Div. 549.

§ 3017, 17 App. Div. 184.

§ 3046, 20 Misc. 369.

§ 3047, 20 Misc. 589.

§ 3053, 19 Misc. 541.

§ 3063, 10 App. Div. 604 ; 14 Id. 585 ; 18 Misc. 248 ; 19 Id. 194.

§ 3064, 20 Misc. 73.

§ 3068, 18 App. Div. 566.

§ 3070, 18 Misc. 508 ; 20 App. Div. 302.

§ 3071, 10 App. Div. 476.

§ 3073, 18 Misc. 508.

§ 3084, *et seq.*, 14 App. Div. 56.

§ 3118, 18 App. Div. 331.

§ 3151, 17 App. Div. 205.

§ 3169, (subd. 4), 18 Misc. 429.

§ 3189, 20 Misc. 431.

§ 3191, (subd. 2), 19 Misc. 10.

§ 3204, (subd. 4), 16 App. Div. 39.

§ 3210, 20 Misc. 367.

§ 3212, 18 Misc. 241.

§ 3213, 19 Misc. 32 ; 20 Id. 617.

§ 3214, 13 App. Div. 47.

§ 3216, 18 Misc. 196.

§ 3226, 12 App. Div. 25, 64 ; 14 Id. 10 ; 20 Id. 204.

§ 3227, 12 App. Div. 25 ; 20 App. Div. 204.

§ 3228, 18 Misc. 600, 688 ; 19 Id. 351, 593 ; 20 Id. 431 ; (subd. 4), 19 App. Div. 59.

§ 3229, 19 Misc. 351, 593.

§ 3229, 19 App. Div. 59.

§ 3232, 19 Misc. 264.

§ 3236, 11 App. Div. 602.

§ 3240, 18 Misc. 661 ; 17 App. Div. 63 ; 20 Id. 272, 273.

§ 3245, 12 App. Div. 595 ; 4 N. Y. Ann. Cas. 183, *n*.

§ 3246, 12 App. Div. 81 ; 18 Misc. 437 ; 19 Id. 555.

§ 3247, 14 App. Div. 467.

§ 3251, 11 App. Div. 602.

§ 3253, 4 N. Y. Ann. Cas. 164; 17 App. Div. 266, 630; 19 Misc. 233, 411.

§ 3253, (subd. 1), 152 N. Y. 610.

§ 3262, 19 Misc. 264.

§ 3263, 13 App. Div. 606.

§ 3264, 13 App. Div. 606; 19 Misc. 351.

§ 3265, 19 Misc. 351.

§§ 3268, 3272, 19 Misc. 279.

§ 3277, 18 Misc. 564.

§ 3280, 20 App. Div. 490, 492.

§ 3290, 12 App. Div. 140.

§ 3296, 4 N. Y. Ann. Cas. 48, n.

§ 3304, 12 App. Div. 141.

§ 3307, (subd. 2), 19 Misc. 52

§ 3311, 20 Misc. 233.

§ 3318, 19 Misc. 281, 379.

§ 3333, 18 Misc. 241.

§ 3334, 18 Misc. 241; 20 App. Div. 272.

§ 3339, 11 App. Div. 49.

§ 3343, (subd. 2), 10 App. Div. 27; (subd. 9), 15 App. Div. 441; (subd. 18), 20 App. Div. 167.

§ 3347, (subd. 4), 16 App. Div. 618; (subd. 6), 4 N. Y. Ann. Cas. 200, 205; 19 Misc. 598.

§ 3347, (subd. 8), 16 App. Div. 618.

§ 3358, 20 App. Div. 636.

§ 3367, 13 App. Div. 602.

§ 3371, 16 App. Div. 516.

§ 3372, 19 Misc. 232; 20 App. Div. 273.

CODE OF CRIMINAL PRO-
CEDURE.

§ 4, 14 App. Div. 507.

§ 56, 14 App. Div. 506; 16 Id. 463; 19 Misc. 682; 20 Id. 154.

§ 56, (subd. 33), 11 App. Div. 409.

§ 57, 11 App. Div. 409; 16 Id. 464.

§ 58, 11 App. Div. 409 ; 16 Id. 464.

§ 74, 20 Misc. 154.

§ 134, 11 App. Div. 543.

§ 144, 20 Misc. 165.

§ 145, 11 App. Div. 610; 19 Misc. 681.

§ 148, 11 App. Div. 610; 18 Id. 589.

§ 149, 19 Misc. 681.

§§ 150-152, 11 App. Div. 611.

§ 152, 13 App. Div. 2.

§ 154, 11 App. Div. 448; 20 Misc. 467.

§ 177, 11 App. Div. 448, 610; 19 Misc. 450.

§ 183, 19 Misc. 450.

§ 180, 11 App. Div. 610.

§ 188, 11 App. Div. 611; 19 Misc. 681.

§ 189, 19 Misc. 681.

§ 194, 11 App. Div. 611.

§§ 196-198, 11 App. Div. 612.

§ 201, 11 App. Div. 612.

§ 204, 152 N. Y. 136; 12 App. Div. 498.

§ 211, 16 App. Div. 465; 19 Misc. 682.

§ 258, 19 Misc. 299.

§§ 278, 279, 151 N. Y. 403.

§ 284, 13 App. Div. 432.

§ 313, 19 Misc. 299.

§ 389, 11 App. Div. 498; 15 Id. 194.

§ 392, 19 App. Div. 349.

§ 411, 4 N. Y. Ann. Cas. 23.

§ 465, 151 N. Y. 607.

§ 484, 20 Misc. 131.

§ 485, 151 N. Y. 403, 543, 607.

§ 488, 13 App. Div. 137.

§ 515, 151 N. Y. 58.

§§ 517, 519, 151 N. Y. 403, 607.

§ 523, 14 App. Div. 540.

§ 527, 19 Misc. 556; 20 App. Div. 444.

§ 528, 151 N. Y. 607.

§ 529, 14 App. Div. 540.

§ 542, 151 N. Y. 210; 11 App. Div. 449, 550; 12 Id. 472; 13 Id. 436; 19 Id. 348; 20 Id. 160.

§ 590, 14 App. Div. 540.

§ 592, 14 App. Div. 540.

§ 616, 19 Misc. 280.

§ 671, 19 Misc. 299.

§ 684, 11 App. Div. 550.

§ 695, 14 App. Div. 538.

§ 699, *et seq.*, 152 N. Y. 136.

§ 721, 19 Misc. 692.

§ 749, 151 N. Y. 58; 12 App. Div. 496; 15 Id. 45.

§ 751, 152 N. Y. 141; 15 App. Div. 45.

§ 756, 12 App. Div. 498.

§ 771, 151 N. Y. 54.

§ 749, 152 N. Y. 136.

§§ 749–770, 151 N. Y. 59.

§ 839, 20 Misc. 161.

§ 842, 151 N. Y. 573.

§ 848, 151 N. Y. 574.

§ 849, 151 N. Y. 570.

§ 851, (subd. 2), 20 Misc. 161.

§§ 861–880, 14 App. Div. 46.

§ 864, 15 App. Div. 44.

§ 899, 151 N. Y. 55; 20 Misc. 150.

§ 913, 20 Misc. 150.

§§ 914–926, 13 App. Div. 437.

§ 920, 151 N. Y. 534.

§ 950, 151 N. Y. 55.

§ 962, 14 App. Div. 508.

CODE OF PROCEDURE.

§ 11, (subd. 3), 10 App, Div. 568.

§ 22, 18 App. Div. 163.

§ 23, 18 App. Div. 163, 165.

§ 69, 11 App. Div. 49.

§ 85, 12 App. Div. 116.

§ 91, 152 N. Y. 529.

§ 112, 15 App. Div. 601.

§ 121, 11 App. Div. 48.

§ 132, 10 App. Div. 147.

§ 294, 19 Misc. 668.

§ 298, 299, 19 Misc. 670.

§ 349, 10 App. Div. 568.

§ 366, 10 App. Div. 604.

§ 399, 18 App. Div. 492.

§ 427, 4 N. Y. Ann. Cas. 247.

PENAL CODE.

Tit. 10, chap. 8, 16 App. Div. 478.

Tit. 10, chap. 1, 20 App. Div. 206.

§ 29, 11 App. Div. 496.

§ 30, 19 Misc. 301.

§ 51, 17 App. Div. 473.

§ 90, 19 Misc. 296.

§ 97, 19 Misc. 675.

§ 148, 20 Misc. 164.

§ 165, 19 Misc. 99.

§ 168, 19 Misc. 294.

§ 170, 152 N. Y, 36.

§ 221, 13 App. Div. 136.

§ 242, 11 App. Div. 167.

§ 259, 18 Misc. 718.

§ 264, 18 Misc. 718.

§ 271, 20 App. Div. 204.

§ 274, 14 App. Div. 506.

§ 275, 14 App. Div. 506.

§ 278, 11 App. Div. 204; (subd. 5), 12 Id. 464.

§ 283, 12 App. Div. 468.

§ 291, 152 N. Y. 136; 12 App. Div. 499; (subd. 2), 19 Misc. 562.

§ 292, 19 App. Div. 149.

§ 293, 19 Misc. 564.

§ 299, 20 Misc. 250.

§ 316, 13 App. Div. 70.

§ 317, 14 App. Div. 306.

§ 322, 11 App. Div. 609; 18 Id. 241; 19 Misc. 681.

§ 323, 152 N. Y. 12.

§ 323, *et seq.*, 16 App. Div. 478.

§ 325, 14 App. Div. 74.

§ 343, 152 N. Y. 6.

§ 351, 152 N. Y. 1 ; 16 App. Div. 20.

§ 352, 152 N. Y. 12.

§ 363a, 19 App. Div. 506.

§ 383, 18 App. Div. 233.

§ 385, 14 App. Div. 118; 19 Misc. 457.

§§ 396, 397, 19 Misc. 494.

§ 408a, 18 App. Div. 589.

§ 421, 13 App. Div. 581.

§ 505, 151 N. Y. 403.

§ 508, 18 Misc. 339.

§ 528, (subd. 2), 20 App . Div. 309.

§ 529, 18 Misc. 465.

§ 562, 20 App. Div. 247.

§ 569, 18 Misc. 465.

§ 571, 4 N. Y. Ann. Cas. 384 ; 18 App. Div. 290, 291 ; 19 Id. 292, 293.

§ 577j, 18 App. Div. 298.

§ 579, 19 Misc. 300.

§ 640, (subd. 11), 11 App. Div. 279 ; 17 Id. 464.

§ 652, 19 Misc. 454.

§ 654, 18 Misc. 652.

§ 668, 20 Misc. 463.

§ 672, 19 Misc. 98.

§ 710, 14 App. Div. 191.

§ 714, 20 App. Div. 318.

§ 725, (subd. 3), 20 Misc. 154.

NEW YORK ANNOTATED CASES.

HOEFLER *v.* HOEFLER.

Supreme Court, Fourth Department, Appellate Division; December, 1896.

Husband and wife; divorce; alimony; contempt; action for damages.] Where, in an action for separation, an order had been made requiring the defendant husband to pay alimony, and it appeared that the mother of the defendant, with knowledge of the separation suit and of the order for the payment of alimony, had induced him to depart from the State and had furnished him with the means of so doing, for the purpose of avoiding the payment of the alimony and getting beyond the jurisdiction of the court,—*Held*, that an action could be maintained by the wife against her mother-in-law for the damages caused by the non-payment of the alimony.[*]

Motion by the plaintiff, Mary E. Hoefler, for a new trial upon a case containing exceptions, ordered to be heard at the Appellate Division in the first instance upon a nonsuit granted by the court after a trial at a Trial Term, Monroe County.

The plaintiff Mary E. Hoefler is the wife of the defendant's son, John C. Hoefler, whom she married in

---

[*] See the following cases of Sorensen *v.* Balaban, and Kujek *v.* Goldman, with Note on Actions without Precedent.

June, 1888, and by whom she had two children. They lived for a while in Geneva, N. Y., and in February, 1892, the plaintiff left her husband, returned to her parents in Rochester and commenced an action against her husband for separation and support. On April 25, 1892, the Monroe special term made an order upon the hearing of the parties, requiring John C. Hoefler to pay the sum of twenty-five dollars counsel fees and the sum of four dollars per week to his wife for alimony during the pendency of the action, which allowance was to commence April 25, 1892. The plaintiff's husband was a letter carrier in Geneva, receiving a salary of $600 per year. He paid the weekly allowance as required by the order up to September 1, 1892. This action is still pending.

John C. Hoefler departed from the State December 25, 1892, and went to Lincoln in the State of Nebraska, where he has since remained in business, and has not contributed anything toward the support of his wife or family or paid the weekly allowance. The complaint in this action seems to have been intended in a double aspect, to recover damages against the defendant Mary R. Hoefler, for alienating the affections of the plaintiff's husband and depriving her and her children of his support, and, also, to recover for the unpaid alimony ; but it was held upon the first appeal in this action by this court (2 *App. Div.* 8) that if any cause of action existed upon the allegations in the complaint, it was to recover damages against the defendant for advising and procuring the husband to leave the State and remain out of it for the purpose of avoiding the payment of the alimony or support, and that she furnished him money for that purpose, and inasmuch as evidence was received upon the first trial not competent upon the last named issue a new trial was ordered. The complaint, after alleging the existence of the first action and the order for the payment of alimony and the payment by John C. Hoefler of the counsel fees and the weekly allowance up to September 1, continues:

Hoefler *v.* Hoefler.

" When he ceased to pay the same and without making any provision for the support of plaintiff and her said children, or for the payment of said sum of $4.00 each week as provided in said order, and said defendant in this action, well knowing of said order of said court, and wrongfully contriving and intending to injure the plaintiff and to deprive her of the comfort, society and aid of her said husband, John C. Hoefler, maliciously advised and counselled and induced the said John C. Hoefler to secretly leave the State of New York and find a separate residence elsewhere, and furnished the said John C. Hoefler with money and means to leave this State and thereby to disregard said order and avoid it, and avoid paying the moneys thereby ordered to be paid, and thereby deprive plaintiff of the same, and of all efforts to compel the said John C. Hoefler to support plaintiff and their said child Josephine, and that said John C. Hoefler acted on said advice of the said defendant, and upon the money and means furnished by said defendant, and without the knowledge or consent of this plaintiff, the said John C. Hoefler, in pursuance thereof, left this State on or about December 25, 1893, and went to Lincoln in the State of Nebraska, and ever since has remained in Nebraska, claiming his residence there, away from plaintiff, . . . and ever since that time the said John C. Hoefler has been and is now without this State and under the defendant's custody, control and influence . . . with intent to remain without this State."

The defendant answered, admitting the order for alimony and the default after September, 1892, besides other admissions, with denials. The trial court dismissed the complaint and directed the exceptions to be heard in the first instance at the Appellate Division.

Held, that there was sufficient evidence to go to the jury upon the question as to whether the defendant had notice of the order for alimony, and induced John C. Hoefler, plaintiff's husband, to leave the State and remain beyond its jurisdiction to avoid the payment for support provided by the order, and that a cause of action was thereby created in favor of the plaintiff against the defendant to recover the damages sustained by the plaintiff. There was evidence that the defendant was aware of the action for a separation.

The defendant's counsel strenuously contends that the plaintiff has no remedy by action against the defendant; that it does not appear that the alleged tort of the defendant caused any damage whatever to the plaintiff, and if any damage did arise it was too remote, indefinite and contingent to be recovered, and he cites Lamb *v.* Stone (11 *Pick.* 527), where a Massachusetts court holds, in effect, that, where a defendant had fraudulently purchased the property of a debtor, and had induced him to leave the State of his residence, a creditor of that debtor who had intended to attach the property of the debtor to secure his debt, and who had intended to arrest the debtor, but had never carried his intention into execution, or procured any attachment against the debtor until the property was sold and he had left the State, had no cause of action, for the excellent reason, as the court says, that the creditor had obtained no lien upon the property by attachment. The claim of the plaintiff consisted, simply, in an intention to effect the lien which was never consummated.

In the case at bar the husband was in contempt for violating an absolute order of the court in the plaintiff's favor requiring the husband to pay her money. There was no contingency about it. Under the statutes of this State the plaintiff was entitled to proceedings against the husband to compel its payment and to punish him for contempt. Of this right the plaintiff was deprived by the intermeddling of the defendant in placing the husband beyond the jurisdiction of the court. The damage in this case (the loss of the alimony) was not remote nor contingent. The grasp of the law was upon this husband and

Hoefler *v.* Hoefler.

upon his property and earnings for the benefit of the wife, which the husband could not escape unless he was placed beyond the jurisdiction of the court so that its order could not be enforced against him, so that the direct consequence of the defendant's acts was that she lost her support and the remedy to compel its payment. The damages were, therefore, the natural and legitimate result of the defendant's acts.

In Porous Plaster Co. *v.* Seabury (43 *Hun*, 611), it appears that the plaintiff in the action had brought a prior action against the same defendants to establish a trade-mark, in which it was successful, and had obtained a permanent injunction enjoining the defendants from violating the trade-mark. The action in that case was brought, among other things, against the defendants to recover damages for a violation of this injunction which had accrued since the judgment in the first action, but it was held that notwithstanding the violation of the injunction order subjected the defendants to contempt proceedings, and they might be proceeded against and fined and the damages collected in that way, there was nothing in the Code which restricts the plaintiff to this form of procedure, but it had a right of action for the damages.

In King *v.* Barnes (113 *N. Y.* 476), where a final judgment required the president and directors of a corporation to transfer its stock upon the books of a corporation, and one Barnes, who was a defendant in the action, though not called upon personally to perform the act required, but who advised and aided the defendants, whose duty it was to transfer the stock, to disobey the judgment, and it appeared that Barnes was "supporting them out of the jurisdiction when the fire of the courts became too hot for safety, or their orders could be thwarted by that means," and Barnes was fined and imprisoned for contempt, Judge FINCH (at p. 479), in referring to Code of Civil Pro., § 14, subd. 4, says: "The subdivision specifies certain acts of interference with the due and orderly

Hoefler *v.* Hoefler.

progress of an action or proceeding to its final and ultimate close, and then adds generally a provision which covers any other interference with it. So that any person who
interferes with the process or control or action of the
court in a pending litigation, unlawfully and without
authority, is guilty of a civil contempt, if his act defeats,
impairs, impedes or prejudices the right or remedy of a
party to such action or proceeding." Here is a clear intimation that the damages may arise from such an interference, which the injured party is entitled to recover in
contempt proceedings, and the case cited in *Hun* holds,
as we have seen, that such damages may be recovered by
action. The act of this defendant, complained of, certainly tended to defeat, impede or prejudice the right or
remedy of the plaintiff in the action for a separation.
The defendant finally claims that no precedent can be
found for this action. This action would, under the old
system, when actions had names, have been an action
upon the case, which is said to be a remedy adapted to
every special invasion of one's rights. Miller *v.* Taylor, 4
Burr. 2345. And in all cases where a man has a temporal
loss or damage by the wrong of another, he may have an
action on the case to be repaid in damages. *Com. Dig. Action
on Case;* County Commissioners *v.* Duckett, 20 *Md.* 468.
To maintain an action on the case it is not necessary that
it should be supported by instances or precedent; it is
sufficient if the case in question is covered by principle.
M'Farlane *v.* Moore, 1 *Overton* (*Tenn.*), 174. In Hurwitz
v. Hurwitz (9 *Misc.* 201 ; s. c., 30 *Supp.* 208), the general
term of the New York city court held that a judgment
creditor might maintain an action at law against the judgment debtor and another to recover damages for conspir-
ing to prevent the collection of the judgment by removing and disposing of such debtor's property and placing it
beyond the reach of execution. In Michalson *v.* All (21
S. E. Rep. [S. C.] 323), it was held that where a person
with the connivance of the owner converts to his own use

farm products subject to an agricultural lien and places
them beyond the reach of the lienee under the statutory
proceedings, the latter may, in an action similar to case
at common law, recover his damages.

Opinion by WARD, J.   All concurred, except ADAMS,
J., not sitting.

Plaintiff's exception sustained and a new trial ordered
with costs to abide the event.

William E. Edmonds, for the plaintiff.

Thomas Raines, for the defendant.

SORENSEN *v.* BALABAN.

*Snpreme Court, Second Department, Appellate Division;
December,* 1896.

1. *Negligence; physician; mother's action for child's death.*]
   While the mother of an unmarried daughter who is an infant
   and in her service, the father being dead, may maintain an action against a physician for malpractice, resulting in the child's
   death, the recovery must be limited to loss of service intermediate the injury and the death, and the fact of death cannot be
   taken into account either as a ground of action or as an aggravation of damages.*

2. *Slander; action by mother of defamed child.*]   No action lies by
   the mother of a deceased daughter for maligning the memory
   of the deceased by slanderous statements, as by charging that
   the daughter had been pregnant, and had had a miscarriage.

3. *Appeal; error considered though no excepction.*]   Where, upon
   an appeal from a judgment and an order denying defendant's

---

* Compare the preceding and following cases and see Note on
Actions without Precedent, *post,* p. 15.

Sorensen *v.* Balaban.

motion for a new trial, there is no exception, in the record, to
an erroneous charge of the trial judge, it is within the discretion of the court whether or not to consider such error.*

Appeal by the defendant, from a judgment of the Supreme Court in favor of the plaintiff, entered upon the
verdict of a jury rendered after a trial at a Trial Term of
the Supreme Court, Queen's County, and also from an
order denying the defendant's motion for a new trial made
upon the minutes.

The plaintiff, Ida C. Sorensen, was the mother of one
Clara O. Nelson, now deceased. The deceased was an
infant, unmarried, in the service of her mother, her father
being dead. The defendant, Siegbert Balaban, is a physician and attended said Clara in her last illness. The action is brought on substantially two causes of action. The
first charges the defendant with malpractice in his attendance on the patient, by reason of which said Clara died.
The second cause of action charges that, after the death
of Clara O. Nelson, the defendant maligned her memory
by repeating to the plaintiff and to divers other persons,
a false, untrue and malicious charge that the said Clara
had been pregnant and had had a miscarriage. The
plaintiff recovered a verdict for $5,000.

Held, as stated in headnotes. It clearly was the rule
at common law that no civil action would lie for causing
the death of a human being. While a husband or
parent might maintain an action for a wrong causing
loss of service from a wife or child, if the injury resulted
in death, this could not, at the common law, be taken into
account either as a ground of action or as an aggravation
of damages, and the plaintiff's recovery would be limited
to loss of service intermediate the injury and the death.
The exact question was determined by the Court of Appeals in Green *v.* Hudson River R. R. Co. (2 *Abb. Ct.*

* See Note on Necessity of Exception to Erroneous Charge, **3**
N. Y. Ann. Cas. 234.

Sorensen *v.* Balaban.

App. Dec. 277). Since the time of that decision, I cannot find that there has ever been in this State a contention for the contrary rule. Of course, for many years the statute has prescribed a remedy for such wrongs. An action for a wrongful act causing the death of any person may be maintained by the executor or administrator of such person for the benefit of his next of kin. *Code Civ. Pro.* § 1902. The plaintiff, however, has not brought this action in such capacity. But, though the trial court erred in assuming that the plaintiff could maintain an action for the death of her daughter, still there was enough in the complaint and in the evidence to show that the daughter was sick for some few days prior to her decease. For loss of services during this period and the expense of care and attendance during the like time, the plaintiff was entitled to recover. Therefore, the defendant's motion to dismiss the complaint as to this cause of action was properly denied. When the cause was submitted to the jury, the court charged that the plaintiff could recover for loss of the services of her daughter from her daughter's death to the time she would have arrived at the age of twenty-one years. The defendant asked the court to charge that the plaintiff could not recover damages for the death of the deceased. The court charged this, " except so far as she loses her personal services." This qualification was error. The plaintiff could not recover any damages caused by the daughter's death. She could recover, as already stated, for loss of service during the period the daughter was ill, but such damages were damages not resulting from the death, but from the malpractice. I can find no exception to the failure of the court to charge as requested. As the appeal before us is not only from the judgment, but also from the order denying defendant's motion for a new trial, it is within our discretion to take notice of the error, though without exception.

This brings us to the question whether the second cause of action stated in the complaint is a good cause of action which the plaintiff can maintain. The action is for damages suffered by a living person from maligning the memory of a deceased relative. No authority for the maintenance of such an action is to be found. As stated by the counsel for the respondent, the lack of precedent is not necessarily conclusive that such an action cannot be sustained, but certainly it militates strongly against the proposition. I think, too, that an analysis of the character of an action for slander will show that on principle no such action as the present one can be supported. The action of slander is not to redress or punish the indignity or outrage on one's feelings when he is falsely charged with an offense, but to redress his reputation or character with others. *Cooley on Torts,* *193; Wilson *v.* Goit, 17 *N. Y.* 442. So far, therefore, as a false aspersion on her daughter's memory, made to the plaintiff, was an insult and an outrage upon the mother's feelings, it could no more give the plaintiff a right of action than if the defendant had aspersed to the plaintiff her own character. It would seem plain that the imputation on the character of the daughter did not necessarily or naturally affect the reputation or character of the plaintiff, and as it is only injury to reputation which gives a right of action, it is apparent that the present action in this respect cannot be maintained. *Newell on Defamation,* 369; *Odgers on Lib. and Sland.* 406.

Opinion by CULLEN, J. All concurred.

Judgment and order reversed and a new trial granted, costs to abide the event.

Stephen C. Baldwin, for the defendant, appellant.

Herbert Kettell and *J. Edward Swanstrom,* for the plaintiff, respondent.

KUJEK *v.* GOLDMAN.

Court of Appeals; October, 1896.

[Affirming 9 *Misc.* 34.]

Husband and wife; marriage induced by fraud of third party; damages.] Where the plaintiff was induced to marry a woman by the false and fraudulent representations of the defendant that she was virtuous, when in fact she was pregnant by the defendant,—*Held,* that the plaintiff could maintain an action for damages because of the fraud practised upon him.*

The same; novel action.] It is no objection to the maintenance of an action that it is novel and has no precedent, when it is based on legal principles clearly applicable to the new state of facts.†

Appeal, by permission, from a judgment of the General Term of the Court of Common Pleas for the city and county of New York, entered upon an order affirming a judgment of the General Term of the City Court of New York, which affirmed a judgment in favor of plaintiff entered upon a verdict.

Prior to January 17, 1891, the defendant Katie Kujek, then named Katie Moritz, was an unmarried woman employed as a domestic in the family of the defendant Goldman, by whom she had become pregnant. Upon discovering the fact, the defendants, as it is alleged in the complaint, conspired to conceal their disgrace and to induce the plaintiff to marry the said Katie, and to that end represented to him that she was a virtuous and respectable woman, and he, believing the same, did marry her on the day last named. The plaintiff, as it was further alleged, would not have contracted said marriage if he had known the facts. Subsequently, and on July 29th, 1891, owing

---

* See Note on Annulment of Marriage for Fraud, 1 *N. Y. Ann. Cas.* 382.

† See note at the end of this case on Actions without Precedent.

Kujek *v.* Goldman.

to such pregnancy, she gave birth to a child of which said Goldman was the father. The answer of Goldman was, in substance, a general denial. No answer was served by the other defendant and no judgment was taken against her.

The case was submitted to the jury upon the theory that if Goldman, knowing that Katie was unchaste, by false representations that she was virtuous induced the plaintiff to marry her, he was entitled to recover damages, and the jury found a verdict in his favor for $2,000.

Held, that the judgment should be affirmed. While no precedent is cited for such an action, it does not follow that there is no remedy for the wrong, because every form of action when brought for the first time must have been without a precedent to support it. Courts sometimes of necessity abandon their search for precedents and yet sustain a recovery upon legal principles clearly applicable to the new state of facts, although there was no direct precedent for it, because there had never been an occasion to make one. Winsmore *v.* Greenback, *Willes*, 577, 580. As was recently said by this court in an action then without precedent : " If the most that can be said is that the case is novel and is not brought plainly within the limits of some adjudged case, we think such fact not enough to call for a reversal of the judgment." Piper *v.* Hoard, 107 *N. Y.* 73, 76 ; s. c. 11 *St. R.* 371.

The question, therefore, is not whether there is any precedent for the action, but whether the defendant inflicted such a wrong upon the plaintiff as resulted in lawful damages. The defendant, by deceit, induced the plaintiff to enter into a marriage contract whereby he assumed certain obligations and became entitled to certain rights. Among the obligations assumed was the duty of supporting his wife in sickness and in health, and he discharged this obligation by expending money to fit up rooms for housekeeping, in keeping house with his wife and caring for her during confinement, when she bore

Kujek *v.* Goldman.

a child not to him but to the defendant. Among the rights acquired was the right to his wife's services, companionship and society. By the fraudulent conduct of the defendant, he was not only compelled to expend money to support a woman whom he would not otherwise have married, but was also deprived of her services while she was in child-bed. He thus sustained actual damages to some extent, and as the wrong involved not only malice but moral turpitude also, in accordance with the analogies of the law upon the subject, the jury had the right to make the damages exemplary. By thus applying well-settled principles upon which somewhat similar actions are founded, this action can be sustained, because there was a wrongful act in the fraud, that was followed by lawful damages in the loss of money and services. Fraudulent representations with reference to the amount of property belonging to either party to a proposed marriage, made by a third person for the purpose of bringing about the marriage, are held to constitute an actionable wrong, and the usual remedy is to require the person guilty of the fraud to make his representations good. Piper *v.* Hoard *supra ;* Montifiori *v.* Montifiori, 1 *Wm. Bl.* 363. In such cases the injury is more tangible and the measure of damages more readily applied than in the case before us, but both rest upon the principle that he who by falsehood and fraud induces a man to marry a woman, is guilty of a wrong that may be remedied by an action, the amount of damages to be recovered depending upon the circumstances of the particular case.

We have thus far considered the right of action as resting upon some pecuniary loss, which, although, trifling in amount, may be recovered as a matter of right, leaving it to the jury in their sound discretion, as in a case for the seduction of a child or servant, to amplify the damages by way of punishment and example. We think, however, that the action can be maintained upon a broader and more satisfactory ground, and that is, the loss of consortium, or the right of the husband to the conjugal fellowship and society of his wife. The loss of the consortium through the misconduct of a third person has long been held an actionable injury, without proof of any pecuniary loss. Bennett *v.* Bennett, 116 *N. Y.* 584 ; Hutcheson *v.* Peck, 5 *Johns.* 196 ; Hermance *v.* James, 32 *How. Pr.* 142.

Where false representations are willfully made as to a material fact for the purpose of inducing another to act upon them and he does so act to his injury, he may recover such damages as proximately result from the deception. The representations in this case, as the jury has found, were made to promote the marriage, and they were false as the defendant well knew. They were clearly material. The plaintiff acted upon them and was thereby injured, for he made a contract entitling him to certain rights, which he has not received and which the defendant knew he could never receive. Here are all the elements of a good cause of action founded upon fraud resulting in damage. If he had induced the very marriage contract under consideration by representing to the plaintiff that he owed his proposed wife a certain sum of money, according to the common law, which entitles the husband to the personal property of his wife, he could have been compelled to make his representations good by the payment of that sum. Montifiori *v.* Montifiori, *supra ;* Redman *v.* Redman, 1 *Vern.* 348 ; Neville *v.* Wilkinson, 1 *Brown's Ch. Cas.* 543 ; Scott *v.* Scott, 1 *Cox,* 378.

Opinion by VANN, J. All concur, except BARTLETT, J., not voting.

Judgment affirmed, with costs.

Wheeler H. Peckham, for the defendant, appellant.

August P. Wagener, for the plaintiff, respondent.

NOTE ON ACTIONS WITHOUT PRECEDENT.

The case in the text affords a striking illustration of the principle of late applied with increasing frequency by our courts, that the mere novelty of an action is no ground for refusing redress for a legal wrong, and shows the radical change brought about in the principles underlying the law, as administered in this country, and particularly in this State, at the present time, in comparison with the doctrines of the Civil Law, and later of the Common Law. Both of these systems of jurisprudence, while they differed widely in the fact that in the former precedent did not have that binding force on later cases that was insisted upon so strenuously in the latter, they were both alike in the fact that for a long time in the history of each the *form* of the action was considered of the first importance. In the Civil Law if a particular case could not be classified so as to come under one of the forms prescribed by the Twelve Tables, no matter how great the wrong, the suitor must suffer his grievance to go unredressed. Likewise, in the Common Law it was absolutely necessary, in the somewhat early stages of its development, that every action should be capable of being begun by one of the regular forms of writs then in use. Both of these systems were modified from time to time, as it was found that a strict adherence to these forms frequently worked great injustice. Finally, in the Common Law there was established a form of action which was known as an action on the case, and generally speaking, all actions that could not be begun by any one of the regular forms of common-law writs was so styled, until after years of gradual development it became a maxim that there was no wrong without a remedy. This maxim is not strictly true, and should be qualified to the extent of declaring that the law furnishes a remedy for legal wrongs only, and so the important question is whether or not the action in any particular case is brought to secure redress for a legal, as distinguished from a moral wrong.

There is also another class of injuries for which the law of this State furnishes no remedy ; that is injuries caused by mental distress or fright. Although physical injuries may result from these causes, if there is no direct physical injury, there can be no recovery. Mitchell *v.* Rochester Ry. Co., 3 *N. Y. Ann. Cas.* 283 ; Curtin *v.* Western Union Tel. Co., *Id.* 286.

In Schuyler *v.* Curtis, 147 *N. Y.* 434, it was held that

the mere fact that a person's feelings may be injured by the erection of a statue to a deceased relative is not ground for an injunction against its erection unless there is reasonable and plausible ground for the existence of this mental distress and injury. It must not be the creation of mere caprice, nor of pure fancy, nor the result of a super-sensitive and morbid mental organization dwelling with undue emphasis upon the exclusive and sacred character of the right of privacy. The court reversed a judgment granting an injunction, not on the ground that the action was without precedent, however, but for the reasons stated above.

In cases of first impression where the question is whether or not a legal wrong has been committed, the courts have laid down general principles which were well stated by Mr. Justice BISCHOFF in writing the opinion of the court below in the case in the text (9 *Misc.* 34), where it is said at page 37 : " Not every wrong perpetrated by one person upon another is actionable. To be actionable the wrong must be accompanied by an injury to the person, reputation, property or marital rights of the plaintiff. For the wounded moral sensibility of a person, unaccompanied by an injury to his person, reputation, property or marital rights, the law will not afford relief by way of damages. A mere moral outrage inflicted by one person upon another is *injuria sine damno*, and the legal aphorism, *ubi jus ibi remedium*, must be accepted with the qualification that it applies only to a legal right as distinguished from a moral right."

Thus, it has been held, that if A. has agreed to sell property to B., C. may at any time, before the title has passed, induce A. to sell it to him instead, and if not guilty of fraud or misrepresentation, he does not incur any liability, and this is so although C. may have contracted to purchase the property of B. Ashley *v.* Dixon, 48 *N. Y.* 430. In that case the court says, at page 432 : " While, by the moral law, C. is under obligation to abstain from any interference with the contract between A. and B. yet it is one of those imperfect obligations which the law, as administered in our courts, does not undertake to impose."

A simple conspiracy, however atrocious, unless it results in actual damage to the party against whom it is aimed, is not the subject for a civil action. BARKER, J., in Buffalo Lubricating Oil Co. *v.* Everest, 30 *Hun*, 586 ; aff'd 95 *N. Y.* 674.

The case of Johnson *v.* Hitchcock (15 *Johns.* 185), has been cited a number of times as authority for the principle that grievances, imaginary or real, which are the result of rivalry or competition in business are not grounds for damages in an action at law. In this case it appeared that the defendant had induced numerous intending passengers to cross one of two rival ferries, by representing that one ferry was better than the other. The plaintiff was allowed to recover below, the defendant putting in no evidence, and the court in reversing the judgment said : "If an action would lie in this case, it would in all cases of rival business, where any means are used to draw custom ; and if this were once admitted it would be difficult to know where to stop."

In Corrigan v. Coney Island Jockey Club (27 *Abb. N. C.* 294), a mandatory injunction was allowed requiring the defendant to refrain from preventing the plaintiff to run his horses which had been entered in a race called the Futurity, and McADAM, J., there says that the novelty of the application was no argument against it. This case was reversed in 48 *St. R.* 582 ; s. c., 20 *Supp.* 437, but not on the ground that such relief could not be granted in any case, but because under the facts in that case the plaintiff had not shown himself entitled to the relief demanded.

Where there has been a legal wrong committed, however, it is not necessary to show that the wrongdoer has derived any benefit from his act. It is sufficient if the plaintiff has been damaged. The leading case to that effect in this State is Brownell v. Flagler, 5 *Hill,* 282. There the owner of a lamb allowed it to escape into the highway where it mingled with a flock of sheep which the defendant was driving along, and he, knowing this fact, made no attempt to separate the lamb from the flock, but delivered the whole in pursuance of a sale previously made to a person by whom they were taken to market, and it was held that these facts were sufficient to authorize a verdict in favor of the plaintiff for the value of the lamb, though it was not included in the sale to the drover, and the defendant received nothing on account of it.

There is another class of cases where the courts admit that technically, there has been a wrong committed, but deny a remedy in the interest of public policy, on the ground that to grant a remedy would lead to much greater abuses. This doctrine applies to actions against judicial officers for acts done in their judicial capacity. Thus it has been held that a judge of a court of record, who sentences a person to imprisonment in good faith without malice, incurs no personal liability, though his judgment be subsequently reversed for want of jurisdiction. Lange *v.* Benedict, 73 *N. Y.* 12. See also East River Gaslight Co. *v.* Donnelly, 93 *N. Y.* 557.

A justice is not liable for false imprisonment by reason of an error in judgment, if he had jurisdiction of the person and the subject matter. Kenner *v.* Morrison, 12 *Hun,* 204.

But a justice is liable for assault and battery and false imprisonment, if he issue a warrant for the arrest of a party in a penal action where the complaint shows no jurisdiction. Warner *v.* Perry, 14 *Hun,* 337.

In Smith *v.* Lewis, 3 *Johns.* 157, it was held that no action would lie against a person in this State for suborning a witness to swear falsely in a cause in another State, whereby a judgment was given against the defendant in that State, contrary to the truth and justice of the case. The reason given by SPENCER, J., for the decision of the court as stated, at page 167, was: " I confess that I should be afraid to make a precedent that would be so productive of litigation, and that would open the door to so much perjury, as the one we are now called upon to establish."

In Dampton *v.* Sympson, *Cro. Elis.* 520, the defendant had committed perjury at a trial, in falsely swearing that a certain silver fountain was worth only £180, when in fact it was worth £500, and it was held that an action would not lie on such ground, mainly because there was no precedent for it.

There is a class of actions which are somewhat unusual and which are referred to in Hoefler *v.* Hoefler, *ante,* page 1, where damages are allowed for abuse of the process of the court or other actions of the defendant amounting to a contempt, the defendant not being precluded from his remedy by an action by the fact that proceedings for a contempt might have been taken.

A person is not debarred from the vindication of a legal right because he is actuated by an improper or a malicious motive. Phelps *v.* Nowlen, 72 *N. Y.* 39.

ROST *v.* BROOKLYN HEIGHTS R. R. CO.

Supreme Court, Second Department, Appellate Division;
December, 1896.

*Evidence; physical exhibits; foot cut off in accident preserved in
alcohol.*] Where, upon the trial of an action for personal injuries,
the plaintiff produced and exhibited the foot of the child who
had been injured, preserved in alcohol, and it did not appear
that such exhibit tended to make clear any disputed question of
fact, but was rather intended to affect the jury in plaintiff's favor,
—*Held*, that it was reversible error to overrule the defendant's
objection to such exhibition.*

Appeal by the defendant from a judgment of the
Supreme Court in favor of the plaintiff, entered upon the
verdict of a jury for $27,500 rendered after a trial at a
Trial Term, Kings County, and also from an order
denying the defendant's motion for a new trial made upon
the minutes.

The action was brought by Clara Rost, an infant, by
her guardian, to recover damages resulting from personal
injuries caused by the alleged negligence of the defendant.
The plaintiff, a little girl five years and nine months old,
was run over by one of defendant's trolley cars and her left
leg was cut off by the wheel of the car. The evidence, the
court say, tended quite strongly to establish that defendant
was grossly negligent in the management of the car which
ran the child down, and every circumstance connected therewith was quite distressing. The legal questions involved
were the negligence of the defendant and the freedom
therefrom of the injured child or her parents, and if these
were found in her favor, the measurement of her pecuniary
loss. These questions exclude sympathy in their deter-

* See note at the end of this case.

Rost *v.* Brooklyn Heights R. R. Co.

mination, rebuke passion and prejudice, and are to be settled in the cold realm of sober judgment. And if the court can fairly see that this has not been accomplished upon the trial had, or if the things which were done render it probable that injustice has been worked, it becomes the duty of this court to interfere and correct the wrong, even though it be difficult or impossible to lay hand upon specific error, for the object of all trials is the accomplishment of justice.* Platt *v.* Munroe, 34 *Barb.* 291 ; Barrett *v.* Third Avenue R. R. Co., 45 *N. Y.* 628. And it is the duty of the court in the disposition of legal controversies, to secure to the parties their legal rights so far as the same may practically be accomplished. Chamberlain *v.* Lindsay, 1 *Hun,* 236.

It appeared upon the trial that the foot of the child, which was amputated, had been preserved by the physician in a glass jar. The physician being upon the stand as a witness was asked by plaintiff's counsel to produce it. Defendant's counsel thereupon stated that it was admitted that the child's leg had been amputated, and that no claim was made that it was not properly done, and objected to its production. Plaintiff's counsel thereupon stated that the object of its production was " to show the size of the child at the time." Objection was made that the production of the foot was not for any legitimate purpose ; this was overruled by the court and the foot was produced.

Held, error. This ruling is now sought to be supported upon the ground that the foot was admissible to show the size of the child at the time of the accident, and also that the discoloration upon it had a tendency to establish that the electrical current had not been shut off at the time the child was run over, and, therefore, bore directly upon the negligence of the defendant in the operation of the car. It is the undoubted rule that the exhibi-

* See Note on Necessity of Exception to Erroneous Charge, 3 *N. Y. Ann. Cas.* 234.

Rost *v.* Brooklyn Heights R. R. Co.

tion of an injury or an injured member of the body to the jury is proper where it is the subject of examination, and when such exhibition is necessary to enable the jury to understand the circumstances surrounding the injury, or to obtain a more comprehensive and intelligent conception of the conditions which existed when the injury was received, or of the character of the injury itself. But where such exhibition is not essential or necessary to enable the jury to better understand the conditions under which it was received, or where the jury may be led to illegitimate considerations on account of it, then it may become improper.

Upon the trial of this case the child was present in the view of the jury; they could judge of her size at the time of the accident from that observation quite as well as they could determine her size from the appearance of this foot which had been preserved. That it would have undergone some change we can readily perceive, and the jury could receive little, if any, aid in that direction. What her size was at the time of the accident was comparatively of little importance in the determination of any issue which the case presented. Whatever the discoloration upon the foot was, whether from a burn or other causes, it had been fully described by the physician, and there was not a pretense that his testimony in this regard was to be controverted. Nor does it appear that the appearance of the discoloration upon the foot aided the jury in arriving at a determination of the question of defendant's negligence in the slightest degree beyond what they obtained from the description given of it by the physician. So far as the suggestion is concerned that the denials in the answer of the amputation and burns, warranted the exhibition, it appears that the defendant admitted the amputation before the foot was produced, and, as before remarked, the testimony of the physician was not expected to be controverted. It may, however, be assumed that, technically, the rule of evidence authorized the exhibition of the foot. Such rule, however, is without force when the legitimate purpose for which the exhibition may be made is slight and the strong tendency is to work improper and illegitimate results. It is perfectly clear, in the present case, that the direct tendency of the exhibition of this mangled foot, coupled with the other considerations already noted, was to arouse the prejudice and inflame the passions of the jury into an angry resentment against the author of the misfortune. This condition far overbalanced any legitimate purpose for which the exhibition might have been made, and made the exhibition of this foot, under the circumstances of this case, improper.

(Some objection was also made to the charge and the court said upon that point:) Without passing upon the question whether technical error was committed in the charge which was the subject of exception, we are of opinion that the charge as a whole conveyed to the jury a wrong impression as to the extent of what would be adequate compensation, which may have led them to award the very large verdict which they did, a verdict which seems excessive in amount, based upon any fair construction of the evidence. Upon the whole case we are satisfied that this verdict may have, and quite likely did, proceed from other considerations than those presented by the testimony, and that justice requires the ordering of a new trial.

The judgment should, therefore, be reversed and a new trial granted, with costs to abide the event.

Opinion by HATCH, J. All concurred, except BRADLEY, J., who concurred in the result.

Judgment and order reversed and new trial granted, costs to abide the event.

Thomas S. Moore, for the defendant, appellant.

Charles J. Patterson, for the plaintiff, respondent.

NOTE ON PHYSICAL EXHIBITS AT THE TRIAL.

The point raised in the case in the text, as to the admissibility of physical exhibits for the information or guidance of the jury in the determination of a disputed question of fact appears to have received very little attention from the appellate courts, so far as can be discovered from the reported cases, although there are a few determinations on the subject. Little or no objection seems to have been made to the practice which is common in negligence cases, of producing models, plans and diagrams of a particular structure for the purpose of demonstrating to the jury the precise manner in which an accident happened.

Under the English practice whenever it appears to the court in actions of waste, trespass *quare clausum fregit*, and other actions, that it is proper and necessary that the jurors who are to try the issue, for the better understanding of the evidence should have a view of the lands and place in question, the court, or judge, will grant a rule or order for such view. The jury, or a part of them, are then taken by the sheriff to the place in question, at some convenient time before the trial, and two persons appointed by the court, frequently the attorneys in the action, thereupon point out to them the matters involved in the controversy. 3 *Wait's Pr.* 124 ; *Tidd's Pr.* 795 : 1 *Archb.* 371. This practice was also in force in this State under the old system, but seems to have fallen into disuse under the restrictions placed upon it by statute. *Grah. Pr.* 880, 881 ; 3 *Wait's Pr.* 124 ; 2 *R. S.* 341, 352.

The Code Civ. Pro. § 1659, provides : " In an action for waste, it is not necessary, either upon the execution of a writ of inquiry, or upon the trial of an issue of fact, that the jury, the judge, or the referee should view the property. Where the trial is by a referee, or by the court without a jury, the referee or the judge may, in his discretion, view the property, and direct the attorneys for the parties to attend accordingly. In any other case, the court may, in its discretion, by order, direct a view by the jury."

The Code Crim. Pro. § 411, provides for the view of premises, where a crime is alleged to have been committed, by the jury.

No case has been found where the precise point raised in the case in the text has been discussed. But in Hiller *v.* Village of Sharon Springs, 28 *Hun*, 344, it was held in an action for personal injuries that it was proper for the plaintiff to exhibit the injured limb to the jury. To the same effect is the case of Jordan *v.* Bowen, 46 *Super. Ct. (J. & S.)* 355.

The Code Civ. Pro., § 873, provides for the physical examination before trial of a plaintiff suing for personal injuries (as to which see Note on Physical Examination of Plaintiff Before Trial, 1 *N. Y. Ann. Cas.* 171), but it does not appear to have changed the rule which is found in Roberts *v.* Ogdensburg & Lake Champlain R. R. Co., 29 *Hun,* 154; Archer *v.* Sixth Avenue R. R. Co., 20 *Super. Ct. (J. & S.)* 378; and McSwyny *v.* Broadway & Seventh Ave. R. R. Co., 27 *St. R.* 363; s. c., 7 *Supp.* 456, to the effect that the defendant cannot insist upon a physical examination at the trial in the presence of the jury. Before the enactment of the provision of § 873, it was settled that no physical examination could be had at the instance of the defendant before trial. Elfers *v.* Woolley, 116 *N. Y.* 294.

The case of McNaier *v.* Manhattan Ry. Co., 4 *Supp.* 310; aff'd without opinion 123 *N. Y.* 664, closely resembles the one in the text. That was an action for an injury to the plaintiff's eye by a hot cinder coming from one of the defendant's engines. The ruling there is best explained in the language of the court itself, at page 311: "The objection of the defendant to the use of a skull to explain to the jury the nature of plaintiff's injuries is not well taken, nor was the objection to the exhibition of the surgical instruments, by which the operation was performed, valid. The examination of the plaintiff in the presence of the jury to see if pus continued to exude from the wound was not objectionable. The object of the trial being to acquaint the jury with the truth of the case, it is not perceived how any of these means, useful for that purpose, could injure the appellant. To suppose that the sight of a skull and the instruments, used, as they were, to explain the injury and the operation necessary to relieve it, should have 'inflamed the passions of the jury,' is quite unreasonable. Their use was a matter in the discretion of the circuit judge, which was wisely exercised."

Upon the trial plaintiff's counsel offered in evidence a photograph of plaintiff showing the manner in which his limbs had contracted, as a result of the accident, proving by a witness, that it was taken in his presence and correctly represented the condition of plaintiff's limbs. The photograph was received under objection and exception. *Held,* no error; that it was competent on the same principle as a map or diagram. Alberti *v.* N. Y. Lake Erie & W. R. R. Co., 118 *N. Y.* 77.

In Corley *v.* N. Y. & Harlem R. R. Co., (12 *App. Div.* 409) a new trial was granted upon the ground of newly-discovered evidence, after a verdict for the plaintiff, in an action for personal injuries caused by the defendant's negligence, where the plaintiff, a boy, had appeared at the trial supported by crutches and, assisted by his father, had proceeded to and from the witness stand with great apparent difficulty, and it was shown by numerous affidavits that he had for more than two weeks before the trial discarded his crutches, and with his mother's consent had played and run about the street like other boys.

DUTTON *v.* SMITH.

Supreme Court, Second Department, Appellate Division; December, 1896.

1. *Judgment ; non-service of process ; action to vacate.*] A defendant against whom judgment has been rendered may maintain an action to set aside the judgment upon the ground that the summons therein was not served upon him ; his remedy is not limited to a motion in the first action.*

---

* In Washbon *v.* Cope (144 *N. Y.* 287) the defendant contended that in a proceeding in a surrogate's court she had never been served with a citation, and that the attorney who appeared for her in that proceeding was unauthorized to do so, and that consequently the surrogate was without jurisdiction as to her in that proceeding. Concerning that contention the court said, at page 294: " We think the objection grounded upon the unauthorized appearance of her attorney, and the non-service of any process upon her cannot prevail in this action. It has been settled by an unbroken line of decisions in this State, running many years back, that, unless under some peculiar and extraordinary circumstances, not existing in this case, the objection that a party was not served and an appearance by an attorney in a court of record for such party was unauthorized, and, hence, that the judgment was without jurisdiction, cannot be taken in a collateral proceeding or action, and that the party is confined to a motion in the original action in order to obtain relief. This was decided in the case of Denton *v.* Noyes (6 *Johns.* 297) and

Dutton *v.* Smith.

2. *Former adjudication; order refusing to vacate judgment.*] An order denying a motion by defendant to vacate the judgment in an action against him upon the ground that the summons was never served upon him is not *res adjudicata*, and does not bar a subsequent action to vacate the judgment upon the same ground.*

---

has been followed by many cases since that time, the last of which in this court is that of Vilas *v.* Plattsburgh & Montreal R. R. Co. (123 *N. Y.* 440), where the whole doctrine was reviewed and affirmed as above stated. The case of Ferguson *v.* Crawford (70 *N. Y.* 256) also contains a discussion of the general doctrine in the opinion by RAPALLO, J."

See Note on Equitable Relief Against Judgments Obtained by Fraud, 2 *N. Y. Ann. Cas.* 382, and Harris *v.* Treu, *Id.* 380.

See also Ward *v.* Town of Southfield, 102 *N. Y.* 287 ; and Stillwell *v.* Carpenter, 59 *N. Y.* 423, for a discussion of the principles governing remedy in equity where a judgment has been obtained by fraud.

Where a party voluntarily pays a judgment after full knowledge that it was procured by fraud a cause of action founded upon the fraud does not survive such payment. Wood *v.* Amory, 105 *N. Y.* 278.

In Converse *v.* Sickles, 2 *N. Y. Ann. Cas.* 16, it was held that an action could be maintained which was in effect to recover money paid under duress in satisfaction of a judgment secured by fraud.

Where the court has jurisdiction of the parties and the subject matter of the action, one party has not an absolute legal right to have an erroneous judgment vacated or set aside on a motion, even though the ground upon which the motion is based is sound. His remedy is by appeal. And if such a motion is denied no appeal lies from such denial to the Court of Appeals. Schaettler *v.* Gardiner, 47 *N. Y.* 404. See, also, Herring *v.* N. Y. Lake Erie & W. R. R. Co., 105 *Id.* 340.

In White *v.* Merritt, 7 *N. Y.* 352, it was held that a defendant could not recover back, in a collateral action, the amount voluntarily paid by him in satisfaction of a judgment which he allowed to be taken by default, because of false and fraudulent statements made to him by the plaintiff in that action, but it was also held that he could maintain an action for damages because of such fraud and deceit.

* In Matter *v.* Parsons, (32 *Hun*, 338) it was held that the denial of a motion, on technical grounds, to open a judgment and for

Dutton *v.* Smith.

Appeal by the plaintiff, from a judgment of the Supreme Court, Kings County, in favor of the defendants, entered upon the decision of the court rendered after a trial at the Special Term, dismissing the complaint.

This action is brought by Stephen A. Dutton to set aside a judgment recovered by the defendant, Lewis M. Smith, against the plaintiff, and entered in the county of Chemung, for a sum of money, upon the ground that the plaintiff in this action was never served with the summons nor appeared in the action. After the entry of the judgment the plaintiff moved in that action to vacate the judgment upon the ground above recited. On that motion a reference was had, witnesses were produced and testimony taken before a referee, and the referee reported that the present plaintiff had in fact been served with process. The special term confirmed this report and denied the motion. Thereafter the plaintiff brought this action. At the close of the plaintiff's evidence the complaint was dis-

---

leave to serve an answer was not a bar to an action to set aside such judgment for fraud.

The general doctrine, with few exceptions, is that the decision of a motion or collateral proceeding in an action does not act with the same strictness as a judgment does as a bar and as *res adjudicata* in a subsequent action concerning the same matter, although it is a bar to another motion or collateral proceeding founded upon the same circumstances. The rule as to subsequent motions is that an order is not conclusive as an adjudication as to a fact which might have been but which was not actually litigated on the motion. Riggs *v.* Purcell, 74 *N. Y.* 370; Easton *v.* Pickersgill, 75 *Id.* 599; Steuben County Bank *v.* Alberger, 83 *Id.* 274; Webb *v.* Buckelew, 82 *Id.* 555; Howell *v.* Mills, 53 *Id.* 322; Keiley *v.* Dusenbury, 77 *Id.* 597; Metropolitan Elevated R. R. Co. *v.* Manhattan Ry. Co., 14 *Abb. N. C.* 103, 215; National Bank of Port Jervis *v.* Hansee, 15 *Abb. N. C.* 488; Matter of Flushing Ave., 98 *N. Y.* 445; Raht *v.* Attrill, 106 *Id.* 423; Place *v.* Haywood, 117 *Id.* 487; Carter *v.* Beckwith, 128 *Id.* 312.

See Note on Renewal of Motion, *post*, p. 35.

missed, as upon a nonsuit, on the ground that the decision on the motion in the first action was conclusive on the right of the plaintiff to maintain the present action.

Held, error. Whatever question there may have been formerly in this State as to the conclusiveness of a judgment on the fact of service of process on the parties thereto, the law was finally settled in Ferguson *v.* Crawford (70 *N. Y.* 253) that a party may attack any judgment collaterally, upon showing that he was never in fact served with process, and the court acquired no jurisdiction of his person. Plaintiff, therefore, was not confined to a motion in the action against him to obtain relief.

The conclusiveness of the decision of the motion upon the issues in this action is a question involved in uncertainty and doubt. That uncertainty is created by the decision of the Court of Appeals in Dwight *v.* St. John (25 *N. Y.* 203). That was an action to have two judgments entered upon confession declared to stand as security for another debt not mentioned in the statement. The defendant had previously made a motion to have the judgments canceled and discharged of record. On that motion a reference was had to take proof of the facts, and upon the coming in of the referee's report the court denied the motion. It was held that the decision on the motion was conclusive in the action. This case has never been in terms overruled and has been once cited as authority. Demarest *v.* Darg, 32 *N. Y.* 281. But I think its effect as a precedent must be strictly limited to the facts of the case. The argument upon which the decision proceeded was not only that the hearing was upon full proofs, but also that the Code of Procedure made the proceeding liable to review. The order in this case, which it is contended operates as a former adjudication, differs from that involved in Dwight *v.* St. John (*supra*).

In Foote *v.* Lathrop (41 *N. Y.* 358) the appeal was from an order denying the motion of the defendant to set aside and vacate a judgment on the ground that she had never been served with process nor appeared in the action. It was held that the order did not affect any substantial right, and the appeal was dismissed. Keck *v.* Werder (86· *N. Y.* 264) was an application by the assignee in bankruptcy of the defendant, who had been adjudged a bankrupt, pending the action, to vacate a judgment entered against the defendant and compel the plaintiff to pay into· court certain moneys which had been received under said. judgment. The motion was denied at the special term· and the order affirmed at general term. The appeal was dismissed.

It would thus appear that the granting or denial of the motion made by the plaintiff was discretionary, and not a matter of right. If this be so, the decision of the motion cannot well be conclusive on the question of fact, for *non constat* but the court regarded the question of fact as so doubtful that it denied the motion as a matter of discretion, leaving the plaintiff to his action or to resist the judgment whenever sought to be enforced against him. Beards *v.* Wheeler, 76 *N. Y.* 213. In fact, Dwight *v.* St. John (*supra*), though not expressly overruled, has been very much cut away by the later cases. In Blank *v.* Blank (107 *N. Y.* 91) the defendant moved to vacate a judgment annulling her marriage and to be let in to defend the action, upon the ground that she had been induced to· let it go by default through fraud. Her motion was denied. Subsequently she brought a direct action to set aside the judgment. It was held below that the decision· on the motion in the first action was conclusive. While the judgment below was upheld on other grounds, it was held on appeal that the decision of the motion was not a bar to the action.

In Riggs *v.* Pursell (74 *N. Y.* 370) it was held that the decision on a motion to compel the purchaser at a judicial sale to complete his purchase did not operate as *res adjudicata* upon a subsequent application where different facts were shown.

Dutton *v.* Smith.

If Dwight *v.* St. John (*supra*) is an authority for the doctrine that a decision on a motion may operate as a former adjudication in subsequent litigation, Riggs *v.* Pursell (*supra*) is authority for the application of such doctrine only when the decision is made on an order affecting a substantial right. The authorities cited above show that the plaintiff's motion was not of such a character. It is further to be observed that the evidence given by the witnesses on behalf of the present plaintiff (there the defendant), on the hearing before the referee on the motion to open the default was rejected and disregarded, both by the referee and by the court in consequence of the failure of such witnesses to sign their testimony as required by the rules. This disposition of the testimony so given was doubtless correct. But it may well be urged that the effect of such action was to deprive the proceeding of the character of a full litigation, which is necessary to make the decision of any motion conclusive, and to reduce it to a mere default. Therefore, the decision of the motion was not conclusive in this action.

Since the foregoing was written I have found the case of O'Connor *v.* Felix (87 *Hun*, 179) * which was not cited before us. The opinion in that case, concurred in by two of the learned justices of the general term of the first department, is to the effect that the jurisdiction of the court over the person of a defendant cannot be attacked collaterally ; that the only remedy is by motion in the action. We should be inclined to follow that decision on the principle of *stare decisis,* did we not regard it as directly opposed to the decision of the Court of Appeals in Ferguson *v.* Crawford (*supra*). The last case, as shown

* This was a motion to compel a purchaser under a sale in foreclosure to take title. The purchaser refused to complete the purchase, upon the ground that one of the defendants in the foreclosure suit had not been served with the summons in that action. The court held that such an objection could not be made in a collateral action or proceeding.

in the opinion in the O'Connor case, has, since its decision, been cited with approval in a number of cases in the Court of Appeals. The cases in that court, referred to by the general term of the first department as in conflict with Ferguson *v.* Crawford (*supra*), are, in our opinion, not inconsistent with the decision in that case, nor can they be considered as overruling it. We are also of the opinion that the conclusion of the learned general term is directly opposed to the decision of the supreme court of the United States in York *v.* Texas (137 *U. S.* 15). There the validity of a statute of Texas, which made an appearance on a motion to set aside a judgment for failure of the court to acquire jurisdiction of the person of the defendant, a general appearance in the action, was upheld. It was based upon the ground that no one had an absolute right to set aside, by motion, a judgment void as to him for failure to serve process, but that he could resist the judgment when it might be sought to be enforced against him or his property, and for this purpose could maintain his own affirmative action.

Opinion by CULLEN, J. All concurred, except BRADLEY, J., who concurred in the result.

Judgment reversed and new trial granted, costs to abide the event.

Henry Daily, Jr., for the plaintiff, appellant.

Abraham Gruber and *Theodore B. Chancellor*, for the defendant, respondent.

SHEEHAN *v.* CARVALHO.

*Supreme Court, First Department, Appellate Division;
December,* 1896.

Motions and orders ; renewal of motion ; different grounds ; leave.]
Where a motion to vacate an order for the examination of witnesses before trial, made on the papers upon which it was
granted, had been denied, and another motion, for the same
relief, was made upon affidavits which involved the merits and
without securing leave of the court to renew the motion,—
Held, that the motion should be denied because of such failure
to secure leave to renew.*

Appeal by the plaintiff from an order of the Supreme
Court, New York Special Term, denying his motion to
vacate an order for the examination of defendant's witnesses before the trial of the action.

This action was brought by John C. Sheehan against
Solomon S. Carvalho and William J. Ward, to recover
damages for an alleged libelous publication in the New
York *World.* The answer alleged that the publications
were true. The action was commenced in 1894. The
order for the examination of the witnesses was granted *ex
parte,* and was made June 30, 1896. The plaintiff made a
motion at Special Term to vacate the order for the examination, on the ground of the insufficiency of the papers
upon which it was granted, and upon the hearing of that
motion, July 16, 1896, an order was made denying the
motion, and directing the examination of the witnesses to
proceed before the referee on a day therein designated.
Thereupon a second motion was made by the plaintiff
upon the papers on which the order for the examination
was made, and all the papers, pleadings and proceedings

---

* See note at the end of this case on Renewal of Motion.

Sheehan *v.* Carvalho.

in the action, and upon additional affidavits served, to vacate and set aside the order for the examination upon the merits, and the examination was stayed until the hearing and determination of the motion. This motion was opposed by the defendants upon additional affidavits, and was denied, the stay vacated, and the examination again ordered to proceed before the referee on a day therein specified, and from this order the plaintiff appealed.

Held, that the motion was properly denied upon the ground that the motion had been once passed upon by the court before another justice; that no leave had been given to renew, and that the facts should have been placed before the court on the former motion. It was not claimed that leave to renew had been given by any order of the court entered in its minutes, but it is said that it is shown by the plaintiff's affidavit that the justice who decided the first motion stated upon the hearing that an independent motion could be made to vacate the order on the merits, no affidavits having been submitted controverting the allegations in the affidavits which were the basis of the order for the examination. This is disputed by the defendants in their affidavits. It was merely the expression of an opinion by that justice as to the practice, if he stated what is claimed. It did not legally constitute leave to renew the first motion or to make another motion. The order made and entered in the minutes can alone be considered in determining what the court did. Its action cannot be shown by, or determined upon, affidavits, nor even by the opinion or memorandum handed down by the justice presiding. If the order as entered was incorrect or defective, the remedy was by application to resettle it.

Again, it is said the two motions were not the same, and the second one might be made after the first one had been denied, without any leave having been given by the court. This position, we think, is not well taken. We think that the mere fact that the grounds were different,

Sheehan *v.* Carvalho.

the relief sought being the same, does not take the motions out of the general rule, that a party cannot make a second motion for the same relief without leave of the court. Lovell *v.* Martin, 21 *How. Pr.* 238; Pattison *v.* Bacon, 12 *Abb. Pr.* 142; s. c., 21 *How. Pr.* 478; Klumpp *v.* Gardner, 44 *Hun*, 515; s. c., 9 *St. R.* 355.

We are aware of no other decisions that seem to bear upon this question more directly than those we have here cited. A question of practice of considerable importance is here involved, and a precedent will be established by the decision of this appeal. We do not desire to recognize a rule that will tend to multiply motions where the courts are already overburdened. We think the better rule is that all questions involved in an application to set aside an order for the examination of witnesses before trial should be presented upon a single motion, and that no second motion like this one should be permitted to be made for the same relief upon different grounds, unless by express leave of the court. The plaintiff may have been misled to his disadvantage by the opinion expressed by the learned judge who heard this first motion; and, indeed, the judge may have refused or failed to grant leave to make the second motion, by reason of his opinion that such leave was unnecessary. The plaintiff should have an opportunity to be heard and to obtain such leave, if he presents a case that entitles him to it.

The order appealed from is, therefore, affirmed with leave to plaintiff to apply at the special term for leave to renew his motion to vacate the order for the examination of these witnesses upon the same affidavits and such additional affidavits and papers as he may desire to present upon such application, with ten dollars costs and disbursements to the respondents to abide event.

Opinion by WILLIAMS, J., RUMSEY, PATTERSON and INGRAHAM, JJ., concurred; VAN BRUNT, P. J., dissented.

Ordered accordingly.

Charles Strauss, for the plaintiff, appellant.

James W. Gerard, Jr., for the defendant, respondent.

NOTE ON RENEWAL OF MOTION.

In general].   The theory upon which two motions have sometimes been allowed heretofore in contesting the validity of an order granting a provisional remedy in an action such as an injunction, order of arrest, attachment, etc., was, that a motion to vacate the order, made on the papers on which it was granted, was in the nature of a demurrer, and a motion made on affidavits contesting the facts set forth in the original moving papers brought the matter before the court on the merits.   The practice as now laid down by the decision in the text is that in moving to set aside such an order the moving party must combine both motions in one, which, obviously, in most cases, would be tantamount to abandoning the remedy of moving on the original papers, (because of the rule that where the party moving to vacate such an order submits affidavits his adversary may submit further affidavits in support of the original order), or move on one ground, and take the risk of having his application for a renewal denied after submitting the matter to the court on either of these grounds.   The practical result of this ruling probably will be that more motions to vacate such orders will be made on the merits, and fewer on technical defects in the original papers.

Although it is said in the case in the text the mere fact that the new motion is made on different grounds from that of the original motion is no excuse for failure to secure leave of court to renew the motion, this doctrine probably refers to cases where the circumstances are similar to this one, and it cannot be assumed to overrule the decisions cited hereafter to the effect that where the second motion is made upon facts arising subsequent to the first motion leave to renew is not necessary.

In Williams *v.* Huber, 5 *Misc.* 488 (Super. Ct., Gen. T.) the following rules were laid down by McAdam, J., governing renewals of motions : " Where parties apply for injunctions and like remedies, it is not too exacting to require : (1) That the papers presented in the first instance conform to the prescribed practice, and state all the grounds relied on for relief. (2) After the application has been once fully argued, carefully considered and decided on such papers, it must be considered finally adjudicated, subject only to the right to appeal. (3) The same matter is not to be again considered without leave first had and obtained from the court which heard the original application. (4) Motions for substantially the same relief are not to be split up and argued or decided upon the installment plan, or they will become interminable as well as confusing."

New facts snbsequently arising.] There is a clear distinction drawn in the cases where the new motion is based upon a new state of facts arising since the first decision was made, and, on the other hand, where it is made on additional evidence only of the same facts as appeared in the first application. In the former case it has been held that it was not necessary to secure leave to renew. Belmont *v.* Erie Ry. Co., 52 *Barb.* 637 ; Erie Ry. Co. *v.* Ramsey, 57 *Id.* 449 ; Bank of Havana *v.* Moore, 5 *Hun*, 624 ; Bank of Rondout *v.* Hamilton, 50 *How. Pr.* 116 ; Wentworth *v.* Wentworth, 51 *Id.* 289 ; and see Goddard *v.* Stiles, 99 *N. Y.* 640 ; German Exchange Bank *v.* Kroder, 14 *Misc.* 179 ; s. c., 35 *Supp.* 380.

In Noonan *v.* N. Y., Lake Erie, & W. R. R. Co., 68 *Hun*, 387, the court says, at page 389 : "The general rule is that a motion once denied at special term cannot be renewed and heard by another special term, unless by the terms of the order it appears that the motion was denied on some technical reason not affecting the merits, or leave is granted to renew the motion. But this rule has exceptions. Where new and different facts have arisen a motion may be renewed without consent." See, also, Smith *v.* Zalinski, 94 *N. Y.* 519, 524.

A motion will sometimes be opened on the question being changed by new material discovered or arising after the decision of the first motion. People *v.* Mercein, 3 Hill, 416; Simpson *v.* Hart, 14 *Johns.* 63.

But if the facts remain essentially the same at the time of the application to renew that they were when the former motion was denied, the court will rarely allow the matter to be reheard on the merits. Greathead *v.* Bromley, 7 *T. R.* 455 ; Allen *v.* Gibbs, 12 *Wend.* 202.

Different property interest.] Where a motion made by a judgment creditor of the attachment debtor, to vacate the attachment, had been denied, and subsequently the same person made a motion to vacate the attachment so far as it affected certain real estate which had been conveyed to her by the attachment debtor since the issuing of the attachment, it was held that it was not necessary to secure leave to make the second motion. Steuben County Bank *v.* Alberger, 83 *N. Y.* 274. The court adds, at page 278 : " The doctrine that a motion once denied cannot be renewed as a matter of right and without leave of the court, except upon facts arising subsequent to the decision of the former motion, cannot apply to a case where the party proceeds in the second motion upon a distinct property interest and right from that involved in the first motion."

Time of obtaining leave to renew.] In People *ex rel.* Wilbur *v.* Eddy, 3 *Lans.* 80, a motion for an order removing a town railroad commissioner for *non-feasance* in office, under *L.* 1859, c. 384, was denied and a new motion was made without leave for the reason as alleged that the ground for the dismissal of the former motion was unfounded in fact. The General Term, Third Department, held that leave was not essential, but even if it was, the special term had power to grant leave on the spot when the motion came up for argument.

Non-payment of costs.] The objection that the renewal of a motion was made without the payment of costs awarded on a previous motion cannot be made for the first time on appeal. Matter of Lotius, 41 *St. R.* 537 ; s. c., 16 *Supp.* 323.

Injunctions.] Code Civ. Pro., §§ 627, 628, provide for making two motions in injunction cases as a matter of right ; one founded on the defects in original papers, and the other upon affidavits.

When leave necessary.] In Standard *v.* Williams, 10 *Wend.* 599, it was held that if the affidavit of the party opposing a motion be shown to be untrue, or if the facts relied upon by him can be subsequently explained so as to show that they ought not to have influenced the court, the party may apply to the court, upon notice, to vacate the rule denying his motion. Under the authority of that case a motion was made in Mitchell *v.* Allen (12 *Wend.* 290), to set aside a rule previously made denying a motion made by the moving party. The second motion was made without leave, and in denying it the court said : " The motion cannot be heard. It is the settled practice that a motion cannot be renewed without leave of the court. The case of Standard *v.* Williams (*supra*) decides nothing to the contrary of such practice. It is there said, the party may apply to the court, upon notice, to vacate the rule denying his motion. So he

may ; but not without leave of the court previously obtained, which is always granted, if, in the circumstances of
the opposition, there is anything to excite suspicion of un-
fairness, or a belief that the party moving is taken by surprise."

Where a party fails in a motion because of some formal
defect or insufficiency in his papers, he should ask leave to
renew the application, or that it be denied without prejudice to another motion, and a motion once denied cannot
be renewed unless leave be first obtained from the court
either at the time of the denial or afterwards. Doelfus *v.*
Frosch, 5 *Hill,* 493. In that case a motion had been made
before the circuit judge for a commission, and the motion
denied because of a formal defect in the papers. The motion was renewed and a commission granted at special
term without leave having been previously secured, but the
court in that case allowed the order to stand because of
the special circumstances in the case, upon the payment of
costs by the moving party.

In Klumpp *v.* Gardner (44 *Hun,* 515), cited in the text, it
was held that where a party had once made a motion for a
bill of particulars as to one part of a complaint, and such
motion had been denied, the defendant was precluded from
making another motion for a bill of particulars as to another part of the complaint.

Before another judge.] A motion denied by one judge
cannot be renewed before another judge of co-ordinate
jurisdiction without leave to renew, but the defeated party
must seek his remedy upon appeal. Matter of Livingston,
34 *N. Y.* 555 ; Wilson *v.* Barney, 5 *Hun,* 257 ; People *v.*
National Trust Co., 31 *Id.* 20 ; Talcott *v.* Burnstein, 13 *St.*
R. 552 ; Koehler *v.* Farmer's & Drover's Bank, 14 *Civ. Pro.*
R. 71 ; aff'd 6 *Supp.* 470.

A motion for a reargument should be made before the
same judge who heard the first motion. Averell *v.* Barber,
44 *St. R.* 542 ; s. c., 18 *Supp.* 81.

Where a motion for a compulsory reference had been
denied by the special term and subsequently granted by
the judge at circuit without the party securing leave to
renew the motion,—*held,* that the order must be reversed
for this reason alone. Chamberlain *v.* Dumville, 21 *Supp.*
827 ; s. c., 50 *St. R.* 356.

Where a motion is made upon new evidence only or
evidence tending to show that there was no ground for the
denial of the motion in the first instance, or impeaching
the adversary's evidence, leave must be first obtained.
Hall *v.* Emmons, 39 *How. Pr.* 187 ; Snyder *v.* White, 6 *Id.*

Note on Renewal of Motion.

321 ; Smith *v.* Spalding, 3 *Robt.* 615 ; Bellinger *v.* Martindale, 8 *How. Pr.* 113 ; Mills *v.* Thursby, 11 *Id.* 114 ; Hoffman *v.* Livingston, 1 *Johns. Ch.* 211 ; Ray *v.* Connor, 3 *Edw. Ch.* 478 ; Schultz *v.* Rodewald, 1 *Abb. N. C.* 365 ; Dunn *v.* Meserole, 5 *Daly,* 434 ; Melville *v.* Matthewson, 17 *Super. Ct. (J. & S.)* 388 ; Apsley *v.* Wood, 67 *How. Pr.* 406 ; Seaman *v.* McReynolds, 20 *Super. Ct. (J. & S.)* 543 ; Bode *v.* Maiberger, 12 *Civ. Pro. R.* 53.

But a motion cannot be renewed upon facts known to the party when the original motion was made. Pattison *v.* Bacon, 12 *Abb. Pr.* 142 ; s. c., 21 *How. Pr.* 478 ; Crocker *v.* Crocker, 1 *Sheld.* 274.

And it is within the discretion of the court to hear a renewal of a motion on the same papers. White *v.* Monroe, 12 *Abb. Pr.* 357 ; s. c., 33 *Barb.* 650.

See Willett *v.* Fayerweather, 1 *Barb.* 72, for discussion of circumstances under which the court will grant leave to renew a motion upon the same papers.

As to renewal after default see Bowman *v.* Sheldon, 5 *Sandf.* 657 ; Fowler *v.* Huber, 7 *Robt.* 52.

Prior motion undecided.] A motion cannot be made without leave of court while a prior motion for the same relief is pending undetermined. Hoover *v.* Rochester Printing Co., 2 *App. Div.* 11 ; s. c., 37 *Supp.* 419 ; 72 *St. R.* 717.

Extension of time by leave.] Where a motion to vacate an order of arrest was denied with leave to renew and the new motion was made after the expiration of twenty days from the entry of judgment in the action,—*held*, that the leave to renew, did not extend the time within which the motion could be renewed until after the time prescribed by the Code within which such a motion could be made. Wheeler *v.* Brady, 2 *Hun,* 347.

Where a motion to correct a judgment is made within a year after the entry of the judgment, and is denied with leave to renew, a renewal of the motion pursuant to such leave cannot be objected to because not made within a year. Oliver *v.* French, 41 *Supp.* 106.

Effect of leave to renew on right to appeal.] Where an order denying a motion contains leave to renew upon the same or additional affidavits, the order is not appealable until the moving party has exhausted his remedy at special term by renewing the motion. Wells, Fargo & Co. *v.* Wellsville, Condersport & P. C. R. R. Co. 12 *App. Div.* 47 ; Robbins *v.* Ferris, 5 *Hun,* 286 ; and by appealing from an order with leave to renew the party waives the right to renew. Harrison *v.* Neher, 9 *Hun,* 127.

STEVENS v. DEWEY.

Supreme Court, First Department, Appellate Division; January, 1897.

Supplementary proceedings; contempt; after-acquired property; rents from lease.] Where a judgment debtor who was enjoined by an order in supplementary proceedings from disposing of his property, etc., held a lease as lessee upon which he collected rents from a sub-tenant which became due after the service of the order, and applied them to the payment of a debt other than that of the judgment creditor,—*Held*, that he was guilty of contempt, for the reason that such payment tended to depreciate the value of the property which he had when the order was served, and could not be said to be property acquired after the service of the order.*

---

* In Beamish *v.* Hoyt (2 *Robt.* 307), it was held, where an estate by the curtesy held by the judgment debtor passed to a receiver, that the rents accruing after the receiver was appointed also passed to him.

Rents and profits of real estate which become due after the granting of the order are not after-acquired property. Farnham *v.* Campbell, 10 *Paige,* 598 ; Albany City Bank *v.* Schermerhorn, 9 *Id.* 372.

In Stevenson *v.* Stevenson, 34 *Hun,* 157, it was held, in a creditor's action, that alimony directed to be paid to the judgment debtor could be reached where the judgment was secured after the order for the payment of alimony had been made.

This case was distinguished in Romain *v.* Chauncey (129 *N. Y.* 566 ; aff'g 60 *Hun,* 477), where it was held that alimony which was payable under an order made after the judgment was secured could not be reached by the creditor.

For a full discussion of what property may be taken in supplementary proceedings see Note on Procedure where Property is Disclosed in Supplementary Proceedings. 1 *N. Y. Ann. Cas.* 152. See also Weiss *v.* Ashman, *Id.* 314 ; People *ex rel.* Goetchius *v.*

Stevens *v*. Dewey.

Appeal by the defendant from an order of the Supreme Court, New York Special Term, committing him to the county jail for contempt of court.

On June 13, 1896, one of the justices of this court in an action by John Crawford Stevens against Sturges Dewey granted an order in supplementary proceedings for the examination of the defendant as a judgment debtor. The order contained the usual injunction forbidding the judgment debtor from making any transfer or disposition of his property, or in any manner interfering therewith, until the further order of the court. It was duly served and the examination was had. At the time of the service of the order the defendant was the owner of a lease of certain premises which he had rented to sub-tenants. The rent which became due from the defendant's sub-tenants, after the order was served and while the examination was progressing, was collected by the defendant and paid upon other debts than that of the plaintiff in this action. Upon proof being made of that fact an order was granted at special term directing the defendant to show cause why he should not be punished for his misconduct in disposing of this money, and upon the return of that order it was adjudged that the defendant was guilty of contempt in disobeying the order in supplementary proceedings, for the reason that he had collected $195 of rent from his sub-tenants after June 17, 1896, and disposed of it without permission of the court, and he was fined for such misconduct in the sum of $166.87, with interest from April 13, 1896, which was the amount of the plaintiff's judgment

McGoldrick, *Id*. 401 ; Stephens *v*. Perrine, *Id*. 81 ; Matter of Crane, *Id*. 148.

See Blake *v*. Bolte, 1 *N. Y. Ann. Cas.* 78, for form of order punishing judgment debtor for contempt.

See Note on Limitation of Supplementary Proceedings, 1 *N. Y. Ann. Cas.* 24 ; following Importers' and Traders' National Bank *v*. Quackenbush, *Id*. 20.

upon which the order in supplementary proceedings was issued, besides ten dollars costs of the motion. From that order the defendant has taken this appeal.

Held, that the appeal could not be sustained. The lease was property belonging to the defendant at the time when the order was served upon him. By virtue of the lease he was the owner of the right to receive from his sub-tenants the rents as they should accrue, and that right was the only valuable thing connected with the lease. It not only had a present value, but it was a thing which the court might have directed to be turned over to a receiver and the proceeds applied to the payment of the judgment. Hence, the conduct of the defendant in collecting those rents as they became due was directly calculated to impair the right of the plaintiff and to deprive him of property which he was entitled to have devoted to the payment of his judgment.

It is claimed that the rents were after-acquired property, and, therefore, not subject to the order of the court in supplementary proceedings. But in this the defendant is mistaken. The property is the lease, and the right to the money which should grow due from his sub-tenants as rent, from time to time. That was owned by the defendant at the time the order for his examination was served upon him. It was precisely like a bond and mortgage, or any other chose in action which has an immediate value, although what is to be paid upon it is not yet due. The collection of the money which is to be paid necessarily depreciates the value of the right. The defendant claims that it is like the future earnings of a judgment debtor, but there is no analogy between the two things. The right to be paid for labor to be performed is a thing which does not exist until the labor has been performed, and the statute expressly exempts earnings already due from the lien acquired by the service of the order in supplementary proceedings. The case cannot be distinguished from that of Mulford *v.* Gibbs (9 *App. Div.* 490), in which a judgment debtor, after the order had been served upon him, collected debts due for property which he had sold before. That was held to be a violation of the order, and he was punished for contempt. Precisely the same principle applies here.

Opinion by RUMSEY, J. VAN BRUNT, P. J., BARRETT, WILLIAMS and PATTERSON, JJ., concurred.

Order affirmed, with ten dollars costs and disbursements.

John R. Benner, Jr., for the defendant, appellant.

Herbert Reeves, for the plaintiff, respondent.

MALONE *v.* THIRD AVENUE R. R. CO.

Supreme Court, First Department, Appellate Division ; December, 1896.

Trial by jury ; requests to charge ; when to be made.] Where, after the court had charged the jury and had considered all the written requests to charge, the defendant's counsel made a further and proper request to charge, and the trial judge refused to hear the request,—*Held*, error, for which the judgment must be reversed.*

---

* In Chapman *v.* McCormick, (86 *N. Y.* 479), as the jury were about to retire to deliberate, the defendant's counsel requested that they wait a minute as he wished to make a further request to charge. The court refused to hear what the request was and directed the jury to retire. The Court of Appeals held that this was reversible error, and that the trial judge should not have anticipated the request which the counsel was about to make by denying

Appeal by the defendant, from a judgment of the Supreme Court in favor of the plaintiff, entered upon the verdict of a jury rendered after a trial at the New York Trial Term, and also from an order denying the plaintiff's motion for a new trial made upon the minutes.

the request before he had heard it. And it is there said that the mere fact that the jury had risen from their seats and are about to retire is not sufficient reason why a further request to charge should be denied, if it is a proper request upon which the party making has a right to have the jury instructed.

In Pfeffele *v*. Second Ave. R. R. Co. (34 *Hun*, 497), the defendant's counsel requested the judge to charge further concerning certain evidence in the case, after having handed up written requests to charge, and the court refused to so charge or to allow an exception from his ruling, on the ground that he had already considered the counsel's written requests to charge, and the court held that this was error for which the judgment must be reversed.

In Gallagher *v*. McMullin (7 *App. Div.* 321), a judgment was reversed because the trial judge had refused to consider requests to charge not embodied in the written requests.

In De Bost *v*. Albert Palmer Co. (35 *Hun*, 386), the defendant's counsel submitted to the court what the general term declared was "a volume of requests to charge unreasonable and unnecessary in number." The trial judge did not embody all these requests in his charge and the defendant's counsel requested the court to allow him to specify and point out certain propositions in his requests upon which he wished to have the jury instructed. The court refused this request and declined to make any further charges, and it was held that this was error; that the counsel ought to have been permitted to point out the specific charges which he wished the court to make.

In O'Neil *v*. Dry Dock, East Broadway & B. R. R. Co. (129 *N. Y.* 125), Chapman *v*. McCormick (*supra*) was distinguished. In the former case both plaintiff and defendant had handed up written requests to charge upon which the court either charged or refused to charge. The plaintiff's counsel then made further requests to charge which the court also either charged or refused to charge and a like disposition was made of further requests to charge by the defendant's counsel. The plaintiff's counsel then attempted to make further requests to charge and the court refused to hear them. —*Held*. no error. And the court said, at page 131 : " Here the judge

Malone *v.* Third Avenue R. R. Co.

The action was brought by James Malone to recover damages for the negligent killing of the wife of the plaintiff. Before the charge to the jury the defendant's counsel submitted several requests to charge, which presented all the law claimed by him to bear upon the case in his favor, so far as he desired to present it at that time. After passing upon these requests, the court proceeded to charge the jury. In the course of the charge the court commented somewhat upon the testimony of a certain witness. At the close of the charge the following colloquy occurred : " Defendant's counsel: I will ask your honor to charge . . . and if any witness has knowingly testified falsely ——. The court: ' If there is any other request on the general law of the case it ought to have been handed up. I do not like, after you exhaust your written requests, to have others asked orally. I do not entertain it.' Defendant excepts. The jury then retired." After the jury had retired the defendant's counsel procured the request which he had undertaken to make, and which the court refused to entertain, to be entered upon the minutes, and excepted again to the refusal to entertain it. The request is as follows : " If any witness has knowingly testified falsely in any material particular, he is guilty of perjury, and you may disregard his entire testimony."

Held that the court erred in refusing to entertain the request, which was a correct statement of the law. There

did not abuse his discretion. His refusal to hear or receive the further requests was not arbitrary. He had fully and fairly laid down the law applicable to the facts of the case. The counsel for the defendant Westing had had full opportunity to make his requests, and he had made them so far as he deemed important, both before and after the charge was made, and whether after that he should be permitted to prolong the trial and still further vex the judge with requests rested in his discretion."

Where, however, the request to charge is covered by the charge already made the court is not required to repeat it. Tucker *v.* Ely, 37 *Hun,* 565 ; Esmond *v.* Kingsley, 3 *Supp.* 696 ; s. c., 19 *St. R.* 665.

is no doubt that it is not only the duty, but the legal right, of counsel to present to the court for its consideration every proposition of law which is material for the instruction of the jury upon the case, nor is there any doubt of the correlative duty of the court to instruct the jury upon each of such propositions, which is submitted by counsel, as bear legitimately upon the evidence. Chapman *v.* McCormick, 86 *N. Y.* 479. Counsel have a right to assume that the court will fully instruct the jury, not only as to every proposition of law bearing upon the case, but that it will also advise the jury, so far as may be necessary as to the manner of considering the evidence, and the rules to be adopted upon such consideration. How far these instructions shall go is to a very considerable extent in the discretion of the court, and no counsel can foresee what will be said on these subjects in any given case. For that reason counsel cannot be expected to present to the court requests to charge on those points, or to anticipate any failure on the part of the court to give such full directions to the jury with regard to the application of legal rights for the consideration of evidence, as will enable them to interpret the evidence understandingly. Whether requests are needed upon these points depends entirely upon the nature of the charge to the jury.

In thus holding we do not wish to be understood that the right of counsel to present requests to charge is unlimited, or that it may not be controlled by the court. As is said by Judge WOODS in L. & N. Railroad Co. *v.* Kelly (24 *U. S. App.* 103, 107), "There must be a point—it may be difficult to locate—where out of sheer self-defense, as well as out of regard for the due administration of justice, a court may refuse to entertain such requests, merely because of their excessive number or quantity." When the charge is adequate and covers every subject as to which it is proper to instruct the jury, further requests are useless and generally confusing. They then become a mere intellectual duel between the court and counsel,

Duhrkop *v.* White.

which should not be permitted. Garbaczewski *v.* Third Ave. R. R. Co., 5 *App. Div.* 186, 189. It must be left very largely to the discretion of the trial court to decide when that point shall have been reached, and an appellate court will be loth to interfere with that discretion, unless it is clear that it has been improperly exercised.

Opinion by RUMSEY, J. VAN BRUNT, J., BARRETT, O'BRIEN and INGRAHAM, JJ., concurred.

Judgment and order reversed and new trial granted, with costs to the appellant to abide the event.

Henry L. Scheuerman, William N. Cohen and *John Vernon Bouvier, Jr.,* for the defendant, appellant.

Emanuel J. Myers, for the plaintiff, respondent.

DUHRKOP *v.* WHITE.

Supreme Court, First Department, Appellate Division ; January, 1897.

Reference; referee's fees; taxation; over-payment; order for repayment.] While a referee has a right to insist upon his fees being paid before delivering his report to the successful party, the amount of such fees depends upon the sum at which they are taxed by the clerk or the court, and when the amount paid is greater than that allowed upon taxation the referee will be required to refund the surplus paid to him.*

---

* Where there is any dispute as to the amount of a referee's fees they must be taxed like any other disbursement in the action. Richmond *v.* Hamilton, 9 *Abb. Pr.* 71, *n.*

And the length of time spent by the referee must be established affirmatively by affidavit, the same as any other disbursement allowed in the taxation of costs, and only those days when he was present personally conducting the reference can be charged. Shultz *v.* Whitney, 17 *How. Pr.* 471 ; s. c., 9 *Abb. Pr.* 71.

It was formerly held that referee's fees could not be taxed as

Duhrkop v. White.

APPEAL by Louis Hanneman, as referee, from an order of the Supreme Court, New York Special Term, directing him to return to and pay over to the plaintiff's attorney the sum of $300, being the amount theretofore alleged to have been paid to him by the plaintiff's attorney in excess of the fees to which it was alleged that he was entitled as referee in the action.

The appellant here was referee in the action above entitled. When his report was ready for delivery he advised the plaintiff of the fact, and the plaintiff's attorney on applying for the report was informed that the referee's fees were $500, which he paid, considering it to be a reasonable and proper charge. The bill of costs, as served with notice of taxation, contained as a disbursement this item of $500. It was objected to by the defendant's attorney, and was reduced upon the taxation to $200. At the request of the referee a motion was made for a re-

part of the costs upon a motion when it was referred. Concklin v. Taylor, 68 *N. Y.* 221. But Code Civ. Pro. § 325, now provides for the taxation of such fees.

A referee's compensation may be settled by the court when not governed by statute in a particular case. Hobart v. Hobart, 86 *N. Y.* 636.

See Code Civ. Pro. § 3296, as amended by L. 1896, c. 90, providing that referee's fees shall be $10 a day, unless the parties stipulate that they shall be more.

A party cannot be imprisoned for non-payment of referee's fees. People v. Grant, 11 *St. R.* 558.

A referee in foreclosure can be punished as for a contempt for disobeying an order of the court as to the disposition of the money which comes into his hands. People *ex rel.* Day v. Bergen, 53 *N. Y.* 404 ; Steele v. Gunn, 19 *St. R.* 654.

In Hobart v. Hobart, (86 *N. Y.* 636) it was held that where an order, in a partition action, fixing the referee's fees had deprived him of the amount to which he was entitled by law, the referee might appeal to the Court of Appeals from the order. Under the constitution of 1895 and the amendments of the code in accordance therewith, it is probable that such an appeal would not be allowed.

Duhrkop *v.* White.

hearing upon the taxation, which was denied, and upon that motion the disbursement for referee's fees in the sum of $200 was confirmed as a reasonable and proper charge, and it was ordered that the referee should, within ten days, pay over to the plaintiff's attorney, from whom he had received payment of his fees, $300, the excess paid above what was fixed as the amount of his fees. It is from that order that the appeal is taken.

Held, no error. The referee is an officer of the court. The statute prescribes the rate at which he is to be paid for services he performs as such an officer, and he can charge only at that rate for what he does in the action. The parties are at liberty, if they see fit, to vary that amount by stipulation entered upon the minutes, but the stipulation must fix the rate of compensation (First Nat. Bank of Cooperstown *v.* Tamajo, 77 *N. Y.* 476), and, when it is so fixed, his right to compensation is determined by the stipulation. But, while the rate of compensation may be fixed by the agreement of the parties, the total amount to which he is entitled for his services at that rate cannot be finally determined until the costs in the action have been taxed. The referee's fees are a disbursement, and the amount to be allowed for that disbursement, like every other one, is to be determined by the evidence presented to the taxing officer. When the referee has completed his report and has it ready for delivery, he is entitled, if he sees fit, to insist that his fees shall be paid as a condition of the delivery of the report, because, after the report has been delivered, he has no lien for his fees, and must depend for their recovery upon the solvency of the party whose duty it is to pay. The fees being payable before the delivery of the report, the amount, in the nature of things, must depend largely upon what is claimed by the referee. While the referee has the right to demand his fees, it must be, we think, upon the implied condition that they shall be adjusted, at the time of the taxation of costs, exactly as they might have been fixed

Tillinghast *v.* Merrill.

by the court before, if an application for that purpose had been made, and an understanding between the parties must be implied that if, for any reason, the amount paid to the referee shall prove to be greater than the court thinks is a proper allowance, the excess will be returned. No other rule can be established which would enable an attorney, who had occasion to take up a report, to do so with safety to himself or with justice to his client. While the referee ceases to be an officer of the court after the report has been delivered and the action disposed of, he still is responsible to the court for what he has done while the relation existed, and that relation surely exists after the report is made and until it is finally delivered.

Opinion by RUMSEY, J. VAN BRUNT, P. J., BARRETT, WILLIAMS and PATTERSON, JJ., concurred.

Order affirmed, with ten dollars costs and disbursements to be paid by the appellant.

James P. Niemann, for the appellant.

Frank J. Dupignac, for the respondent.

TILLINGHAST *v.* MERRILL.

Court of Appeals; December, 1896.

[Affirming 77 *Hun*, 481.]

Officers; town supervisor; liability for public money lost by failure of bank.] Where a town supervisor lost certain moneys, which were in his custody as such officer, by reason of the failure of the bank where such moneys were deposited,—*Held*, that the officer and his bondsman were liable therefor although no fault or negligence was attributable to such officer.*

---

* In Village of Oneida *v.* Thompson, (92 *Hun*, 16) the same principle is announced as is found in the text. In fact the last mentioned

Tillinghast *v.* Merrill.

Appeal from a judgment of the General Term of the Supreme Court, Fourth Department, which affirmed a judgment in favor of plaintiff entered upon a decision of the court on trial at circuit without a jury.

case followed the decision of the general term in the case reported (77 *Hun,* 481). There the officer was a tax collector and the bank where he deposited the funds in his hands failed and the action was brought on his bond.

In United States *v.* Prescott (3 *How.* [*U. S.*] 578), cited in the text, it was said : " Every depositary of public money should be held to a strict accountability ; not only that he should exercise the highest degree of vigilance, but that he should keep safely the moneys which come to his hands. Any relaxation of this condition would open a door to fraud which might be practised with impunity. A depositary would have nothing more to do than to lay his plans and arrange his proofs so as to establish his loss, without laches on his part. Let such a principle be applied to our postmasters, collectors of the customs, receivers of public moneys, and others who receive more or less of the public funds, and what losses might not be anticipated by the public ?"

In United States *v.* Thomas, 15 *Wall.* 337, the principle referred to in the text, that a public officer might be relieved from liability for losses caused by the act of God or the public enemy, was applied and it was held that a collector or receiver of public moneys, under a bond to keep it and pay it when required, was excused from rendering the same where it was forcibly seized by the rebel authorities against the will of the collector and without his fault or negligence.

The case of Bronson *v.* Woolsey, (15 *Johns.* 46), is somewhat analogous in principle to that of United States *v.* Thomas, (*supra*). In the former, a military officer, in time of war, to prevent a vessel loaded with munitions of war from falling into the hands of the enemy ordered the vessel to be sunk. It was held that he was not liable to the owner of the vessel for its value.

A public officer who uses the funds which come into his hands in his private business is guilty of conversion. Bissell *v.* Saxton, 66 *N. Y.* 55.

A collector of taxes becomes a debtor to the county immediately upon the receipt of his warrant as collector for the amount of taxes specified in the warrant. Fake *v.* Whipple, 39 *N. Y.* 397.

Tillinghast *v*. Merrill.

The defendant, J. Herman Merrill, while supervisor of the town of Stockbridge, in the county of Madison, deposited with a firm of private bankers to his credit, as supervisor, certain of the public moneys in his hands; the banking firm afterwards failed and the money was totally lost. This action was brought by George S. Tillinghast as county treasurer, to recover the money of Merrill and his bondsmen, upon the theory that Merrill on receiving the money became the debtor of the county, and that the deposit of the same was at his own risk. The trial judge found that Merrill acted in good faith and without negligence in all that he did in the premises.

Held, that the judgment should be affirmed. The question of the measure of liability to be applied to a supervisor under the circumstances stated is an open one in this state, and as the case at bar presents a claim against a supervisor who acted in good faith and without negligence, we are permitted to consider and decide this appeal upon general principles and in the light of public policy. It is rather remarkable that in a great business State like New York this question should not have been decided long since by the court of last resort. In 1841 the case of Supervisors of Albany County *v*. Dorr (25 *Wend*. 440) came before the Supreme Court, composed of NELSON, Ch. J., and Justices BRONSON and COWEN. Dorr was county treasurer and had given a bond to faithfully execute the duties of his office and pay according to law all moneys. The declaration was on the bond, alleging breaches in not paying over and in not accounting. Dorr pleaded that the identical money received by him was stolen from his office without negligence on his part. To this plea the plaintiff demurred. Chief Justice NELSON, delivering the opinion of the court, stated that the question was "whether an officer concerned in the receipt and disbursement of the public funds is an insurer of the same, *ex virtute officii*, whilst they necessarily remain in his custody." He then stated that "the principle was

Tillinghast *v.* Merrill.

decided in favor of the defendant in Lane *v.* Cotton & Frankland, (1 *Ld. Raym.* 646,) and subsequently confirmed in Whitfield *v.* Le Despencer (*Cowp.* 754), and is in conformity with the general rule of daily application that in order to subject the officer it is necessary to prove misconduct or neglect in the execution of his duties." Justices BRONSON and COWEN concurred. An appeal was taken to the Court of Errors, and that court equally divided upon the question, the effect of which was to affirm the judgment below, and the case stands with no more force as a precedent than a unanimous opinion of the supreme court. Chancellor WALWORTH, in the Court of Errors, wrote for affirmance, thus adding his name to those of the distinguished justices of the supreme court, who had decided to limit the liability of a public officer by the rule of the common law.

It has been a mooted question whether this case was overruled by Muzzy *v.* Shattuck (1 *Denio,* 233), decided in 1845. Mr. Hill in his note to Supervisors *v.* Dorr, in Court of Errors (7 *Hill,* 584), says that in Muzzy *v.* Shattuck the law seems to have been settled, and properly, directly the other way. On the other hand, Judge EARL, in People *ex rel.* Nash *v.* Faulkner (107 *N. Y.* 486), in referring to Supervisors *v.* Dorr says : "The doctrine of that case has been erroneously supposed to have been overruled by the decision in Muzzy *v.* Shattuck. The question here involved was not decided in the Faulkner case, however."

It, therefore, comes to this, that for forty-five years the case of Supervisors *v.* Dorr (25 *Wend.* 440) has stood without being directly overruled by any case in this State, and the rule of the limited liability of the common law approved therein by four of our most distinguished judges. It must be admitted, however, that the weight of authority in the Federal and State courts is in favor of holding officials having the custody of public moneys liable for its loss, although accruing without their fault or negligence.

In many of these cases the decision turned upon the construction of the local statute or the official bond, but others squarely decide the question on principles of public policy.

In the case at bar, the defendant Merrill is sought to be held liable for school moneys paid to him by the county treasurer to disburse in payment of the salaries of school teachers upon the orders of the trustees. The statute imposing this duty reads as follows, viz: " It is the duty of every supervisor, 1. To disburse the school moneys in his hands applicable to the payment of teachers' wages upon and only upon the written orders of a sole trustee, or a majority of the trustees, in favor of qualified teachers. . . ." (2 *R. S.* [8th *ed.*] page 1283, section 6.)

By paragraph 8 of the same section a supervisor is required to pay to his successor all school moneys remaining in his hands. In this statute it will be observed that there are no explicit declarations of the legislative intent, as in the case of town collectors, to create a supervisor the debtor of the county for public moneys in his hands, and the condition of the bond to safely keep, faithfully disburse and justly account for the same does not add to the liability created by statute. Without regard to decisions outside of our own jurisdiction, we think the weight of the argument, treating this as an original question, is in favor of the rule of strict liability which requires a public official to assume all risks of loss, and imposes upon him the duty to account as a debtor for the funds in his custody. We do not wish to be understood as establishing a rule of absolute liability in any event. The United States Supreme Court, in United States *v.* Thomas (15 *Wallace*, 337), held the surveyor of customs for the port of Nashville, Tennessee, and depositary of public money at that place, not liable when prevented from responding by the act of God or the public enemy. If that state of facts is hereafter presented to this court it will doubtless be carefully considered whether it does not present a proper exception to the general rule. It would not be profitable to refer in detail to the many cases, Federal and State, which sustain the strict rule of liability, and we content ourselves with a reference to a number of them involving losses by robbery, burglary, bank failure and the like. U. S. *v.* Prescott, 3 *How.* [U. S.] 578; U. S. *v.* Morgan, 11 *How.* (U. S.) 154; U. S. *v.* Dashiel, 4 *Wall.* 182; U. S. *v.* Keehler, 9 *Wall.* 83; Boyden *v.* U. S., 13 *Wall.* 17; Bevans *v.* U. S., 13 *Wall.* 56; Inhabitants of Hancock, *v.* Hazzard, 12 *Cush.* 112; Commonwealth *v.* Comly, 3 *Penn.* 372; Inhabitants of New Providence *v.* McEachron, 33 *N. J. L.* 339; State *ex rel.*, etc., *v.* Powell, 67 *Mo.* 395; Lowry *v.* Polk County, 51 *Iowa,* 50; Perley *v.* County of Muskegon, 32 *Mich.* 132; Nason *v.* Directors of the Poor, 126 *Penn. St.* 445; Supervisors of Omro *v.* Kaime, 39 *Wis.* 468; Redwood County *v.* Tower, 28 *Minn.* 45; State *v.* Harper, 6 *Ohio,* 607; Halbert *v.* State, 22 *Ind.* 125; Ward *v.* School District, 10 *Neb.* 293.

Opinion by BARTLETT, J. All concur except GRAY, J., dissenting, and MARTIN, J., not sitting.

Judgment affirmed.

Henry B. Coman, for defendants, appellants.

John E. Smith and *Joseph Mason,* for plaintiff, respondent.

FLANDROW v. HAMMOND.

Supreme Court, First Department, Appellate Division; January, 1897.

Executors and administrators; foreign; capacity to sue; substitution after death of testator.] Under the doctrine that a foreign executor cannot sue or be sued purely in his representative capacity in the courts of this State, the court has no power to make an order substituting a foreign executor, to whom no ancillary letters have been issued in this State, as a party defendant in an action, for the purpose of appealing, where the testator died after judgment was rendered against him.*

---

* An action may be maintained in equity against a foreign executor for an accounting where property has been brought within this State. Gulick *v.* Gulick, 33 *Barb.* 92 ; Field *v.* Gibson, 20 *Hun*, 274 ; Brown *v.* Brown, 1 *Barb. Ch.* 189 ; McNamara *v.* Dwyer, 7 *Paige*, 239.

And an action at law can be maintained against a foreign executor who has taken out ancillary letters in this State although there is no property here. Hopper *v.* Hopper, 125 *N. Y.* 400 ; aff'g 53 *Hun*, 394 ; s. c., 25 *St. R.* 132 ; 6 *Supp.* 271 ; which rev'd 3 *Supp.* 640.

A foreign executor may assign a chose in action and the assignee can maintain an action upon such assigned claim in the courts of this State. Peterson *v.* Chemical Bank, 32 *N. Y.* 21 ; Middlebrook *v.* Merchants' Bank, 41 *Barb.* 481.

Where a foreign executor makes a contract in this State he can be sued here. Johnson *v.* Wallis, 112 *N. Y.* 230.

In Smith *v.* Second National Bank, 70 *Hun*, 357, it was held that a foreign executor who had received ancillary letters here had no authority to pledge the property of the estate to secure money in advance of income from the estate.

Code Civ. Pro., § 2695, provides for the granting of ancillary letters to foreign executors, etc., upon the production to the surrogate of an exemplified copy of the foreign will and the foreign letters of probate issued to such executor.

Section 764 of the Code of Civil Procedure provides for the continuance of an action by the personal representatives of the deceased even where the cause of action does not ordinarily survive, if

Flandrow *v.* Hammond.

Appeal by the plaintiff, from an order of the Supreme Court, made at the New York Special Term, reviving and continuing the action against Elenore B. Hammond, as executrix under the last will and testament of Henry B. Hammond, deceased, who was appointed such executrix by the Probate Court of Norfolk county, in the Commonwealth of Massachusetts.

This action was brought to recover the consideration paid for a judgment transferred by defendant to plaintiff, to which judgment defendant had no title. The answer was, in substance, a general denial. A judgment was recovered in the action against the defendant. Before the time to appeal had expired the defendant died, and the executrix was appointed in the State of Massachusetts. No ancillary letters were granted in this State. The foreign executrix thereupon made the motion resulting in the order appealed from.

Held, error. The general rule is well settled that a foreign executor cannot sue or be sued purely in his representative capacity in the courts of this State. Matter of

---

the action has proceeded to judgment before the testator's death. These provisions are discussed in a Note on Abatement by Death After Verdict, 3 *N. Y. Ann. Cas.* 310 ; following the case of Vitto *v.* Farley, *Id.* 308, where it was held in an action for personal injuries caused by the defendant's negligence that the action did not abate where the defendant died after verdict rendered against him.

In Palmer *v.* Phoenix Mutual Life Ins. Co., (84 *N. Y.* 63) where the executor, who resided in this State, had taken out letters testamentary in Connecticut, where the decedent died, and had subsequently caused the will to be proved and admitted to probate and had received letters testamentary here, it was held that such an executor could maintain an action in this State against a foreign corporation on a policy of insurance on the testator's life. "But," it is said in that case, at page 67, "he could not have sued without letters issued to him here." Thus the rule seems to be that the mere fact that a foreign executor resides in this State, does not give him a standing to sue here unless he has taken out letters here.

Webb, 11 *Hun*, 124; Vermilya *v.* Beatty, 6 *Barb.* 429;
Field *v.* Gibson, 20 *Hun*, 274; Hopper *v.* Hopper, 125 *N.
Y.* 400; Johnson *v.* Wallis, 112 *Id.* 230; Dolittle *v.* Lewis,
7 *Johns, Ch.* 45; Petersen *v.* Chemical Bank, 32 *N. Y.* 21;
Lawrence *v.* Lawrence, 3 *Barb. Ch.* 74. It will not do to
say that a foreign executor may sue or defend in this State
if he voluntarily submits himself to the jurisdiction of our
courts, because the rule is that he may no more sue than
be sued in our courts. He would certainly submit himself to such jurisdiction if he were to bring a suit here, but
this he cannot do by reason of this well-settled rule.

In Lawrence *v.* Lawrence (*supra*) the action was
brought by the foreign executor to foreclose a mortgage
given to a co-executor after the death of his testator, and
it was said: "As a general rule, a foreign executor is not
entitled to sue in our courts . . . These rules, however, are only applicable to suits brought by executors for
debts due to the testator, or where the foundation of the
suit is based upon some transaction with the testator in
his lifetime. And they do not prevent a foreign executor
from suing in our courts upon a contract made with him
as such executor."

In this case the executrix asked to be made a party in
her purely representative capacity, the subject matter of
the suit being a transaction had with the testator in his
lifetime. Under the rule we have stated, she cannot be a
party either plaintiff or defendant in the action. It is
said that letters ancillary in this State cannot be issued
because there is no property of the estate here, and, therefore, the estate will be without remedy to review the
judgment in this case, if the rule we have stated is applicable here. The appellant seeks to answer this by the
suggestion that property of the estate might be brought
here so as to confer jurisdiction upon our courts to grant
letters ancillary, if the executrix is inclined to bring such
property here. Without passing upon the question which
might arise in case this were done, it is sufficient to say

Leonard *v.* Buttling.

that there is nothing in the present record to vary the long settled and established rule to which reference has been made, and that rule cannot be disregarded for the purpose of any particular case. The order was clearly unauthorized.

Opinion by WILLIAMS, J.   VAN BRUNT, P. J., BARRETT, RUMSEY and PATTERSON, JJ., concurred.

Order reversed, with ten dollars costs and disbursements, and motion denied, with ten dollars costs.

Abram Kling, for the plaintiffs, appellant.

Nelson S. Spencer, for the defendant, respondent.

LEONARD *v.* BUTTLING.

Supreme Court, Second Department, Appellate Division ; January, 1897.

Conversion ; sheriff ; substitution of indemnitors.]   Where the plaintiff sued a sheriff for conversion of property which the officer took pursuant to a requisition in replevin, and the plaintiffs in the replevin suit furnished the sheriff with an indemnity bond,—*Held*, that the indemnitors in said bond could not be substituted as defendants in the action for conversion in place of the sheriff, on the motion of the sheriff only ; that such substitution conld only be made upon motion of the indemnitors, under Code Civ. Pro. § 1710.[*]

Appeal by the defendant, William J. Buttling, sheriff of Kings County, from an order of the Supreme Court, made at the Kings County Special Term, denying his motion to substitute his indemnitors as defendants in the action in his place and stead.

---

[*] See note following this case.

Leonard v. Buttling.

This is an action by John J. Leonard and another, in which the defendant is charged with taking and coverting to his own use a quantity of brick. The property was taken by the defendant, as sheriff, by virtue of requisitions in two actions, one brought by Milton A. Fowler against John and James Glanfield, and the other by Alonzo and William Covert against the same defendants, to recover the possession of the property in question. Thereupon the plaintiffs in the present action, claiming the right to the possession of the property, delivered to the sheriff an affidavit, as provided by Code Civ. Pro. § 1709, and the plaintiffs in those two actions furnished to the sheriff indemnity, as provided in the same section. The sheriff moved to have his indemnitors substituted as defendants in this action. The motion was denied and the sheriff appealed.

Held, no error. The only statute upon the subject is that " the sureties are entitled to be substituted as defendants in an action brought as prescribed " in Code Civ. Pro. § 1710, " as if the chattel had been levied upon by virtue of an execution." *Id.* § 1711. As the plaintiffs proceeded to assert their claim to the property with a view to having it delivered by the sheriff to them, pursuant to the statute (*Id.* § 1709), and notwithstanding the conflicting affidavits as to the question whether the property was in the possession of the defendants in the replevin actions at the time it was taken by the sheriff by virtue of the requisitions, it is for the purpose of the questions on this review assumed that it was then in the possession of the defendants in those actions, and that this action is one brought as prescribed in such section 1710.

The power of the court to substitute sureties as defendants in an action within that section is dependent upon the statute before referred to, which does not provide that they may be required to submit to such substitution, but merely gives them the right to assume that relation to such an action brought against their principal,

Leonard *v.* Buttling.

whom they have undertaken to indemnify. The ultimate liability of the sureties, in the event of recovery by the plaintiff in an action where the defendant is so indemnified, furnishes some reason why it may be desirable for them nominally and in fact to have the control, as well as the responsibility of the defense. This we have seen is their right. And the plaintiff can make no effectual objection to its exercise. Hein *v.* Davidson, 96 *N. Y.* 175.

The statute, however, is in contravention of the common law, and will not by construction be extended beyond the plain import of its terms. The plaintiff in such case cannot be required, on application of the defendant, to submit to his discharge and the substitution of his sureties as defendants. It is their right alone and is to be granted by the court (without the consent of the plaintiff) only on motion made by them or in their behalf. It does not appear that the defendant's indemnitors elected or consented to take substitution. It is true that service of the motion papers was admitted by attorneys who assumed to represent the sureties, but this did not purport their consent, nor does it appear that the sureties even consented that the motion should be granted ; and it may be that, so far as they were concerned, no consent on their part was necessary to charge them with the effect of an order substituting them as defendants. Dyett *v.* Hyman, 129 *N. Y.* 351. They were not represented in court upon the hearing of the motion. It apparently was made in behalf of the defendant only, and, being resisted by the plaintiff, was properly denied.

In relation to indemnitors of a sheriff on account of the levy by him of an execution upon a chattel, it may be observed that the provision of the statute on the subject, as it existed at the time of the adoption of section 1711, was to the effect that the sureties might apply to the court to substitute themselves as defendants in an action brought against the sheriff, and that afterwards, in 1887, (*L.* 1887,

c. 182), the right to have his sureties so substituted was by amendment of the statute extended to the officer. Code Civ. Pro. § 1421. This amendment has no bearing upon the construction of the provision of section 1711.

Opinion by BRADLEY, J. All concurred.

Order affirmed, with ten dollars costs and disbursements.

Hugo Hirsh, for the sheriff, appellant.

Josiah T. Marean, for the plaintiffs, respondents.

NOTE ON SUBSTITUTION OF SHERIFF'S INDEMNITORS.

The case in the text raises a new point as to the substitution of the sheriff's indemnitors as defendants in actions brought against that officer for a levy on property where such property is claimed by others than those against whom the process runs. From the cases cited hereafter it will be seen that prior to the amendments of Code Civ. Pro., §§ 1421, 1427, contained in *L.* 1887, chaps. 182, 453, it was held that such a substitution could only be made upon the application of the indemnitors, and that it could not be made at all where there were several levies under successive attachments, executions, etc.

But after the amendment of 1887, it was decided in cases of attachment and executions that such substitution could be had upon the application of the sheriff or of the indemnitors, and the fact that there were successive levies did not prevent the substitution. The court now holds that so far as replevin is concerned the amendment of 1887 does not apply, and that the application for substitution in such a case must be made by the indemnitors.

In the leading case of Hein *v.* Davidson (96 *N. Y.* 175), cited in the text, the court apparently did not look with approval upon the legislation allowing this procedure, but notwithstanding held the act to be constitutional, and that it was the legal right of such indemnitors, upon their own motion, to be made defendants in the place of the sheriff.

In McBride *v.* Tappen, (10 *Supp.* 137 ; s. c., 31 *St. R.* 477) the court frankly criticised the decision of Hein *v.* Davidson (*supra*), but felt compelled to follow it. In the McBride case the seizure had been made under an execution. The plaintiff also sued the sheriff for an abuse of process for seizing more property than was necessary to satisfy the execution. The substitution was made on the motion of the sheriff and the indemnitors did not appeal, but appeared and argued in support of the order. The court said that had it not been for the consent of the indemnitors to assume any liability of the sheriff for the alleged abuse of process another question might have been presented.

Later, however, it was held that the liability of the indemnitors was not limited to the amount in which they would be held in an action by the sheriff on the bond ; their liability rests wholly upon their implied participation in the original trespass. Dyett *v.* Hyman, 129 *N. Y.* 351 ; Ebenreiter *v.* Dahlman, 19 *Misc.* 9.

The indemnitors are liable for the original trespass committed by the sheriff as principals. Those thus connected with the original wrong are jointly and severally liable with the sheriff, and it is no defense, in an action by the owner of the property against one or more of the wrongdoers that others were not joined as defendants who are also liable. Dyett *v.* Hyman (*supra*).

Indemnitors in a bond given to the sheriff are principals and severally liable with him for the wrong committed. Jacobi *v.* Gorman, 1 *Misc.* 222. And where indemnitors are allowed to intervene it is not necessary for the plaintiff to have any cause of action against them ; by giving the bond and being substituted as defendants they make themselves liable for the original trespass. Pool *v.* Ellison, 30 *St. R.* 135 ; Kerner *v.* Boardman, 14 *Supp.* 787.

In Hayes *v.* Davidson (98 *N. Y.* 19 ; rev'g 34 *Hun.* 243) it was held that the indemnitors could not be substituted unless it appeared by the moving papers that they became such before the commencement of the action ; but the effect of that decision was annulled by the amendment of 1887, which provided that the application for substitution could be made before or after the commencement of the suit. It was also decided in that case that where there had been several seizures as to only a part of which indemnity had been furnished, and only a portion of the indemnitors applied for substitution, the order could not be granted. That ruling also seems to have been annulled by the amendment of 1887. Corn *v.* Tamsen, 16 *Misc.* 670.

Note on Substitution of Sheriff's Indemnitors.

In Isaacs *v.* Cohen (2 *N. Y. Ann. Cas.* 99 ; s. c., 86 *Hun,* 119) there is a dictum to the effect that if the sheriff moved to substitute all his indemnitors the court was authorized to divide the action and limit each action to the part of the property for which each class of indemnitors was responsible. But the court further said that if this is not requested and done and the substitution made is general and the whole body of indemnitors are treated as responsible for the entire trespass complained of in the original action against the sheriff, the action cannot thereafter be segregated. The principal question involved in that case was one of costs, the court holding, in effect, that where the substitution was general as in that case only one bill of costs could be allowed if the plaintiff in the action against the sheriff was defeated.

In Carter *v.* Bowe (47 *Hun,* 628), there had been several attachments and seizures and a number of indemnitors. The plaintiff claiming the property had sued the sheriff and after two trials and when the case was on the day calendar for the third time the indemnitors on one of the bonds given to the sheriff, moved to have the action divided and to be substituted as defendants in place of the sheriff, so far as the latter was liable for the portion of the property seized upon the attachment in which the moving parties became indemnitors. The court held that although the delay in moving was sufficient reason for denying the motion, Code Civ. Pro. §§ 1421–1427 did not empower the court to split up the action under such circumstances.

The last mentioned case was decided after the amendments of 1887 (*L.* 1887, chaps. 182, 453), providing for a substitution where there were successive attachments and the court discussed the amendments saying : " But they will not be required to be so far enlarged and extended as to include a case of this description, to which they could not be applied without danger of subjecting the plaintiff in the action to very great injustice. To divide her action in the manner directed by the order would be to subject her to a greater state of confusion and uncertainty in the determination of it, than the law has either provided for or contemplated." The court places its decision mainly on the ground that it was not clearly shown what part of the property seized by the sheriff was affected by the bond given or the indemnitors who asked to be substituted.

It was held, however, in Corn *v.* Tamsen, (16 *Misc.* 670 ; s. c., 25 *Civ. Pro. R.* 129 ; 39 *Supp.* 129), that since the amendment of 1887 there could be a substitution of the sheriff's indemnitors although there were successive levies, where only the first execution was levied on the goods, the subsequent ones being levied on a possible excess of proceeds ; but that only the indemnitors under the first levy should be substituted. The court cited Carter *v.* Bowe (*supra*) as an authority for its decision.

As a general rule the indemnitors have an absolute right to a substitution in attachment cases and it is not within the discretion of the court to deny a motion for substitution. Cantor *v.* Grant, 23 *Abb. N. C.* 424 ; s. c., 10 *Supp.* 223.

Where the application for a substitution is made by the sheriff, notice must be given to the indemnitors or their attorneys, as well as to the plaintiff's attorney. Hero Fruit Jar Co. *v.* Grant, 11 *Supp.* 28 ; s. c., 32 *St. R.* 209.

MANDA *v.* ETIENNE.

Supreme Court, First Department, Appellate Division ; January, 1897.

1. *Attachment ; amount of undertaking by plaintiff ; increase.*] Under Code Civ. Pro. § 682, as well as by virtue of its inherent power to regulate and control provisional remedies, the court may, upon the application of the defendant in attachment, require the plaintiff to give additional security upon the warrant of attachment.*

---

* The power of the court to protect the defendant whose property is attached upon an undertaking insufficient in amount by requiring an increase in the security seems too clear for serious contention, in view of the provisions of section 682 of the Code. This provides that " the defendant, or a person who has acquired a lien upon, or interest in, his property, after it was attached, may, at any time before the actual application of the attached property, or the proceeds thereof, to the payment of a judgment recovered in the action, apply to increase the security, given by the plaintiff."

But although the amount may be thus increased, there seems to be no provision for ascertaining by exception to the sureties upon the undertaking on attachment whether the sureties are in fact sufficient. Under Rule 4 of the General Rules of Practice, the justice.

Manda *v.* Etienne.

2. *The same; unliquidated damages claimed.*] Where plaintiff's
original undertaking on attachment against a non-resident was
for $300, and the plaintiff claimed $20,000 damages for alleged
breach of a vendor's contract of sale, claiming large prospective
profits and speculative and unliquidated damages,—*Held*, that
the court properly increased the security to $2,500, and that the
court might properly require security to the full value of the
property attached.

must require the sureties to justify when he grants the warrant, but
this affords only the formal affidavit of qualification provided for
by the general provisions of section 812. On the other hand, if the
defendant gives an undertaking to discharge the attachment, the
plaintiff may except to the sureties thereon and require them to
submit to an examination as to their property, under Code Civ.
Pro. § 687–690.

A false justification by sureties to an undertaking is a contempt
of court. McAveney *v.* Brush, 1 *N. Y. Ann. Cas.* 414, and notes ; s.
c., on another appeal, 3 *N. Y. Ann. Cas.* 143, and notes.

Where an order has been made requiring the plaintiff to give
additional security the court has power to vacate the attachment
unless such additional security is given, and in case the original attachment is vacated for this reason the sureties on the undertaking
become liable. Corbit *v.* Nicoll, 12 *Civ. Pro. R.* 235 ; s. c. 9 *St.
R.* 525.

Where the defendant gives a bond under Code Civ. Pro., § 688,
to relieve the property from the lien of the attachment this is not
a waiver of the right to move to increase the security under the
attachment. Dusseldorf *v.* Redlich, 16 *Hun,* 624.

The court has power to amend the warrant of attachment as to
the amount on the application of the plaintiff. Sulzbacher *v.*
Cawthra, 14 *Misc.* 544.

Where a large amount of property has been levied upon the
amount of security to be furnished by the plaintiff may be increased
although the defendant is insolvent. Riggs *v.* Cleveland R. R. Co.,
21 *W. Dig.* 45.

Where plaintiff in an action for $14,200, obtained an attachment
upon an undertaking for $200, and the defendant deposited $20,000
with the sheriff and secured a discharge of the attachment, it was
held error to deny a motion of the defendant for an increased security, and the appellate court directed a new undertaking to be given
in lieu of the old in the sum of $1,400, saying that the amount should
be one-tenth the amount claimed by the plaintiff. Bamberger *v.*
Duden, 9 *St. R.* 686.

Manda *v.* Etienne.

Appeal by the plaintiff, Albert A. Manda, from an order of the Supreme Court, New York Special Term, requiring the plaintiff to give additional security in the sum of $2,500 upon the warrant of attachment herein. The attachment was for $20,000, and the original undertaking thereon was for but $300.

Held that the order was properly made. The plaintiff's main contention is that the special term " was wholly without jurisdiction, power or authority to make " the order in question. He seems to overlook section 682 of the Code of Civil Procedure, where this power is expressly conferred. It is a power which is frequently exercised. Before it was thus expressly conferred it was held to be an incident to the regulation and conduct of provisional remedies. Whitney *v.* Deniston, 2 *Supm. Ct.* (*T. & C.*) 471. What the plaintiff really complains of is not the want of power, but an abuse of discretion. That is, indeed, the substance of his argument. But this complaint is equally unfounded. Its presentation calls attention to the plaintiff's own attitude, which is certainly not lacking in boldness. He obtained this attachment for an alleged breach of the defendant's contract to sell and deliver to him certain bulbs. The bulbs were to be shipped by the defendant from France, and were to be paid for by the plaintiff here (immediately after inspection) by accepting drafts at three and four months for the contract price. Some of the bulbs were shipped, and these bulbs in due course reached the defendant's agent in this city, Messrs. Sheldon & Co. Other bulbs were shipped, and the bills of lading therefor were in the hands of these agents when the attachment was issued and served. The disagreement was about the contract price. The plaintiff claimed that the drafts which he was called upon to accept were forty per cent. in excess of the contract price. Sheldon & Co. were unwilling to deliver the goods or the bills of lading without acceptance of the specific drafts which the defendant had forwarded. Thereupon the plaintiff brought this action, and he at once obtained an attachment against the defendant as a non-resident for the sum of $20,000. This was a remarkable sum under the circumstances. It was made up, not of the difference between the contract price of the bulbs and the sum required to obtain them in the market—the plaintiff deposing that they could not be obtained in the market—but of the difference between such contract price and the price at which the plaintiff had contracted to sell them to his customers; in other words, of his prospective profits. But that was not all.. The plaintiff claimed but $10,000 for these profits. His further claim was for speculative and unliquidated damages to the amount of another $10,000. It is plain that the amount for which this attachment was issued was grossly excessive. The plaintiff has the bulbs for which he has not paid, and, in addition, he has his action for $20,000 for failure to deliver these self-same bulbs. The special term upon these facts might well have increased the security to the full value of the goods which this non-resident plaintiff has thus managed to capture. These goods were turned over to him either in fulfillment of the contract, or as custodian (in place of the sheriff) pending this action for the breach. If the former, this action must fail, at least in its most essential features, for how can the plaintiff obtain substantial damages for the breach of the contract after he has accepted the goods in fulfillment? As, however, the plaintiff is steadily proceeding with this action, and indeed exhibits a marked aversion to stipulating to vacate his attachment, it is evident that he insists upon substantial damages for the breach, and consequently holds the goods as security for any judgment he may obtain herein. The least that the court could do, therefore was to require him to give security for the value of these goods under penalty of vacating his attachment. This the court did not do, but the defendant has not appealed upon the ground that the required amount was

Manda *v.* Etienne.

still insuffic:ent.   It he had done so we might have required more adequate security.   As it is we can only affirm the order.*

Opinion by BARRETT, J.   VAN BRUNT, P. J., RUMSEY, WILLIAMS and PATTERSON, JJ., concurred.

Order affirmed, with ten dollars costs and disbursements.

Hector M. Hitchings, for the plaintiff, appellant.

Henry W. Rudd, for the defendant, respondent.

---

* Following this decision the defendant moved at the special term to further increase the amount of the plaintiff's undertaking. That motion was denied by BEEKMAN, J., in the following memorandum opinion :

" The defendant has obtained an order requiring the plaintiff to furnish further security upon his attachment, which order has been sustained on appeal, taken by the plaintiff, and the required security has been given. He cannot now, on substantially the same facts, obtain a further order for the same purpose because he is dissatisfied with the amount of the security which the court has fixed. Defendant's attorney, in justification of this motion, relies upon certain new matter, which he sets forth in his affidavit, tending to show that the plaintiff is irresponsible, and of which he was ignorant at the time the first motion was made. This, however, seems to be so far met by the plaintiff's answering affidavit, that I do not think it presents sufficient ground for so serious a step as the reopening at special term of a question which has already been settled by the order which has been made, and in which the defendant acquiesced by not appealing from it. Motion denied, without costs."

Hill *v.* Schneider.

HILL *v.* SCHNEIDER.

Supreme Court, First Department, Appellate Division ;
January, 1897.

1. *Negligence ; blasting ; injury to property ; injunction.*] Where
   it appeared that the defendant in blasting rock in a lot adjoining premises occupied by the plaintiff, used large charges of
   giant powder and discharged heavy blasts which shook the
   walls and made the building unsafe in which plaintiff had his
   place of business, and it further appeared that the blasting could
   be done in a different manner, which would not have injured
   said building, although this would have entailed greater expense on the part of the defendant,—*Held*, that the plaintiff
   was entitled to an injunction restraining further prosecution of
   the work in the manner described.

2. *The same ; adequate remedy at law.*] Although under such circumstances the plaintiff could maintain an action for damages
   for the injury caused to his property, where the effect of the
   blasting would be to shake down the plaintiff's house and
   make it entirely uninhabitable, with the necessary result that
   the plaintiff would be obliged to abandon his place of business
   and go elsewhere, the remedy at law would be entirely inadequate.

3. *The same ; liability of contractor and principal.*] Where it appeared that the owner of the premises where the blasting was
   being carried on had made a contract with another person to
   do the work, but the owner was to have no control over the
   contractor or his men in performing the work,—*Held*, that a
   preliminary injunction should not be granted against such
   owner as it did not appear that he took any part in the acts
   which violated the plaintiff's rights.*

---

* This case is not entirely without precedent in allowing relief
in equity by way of an injunction restraining a person from continuing the work of blasting where injury is caused thereby to the
property of the plaintiff. In Rogers *v.* Hanfield (14 *Daly*, 399 ; s. c.,
12 *St. R.* 671), the defendant was enjoined from blasting so near to
plaintiff's premises that rocks were thrown thereon, although the
blasting was being done in accordance with the requirements of a
city ordinance.

Hill *v.* Schneider.

Appeal by the plaintiff, from an order of the Supreme Court, New York Special Term, denying his motion for an injunction *pendente lite.*

The plaintiff William R. Hill, is the lessee and in the possession of the premises known as No. 103 West Thirty-Sixth Street, under a lease which expires May 1, 1897. He carries on at that place the business of plumbing and other business, and has done so for several years. The defendant Douglas Schneider is the owner in fee of the premises. He also owns the land on Thirty-Sixth Street, between Broadway and Sixth Avenue, extending northerly about 100 feet. He is engaged in work preliminary to the construction of a large hotel building on these premises, and, to that end, has entered into a contract with a person who is not a defendant in this action, to

In Marvin *v.* Brewster, Iron Mining Co. (55 *N. Y.* 538), the court refused to grant an injunction to restrain the defendant from blasting in the night time beneath the plaintiff's premises, although such blasting disturbed the sleep and affected the health of the plaintiff and his family. But the denial of relief was put on the ground that the defendant in buying the ore in the ground secured the right to take it out in the usual method, and it did not appear that there was any other way of performing the work.

Where an owner of premises lets the entire work of clearing them or doing other work thereon which requires blasting, and he has no control over the contractor or the manner in which the latter does the work, the owner is not, as a general rule, liable for the negligence of the contractor. McCafferty *v.* Spuyten Duyvil & P. M. R. R. Co., 61 *N. Y.* 178 ; Ferguson *v.* Hubbell, 97 *N. Y.*, 507.

But a person is bound to use due care in engaging a person to do blasting, and where there is a conflict of evidence as to the extent of the inquiries made by the defendant as to the competency of a person engaged by him to do such work on his premises and as to the qualifications of such contractor, the question should be submitted to the jury. Berg *v.* Parsons, 90 *Hun,* 267 ; s. c., 35 *Supp.* 780 ; 70 *St. R.* 284.

For a full discussion of this subject see Note on Trespass by Blasting, 3 *N. Y. Ann. Cas.* 328 ; following the case of Sullivan *v.* Dunham, *Id.* 324.

make the necessary excavations and to erect the building. The original contractor has caused the buildings upon a large portion of said land to be removed, and has entered into a contract with the defendant William Bradley to make such excavations upon the whole of said land, including the premises occupied by the plaintiff's building, as are necessary for the construction of the hotel which Schneider intends to build. Over a large portion of this area blasting has been in progress to a considerable extent. It appears that during the progress of the work a notice was served upon the defendant Schneider by the department of buildings, that the building occupied by the plaintiff was unsafe and dangerous in certain respects specified in the notice, and Schneider was required to take steps to secure the building by properly shoring it up, or to take it down. In pursuance of that notice he proceeded to take down the wall of the two upper stories, but the remainder of the building which is occupied by the plaintiff, has been permitted to stand, having, as it seems, a temporary roof over it, so that it is not entirely uninhabitable. A large amount of blasting has already been done in such a way and with such unnecessary force as to shatter the walls of the building, and plaintiff says that the insecurity complained of by the department of buildings was brought about by the excessive blasts used in causing the explosions in the course of the excavations. He alleges in his affidavits that this was done, and that the notice was procured to be sent by the department of buildings, in pursuance of a scheme of Schneider's to drive the plaintiff away from the premises so that Schneider and his contractors could take possession of them for the purpose of proceeding with the construction of the hotel. This is denied by the defendants. [After reviewing the facts set forth in the affidavits.] Therefore, the case presents itself substantially in this way: The plaintiff's building has already been seriously injured by blasts let off in the course of making this excavation. The defendant

Hill *v.* Schneider.

Bradley proposes to let off further blasts in the course of the same work nearer to the plaintiff's building than those already exploded. The blasts already let off have shattered the wall of the plaintiff to some extent. The ones to be let off are almost certain to do the same thing to a greater extent. The course of work pursued by Bradley is not necessary to the making of the excavation, but it is easy to do it in a different way with the use of smaller blasts so as not to injure the wall of the plaintiff's building, although at perhaps a somewhat greater cost to the contractor, and such is the usual way of doing that work where there is danger of injuring a neighbor's premises.

Held, that upon that state of facts the plaintiff is entitled to an injunction restraining this blasting in the way in which Bradley proposes to do it. The rule *sic utere tuo ut alienam non lædas* is of wide application, and it is a maxim of the law to which the exceptions are few. It is not intended of course, in the application of this maxim, to take away from any person the right to improve his own property in a lawful manner, but the law requires that when he shall attempt to do so he must exercise his right with a due regard for the rights of other people, and in every way legally possible he must avoid injury to those rights. One living in a city must necessarily submit to considerable inconvenience which arises from the proximity of other people, and from the carrying on of unpleasant trades and businesses near him, and such things will be restrained only when it is absolutely certain that the person engaged in them is going beyond his legal right, to the injury of his neighbor. But when one has occasion, in a crowded community, to do upon his own premises anything which is likely to injure his neighbor, he is called upon to use the utmost care and the most approved methods, so as not to inflict any injury beyond what is necessary for the performance of his lawful work in a lawful manner. If he goes beyond that he makes himself liable to respond to his neighbor in damages. Morgan *v.* Bowes, 62 *Hun*, 623; S. C., 17 *Supp.* 22.

The case of Booth *v.* Rome, W. & O. T. R. R. Co., (140 *N. Y.* 267), was evidently decided upon the special facts made to appear upon the trial, and it is undoubtedly an authority for any other case where the same conditions exist. But the rule laid down in that case, while supposed by the court to be necessary for the protection of persons improving their land, ought not to be extended so as to give those persons the privilege of unnecessarily destroying the buildings of their neighbors. The true rule must be that, while any person is at liberty to improve his own land, yet in the doing of that he must use every practicable means to avoid injury to his neighbor, and he will not be permitted by the use of powerful explosives upon his own land to injure the house of his neighbor. Certainly is this so, when, by the use of smaller quantities of the explosives or in some other way, even at a greater expense, he can avoid such a result. In this case it is very clear that the blasting in the way proposed to be done by Bradley is not necessary, even within the exceedingly broad rule in favor of builders laid down in the Booth case (*supra*).

But it is claimed on the part of the defendants that this injury is not irreparable. The effect of the blasting will be to shake down the house and make it entirely uninhabitable, with the necessary result that the plaintiff will be obliged to leave it, to abandon his business and go elsewhere. While in a sense this may be compensated for in damages, yet the remedy at law will be entirely inadequate within all the authorities, and the injury will be irreparable. *Pom. Eq. Juris.*, § 1357, note; *High on Injunc.* §§ 701, 704; Livingston *v.* Livingston, 6 *Johns. Ch.* 497.

But the defendant Schneider stands in an entirely different position. While he is the owner of these premises and is desirous of obtaining possession of them, and it is fair to infer that he has used every means in his power to do so, and even that he is not unwilling to see this house destroyed so that he may have possession of his land, yet we cannot see from the affidavits here that he has been a party to the blasting so as to warrant an injunction against him. It appears that he has made a contract with the Chas. S. Kendall Company to do this work. So far as appears, in making this contract he did nothing to violate the rights of the plaintiff. Certainly the making of the contract itself was not in violation of the rights of the plaintiff, for it was not necessary, under the contract, for the contractors to take possession of this land, or to do anything to which the plaintiff could object. The plaintiff does not show that any portion of this blasting has been controlled by the defendant Schneider. He has nothing to do with it upon the facts stated in the papers presented to the court. He has no control over Bradley and no privity of contract with him, and could not in any way restrain his action. For that reason we are of the opinion that the plaintiff has not shown anything to entitle him to a preliminary injunction against Schneider, because there is nothing in the case which would warrant a finding that Schneider either has done or could do any act about the blasting out of the excavation which would affect the plaintiff's rights, or, indeed, that he has any control over the excavation whatever.

Upon the facts which were made to appear, there was no privity between Bradley and Schneider. Schneider made a contract with the Kendall Company to accomplish a certain result, leaving it to them to use the ordinary means to complete the work which they agreed to do. He had, so far as appears, no right to control them as to their manner of doing the work. They were responsible to him only for the results to be obtained, and the thing to be done was lawful in itself. That being the case, neither the Kendall Company nor Bradley occupied toward Schneider the relation of a servant. Hexamer *v.*

Webb, 101 *N. Y.* 377. So long as the work which was to be done did not necessarily involve an infringement of the rights of the plaintiff, but might have been done with due regard to them, Schneider is not responsible for any violation of those rights, unless it has been proved that he personally directed it. There is a class of cases where the owner is equally responsible with the contractor for injuries done in the progress of the work, but those are cases where the contractor is employed to do an act which is illegal in itself, or which is likely to infringe upon the rights of the plaintiff, however skillfully it is performed. Joliet *v*. Harwood (86 *Ill.* 110), but, upon the facts shown, this is not one of those cases.

Opinion by RUMSEY, J. VAN BRUNT P. J., BARRETT, O'BRIEN and INGRAHAM, JJ., concurred.

Order affirmed as to the defendant Schneider, with $10 costs and disbursements, to be paid by the plaintiff to him; and reversed as to the defendant Bradley, with $10 costs and disbursements, to be paid by Bradley to the plaintiff; and, as to Bradley, injunction granted, with $10 costs to abide event.

Charles De Hart Brower, for the plaintiff, appellant.

John Frankenheimer, for the defendant, respondent Bradley.

Julien T. Davies and *Herbert Barry*, for the defendant, respondent Schneider.

SMITH *v.* CROCKER.

Supreme Court, First Department, Appellate Division;
February, 1897.

1. *Defense; former action pending ; different State.*] The pendency
of an action in a different State, by the same plaintiff against the
same defendants, to recover a debt due upon a contract, cannot be pleaded in abatement of an action in the courts of this
State ; it is only where one of the actions has ripened into a
judgment that it can be pleaded in bar of the other action.*

2. *Jurisdiction; action on contract; non-resident parties.*] The courts
of this State have jurisdiction in an action upon a contract
made in another State, although both parties to the action are
non-residents; but in an action founded upon a tort, committed
without the State, our courts will not take jurisdiction where
the parties are non-residents, unless special reasons are shown
to exist which make it necessary or proper that they should do
so.†

---

* "At common law the pendency of another suit for the same
cause could, at most, only be pleaded in abatement ; but where the
former action is in a court of the United States or a sister State, it
is no stay or bar to a suit in the courts of this State. A recovery in
one might be pleaded to the further continuance of the other, but
until that was obtained, each might proceed to judgment and
execution, when satisfaction of either would require a discharge of
both." Oneida County Bank *v.* Bonney, 101 *N. Y.*173, at page 175.

The pendency of a prior suit in a State court is not a bar to a
suit in a circuit court of the United States, or in the Supreme Court
of the District of Columbia, by the same plaintiff against the same
defendant for the same cause of action.   Stanton *v.* Embrey, 93 *U.
S.* 548.

It is no ground for staying proceeding in an action in England,
that proceedings are pending between the parties for the same
cause of action in the United States.   Cox *v.* Mitchell, 7 *C. B.* (*N.
S.*) 55.

See Note on Defense of Former Action Pending, 3 *N. Y. Ann.
Cas.* 215 ; following the case of Parker *v.* Selye, *Id.* 210.

† In Reed *v.* Chilson, 142 *N. Y.* 152, an action was brought by a

Smith *v.* Crocker.

Appeal by the defendant Crocker, from a judgment of the Supreme Court, New York County, entered upon the verdict of a jury, and also from an order denying the

non-resident against non-residents of this State to recover upon a judgment of the courts of the State of Michigan. The summons was served without the State pursuant to an order of publication. The defendants appeared in the action by attorney and served an answer setting up the alleged lack of jurisdiction of the courts of this State on the ground that all the parties to the action were non-residents and that the defendants had no property here. It was there held that the court had jurisdiction and a judgment of the lower court (16 *Supp.* 744 ; S. C., 40 *St. R.* 960), in favor of the plaintiff was affirmed.

The law seems to have been settled in Burdick *v.* Freeman (120 *N. Y.* 420), that the courts of this State may in their discretion, entertain jurisdiction of actions of tort where the parties were both non-residents and the act complained of was committed without the State. The court there cited with approval and as authorities for the principle of its decision, Gardner *v.* Thomas, 14 *Johns.* 134 ; Johnson *v.* Dalton, 1 *Cow.* 543 ; Dewitt *v.* Buchanan, 54 *Barb.* 31 ; McIvor *v.* McCabe, 26 *How. Pr.* 257 ; Newman *v.* Goddard, 3 *Hun*, 70 ; Mostyn *v.* Fabrigas, 2 *Smith's L. C.* (9th ed.) 916 ; Story on Conflict of Laws, § 582 ; *Whart. on Conf. Laws,* §§ 705, 707, 743 ; 4 *Phil. on Int. Law,* 701 ; and the court also expressly overrules the cases of Molony *v.* Dows, 8 *Abb. Pr.* 316, and Latourette *v.* Clark, 30 *How. Pr.* 242.

Very different rules apply to actions by and against non-resident natural persons from those which govern actions where the plaintiff or defendant is a foreign corporation. The latter are governed entirely by statute.

In Robinson *v.* Oceanic Steam Nav. Co. (112 *N. Y.* 315), it is said, on this point, at page 321 : " It is true that the plaintiff's cause of action (for causing the death of his intestate by the negligence of the defendant) is transitory, and that a plaintiff may bring a suit upon such a cause of action wherever he may be, provided he can find a court which has jurisdiction of the action and can obtain jurisdiction of the defendant. But a cause of action, even if transitory, must always arise somewhere, and this cause of action arose where the tort was committed which caused the death of plaintiff's intestate. That this is a cause of action for a tort is too clear for reasonable dispute. It exists only by virtue of the statute (Code Civ. Pro. § 1780) referred to, and is based entirely upon the negligence and tortuous conduct attributable to the defendant. We, therefore, have a case where the plaintiff is a non-resident, the de-

Smith *v.* Crocker.

defendant's motion for a new trial made upon the minutes.

The complaint in this action alleged that the defendants, Henry J. Crocker impleaded with others, desiring to have a test made of a certain process for the manufacture of champagne and other wines in the State of California, with a view to purchasing the same, on or about April 18, 1891, promised and agreed to and with the International Wine Company that, if said company would ship a plant for the demonstration of said process to California, and there make a demonstration of the same by the manufacture of one hundred cases of champagne, upon the delivery of said one hundred cases of champagne to them they would at once pay to said company the sum of $5,000, for, and in consideration of the said company's shipping said plant and making said demonstration as aforesaid. That thereafter the said International Wine Company did ship such plant to California, and did make such demonstration of its process, and manufactured and tendered to the said defendants the one hundred cases of champagne so agreed to be manufactured by it, and duly performed all the conditions precedent upon its part. That thereupon the said defendants became indebted to

fendant a foreign corporation, and the cause of action did not arise within this State; and, therefore, no court within this State has jurisdiction of the action."

The Code Civ. Pro. § 1780, reads as follows: "An action against a foreign corporation may be maintained by a resident of the State, or by a domestic corporation, for any cause of action. An action against a foreign corporation may be maintained by another foreign corporation or by a non-resident, in one of the following cases only:

1. "Where the action is brought to recover damages for the breach of a contract, made within the State, or relating to property situated within the State, at the time of the making thereof.

2. "When it is brought to recover real property situated within the State, or a chattel, which is replevied within the State.

3. "Where the cause of action arose within the State, except where the object of the action is to affect the title of real property situated without the State."

Smith *v.* Crocker.

the said International Wine Company in the said sum of
$5,000, no part of which has been paid. That prior to
the commencement of this action the said International
Wine Company, for a good and valuable consideration,
duly sold, assigned and transferred to this plaintiff all its
right in and to said claim for $5,000 against said defend-
ants.

Upon a former trial the complaint was dismissed and
upon appeal a new trial was ordered. 3 *App. Div.* 473.
The defendants pleaded in abatement of this action
the pendency of a former action against part of the
defendants here upon the same contract, and also that
the court was without jurisdiction because the contract
was made in another State and both parties thereto were
non-residents. The defendants asked for a dismissal of
the complaint on these grounds and the motion was
denied.

Held (after considering the evidence and holding that
there was sufficient to go to the jury on the question of
the breach of the contract), that the motion for a dismissal
was properly denied. It appears that this plaintiff sued
Ferris and McCondry in California upon the same contract, and to obtain the same relief as by the verdict of
the jury has been accorded to him here. Having made
this appear, the defendants asked the trial judge to
charge, in effect, that, by suing the parties named in California on the same cause of action, the plaintiff elected,
and that, therefore, he is prevented from maintaining an
action against the defendants in our courts, the reason
assigned being that the plaintiff could not sue on the same
cause of action two different people in two different jurisdictions. This request, we think, was properly refused.
A party may have pending actions against the same
defendant to recover the same indebtedness in different
States at the same time, and the pendency of an action in
one State to recover a debt cannot successfully be pleaded
in abatement in an action in another State to recover the

Smith *v.* Crocker.

same debt. It is only where one of the actions has ripened into a judgment that such judgment can be pleaded in bar in the other action.

The contention that, because both the plaintiff and the defendant Crocker are non-residents, the trial court should have refused to entertain jurisdiction of the cause, we regard as equally untenable. We are referred to a number of cases (Ferguson *v.* Neilson, 33 *St. R.* 814; Robinson *v.* Oceanic Steam Nav. Co., 112 *N. Y.* 315) in which it was held that the courts of this State will not retain jurisdiction of and determine an action for tort between parties residing in other States on causes of action arising out of the State, as a matter of public policy, unless special reasons are shown to exist which make it necessary or proper so to do. An examination of the cases cited, as well as of all to which our attention has been called where that rule has been applied, were actions in tort, and not actions upon a contract. Our courts have never refused to entertain jurisdiction of a cause of action arising upon contract. In the case of Davidsburgh *v.* Knickerbocker Life Ins. Co. (90 *N. Y.* 526) it was held that as the city court of Brooklyn was a local court of limited jurisdiction, unless the defendants came within the classes over which the statute had conferred jurisdiction upon that court, the parties could not confer jurisdiction by consent. This case is in no respect an authority for the rule contended for by the appellants. Whether, therefore, this contract was made in California or New York—upon which question much in favor of the view that it was a New York contract might be said—we do not think it is necessary to determine; as it appears that the action was one upon contract, the court committed no error in entertaining jurisdiction of the cause.

Having concluded that, upon the questions of law, the appellant's contentions cannot be sustained, and that we would not be justified in interfering with the verdict of the jury, it follows that the judgment should be affirmed, with costs.

Opinion by O'BRIEN, J.   VAN BRUNT, P. J., WIL. LIAMS, PATTERSON and INGRAHAM, JJ., concurred.

Judgment affirmed, with costs.

Charles K. Beekman and *Charles C. Alexander*, for the defendant, appellant.

J. A: Dennison, for the plaintiff, respondent.

LEHMAIER *v.* BUCHNER.

Supreme Court, First Department, Appellate Division; February, 1897.

Attachment ; affidavit ; positive averments upon undisclosed sources of information.] Where one of the plaintiffs, in an affidavit to secure a warrant of attachment, averred positively the material facts, but the affidavit did not disclose how the deponent could have this personal knowledge, and from all the circumstances of the case he could not be presumed to have it,—*Held*, that the affidavit was insufficient and the attachment should be vacated.*

---

* This case, with that of Tucker *v.* E. L. Goodsell Co., *post,* page 86, lends emphasis to the view before expressed (see Note on Affidavits on Information and Belief, 2 *N. Y. Ann. Cas.* 58), that the courts have shown recently an increasing tendency to give but little probative force to affidavits made on information and belief. The question was there discussed more particularly with reference to cases where it appeared from the face of the affidavit that the statements therein contained were made on information and belief. Since that note was written several cases have been decided wherein it was held, as in the cases in the text, that not only would the court look with disfavor upon affidavits where the statements were al-

Lehmaier *v.* Buchner.

Appeal by the defendant, from an order of the Supreme Court, New York Special Term, denying his motion to vacate an attachment.

The attachment was granted upon the ground that the defendant, David Buchner, a resident of this State, has assigned and disposed of his property with the intent to defraud his creditors, the affidavit to prove such fraudulent assignment and disposition of his property being made by one of the plaintiffs, Albert Sichel, impleaded with Martin Lehmaier and others. In his affidavit he makes certain statements as to the acts of the defendant, as to the organization of a company by the defendant, as to the intention of the defendant in organizing the company, and as to the acts of the defendant in making transfers to the company. There is no intimation in this affidavit as to the sources of the affiant's knowledge, as to his opportunity of ascertaining the intention of the defendant, the condition of his property or its value, nor as to the amount of his indebtedness. There is hardly an allegation in the affidavit which is a distinct statement of a fact, all of the statements being conclusions or expressions of opinion or statements of the intentions of the defendant, with nothing to show upon what such conclusions

leged to be made on information only, but would go further and scan the affidavit to see if the one making it could, from all the circumstances, be presumed to have knowledge of the facts which were sworn to positively. This rule has been held to apply to cases where the facts constituting the cause of action have been sworn to by an agent, attorney, or assignee of the plaintiff. See Note referred to above ; Everitt *v.* Park, 2 *N. Y. Ann. Cas.* 205 ; Ladenburg *v.* Commercial Bank, *Id.* 397 ; Hoorman *v.* Climax Cycle Co. 3 *Id.* 201 ; Einstein *v.* Climax Cycle Co., *Id.* 203.

The court now extends this rule as to positive averments concerning acts of the defendant which entitle the plaintiff to an attachment, and holds that it must appear how the affiant secured the personal knowledge of the facts sworn to when it cannot be presumed that he had such knowledge.

are based, or how the affiant ascertained the defendant's intentions.

Held, that such an affidavit was insufficient and the attachment should be vacated. It is impossible for us to conceive how this plaintiff should have had personal knowledge as to the assets and liabilities of the defendant. It might be that the defendant had made a statement to him as to the amount of his assets or liabilities. It might be that he had seen a stock of goods in the defendant's store which he would estimate as of the value stated, or that in some other way he had been told, or had ascertained facts upon which his conclusions are based, but we are entirely in the dark as to how he arrives at the conclusions stated, and how his statement of such assets and liabilities, without any statement of the method by which he obtained this knowledge, can be said to be competent evidence of the fact that the defendant had in his possession at any time the assets, or that he owed the amount stated. So it is not stated how the affiant knew that the defendant caused a corporation to be incorporated. It is not stated that this affiant ever saw the certificate of incorporation, nor is the said certificate annexed to the affidavit. The affiant also states that two of the incorporators had no actual pecuniary interest in the pretended incorporation, and merely allowed the use of their names for the accommodation of the defendant and the accomplishment of his unlawful purpose to defraud his creditors. How the affiant could know of this fact it is a little difficult to conceive. He states no fact of which he has personal knowledge which would lead him to this conclusion, but boldly states a conclusion without stating anything to justify it. His affidavit then states that the defendant caused all of his property and effects to be transferred to the said corporation. How he knows this is not stated. In fact, there is nothing stated to justify the granting of this warrant based upon the personal knowledge of the defendant; nothing but his conclusions, surmises and suspicions, without stating any fact upon which he bases them or upon which the court can determine whether or not they are justified.

A creditor may have knowledge of statements made by his debtor as to his assets and liabilities. He may have knowledge of statements made by the debtor's representatives or employees. He may have knowledge of his debtor's credit in the business in which he is engaged. He may have some knowledge of the amount of stock a debtor is carrying, but there is certainly no presumption that every creditor has personal knowledge of the amount of the assets or liabilities of a debtor. On the contrary, it would seem that no third party not an employee, or having some confidential relation to a business firm, could possibly have knowledge of the exact amount of the firm's liabilities or its assets; and when such a person comes into a court of justice to obtain relief, which is based upon the extent of a debtor's assets and liabilities, something more is required than that he should merely swear to the amount of such assets and liabilities, or swear to the debtor's intentions in the doing of certain acts, without showing how his knowledge is acquired, or upon what he bases his conclusions.

Opinion by INGRAHAM, J. VAN BRUNT, P. J., BARRETT, RUMSEY and O'BRIEN, JJ., concurred.

Order reversed, with ten dollars costs and disbursements, and motion granted to vacate attachment, with ten dollars costs.

Franklin Bien, for the defendant, appellant.

Samuel Untermyer, for the plaintiff, respondent.

TUCKER *v.* E. L. GOODSELL CO.

Supreme Court, First Department, Appellate Division; February, 1897.

Attachment ; affidavit by assignee of claim ; mere averment of positive knowledge, insufficient.] An affidavit for attachment by an assignee of the cause of action, though he expressly avers that the facts alleged are true to his own knowledge, is insufficient, without evidence in support of the averments relating to transactions with which he was not apparently connected.[*]

Appeal by the defendant from an order of the Supreme Court, New York Special Term, denying a motion to vacate an attachment upon the papers on which it was granted.

Action by Robert A. Tucker, Jr., against the E. L. Goodsell Company, upon a complaint setting forth that a

---

[*] It will be noticed that this decision goes a step further than the case of Hoorman *v.* Climax Cycle Co. (9 *App. Div.* 579 ; aff'g 3 *N. Y. Ann. Cas.* 201) where the affidavit of the assignee of the claim was held insufficient, because, though positive in form, it did not expressly allege the affiant's personal knowledge of the facts. It seems, in the light of the case in the text, that such an averment of personal knowledge would have been wholly nugatory, unless supplemented by evidence—a statement of the facts and circumstances which show how the affidavit could have had personal knowledge of transactions apparently occurring between third parties.

It results from this ruling that the affidavit for attachment should show either : (1) that the affidavit was an actor in the transaction about which he testifies, so as to justify an absolute averment thereof, or an express affirmation of knowledge; or (2) if he was in fact disconnected with the transaction, the grounds of his information and sources of his belief as to the material facts.

Compare the preceding case of Lehmaier *v.* Buchner, *ante*, p. 82, and see Note on Affidavits on Information and Belief, 2 *N. Y. Ann. Cas.* 58.

Tucker *v.* E. L. Goodsell Co.

firm doing business in London, England, under the name of Greenwood, Haro & Co., placed "certain" goods in the hands of the defendant corporation for sale by it in the city of New York, upon an agreement that such sale should be at public auction, and that the defendant should pay over the proceeds to such English firm, after deducting its reasonable commissions and charges; that the defendant sold the goods and received the proceeds, which amount, over and above its reasonable commissions and charges, to the sum of $790; and that the defendant neglects and refuses to pay over the latter sum to Greenwood, Haro & Co., or to the plaintiff as their assignee.

The attachment was granted upon the complaint and an affidavit of the plaintiff deposing that the facts alleged were true "to his own knowledge."

Held, that the affidavits were insufficient, and the attachment should have been vacated. The affidavits simply contain verified allegations of fact, and no proof of the facts so alleged. It is doubtful whether certain of these allegations would be sufficient as proof even if verified by Greenwood, Haro & Co.; some, at least, are but bald assertions. There is no averment, much less evidence, of what the goods consisted of, or what they sold for, or what the defendant's reasonable charges and commissions were; nothing whatever which would enable the court to ascertain the proper balance. But the affiant here is apparently a total stranger to the transactions between Greenwood, Haro & Co. and the defendant. If ever a plaintiff affiant should be held to proof of facts, rather than to mere verified averment of facts, it is here. The court cannot overlook the almost incredible character of the affiant's statement. We may not deny its efficacy as a properly verified averment. But we should attribute to it no value whatever as proof. " Proof by affidavit," as Justice JAMES well said, speaking for the general term in Town of Duanesburgh *v.* Jenkins (40 *Barb.* 584), " can only be made by a statement and verification of such facts as are requisite to establish the principal fact sought to be maintained." Or as Presiding Justice VAN BRUNT put it in Mechanics & Traders' Bank *v.* Loucheim (55 *Hun*, 396; s. c., 8 *Supp.* 520): "The office of an affidavit is to set forth the evidence from which the court may draw conclusions of fact, differing in this respect radically from a complaint, which should only set forth conclusions of fact and not the evidence of the correctness of these conclusions."

We distinctly held in Hoorman *v.* Climax Cycle Co. (9 *App. Div.* 579; aff'g 3 *N. Y. Ann. Cas.* 201), that the averment of facts as upon personal knowledge, by an assignee who was an apparent stranger to the transaction between the original parties, was not sufficient to entitle the plaintiff to an attachment without proof of the facts as averred. That rule applies with equal force whether such an assignee makes his averments positively as upon personal knowledge—though without direct affirmation thereof —or whether he makes them positively, with direct affirmation of such knowledge. In either case—whether the affirmation of what he calls knowledge be express or implied—the assignee affiant must furnish evidence in support of such of his averments as relate to transactions with which he was not apparently connected.

Some allegations of fact, as pointed out in the Hoorman case, may, of themselves, amount to quite satisfactory proof. For example, the plaintiff's allegation here that the claim was assigned to him. His verified statement upon that head sufficed without the production of the instrument, if the assignment was in writing, or without narrating what took place between himself and his assignors, if the assignment was by parol; so, too, would the verified statement of a member of the firm of Greenwood, Haro & Co., that that firm had made a contract with the defendant for the sale of their goods. But even their statement, though upon affirmation of knowledge, that the proceeds of the sale, over and above the defendant's reasonable commissions and charges, amounted to some particular sum, would hardly suffice, without proof. Such a statement might be barely sufficient to confer jurisdiction and to uphold the attachment as against a junior attaching creditor (Haebler *v.* Bernharth, 115 *N. Y.* 459), but it would scarcely stand the test upon an application to vacate made by the defendant in the action.

The court has repeatedly held that to entitle a plaintiff to this severe and summary remedy he must show the proper facts by affidavit; that is, he must furnish satisfactory proof of such facts. Where the affiant, owing to his relation to the parties and to the cause of action, plainly speaks as an actor in the transaction, the court frequently treats his verified averments of facts, which may naturally have come within his actual observation or personal action, as satisfactory proof thereof, as in Ladenburg *v.* Com. Bank (2 *N. Y. Ann. Cas.* 397 ; s. c., 5 *App. Div.* 220). Where, however, he does not speak as such a direct actor, where, in fact, he speaks apparently as a stranger to the transaction, it matters not how positively he so speaks, how firmly he asserts his personal knowledge of the facts averred, he must still furnish the evidence of such facts. Under such circumstances, his verified allegation " shows " nothing " by affidavit." He simply pleads the facts. He pleads them positively, it is true, and upon personal knowledge. But he does not prove them. And a person standing as he does in relation to the cause of action must prove them.

Opinion PER CURIAM. Present—VAN BRUNT, P. J., WILLIAMS, PATTERSON, O'BRIEN and INGRAHAM, JJ.

Order reversed, with ten dollars costs and disbursements, and attachment vacated, with ten dollars costs.

Dallas Flannagan, for the defendant, appellant.

Thaddeus D. Kenneson and *Thomas C. T. Crain*, for the plaintiff, respondent.

ALBANY HARDWARE & IRON CO. *v.* DAY.

Supreme Court, Third Department, Appellate Division; December, 1896.

Former adjudication; judgment for goods sold and delivered; subsequent action for fraud.] Where a purchaser of goods induced the plaintiff to make the sale by means of false representations as to his solvency, and the vendor did not discover such fraud until after recovering a judgment for the price of the goods, —*Held*, that the recovery of such judgment was not a bar to a subsequent action founded upon the fraud.*

Appeal by the plaintiff from an order of the Supreme Court, Albany Special Term, vacating an order of arrest of the defendant.

The plaintiff sold goods to the defendant upon credit. When the purchase price became due the defendant defaulted in its payment, and the plaintiff thereupon brought an action for the same, recovered a judgment by default and issued execution thereon. Such execution was returned wholly unsatisfied. By supplementary proceedings instituted thereon the plaintiff discovered that the representations to the effect that the defendant, George H. Day, was solvent, was worth $1,800 and that his liabilities did not exceed $100, by which it had been induced to make the sale were utterly false and fraudulent. It thereupon brought this action to recover damages for the fraud and deceit so practiced upon it. It procured an order of arrest against defendant from the county judge of Albany county, which was vacated by an order of the special term. From such latter order this appeal is taken.

Held, that, as at the time the plaintiff recovered the judgment for the purchase price of the goods sold it had no knowledge of the fraud which defendant had perpetrated upon it, that the action on its part could not, therefore,

---

* See note following this case.

Albany Hardware & Iron Co. *v.* Day.

be deemed an election of remedies, so as to bar its maintaining an action to recover damages for that fraud.
Rochester Distilling Co. *v.* Devendorf, 72 *Hun*, 428;
Equitable Co-Operative Foundry Co. *v.* Hersee, 103 *N. Y.*
25 ; Hays *v.* Midas, 104 *Id.* 602.

Held, also, that the plaintiff could maintain an action
for the fraud without first discharging the judgment which
it still holds for the purchase price. If the plaintiff were
seeking to repossess itself of the goods, it would have to
disaffirm the contract of sale on the ground of the fraud
and restore all that had been received under it in order to
obtain such relief. Thus, if, at the time of the sale, part
of the purchase price had been paid and credit had been
given for the balance only, the plaintiff could not recover
the goods without restoring the amount so paid. Nor
could it reasonably hold a judgment for that purchase price
and also retake possession of the goods. But the relief
which it asks in this action is not at all inconsistent with
its affirmance of the contract. It is to recover the damages which have been sustained by reason of its relying
on certain false and fraudulent statements of defendant,
to the effect that he was the owner of certain property
and owed no debts—statements which, if true, showed him
to be solvent, and authorized plaintiff to believe that if
the defendant defaulted in payment of such purchase
price it could be recovered from him by the very process
of judgment and execution which the plaintiff has already
taken. The subject-matter of the fraud was the ability of
the defendant to pay such an execution.

If the plaintiff in this action should aver the sale of
the goods, the representations of solvency which induced
it, that upon default in paying for them it had recovered
judgment and issued execution, which was returned wholly
unsatisfied, and that thereupon it discovered that such
representations were false and fraudulently made, and then
ask for the damages which is thereby sustained, such averments would be but a concise statement of the facts con-

stituting its cause of action, and none of them would be inconsistent with the relief asked. In estimating these damages the purchase price would be the principal element. If anything had been paid upon that, or collected by the execution issued, the damages would be diminished in accordance with the proofs made upon such subjects. But the mere fact that a worthless judgment for the purchase price was outstanding when this action was commenced, neither satisfies the damages occasioned by the fraud nor bars an action therefor. The case of Rochester Distilling Co. *v.* Devendorf (72 *Hun*, 622) is not an authority against this conclusion. In that case it appeared upon the trial that the judgment theretofore recovered for the purchase price of the goods had been paid and discharged, thus showing that the damages which the plaintiff was then seeking to recover had been fully satisfied. A judgment for the purchase price is not as full and complete a remedy for the damages sustained as is a judgment rendered in an action for the fraud. In the latter action an execution issues against the body of defendant, and thus affords a much more effective remedy than one against the property merely. In this respect a distinction exists between actions against corporations, where no process against the person can issue, and one against the individual, and hence the case of Caylus *v.* N. Y., Kingston & S. R. R. Co. (76 *N. Y.* 609, 611) is not an authority applicable to this case.

It is objected that the plaintiff should not have two judgments for the same demand. No difficulty need arise on that account. Inasmuch as the plaintiff is not barred by the election of remedies from maintaining this action, there is no reason why it may not upon the trial, or whenever the damages are assessed, tender a discharge of the judgment for the purchase price; or, indeed, if no such tender was made it is manifest that it would not be allowed to collect both. Payment or satisfaction of either would be satisfaction of the other. And the court not infrequently is called upon to stay the collection of a judgment against one defendant because it has been collected from the property of another.   Inasmuch as the action can be sustained, there is no reason apparent why an order of arrest therein might not be issued.

Opinion by PARKER, P. J.   All concurred, except PUTNAM, J., not voting.

Order of Special Term reversed, with ten dollars costs and disbursements.

A. Page Smith, for the plaintiffs, appellant.

Henry A. Peckham, for the defendant, respondent.

NOTE ON REMEDY FOR FRAUD AFTER SUIT ON CONTRACT.

The case in the text apparently goes a step further than any of the prior decisions on the point there involved. Heretofore it has been held that a second action could be maintained for fraud subsequently discovered where the first action on a contract was discontinued before it went to judgment, or the second action would lie where the first one had gone to judgment and the judgment had been discharged.

It is somewhat difficult, moreover, to see how the decision in the text can be harmonized with the case of Cormier *v.* Hawkins, 69 *N. Y.* 188.   There the plaintiff sued on an undertaking given on an injunction in a former action. The suit went to judgment and the plaintiff failing to secure satisfaction of the judgment sued in tort because of the false affidavit of the surety, and secured an order of arrest in the second action.   The Court of Appeals vacated the order of arrest, and said, at page 190 : " The action is novel and unprecedented, unless the case of Wonzer *v.* De Baun, (1 *E. D. Smith,* 261) in which *Woodruff, J.,* intimates that such an action may be maintained, shall be regarded as a precedent.   Dyer *v.* Tilton, (25 *Vt.* 313), is an authority against it, and the doctrine of this case accords with the current of judicial expression.   The code provides that a party may be held to bail when he fraudulently contracted the debt for which an action is brought; and the defendant might have been held to bail in the action upon the undertaking. Instead of availing himself of this remedy, in the manner provided, the plaintiff seeks to accomplish the same result by an independent action. The question involved is very important and should not be adjudged upon a special motion. The facts should be proved at the trial, and the questions presented upon exceptions. We think there is too much doubt about the right to maintain the action to justify a preliminary order of arrest."

That case has never been distinctly overruled or criticised by later decisions, in this State at least. Some of the later cases have allowed the two remedies, but in all of them the plaintiff has either discontinued the first action, or caused the judgment to be vacated if the first action had proceeded to judgment.

In Equitable Co-operative Foundry Co. *v.* Hersee (103 *N. Y.* 25), the first action was discontinued before the second one was brought, and the court held that the plaintiff had a right to disaffirm the contract after discovering the fraud, and that the mere bringing of an action was not such an election as would bar the subsequent suit founded upon the fraud.

In Hays *v.* Midas (104 *N. Y.* 602), the plaintiff also discontinued the first action before it went to judgment.

In Rochester Distilling Co. *v.* Devendorf, (72 *Hun*, 428) the plaintiff first brought an action for goods sold and delivered in which it secured a judgment. Upon examination of the defendant in supplementary proceedings the plaintiff discovered that certain representations which had been made to it before the sale, were false, and thereupon began a second action in replevin to secure the goods sold, after giving notice of the disaffirmance of the sale, and after demanding a return of the goods. The plaintiff also discharged the first judgment and dismissed the supplementary proceedings. It was there held that under these circumstances the second action could be maintained.

In Caylus *v.* N. Y., Kingston & S. R. R. Co., (76 *N. Y.* 609) it was held that, where a judgment had been secured against a corporation for goods sold and delivered, a subsequent action could not be maintained against it because of the fraud of the directors in contracting the indebtedness. The court says that a judgment in the second action, the defendant being a corporation, would not afford any greater relief to the plaintiff than the one already recovered.

Note on Remedy for Fraud after Suit on Contract.

In Underhill *v.* Ramsey (2 *Supp.* 451) ; aff'd without opinion (125 *N. Y.* 681), it was held that the beginning of an action for goods sold and delivered was not a bar to a subsequent action for fraud in making representations as to solvency when the purchase was made, where it did not appear that the plaintiff had knowledge of the fraud when the first action was brought, and the original action was discontinued before judgment.

A party cannot, after securing judgment for goods sold and delivered maintain an action for the conversion of the same goods. Boots *v.* Ferguson, 46 *Hun,* 129.

Where the plaintiff sued as upon a contract one or more persons for the value of goods which had in fact been converted, thus waiving the conversion,—*Held*, that the same plaintiff could not subsequently maintain another action against a person who had been a party to the conversion, in an action for the tort, because of the election in the former suit to treat the transaction as one upon contract. Terry *v.* Munger, 121 *N. Y.* 161.

Where an action was begun by an attachment in another State to recover the price of goods sold on the ground that the sale was induced by reason of fraudulent representations on the part of the defendant,—*Held*, that the pendency of such action, while it could be pleaded in abatement of a subsequent action against third parties on notes given in payment for the same goods, was not an absolute bar to such second action, and the plaintiffs could show that they had not recovered anything from the first action or that they had discontinued it, in which case it would not abate the second action. Crossman *v.* Universal Rubber Co., 127 *N. Y.* 35. See same case on another appeal, 131 *N. Y.* 636.

In Conrow *v.* Little, (115 *N. Y.* 387, rev'g. 41 *Hun,* 395) the plaintiff was induced to sell paper to certain of the defendants upon forged notes with which the defendant paid for the paper. Upon discovering the forgery the plaintiff secured an attachment against the defendant who had been guilty of the fraud, and subsequently learning that the paper was in the hands of the other defendants, discontinued the first action and the attachment proceedings, and brought an action in replevin against those who had been guilty of the fraud and those who had the property ; and it was held that the first action was a bar to the replevin suit, on the ground of the election of remedies. Equitable Co-operative Foundry Co. *v.* Hersee (*supra*) and Hays *v.* Midas (*supra*) were distinguished in the last mentioned case, and the court said at page 394 on this point :

"The two remedies are inconsistent. By one the whole estate of the debtor is pursued in a summary manner, and payment of a debt sought to be enforced, by execution; by the other specific articles are demanded as the property of the plaintiff. One is to recover damages in respect of the breach of the contract, the other can be maintained only by showing that there was no contract. After choosing between these modes of proceeding the plaintiffs no longer had an option. By bringing the first action after knowledge of the fraud practised by Branscom, the plaintiffs waived the right to disaffirm the contract, and the defendants may justly hold them to their election."

The same doctrine is found in Bach *v.* Tuch, 126 *N. Y.* 53.

It seems that an action to rescind a contract for fraud would be a bar to a subsequent action for a specific performance of the same contract. Roberge *v.* Winne, 144 *N. Y.* 709.

But an unsuccessful action to rescind a sale of land for fraud, does not bar an action to foreclose a purchase money mortgage given on the sale to the plaintiff. Koke *v.* Balkew, 15 *App. Div.* 415.

WILLIAMS *v.* COLWELL.

Supreme Court; Fourth Department; Appellate Division; February, 1897.

Newspaper; what is; notice of judicial sales.] A paper issuing two
editions daily, and having a general circulation, though not
sold by newsboys or at news stands, but only by subscription
and on application at the publisher's office, and publishing
principally news of especial value to attorneys, bankers,
brokers, commission merchants and those engaged in the
real estate business, but also containing several columns devoted
to general advertising, and to the publication of local and
general news, and printed in sheet form,—*Held,* on motion to
compel a purchaser at a foreclosure sale advertised therein to
complete, to be a "newspaper" within Code Civ. Pro. § 1434,
requiring publication of notices of judicial sales in a newspaper.[*]

---

[*] In Mass *v.* Hess (41 *Ill. App.* 282), it was held that the *National Corporation Reporter,* a weekly publication, containing advertisements and reading matter mainly, but not exclusively, relating to

Williams *v.* Colwell.

Appeal from an order of the Supreme Court, Erie Special Term, directing E. C. Hazard, the purchaser at a foreclosure sale had in this action, to complete his purchase.

law and finance, of interest to corporations, was a newspaper within the Illinois statute.

In Railton *v.* Lauder (26 *Ill. App.* 655; aff'd. 126 *Ill.* 219), it was held that the *Chicago Daily Law Bulletin,* which it was shown was in general circulation throughout Illinois among judges, lawyers, real estate dealers, brokers, merchants and business men generally, and contained legal matters, court notices and various advertisements, and general news matter, was a "secular newspaper of general circulation" within the statute.

In Kerr *v.* Hitt (75 *Ill.* 51), it was held that the *Chicago Legal News,* published weekly and devoted principally to the dissemination of legal intelligence, but containing brief reference to passing events of general interest, was also a "secular newspaper of general circulation."

In Beecher *v.* Stephens (25 *Minn.* 146), it was held that the publication of a summons in the *Northwestern Reporter,* a twelve-page, weekly publication, somewhat different in size and shape from an ordinary newspaper, devoted specially to the legal profession, in which was published the general laws of the State, the decisions of the supreme court of that State and of Wisconsin and occasionally of other States, court directory, cards of attorneys, land transfers, advertisements and notices of law books and miscellaneous advertisements, was not a compliance with the statute requiring publication in a newspaper.

In Hull *v.* King (38 *Minn.* 349), it was held that the *Northwestern Presbyterian,* a religious weekly publication, was a newspaper within the meaning of the statute, and the court said: "According to the usage of the business world, and in ordinary understanding a newspaper is a publication usually in sheet form, intended for circulation and published regularly at short intervals, containing intelligence of current events and news of general interest."

In Matter of Application for Charter (11 *Phila.* 200), it was held that the publication of a notice in the *Legal Intelligencer,* a periodical, the circulation of which was mainly, if not entirely confined to the legal profession, did not comply with a statute requiring notice of application by corporations for a charter to be published "in two newspapers of general circulation."

In Lynch *v.* Durfee (24 *L. R. A.* 793), the supreme court of Michi-

Williams *v.* Colwell.

The purchaser declined to complete his purchase solely upon the ground, that the *Daily Mercantile Review,* in which the notice of sale was published was not a "newspaper" within Code Civ. Pro. § 1434, which required that notice of a sale of real estate on execution " be published at least once in each of the six weeks immediaetly preceding the sale, in a newspaper published in the county." Section 1678 of the Code requires that notice of a sale in foreclosure be published in the same manner.

In behalf of the plaintiff, the affidavit of the publisher of the *Daily Mercantile Review* and a stipulation of the parties were presented, which show that two editions of the *Review* are published daily, excepting Sundays, and that it has a circulation in the city of Buffalo of 1,000, and in the county outside the city of 500, and in other parts of the State of New York and in twenty-four other States and in the Province of Ontario, Canada, of 3,600; that it publishes the records from the county clerk's office of judgments, satisfactions of judgments, chattel mortgages, real estate mortgages, assignments and discharges of same, deeds, mechanics' liens and discharges

gan held that the *Wayne County Legal News,* a weekly publication devoted primarily to the legal profession, but also containing matters of general interest, was a newspaper.

In Kellogg *v.* Carrico (47 *Mo.* 157), a trust deed provided for a sale of land after thirty days notice in some newspaper, and it was held that such a notice published in the *Legal Record and Advertiser,* printed in St. Louis in the form of a newspaper, and issued to subscribers daily except Sunday and containing general legal intelligence and advertising, notices of judicial sales and sales on execution, and circulating particularly among real estate dealers, lawyers and others interested in real estate, complied with the terms of the deed. Benkendorf *v.* Vincenz (52 *Mo.* 441) is to the same effect.

In Knight *v.* Alexander (38 *Minn.* 384), it was held that the designation of a newspaper for the publication of a delinquent tax list, named in a resolution of the board of county commissioners as the *Enterprise* sufficiently designated the *Glencoe Enterprise,* there being no other newspaper published in the county of that name.

Williams *v.* Colwell.

of same, notices of pendency of actions, bills of sale, the
court calendars and decisions, a synopsis of the proceedings of the courts in Erie county, also a review of the
New York and Chicago stock, grain and produce markets,
of the Buffalo flour and grain markets, of the Buffalo
prices of local securities and bank stocks, railway time
cards, official time table of the departure of the mails,
the live-stock markets of Buffalo, New York, St. Louis,
Kansas City and Omaha, the Buffalo coal, hide and
leather, wool and sheep, produce and grocery markets,
and prices of the various building materials, together
with news of a general character each day, relating to
financial and mercantile matters and local affairs, and ex-
tensive reports of telegraphic news from all portions of
the United States and abroad, containing matters of
general interest to the public ; and also reports of sport-
ing news and other items of general public interest, and
that other items of general interest cover from two to
three columns of said paper, also, many advertisements
of all kinds and descriptions ; and that it has among its
subscribers two hundred and fifty lawyers and law firms,
sixteen bankers, one hundred and ninety real estate men,
and many merchants, contractors, manufacturers, builders and commission men, and that a large number of
legal notices have already been published in said papers ;
that more than four hundred and fifty have been published therein since February, 1894, the great majority thereof having been published during the past six months, and
that more than one hundred and fifteen different law firms
in Buffalo cause their legal notices, including notices of
sale of real estate under foreclosure, to be published
therein, and it appears that the *Review* has been frequently designated by the different judges of the courts
of record as a newspaper for the publication of legal
notices.   These facts are not controverted by the purchaser, but are in fact stipulated by him to be true, and
he presents no affidavit in opposition to the motion, but

merely a stipulation to the effect that the paper is not sold by the newsboys or at the news stands, but only by subscription and on application at the office of the publisher.

The *Special Term*, (LAUGHLIN, J.) *held*, that the *Review* was a newspaper within the Code, and that the publication of the notice of sale was therefore sufficient, and granted the motion. The Century Dictionary defines a newspaper as " a paper containing news ; a sheet containing intelligence or reports of passing events, issued at short but regular intervals and either sold or distributed gratis ; a public print, or daily, or weekly, or semi-weekly periodical, that presents the news of day, such as the doings of political, legislative or other public bodies, local, provincial or national current events, items of public interest on science, religion, commerce, as well as trade, market and money reports, advertisements and announcements, etc. Newspapers may be classed as general, devoted to the dissemination of intelligence on a great variety of topics which are of interest to the general reader, or special, in which some particular subject, as religion, temperance, literature, law, etc., has prominence, general news occupying only a secondary place." Other lexicographers employ other language, but of substantially the same import, in defining this word. Burrill, in his Law Dictionary, gives the following definition of newspaper: "A paper or publication conveying news or intelligence. A printed publication issued in numbers at stated intervals conveying intelligence of passing events. The term newspaper is popularly applied only to such publications as are issued in a single sheet and at short intervals, as daily or weekly." The same definition is given in Abbott's Law Dictionary, and was long ago given by the attorney-general of the United States with respect to the postal laws. 4 *Op. Atty.-Gen.* 10. In 1851 the same definition was given by the English Court of Exchequer in interpreting the Duty Laws. Attorney-General *v.* Bradbury, 7 *Ex.* (*W. H. & G.*)

Williams v. Colwell.

97. See Kellogg v. Carrico, 47 *Mo.* 157; Benkendorf v. Vincenz, 52 *Mo.* 441; Kerr v. Hitt, 75 *Ill.* 51; Hernandez v. Drake, 81 *Ill.* 34; Matter of Application for Charter, 11 *Phila.* 200; Beecher v. Stephens, 25 *Minn.* 146; Hull v. King, 38 *Minn.* 349; Railton v. Lauder, 26 *Ill. App.* 655; aff'd. 126 *Ill.* 219; Maas v. Hess, 41 *Ill. App.* 282; Lynch v. Durfee (*Mich.*), 24 *L. R. A.* 793.

While the principal news published in the *Daily Mercantile Review* is of especial value to attorneys, bankers, brokers, commission merchants and those engaged in the real estate business, yet it is shown by the affidavit and stipulation that several columns are devoted to general advertising, and to the publication of local and other news of general interest, and that it has a general circulation; it is printed in sheet form, like other news-papers, and at frequent intervals.

The *Appellate Division*, Fourth Department (HARDIN, P. J., FOLLETT, ADAMS, GREEN and WARD, JJ.) affirmed the order upon the opinion of LAUGHLIN, J., delivered at special term, all concurring.

Charles E. Forsyth, for the purchaser, appellant.

Arthur H. Williams for the plaintiff, respondent.

WYCKOFF *v.* TAYLOR.

Supreme Court, First Department, Appellate Division;
January, 1897.

1. *Contracts; time, when of the essence; building contract.*] Time
is to be deemed of the essence of a contract to complete a
building on or before a specified date, since from its nature delay means loss of rents, and an unexcused delay (in this case, of
three weeks) justifies a termination of the contract.*

2. *The same; waiver of delay.*] Mere neglect to terminate the
contract at once when the contractor runs over his time is not
a waiver of the delay, but the continued failure on the contractor's part to complete the work is a continuous breach of which
the owner may avail himself at any time.

3. *Evidence; value; action on quantum meruit; special contract.*]
In an action upon *quantum meruit* to recover for work done in
part performance of a special contract, the contract price is no
evidence of value, and if no proof of value is given, the complaint should be dismissed.

Appeal by the defendant from a judgment of the
New York Court of Common Pleas in favor of the plaintiff, entered upon the report of a referee.

The original plaintiff, Emily F. Wyckoff, brought
this action as assignee of John J. Kierst and William F.
Morgan, to recover for work done and material furnished
to the defendant upon land owned by her in the city of
New York. The complaint alleges, for the first cause of
action, that Kierst made a contract with the defendant
on January 20, 1885, to furnish certain labor and material,
and "that said Kierst furnished the materials and performed the work provided in said contract, so far as he
was allowed to do so by defendant, and on or about
April 20, 1885, said defendant prevented said Kierst

---

* See Note on When Time is of the Essence of a Contract, at
the end of this case.

Wyckoff *v.* Taylor.

from completing said work under said contract, leaving due and unpaid the sum of $1,900, which sum is still due and unpaid." The contract was a written one, and is in evidence. By it Kierst agrees with the defendant that he " shall and will, for the consideration hereinafter mentioned, on or about March 20, 1885, well and sufficiently erect and finish " a certain building—an extension to another building owned by the defendant—in accordance with certain plans and specifications, and to the satisfaction of the architect ; also, that he will do certain work upon the old building. The contract price is $4,900, to be paid in four installments, as the work progressed, upon the architect's certificate, approved by the building department. At the trial the plaintiff, after introducing the contract in evidence, put the assignor Kierst upon the stand. He testified to an additional agreement to do certain extra work for $300 ; that the defendant expelled him and his men from the premises ; but that, at the time of such expulsion, he had substantially completed all the work. On this evidence, coupled with proof as to ownership of the cause of action, the plaintiff rested. The defendant moved to dismiss the complaint on account of failure to plead and prove that the necessary certificate had been given by the architect. The motion was denied and the defendant excepted. She then gave evidence as to the amount and value of the work which Kierst had left undone, and which she was obliged to supply. The plaintiff gave rebutting evidence on these heads. The case was then closed, the defendant renewed her motion to dismiss it which was again denied, and an exception taken. The referee awarded the plaintiff the full contract price of $5,200. less such sums as had been paid, and such as he found that the defendant had been compelled to expend in order to complete the work.

Held, that the complaint should have been dismissed. There can be no doubt from the complaint that the action was to recover upon a *quantum meruit* for the reasonable value of the work and material furnished by Kierst, not for damages for breach of contract. But the proof did not conform to the pleading and admission. No detailed evidence was given of the work and material, and its value. Kierst simply testified, generally, to fulfillment of the contract on his part. The plaintiff thus made out a *prima facie* case for a recovery of the full contract price, less the sums paid thereon. He made out no other cause of action, nor did he attempt to do so. The defendant had a perfect right to hold him to the position thus deliberately taken, and the complaint should have been dismissed, unless facts were shown dispensing with the necessity for the architect's certificate. It was not necessary to base the motion to dismiss upon the specific ground that the evidence was insufficient for a recovery upon a *quantum meruit*. It appeared, beyond dispute, that the proof had been confined to what was requisite for a recovery upon a different ground, namely, substantial fulfillment of the contract. The most that could be required of the defendant's counsel was that he should point out the change in the theory of the action, and state that his motion was made in view of it. This he clearly did. No architect's certificate was shown, nor was evidence given that such a certificate was requested and unreasonably refused. This was the condition of the case when the plaintiff rested—as he did—upon Kierst's testimony that the contract had been substantially fulfilled. But this *prima facie* case of fulfillment fell as the trial proceeded; and when the testimony was all in, it appeared beyond a doubt, that the contract had never been fulfilled. Indeed, the trial, after the plaintiff rested, proceeded mainly upon a dispute as to the cost of work which was confessedly unfinished at the time Kierst was stopped; and it was indisputably proved that items of work of prime importance, costing hundreds of dollars to supply, were unfinished when he left. Under this state of the proof, the motion to dismiss was renewed and again denied. This is not, therefore, the common case of a contractor proving full performance to show that the architect's refusal was unreasonable.

The plaintiff's whole claim is based upon an erroneous view of his position at the time he was stopped. Kierst agreed to complete the work "on or about March 20, 1885." He testifies that he was expelled the latter part of April or beginning of May; the defendant, that it was on April fourteenth. In either case it was over three weeks after the work should have been turned over complete to the defendant. No excuse for this delay, having any substance, is given. The defendant was not to blame in any way, and the plaintiff, with great philosophy, treats it as one of the necessary evils which an owner is compelled to put up with when he enters into a building contract. It is impossible, however, for the law to overlook this breach with the same easy good nature. If the provision of the contract as to time is to be overlooked, it must be because the case falls within that narrow class where courts have always held time not to be of the essence of the contract. The defendant testified, without contradiction, that she saw the delay would result in her not being able to rent the building when the season came. But it required no such testimony to show that time was, here, of the essence of the contract. It was manifest from its very nature that delay meant loss of rents.

Nor did the defendant waive her right thus to terminate the contract. It appears that she did not expel Kierst at once when he ran over his time. But this cannot be construed into a consent that he might go on, in any event, until he should get the work done. An owner may be willing to wait for a brief period without being willing to wait indefinitely. The continued failure on the contractor's part to complete the work is a continuous breach of the contract, of which the owner may avail himself at any time. To hold otherwise would put the owner completely at the mercy of a dilatory contractor.

If the plaintiff seeks to recover upon a *quantum meruit*, he must prove what it was he did which was not paid for under the contract, and its value. He cannot throw upon the defendant the burden of showing what he omitted. Nor can he escape this result by contending that the full contract price shall represent the reasonable value of the contract work. It is no evidence whatever of such value. Gumb *v.* Twenty-third St. Ry. Co., 114 *N. Y.* 411; Kennedy *v.* McKone, 10 *App. Div.* 88; S. C., 41 *Supp.* 782.

Opinion by BARRETT, J. RUMSEY, WILLIAMS, O'BRIEN and INGRAHAM, JJ., concurring.

Judgment reversed and order of reference vacated, and new trial ordered, with costs to defendant to abide event.

Benjamin Scharps, for the defendant, appellant.

B. C. Chetwood, for the plaintiff, respondent.

NOTE ON WHEN TIME IS OF THE ESSENCE OF A CONTRACT.

Express stipulation.] Time may be of the essence of a contract if made so by express stipulation of the parties, or from the nature of the agreement. If the parties expressly declare that time shall be of the essence of the contract, they are bound thereby, and the courts will give full effect to the stipulation. Wells *v.* Smith, 2 *Edw. Ch.* 78; aff'd 7 *Paige,* 22; Price *v.* McGown, 10 *N. Y.* 465; Crippen *v.* Heermance, 9 *Paige Ch.* 211; Benedict *v.* Lynch, 1 *Johns. Ch.* 370; Hatch *v.* Cobb, 4 *Johns. Ch.* 559; More *v.* Smedburgh, 8 *Paige Ch.* 600.

The cases just cited seem to indicate that words, in effect, declaring that the time of performance stipulated in the agreement shall be considered of the essence of the contract will be sufficient; and other words have also been held to make time of the essence. Thus, where a contract for the conveyance of land provided that the purchaser should pay the purchase price at a certain date, and that, if the money was not then paid, the contract should be null and void, it was held that the time of payment was of the essence of the contract, and strict fulfillment, unless duly waived or the time was extended, was requisite to give a right to compel specific performance. Fullerton *v.* Mc-Laughlin, 70 *Hun*, 568. But see Edgerton *v.* Peckham, 11 *Paige Ch.* 352 ; cited *infra*.

In Mitchell *v.* Wilson (4 *Edw. Ch.* 695), a landlord agreed to lease certain premises to a tenant then in possession, for a further term on condition that the tenant should give J. C. as surety, and the lease to be executed on February 1, the term to begin on May 1, following. On the day fixed the tenant failed to secure J. C. as surety, but offered another surety whom the landlord refused to accept, and a few days later offered J. C. as such surety. *Held*, that time was of the essence of the contract, and the landlord's refusal to execute the lease was upheld.

Where installments due to a contractor for the construction of a railroad were not paid at the time provided for in the contract,—*Held*, that this did not constitute a breach of the entire contract which would allow the contractor to refuse further performance and recover for prospective profits if the contract had been completed, but he could rescind the contract for such failure and recover for work already performed. Wharton *v.* Winch, 140 *N. Y.* 287 ; Moore *v.* Taylor, 42 *Hun*, 45.

Nature of contract]. Most of the cases, where the question whether or not time was of the essence of the contract depended on the nature of the agreement, have turned upon the further question whether or not the party not in default has been injured by the delay in performance by the other party. Thus the case in the text held that in a building contract it was obvious that a delay meant a loss in rents, and hence the time stipulated for the completion of the building was necessarily of the essence of the contract.

In Yeamans *v.* Tannehill, (15 *Supp.* 958 ; s. c., 40 *St. R.* 548) the defendant agreed to write a play for the plaintiffs and have it completed by September 15th, at which time the plaintiffs agreed to produce it. The play was not finished until September 30th, when the plaintiff refused to accept it and sued to recover the sum of $450 paid in advance, and a judgment for the plaintiff was affirmed. While the decision in this case is not specifically put on the ground that time was of the essence of the contract, it, in effect, so holds.

In Gale *v.* Archer, (42 *Barb.* 320), the contract provided for the sale of the vendor's place of residence, together with horse, cattle, etc., and growing crops, and by the terms of the contract he was to give possession in the middle of the growing season. It was held that from the nature of the contract time was of its essence, and the vendor must give possession on the precise day named.

In Higgins *v.* Delaware, Lackawanna & W. R. R. Co., (60 *N. Y.* 553), the defendant sold a quantity of coal at auction, deliveries to be made at its wharves and yards in October. The plaintiff did not demand the coal until February following, when the defendant refused to deliver it, and in an action by the plaintiff for damages for this refusal the court held that time was necessarily of the essence of the contract under the circumstances there appearing. These circumstances were that the defendant would be compelled to keep a large amount of coal for a long time on its docks and in its yards at the point of delivery, at great expense and inconvenience, in order to comply with the demand of the plaintiff at any time between October and February; and the plaintiff having failed to keep his agreement to accept deliveries in October the defendant was relieved from further obligation. It should be observed that in this case the court held that there had not been a complete sale of the coal, and the court intimates that if there had been, the plaintiff could have recovered.

In Riendeau *v.* Bullock, (20 *Supp.* 976), the defendant agreed to buy the ice in the plaintiff's ice-house at a certain price, deliveries to be made in August. The defendant did not take all the ice in that month and the plaintiff thereupon raised the price, which the defendant refused to pay or to take any more ice, and it was held that the plaintiff could not recover, although if he had rested on his rights when the defendant failed to take the ice as agreed, he then could have recovered such damages as he actually suffered.

Building contracts]. While, as held in the case in the text, time is *prima facie* of the essence of a building contract, various circumstances have been held to excuse the contractor's failure to perform at the stipulated time. Thus, a failure to complete a building within the time specified in the contract will not prevent a recovery of the contract price where such delay was caused by the owner. Murphy *v.* Stickley Simonds Co., 82 *Hun*, 158; s. c., 31 *Supp.* 295; 63 *St. R.* 744.

But the contractor must use due diligence to complete

the contract after the delay, and in the event of his failure to do so the owner can recover damages for the delay after a reasonable time for the completion of the building. Schlachter v. Hopkins, 84 *Hun*, 402.

After the parties to a building contract have waived the performance of it within the time stipulated, and have gone on with the work, the time fixed ceases to be an element in the contract, and each party then has a reasonable time in which to perform. Therefore, a builder who abandons his contract, without having first demanded performance by the owner and giving him a reasonable opportunity to perform on his part, cannot recover on a *quantum meruit* for the work done. Lawson v. Hogan, 93 *N. Y.* 39.

Where a building contract provided for liquidated damages at the rate of $250 a day beyond a date named for the completion of the building, and there had been a delay of about a month in the completion of the building, but the plaintiff (the contractor) proved that a part, at least, of the delay was caused by the acts and omissions of the owner and his agents,—*Held*, that the contract was entire, so far as the indemnity for delay was concerned, and the owner could not recover a proportionate share of the liquidated damages for the delay not caused by him, when part of it was caused by his acts and those of his agents. Willis v. Webster, 1 *App. Div.* 301 ; s. c., 37 *Supp.* 354 ; 72 *St. R.* 743.

The measure of damages for delay in furnishing plumbing material, thereby causing delay in the completion of a building, is the fair and reasonable rental value of the building during the time of the delay less the cost of maintaining the property for the same time. Reich v. Colwell Lead Co., 21 *Supp.* 495. The same rule of damages was applied in Scribner v. Jacobs, (9 *Supp.* 856), where the contract did not provide for the time of completion of the building, and the court held that the damages could be recovered for any delay beyond a reasonable time within which the building should have been completed.

Although material to be furnished to a contractor is of special design and character, unnecessary delay in supplying it will make the one in default liable for the damages suffered by the contractor, although he was ignorant of the time which the contractor had to perform his contract. Murdock v. Jones, 3 *App. Div.* 221.

Equity; vendor and purchaser.] The cases generally apply the rule that time is not, except under special circumstances, of the essence of a contract for the purchase of real estate, although this principle is frequently qualified, as said by Chief Justice MARSHALL, in Brashier v. Gratz) 6 *Wheat*. 533): "The rule that time is not of the essence of a contract has certainly been recognized in courts of equity; and there can be no doubt that a failure on the part of the purchaser or vendor to perform his contract on the stipulated day, does not of itself deprive him of his right to demand a specific performance at a subsequent day, when he shall be able to comply with his part of the engagement. It may be in the power of the court to direct compensation for the breach of contract in point of time, and in such case the object of the parties is effected by carrying it into execution. But the rule is not universal. Circumstances may be so changed, that the object of the parties can be no longer accomplished; that he who is injured by the failure of the other contracting party cannot be placed in the situation in which he would have stood had the contract been performed. Under such circumstances, it would be iniquitous to decree a specific performance, and a court of equity will leave the parties to their remedy at law."

The same doctrine has been announced by courts of this State. Thus it is said: "Although time may not necessarily be of the essence of a contract for the sale of real estate, it is treated in this State as material in such sense that unreasonable or inexcusable delay of the parties to it may deny to him relief; and when during his default or delay circumstances have intervened which will render subsequent performance by the other party prejudicial or detrimental to him, those facts are properly matters of consideration and will ordinarily relieve him from the obligation of the contract." Schmidt v. Reed, 132 *N. Y.* 108, at page 116.

See also Day v. Hunt, 112 *N. Y.* 191.

In general time is not of the essence of a contract in a court of equity. If one party be not bound, there is no estoppel against the other; an estoppel must be reciprocal. Clute v. Jones, 28 *N. Y.* 280.

Where, in a contract for the purchase of real estate time is not specifically made the essence of the contract the court may decree specific performance at a later day, and even a tender of a deed after suit brought for an alleged breach may be sufficient on which to found a suit for specific performance. Brush v. Vandenberg, 1 *Edw. Ch.* 21.

In Willis v. Dawson (34 *Hun*, 492), on the date stipulated in a contract for the purchase of real estate the plaintiff appeared and asked for a postponement on the ground that he had been unable to procure an abstract of the title to the property, which he had agreed to purchase, and asked for more time in which to secure it.   The defendant refused to grant more time and rescinded the contract.   Three weeks later the plaintiff, having secured an abstract, and satisfied himself as to the title, tendered the agreed amount and demanded a deed, and it was held that he was entitled to a decree of specific performance.

Even where a contract for the purchase of real estate provides that if not completed on a day certain it shall be void, courts of equity have interfered in behalf of the party in default, where the circumstances are such that great injustice might be done.   Thus, where the owner of land made a written agreement to sell the same for one third cash down and the residue in one and two years, with interest thereon, possession to be delivered immediately to the vendee ; and a provision was made in the contract that upon default to make either payment, the vendor should be discharged from the contract and the vendee should forfeit all prior payments, and should deliver up peaceable possession of the premises, and the vendee took possession of the premises and made valuable improvements thereon and paid the first two installments and then assigned the contract, and the assignee made other improvements, but did not tender the final payment until a few days after it was due under the terms of the agreement, and in the meantime the vendor had not tendered a deed or demanded the balance of the purchase price,—*Held*, that time was not of the essence of the contract to the extent of defeating an action by the assignee of the vendee for a specific performance. Edgerton *v.* Peckham, 11 *Paige Ch.* 352.

Where two men agreed to exchange farms and were to pay at the rate of $57.50 an acre for the land which one received in excess of that which he gave, and it was mutually agreed that any error as to the number of acres contained in either should be corrected by a proper payment under the agreement if such error was corrected prior to April 1, following the trade, and one of the parties after said date caused the farms to be surveyed, and discovering an error called upon the other party to make compensation therefor, which was refused,—*Held*, that time was not of the essence of the contract, and the plaintiff could recover.   Dumond *v.* Sharts, 2 *Paige*, 182.

Unreasonable delay.]   While as a general rule time is not of the essence of a contract to purchase real estate where the other party is not prejudiced by the delay (Davison *v.* Associates of the Jersey Co. 71 *N. Y.* 333 ; Waters *v.* Travis, 9 *Johns.* 457 ; Benedict *v.* Lynch, 1 *Johns Ch.* 370 ; Cythe *v.*

Note on When Time is of the Essence of a Contract.

La Fontain, 51 *Barb.* 192 ; Seaman *v.* Van Rensselaer, 10 *Barb.* 86 ; Harris *v.* Troup, 8 *Paige,* 423 ; Voorhees *v.* De Meyer, 2 *Barb.* 37 ; Miller *v.* Bear, 3 *Paige,* 466 ; Story's Eq. §§ 775, 776 ; Hubbel *v.* Von Schoening. 49 *N. Y.* 331 ; More *v.* Smedburg, 8 *Paige,* 600 ; Renwick *v.* Renwick, 1 *Bradf.* 237 ; Pinckney *v.* Hagadorn, 1 *Duer,* 98 ; Myers *v.* De Mier, 4 *Daly,* 350 ; Duffy *v.* O'Donovan, 46 *N. Y.* 223), it may be so. As said in Merchants Bank *v.* Thomson, 55 *N. Y.* 7, at page 12 : " Doubtless the later tendency of courts of equitable jurisdiction is to hold that time is material, and is in many cases of the essence of the contract. Inexcusable laches and delay will debar a party from the relief which, they being absent, he might have by a judgment for specific performance. . . . It is not yet the rule, however, that the time fixed in a contract for the performance of it is necessarily of its essence. The mere efflux of time will not of itself always lead to a denial of relief. When the lapse of time is occasioned, or accompanied, by a refusal or failure to claim or act under the contract, and is so great or of such characteristics as to amount to a waiver or abandonment of the contract, the party who comes not into court until after such delay, will have forfeited all claim to equity."

See, also, to the same effect, Page *v.* McDonnell, 55 *N. Y.* 299 ; Roberts *v.* White, 5 *Super Ct.* (*J. & S.*) 168 ; Boyd *v.* Schlesinger, 59 *N. Y.* 301 ; Babcock *v.* Emerick. 64 *How. Pr.* 435 ; McClaskey *v.* Mayor, etc. of Albany, 64 *Barb.* 310 ; Tompkins *v.* Hyatt, 28 *N. Y.* 347 ; Williston *v.* Williston, 41 *Barb.* 635; Beebe *v.* Dowd. 22 *Barb.* 255; Richmond *v.* Foote, 3 *Lans.* 244 ; Waters *v.* Travis, 9 *Johns.* 450 ; Edgerton *v.* Peckham, 11 *Paige,* 352 ; Myers *v.* De Mier, 52 *N. Y.* 647; Benson *v.* Tilton, 41 *Id.* 619 ; aff'g 24 *How. Pr.* 494 ; Delevan *v.* Duncan, 4 *Hun,* 29 ; Buess *v.* Koch, 10 *Id.* 299 ; Von Compton *v.* Knight, 65 *N. Y.* 580 ; McCotter *v.* Lawrence, 4 *Hun,* 107 ; Walton *v.* Meeks, 41 *Id.* 311 ; Day *v.* Hunt, 112 *N. Y.* 191 ; Andrews *v.* Davis, 5 *St. R.* 859; Dieter *v.* Fallon, 34 *Id.* 680 ; McSorley *v.* Hughes, 58 *Hun,* 360 ; Jencks *v.* Kearney, 42 *St. R.* 826 ; s. c., 17 *Supp.* 143, aff'd without opinion, 138 *N. Y.* 634.

Waiver.] In Thorne *v.* French, (4 *Misc.* 436 ; aff'd without opinion, 143 *N. Y.* 679) it is said at page 440 : "A defendant is not bound to take advantage of a delay or forfeiture, and there may be a waiver, if there be conduct indicating an intention to waive a condition as to time, although there are no new considerations, and although there may be no technical estoppel." Citing Prentiss *v.* Knickerbocker Life Ins. Co., 77 *N. Y.* 483 (where it was

Note on When Time is of the Essence of a Contract.

held that no new consideration was necessary to support a waiver by an insurance company of a condition in a policy in respect to the time of serving proof of loss, and that such waiver might be established by acts indicating an intention to waive such condition) ; Goodwin *v.* Massachusetts Mut. L. Ins. Co., 73 *N. Y.* 480, (where it was held that such waiver could be effected by the plaintiff's being induced to refrain from making proof of death in time by misleading statements of the defendant's agent) ; Titus *v.* Glens Falls Ins. Co., 81 *N. Y.* 410 ; Sinclair *v.* Tallmadge, 35 *Barb.* 602.

It is further said in Thorne *v.* French (*supra*) : " Where time is waived a party is not put in default until he has demanded performance and thus restored time as an element of the contract." Citing Lawson *v.* Hogan, 93 *N. Y.* 39 ; Wallman *v.* Society of Concord, 45 *N. Y.* 485 ; Leaird *v.* Fisk, 44 *N. Y.* 618 ; Owen *v.* Evans, 31 *N. E. Rep.* 999 ; Dillon *v.* Masterson, 42 *Super. Ct.* (*J. & S.*) 176.

Where the president of an insurance company indorsed upon a card, giving notice to the insured that a premium was due, an extension of the time of payment until the following October 10, and the insured died on September 19, — *Held*, that the indorsement on the notice constituted a valid waiver of the condition of the policy that it should be void if the premium should not be paid when due. Homer *v.* Guardian Mut. Life Ins. Co., 67 *N. Y.* 478.

Where a contract provides that certain work is to be done within a specified time, and the completion of such work depends upon something being done by the other party, and this is not done, the former is excused from performing within the time specified. Case *v.* Phœnix Bridge Co., 134 *N. Y.* 78 ; Grannis & Hurd L. Co., *v.* Deeves, 72 *Hun*, 171 ; s. c., 55 *St. R.* 674 ; 25 *Supp.* 375 ; Smith *v.* Smith, 7 *Misc.* 37.

A party permitting the completion of a contract after the time for performance has expired, does not, thereby, forfeit his right to damages for a breach of the contract as to the time in which it was to be completed. Ruff *v.* Rinaldo, 55 *N. Y.* 664. (Action to foreclose a mechanic's lien.) Nor to damages caused by changes in the contract by proceeding with and completion of the work according to changes in the plans. Mc. Master *v.* State of *N. Y.*, 108 *N. Y.* 542.

WALTON *v.* STAFFORD.

Supreme Court; First Department; Appellate Division; February, 1897.

1. *Assignment for creditors; assignee's liability; rent.*] Where the monthly rent under a lease for a term of years is payable in advance on the first day of the month, and the lessee makes a general assignment for benefit of creditors on the second day of a given month, the rent for that month is a debt of the assignor and provable against the assigned estate; it is not a claim against the assignee as such, although he remains in occupation the rest of the month.*

2. *Evidence; judicial notice; Sunday; appeal.*] The fact that the first day of a given month fell on Sunday, if not brought to the attention of the trial court, will not be judicially noticed on appeal in order to reverse the judgment directed by the court below, upon a stipulation of the parties as to the facts, including an admission that the rent under a certain lease became due on the first day of the month in question.†

---

* Where a lease contains a clause by which the lessor, if the premises become vacant, may relet for the lessee's account and charge him with any deficiency, and the lessor exercises his option to so relet, the contingent claim for such a deficiency, which cannot be ascertained until the expiration of the lease and may not arise at all, is not provable as a debt or liability of the lessee against his estate under an assignment for benefit of creditors, made prior to the reletting, directing the payment of the assignor's debts and liabilities then due or to grow due. Matter of Hevenor, 1 *N. Y. Ann. Cas.* 144; aff'g 70 *Hun,* 56. And see cases cited in notes to this case, 1 *N. Y. Ann. Cas.* 146.

Under an assignment for the benefit of creditors, which does not provide for the payment or indemnification of persons who subsequently incur liabilities or make advances for the assignor, a claim by a surety for the assignor upon a lease, for money paid by him, subsequent to the assignment, for rent due upon the lease, and as a bonus for its cancellation, cannot be allowed. Matter of Risley, 10 *Daly,* 44.

† In Hunter *v.* N. Y. Ontario & W. R. R.Co. (116 *N. Y.* 615), it

Walton *v.* Stafford.

Motion by the defendants for judgment upon an order of the New York Trial Term of the Supreme Court, directing a verdict for the defendants for $3,013.86, subject to the opinion of the Appellate Division.

was held, in effect, that where facts are proved at the trial from which the court should have taken judicial notice of other facts and failed to do so, the appellate court would notice such facts even though, as in that case, they furnished ground for the reversal of the judgment ; and the court said, at page 621 : "Courts are not bound to take judicial notice of matters of fact. Whether they will do so or not depends on the nature of the subject, the issue involved and the apparent justice of the case. The rule that permits a court to do so is of practical value in the law of appeal, where the evidence is clearly insufficient to support the judgment. In such cases judicial notice may be taken of facts which are a part of the general knowledge of the country, and which are generally known and had been duly authenticated in repositories of facts open to all and especially so of facts of official, scientific or historical character."

In that case the plaintiff was injured, while attending to his duties as brakeman on the defendant's railroad, by his head coming in contact with the top of a tunnel. The question was whether or not from the evidence given on the trial as to the height of the tunnel and the cars, and the distance between the top of the car and the tunnel it was possible for a man of ordinary stature to have been injured in the manner described by the plaintiff, and the Court of Appeals said it would take notice of the fact that such an accident under the facts proved at the trial was impossible.

The case of McKinnon *v.* Bliss (21 *N. Y.* 206), was decided on somewhat similar principles involved here as to the question of evidence, that some proof must be presented to the court even to have it take judicial notice of a fact. It was there held that while the court will take judicial notice of matters of public history, where no proof is given of a historical fact to the jury, the court will not take judicial notice of such fact on appeal.

In Wood *v.* North Western Ins. Co., (46 *N. Y.* 421), which was an action on an insurance policy, the Court of Appeals was asked to take judicial notice of the alleged fact that kerosene oil was "inflammable" so as to avoid a condition of the policy prohibiting the keeping on the premises liquids of that nature. The court refused to do so, putting its refusal on the ground mainly that no motion had been made for such a finding before the referee.

Action by Charles L. Walton, as assignee for benefit of creditors of Francis T. Walton, against Robert Stafford and others for $811.16, the price of goods sold by the plaintiff as assignee to the defendants on January 27, 1894, no part of which sum has been paid.

On February 28, 1893, the defendants leased to plaintiff's assignor, Francis T. Walton, the premises known as the Grand Hotel in the city of New York, for a term of four years and six months, at an annual rental of $51,000, payable monthly in advance on the first day of each month during the term. One installment of rent under this lease became due on January 1, 1894. That installment was not paid. On January 2, 1894, Walton made a general assignment for the benefit of creditors to the plaintiff. Immediately upon the execution of this assignment the plaintiff, professing to act under authority thereof, entered into possession of the demised premises, and continued to operate the same as a hotel until about January 29, 1894, at which time a warrant in dispossess proceedings was issued, and the plaintiff thereupon surrendered possession of the premises to the defendants. During the month of January, while operating this hotel, plaintiff collected rent from sub-tenants, hired the employees, and carried on a general hotel business, but paid no rent therefor. The defendants seek to counterclaim the rent for January, 1894, and claim judgment therefor, after crediting the price of the goods. These facts being admitted, the trial judge directed a verdict in favor of the defendants for the amount of their counterclaim (less $811 and interest), subject to the opinion of this court.

Held, that the counterclaim should not be allowed. The plaintiff, being an assignee for the benefit of creditors, had an election to accept or decline the lease. He had a reasonable time to ascertain whether this lease could be made available for the benefit of the creditors whom he represented. If, thereupon, he found that the term, burdened with the payment of rent and the performance of other conditions, was an interest of no value ; that instead of being a benefit it would probably diminish the amount to which the creditors would otherwise be entitled, his duty was to decline the lease. If, however, his investigation led him to believe that the lease was a valuable asset, he could, as, in fact, he did, accept it. Journeay *v.* Brackley, 1 *Hilt.* 447. Upon its acceptance it became a part of the assigned estate, held by the assignee in his trust capacity subject to the covenants contained therein. While it was so held the assignee, in his representative capacity, was chargeable with all the conditions attached thereto. It was not his contract, either personal or as representative, and his liability upon the covenants was, consequently, not contractual. The liability was the liability of his assignor's estate, legally resulting from its acquisition of the lease as an asset. It was, therefore, the plaintiff's liability *as assignee.*

In the present case the assignee accepted the lease and utilized the demised premises for the benefit of his *cestuis que trust.* Privity of estate was thus established, and, as a sequence, the plaintiff's liability as assignee for the rent falling due during the period of his occupation. This was a liability which ceases upon his eviction by the lessor, or upon his assignment of the lease to a third person, with surrender of possession. His liability while in possession, however, was not for use and occupation (Kiersted *v.* Orange & A. R. R., 69 *N. Y.* 343), or upon a *quantum meruit* (as erroneously held in Foster *v.* Oldham, 4 *Misc. Rep.* 201 ; S. C., 53 *St. R.* 488 ; 23 *Supp.* 1024 ; and Smith *v.* Wagner, 9 *Misc. R.* 122 ; S. C., 59 *St. R.* 710 ; 29 *Supp.* 284 ; aff'g 7 *Misc. R.* 739) but upon the covenants of the lease. Stewart *v.* Long Island R. R. Co., 102 *N. Y.* 601. This liability results not from privity of contract—for there is no such privity—but solely from privity of estate. The lessee's estate is burdened with the covenants running with the land, and the assignee takes the term for this trust estate subject to the burden. It follows that the plaintiff is liable only upon such covenants as matured during the period of his possession. Upon the agreed state of facts it appears that one of the covenants was to pay the January rent upon the first day of the month. The lease was not assigned until the next day. Consequently the assignee, as such, was chargeable with no primary liability for the January rent, upon his assumption of the lease. That rent was a debt of the assignor, existing at the time of the execution of the assignment, and provable as such against the assigned estate.

It is, however, suggested that the first day of January fell on Sunday, and that, therefore, the obligation accrued on the next day (Monday, January second), which was the day when the assignment was executed and delivered. Nothing of the kind appears in the record, and the suggestion is made for the first time upon this appeal. The stipulation is explicit that the assignor was obligated to pay the rent for the month of January on the first day of that month. ' It was upon this agreed fact, and upon that alone, that the learned trial judge made his ruling. We are asked to supplement this fact with another fact which had never been agreed upon, and to do so by taking judicial notice of the coincidence of the first day of the week with this day of the month. We do not think this would be proper upon the present appeal. The matter was not called to the attention of the court upon the trial, nor was the court there asked to take judicial notice of the fact now suggested, or to consider any fact in addition to those agreed upon. That the first day of January fell upon Sunday was a fact like any other fact. It is true that it was not a fact which the defendants were bound to prove in the ordinary way, but it was none the less a fact which they were required—if they desired its consideration—to place in some way before the court and jury. They were, at least, bound to bring the fact to the attention of the court, and to claim for it judicial notice. As they did not do this, the fact

Walton *v.* Stafford.

is not in the case, and it cannot be got into the case without giving the stipulation an effect not contemplated by the parties when they entered into it. It is our duty to give the appropriate judgment solely upon those facts which the defendants chose to present below, and which alone appear in the record. We can neither add independent facts, nor additional facts tending to vary the ordinary effect of those specified in the stipulation; Scheffler *v.* Minneapolis & St. Louis Ry. Co., 32 *Minn.* 521 ; Hunter *v.* N. Y. Ontario & W. R. R. Co., 116 *N. Y.* 621 ; S. C., 27 *St. R.* 729.

How the trial judge here would have acted had the coincidence in question been brought to his notice, we cannot know. There was, as we have seen, no reference thereto before him. Nor was there any offer of an almanac or other chronicle, either upon the trial or upon even this appeal. The effort now is to induce us to ignore these conditions, and upon this appeal to supplement carefully formulated facts which were reduced to writing, and upon which the decision under review was made, with another fact to which the parties have never agreed and to which they might never have agreed. We think it would be unjust to inject this other fact into the stipulation of the parties without their consent, or to decide the controversy upon anything save the precise facts upon which they have specifically agreed.

Opinion by BARRETT, J. VAN BRUNT, P. J., RUMSEY and PATTERSON, JJ., concurred ; WILLIAMS, J., concurred in result.

Judgment directed for plaintiffs for the sum of $811.16, with interest from January 27, 1894, and counterclaim dismissed with costs.

Esek Cowen, for the plaintiff.

James M. Gifford, for the defendants.

BRYER *v.* FOERSTER.

*Supreme Court, First Department, Appellate Division;
February,* 1897.

Creditor's suit'; judgment ; receiver's appointment, when unnecessary.]
In a suit by a judgment creditor solely in his own behalf to
set aside as fraudulent conveyances of real estate only, the judgment should not ordinarily provide for the appointment of a
receiver to sell, but should direct that the conveyances be set
aside so far as they are an obstruction to the plaintiff's judgment and that he shall be permitted to sell the property upon
the execution in the usual way.*

---

* Where an action is brought by a judgment creditor, on behalf
of all other judgment creditors, as well as himself, to set aside as
fraudulent conveyances of the debtor's real estate, a judgment is
not improper adjudging the appointment of a receiver to take a
conveyance of and to sell the real estate.   Shand *v.* Hanley, 71 *N.
Y.* 319.

In Cole *v.* Tyler (65 *N. Y.* 73), it is said, at page 77 :   " It is
objected by the appellants that the judgment in this case was
erroneous in directing a sale by a receiver ; and that the proper
course, if the conveyances were to be set aside, was to have the
plaintiff sell on execution against Crawford, on his original judgment.   This objection cannot be sustained.   The court has power
to order a transfer to a receiver in such cases."

In Union National Bank *v.* Warner, (12 *Hun*, 306), it is said at
p. 309 : " The more usual judgment to be entered in such case (real
estate) is to declare the conveyance fraudulent and void as against
the creditor and his judgment, with the necessary and appropriate
formalities in that regard, leaving the latter to enforce his judgment in the usual way by execution.   But the court may also, in
the exercise of its common law powers, appoint a receiver and
direct and enforce a conveyance to him by the party or parties having the apparent or legal title, and vest him with the power of sale
and with the application of the proceeds."

In Chautauqua County Bank *v.* Risley (19 *N. Y.* 369), it was
held that the court had power in a creditor's suit to require the
debtor to convey his real estate to a receiver appointed therein, but

Bryer *v.* Foerster.

Appeal by the defendants, from a judgment of the Supreme Court in favor of the plaintiff, entered upon the decision of the court rendered after a trial at the New York Special Term.

Action by Peter Bryer against Catherine Foerster, and others, to set aside, as in fraud of creditors, certain conveyances of real estate made by Joseph Foerster, deceased. The judgment in favor of the plaintiff setting aside the conveyances also appointed a receiver of the property.

Held, that the judgment should be modified by striking out the appointment of the receiver. In our opinion, in cases of this kind, where an action is brought by a judgment creditor to reach real estate fraudulently conveyed, the proper judgment to enter is to direct that the fraudulent conveyances shall be set aside, so far as they are an obstruction to the plaintiff's judgment, and that he shall be permitted to issue execution, and sell the property upon the execution, in the usual way. It is quite true that the courts have held that the appointment of a receiver to sell the property fraudulently conveyed, and pay the judgment out of the proceeds, is not improper, but this conclusion was reached after considerable vacillation, and in spite of the serious inconveniences which necessarily resulted from the taking of that course. When a judgment is brought to reach personal property or equit-

---

it was pointed out in that case, that if this was done the real property when conveyed to the receiver was subject to all liens which had accrued prior to the filing of a notice of *lis pendens* of the creditor's suit, and the lien of the judgment on which the creditor's suit was founded was lost in favor of junior judgments when this method of procedure was adopted, if such junior judgments were entered in the county where the real estate was situated prior to the beginning of the creditor's suit.

Where, however, such junior lienor is made a party to a creditor's suit, and the question of the validity of his lien is decided adversely to such lienor, a sale by the receiver gives a title paramount to that of the lienor. Shand *v.* Hanley, 71 *N. Y.* 319.

able assets which have been disposed of with intent to defraud creditors, the appointment of a receiver is not only proper but necessary, because it is only when a receiver has been appointed, and has taken the property into his possession that the creditors acquire an equitable lien upon the assets sought to be reached, and in no other way than by a sale through a receiver can these assets be reduced to money, and applied to the payment of the execution. Storm *v.* Waddell, 2 *Sandf. Ch.* 494.

In an action like this, where the action is brought by one judgment creditor solely in his own behalf, and it is sought to reach only real estate fraudulently conveyed, the proper judgment is to set aside the conveyance, so far as it is an obstruction to the plaintiff's judgment, and permit him to pursue his remedy upon his judgment in the usual way. Hendrickson *v.* Winne, 3 *How. Pr.* 127. It is not necessary to enlarge particularly upon the inconveniences which may result to all parties from a resort to a receiver. They are fully set out by Judge COMSTOCK in the case of Chautauqua County Bank *v.* Risley, 19 *N. Y.* 369. In Union National Bank *v.* Warner (12 *Hun*, 306) it is said that the appointment of a receiver is not the safest practice, for in that case the purchaser at the receiver's sale must trace his title through the conveyance to the receiver, which might let in other liens attaching subsequently to the judgment, which was the foundation of the creditor's suit. The suggestion in that case is that the better practice is to permit the creditor to pursue his usual remedy upon his judgment after the fraudulent conveyance is put out of the way.

The legislature has indicated in a manner not to be mistaken, that, in cases like this especially, the proper mode of procedure is the issue of execution. Code. Civ. Pro. §1380, requires in ordinary cases, after the death of the judgment debtor, an application to the surrogate for leave to issue execution against his property, but that section, as recently amended, excludes cases of this kind

Bryer v. Foerster.

from its provisions, and expressly directs that the judgment creditor of the deceased person may enforce his judgment against real estate which has been fraudulently conveyed, and in regard to which, a judgment declaring the conveyance fraudulent has been entered, by the issue of execution, without application to the court, thus indicating quite clearly the judgment of the legislature as to what is the proper course to pursue in such cases. This indication should be followed, as we think, by the courts, and the judgment entered in this action should be modified by striking out so much of it as provides for the appointment of the receiver and the sale of the property by him, and by giving leave to the judgment debtor to enforce his judgment by execution issued in the manner prescribed by Code Civ. Pro. §1380, and directing the sheriff to sell the property described in the complaint, upon execution, with the same force as though the fraudulent conveyances had not been made. As thus modified, the judgment should be affirmed.

Opinion by RUMSEY, J. VAN BRUNT, P. J., BARRETT, O'BRIEN and INGRAHAM, JJ., concurred.

Judgment modified as directed in opinion, and as so modified affirmed, with costs to the respondent.

George W. Wingate, for the defendant, appellant, Catherine Foerster.

Sumner B. Stiles and *F. L. Wellman*, for the plaintiff, respondent.

TOOLE *v.* SUPERVISORS OF ONEIDA COUNTY.

Supreme Court, Fourth Department, Appellate Division; January, 1897.

1. *Appeal; evidence not in record; certificate of sale for taxes.*] Where, upon the trial of an action to set aside an assessment, taxation, advertisement and sale of real property, the plaintiff failed to introduce in evidence th certificate of sale,—*Held*, that this record might be produced on the hearing on appeal to sustain the judgment, and the court might permit it to be filed as part of the case.*

2. *Taxes; exemption; house bought with pension money.*] Real estate purchased by a soldier with pension money, if necessary or convenient for the support of the pensioner or his family, is exempt from taxation under Code Civ. Pro., § 1393, as no distinction is made between a levy and sale by virtue of an execution and a sale for non-payment of taxes.†

* See Note on Introduction of Evidence on Appeal, following this case.

† Otherwise by *L.* 1897, c. 348, amending § 1393 of the Code, to take effect September 1, 1897.

There was considerable confusion in the reported cases on the question whether or not property purchased with funds which were exempt from levy under an execution, retained that quality, until 1890, when the case of Yates County Nat. Bank *v.* Carpenter (119 *N. Y.* 550), decided the question affirmatively, as a general doctrine. The court, however, distinguished the case of Wiggant *v.* Smith (2 *Lans.* 185), where a pensioner who claimed exemption had embarked in business and had used his pension money therein. In some transactions he had made a profit, and it was impossible to identify the fund or the various articles of property in which the pension money had become invested, and it was held that the rule of exemption no longer applied. The court in Yates County Nat. Bank *v.* Carpenter (*supra*), also reversed the decision of the general term that the property purchased was not exempt, and approved the doctrine of Burgett *v.* Fancher, 35 *Hun*, 647, and Stockwell *v.* Bank of Malone, 36 *Hun*, 583.

Where a soldier received a government draft for pension money and deposited it in bank and drew part of it out,—*Held*, that the

Toole *v.* Supervisors of Oneida County.

Appeal by the defendant from a judgment of the Supreme Court, Oneida County, in favor of the plaintiffs,

balance standing to his credit was exempt under Code Civ. Pro., § 1393. Burgett *v.* Fancher, 35 *Hun*, 647.

In Stockwell *v.* Bank of Malone, 36 *Hun*, 583, a pensioner deposited his pension money in bank, and the bank agreed to pay interest on the deposit. It was held that it was still exempt. See also, Wildrick *v.* De Vinney (18 *W. Dig.* 355), to the same effect.

In Tillotson *v.* Wolcott (48 *N. Y.* 188), it was held that the exemption of a team, provided for a householder, should also apply to a judgment recovered by such householder against one who had tortuously taken and converted it to his own use.

In Andrews *v.* Rowan (28 *How. Pr.* 126), it was held that a receiver of the property of a judgment debtor appointed in supplementary proceedings, did not take title to a claim, or a judgment thereon, for damages accruing to such debtor from one who had wrongfully taken exempt property on execution for debt.

Where a soldier received a bounty n county bonds, which he gave to his wife, it was held that the bonds could not be reached in a judgment creditor's action against the husband and wife. as they were exempt when he gave them to her. Whiting *v.* Barrett, 7 *Lans.* 106.

Property purchased by the committee of a lunatic in his own name but with pension money of the lunatic is exempt from taxation. People *ex rel.* Canaday *v.* Williams, 90 *Hun*, 501 ; s. c., 71 *St. R.* 401 ; 36 *Supp.* 65.

In St. Lawrence State Hospital *v.* Fowler, (15 *Misc.* 159), it was held that when the sole resources of a father were pension moneys and property bought with them, he could not be compelled to support a pauper son upon an application of the State hospital, under *Code Crim. Pro.* §§ 915, 916.

Real estate purchased with a veteran's or a soldier's pension money is exempt from taxation, and an assessment thereof is void. Lapolt *v.* Maltby, 10 *Misc.* 330.

Real estate purchased by a United States pensioner with his pension money and occupied as a home for himself and family is exempt from execution. Buffum *v.* Forster, 77 *Hun*, 27.

When a pensioner buys real estate with pension money and gives a mortgage, it may be assessed for taxation in the amount of the mortgage. Matter of Murphy, 9 *Misc.* 647.

Real estate purchased with the pension money of a widow of a soldier is exempt from taxation. People *ex rel.* Scott *v.* Williams, 6 *Misc.* 185.

entered upon the decision of the court rendered after a trial at Special Term.

This action was brought by Garrett Toole and his wife, to set aside an assessment, taxation, advertisement and sale of certain real property, and to obtain the cancellation thereof, on the ground that the property was purchased with money paid to the plaintiff, Garrett Toole, for a pension from the United States government. The court below held that such property was exempt from taxation under Code Civ. Pro. §1393, and rendered judgment cancelling the assessment and sale.

Held, no error, and that the certificate of tax sale which had not been introduced on the trial might be read on appeal to sustain the judgment. The appellant takes the point that because a certificate of sale was not shown to have been issued to the defendant, the action cannot be maintained. It is alleged in the answer: "And thereafter said county treasurer duly advertised and sold the same to the defendant as provided by law." Tax sales in the county of Oneida are regulated by chapter 91 of the Laws of 1880, the 7th section of which provides that the county treasurer, within forty-eight hours after the sale, shall give to the purchaser a certificate describing the real estate purchased. The presumption is that the county treasurer did his duty and issued the certificate. A record may be produced on the hearing on an appeal from a judgment to sustain the judgment, and were it important, the court might permit it to be filed as part of the case.

The judgment should be affirmed, with costs, on the opinion of MR. JUSTICE VANN.*

Opinion PER CURIAM.

---

* The opinion of Mr. Justice VANN, adopted by the Appellate Division, is reported in full in 16 *Misc.* 653.

Judgment affirmed, with costs.

George C. Morehouse, for the defendant, appellant.

George C. Carter, for the plaintiffs, respondents.

NOTE ON INTRODUCTION OF EVIDENCE ON APPEAL.

Just how far appellate courts will go in admitting evidence not contained in the record to determine a case before them cannot be determined always by any general principles to be deduced from the reported cases. The question appears to be one resting somewhat largely in the discretion of the appellate court. It is well settled, however, that while records are sometimes received on argument in an appellate court to cure an omission through inadvertence of proof on trial, this is only permitted to uphold a judgment, not to reverse it, as a reversal is only for error committed below, and there can be no error in deciding contrary to a record not produced. Stilwell *v.* Carpenter, 2 *Abb. N. C.* 238 ; s. c., 62 *N. Y.* 639.

The same rule is applied on motions. Irving National Bank *v.* Adams, 28 *Hun,* 108.

In Porter *v.* Waring (69 *N. Y.* 250), the plaintiff was not allowed to read on appeal a city ordinance as to the width of certain city streets, which was not put in evidence below, although the ordinance could have been read in evidence at the trial, under the statute. But it was sought to read it for the purpose of reversing a judgment and the court held that this could not be done.

The primary rule is that evidence cannot be produced on appeal which has not been introduced at the trial and regularly proved, except records, or documentary evidence which proves itself, and on which no question can arise in the cause, except such as is apparent on its face. Brooks *v.* Higby, 11 *Hun,* 235 ; Bank of Charleston *v.* Emerich, 2 *Sandf.* 718 ; Dresser *v.* Brooks, 3 *Barb.* 429 ; Burt *v.* Place, 4 *Wend.* 591 ; Armstrong *v.* Percy, 5 *Id.* 535 ; Ritchie *v.* Putnam, 13 *Id.* 524 ; Hugh *v.* Wilson, 2 *Johns.* 46.

But where a party's attention is particularly called to a defect in his proof at the trial he will not be allowed to supply the defect on appeal by introducing documentary evidence not in the case.   Moser *v.* Mayor, etc:, of *N. Y.*, 21 *Hun*, 163.

In Dunford *v.* Weaver (84 *N. Y.* 445), the rule is laid down that an omission in proof of a matter of record may be supplied on appeal to sustain a judgment, where the record cannot be answered or changed.

In Hall *v.* U. S. Reflector Co. (21 *W. Dig.* 37), it was said that the practice which allows the receiving of documentary evidence on appeal is confined to supplying defects in proof given on the trial, of the same facts, and does not sanction independent and additional evidence, particularly if other counter evidence might have been given had the question been raised at the trial.

But where the documents sought to be introduced are deliberately withheld from the trial court the party will not be allowed to read them in the appellate tribunal.   Onderdonk *v.* Voorhis, 2 *Robt.* 623.

In an action to foreclose a mortgage, the mortgage referred to certain leases, and these leases were referred to in the complaint but were not produced or read at the trial, and the appellate court allowed them to be read on appeal to supply defects in the proof.   Catlin *v.* Grissler, 57 *N. Y.* 363.

In Munoz *v.* Wilson (111 *N. Y.* 295), which was an action to foreclose a mortgage, the mortgage was not printed in the case on appeal, and the court allowed an exemplified copy thereof to be produced and submitted as part of the case for the consideration of the court in deciding the appeal.

In Genet *v.* Davenport (66 *Barb.* 412), a mortgage was allowed to be read in the Appellate Court to supply a formal defect in the proof at the trial.

A former judgment between the same parties not pleaded as an estoppel nor given in evidence on the trial cannot be introduced on appeal as a bar to the action. Hebrew Free School Assn. *v.* Mayor, etc., of N. Y., 99 *N. Y.* 488.   But mere insufficiency in the proof of a judgment at the trial may be cured by a production of the judgment on appeal. ' Moore *v.* Williams, 23 *Super. Ct. (J. & S.)* 116 ; aff'd 115 *N. Y.* 586.

It is error, however, for the general term to receive a copy of a judgment roll referred to in the case on appeal as a basis for reversing the judgment appealed from.   Day *v.* Town of New Lots, 107 *N. Y.* 148.

In Scribner *v.* Williams (1 *Paige*, 550), it was held that if the appellant wished to produce further proofs in the

Appellate Court he should ask leave so to do in his petition of appeal.

In Dunham *v.* Townshend (118 *N. Y.* 281 ; aff'g 43 *Hun,* 580), in an action in ejectment, objection was made to the introduction in evidence of a sheriff's deed, because the judgment on which the execution was founded was not produced, and the court on appeal allowed such judgment roll to be introduced as part of the case.

When a former adjudication is set up as a bar to an action, for the purposes of appeal the decision must rest upon what the record in the second action discloses as to the questions passed upon in the former action.   Lorillard *v.* Clyde, 102 *N. Y.* 59 ; 122 *Id.* 41, 498.

In People *v.* Sullivan (2 *Edm.* 294), it was contended that a particular statute affected a writ of error before the court, and the record did not disclose the date of the judgment on which the proceeding was founded ; and the court allowed proof to be introduced as to the date of the judgment.

In Cousinery *v.* Pearsall (8 *J. & S.* 113), the court refused to consider the sufficiency of a memorandum of sale which was offered in evidence at the trial but was not contained in the case on appeal.

PURCELL *v.* LAUER.

Supreme Court, Fourth Department, Appellate Division ; February, 1897.

1 *Negligence; death; proximate cause; question for jury.*]
Where, by reason of the negligence of the defendant, the plaintiff's intestate was injured by tripping over a wire cable stretched across the sidewalk of a city street, over which she was passing in the night time, and in falling injured her knee and spine, and there was evidence tending to show that such injuries brought on a long train of diseases from which she died a year and four months after the accident,—*Held*, that the question whether or not the ultimate result could be traced back through the successive stages of the diseases, and her death could be

Purcell *v.* Lauer.

said to have been approximately caused by the accident, was properly left to the jury.*

2. *The same; common law rule as to the proximate cause of death.*] The common law doctrine in homicide cases that where a person died, from injuries received from another, more than a year and a day after the accident, there was an indisputable presumption that death was not caused by such injuries, has been abrogated in this State, and has no application to civil cases.

3. *The same; measure of damages.*] Where the plaintiff, the father and only next of kin of the deceased, was about eighty-two years old and in good health, and was entirely dependent upon the decedent, his daughter, for his support,—*Held*, that a verdict for $3,000 was not excessive.

Appeal by the defendants, from a judgment of the Supreme Court, Monroe County, in favor of the plaintiff, entered upon the verdict of a jury, and also from an order denying the defendants' motion for a new trial made upon the minutes.

This action was brought by James Purcell against

* In Sauter *v.* N. Y. Central, etc., R. R. Co., (66 *N. Y.* 50), it was held that where a person who had been injured through the negligence of the defendant, but his death resulted from the mistake of a competent physician in performing an operation, that this did not relieve the defendant from the result of its wrongful act, but the question of the proximate cause of the death of the deceased was for the jury.

Where the person injured refused to submit to the amputation of an injured limb and in the opinion of a professional witness such operation would have improved the patient's condition, it was held that this did not bar a recovery, but raised a question for the jury as to whether or not the injury was the proximate cause of his death. Sullivan *v.* Tioga R. R. Co., 112 *N. Y.* 643.

In Ginna *v.* Second Ave. R. R. Co., (8 *Hun,* 494 ; aff'd 67 *N. Y.* 596), through the negligence of the defendant the plaintiff's intestate was thrown from a car, and his arm was broken. The injury resulted in blood poisoning from which he died, and it was held that the injury was the proximate cause of his death.

See Note on Proximate Cause of Death from Wrongful Act, 2 *N. Y. Ann. Cas.* 404 ; following Lyons *v.* Second Ave. R. R. Co., *Id.* 402.

Purcell *v.* Lauer.

Frederick C. Lauer, Jr., and others, to recover damages for the negligence of the defendants in causing the death of Mrs. Wooster. The injury complained of was received by Mrs. Wooster on October 23, 1893, while she was going along a sidewalk in that city, in the evening, by tripping over a cable wire drawn across the walk, which was used as a guard to support the defendants' derrick while they were constructing a bridge. The cable was about two inches above the sidewalk. The deceased was a large, heavy woman, weighing about 180 pounds, and was carrying a number of bundles in her arms. She fell to the sidewalk, greatly injuring her right knee and to some extent her left one, and the evidence tended to show that in the fall, or in the wrench given by it to her body, she seriously injured her spine. She was taken to her home, and there was evidence tending to show that the knee cap of the left limb was injured ; that swelling and inflammation resulted from the injury ; that the accident caused a great shock to her nervous system ; that she was compelled to employ a physician and a nurse and received treatment almost continuously for the injury, until the time of her death ; that an abscess was formed and a suppuration created under her knee ; that evidence of blood poisoning occurred ; that she gradually grew weaker and thinner from the time of her injury until her death ; that at times she had symptoms of fever which appeared to be recurrent or intermittent, and the physician in charge, who seemed to have been an experienced and capable one, attributed her death to the original injury and shock caused by the accident. The deceased was a remarkably vigorous and healthy woman before the injury, about sixty years of age and with great powers of resistance as against disease ; she was a widow ; her husband had been killed in the war for the Union, and she was drawing a pension of about $200 per year, and in addition thereto earned considerable as a music teacher. Her next of kin was her father, a gentleman who, at the time of the trial, was about eighty-two years of age, but a man of vigor and good health and to all appearances likely to live for some time, and almost entirely dependent upon her for his support. She was his housekeeper, took charge of his business and household so far as it pertained to their home, turned her pension in for his support, and seemed indispensable to his comfort and support. The defendants concede that the deceased was not at fault as to the injury, and that there was evidence upon which she might have recovered against the defendant for the injury which she sustained if she had brought the action herself; nor do they question but what the defendants were negligent in the matter; indeed, it appears that they were grossly negligent; but the defendants do claim that, as a matter of law, it did not appear that the injury and her death were so connected as to render the defendants liable to her executor after her death, and the defendants upon this appeal make four points : *First*, that upon the whole evidence the injury was not the proximate cause of the death, nor was the death the natural or probable result of the defendant's wrongful act. *Second*, that there is a conclusive presumption that the injury was not the proximate cause of the death, because it did not occur within a year and a day after the injury. *Third*, that it was shown upon the trial that the origin of the fever that the deceased had was malarial, which comes from matter in the atmosphere, and is an intervening cause of death, and that the court had erred in its charge upon that subject, and, *Fourth*, that the damages awarded by the jury, of $3,000 are excessive.

The immediate cause of the death seems to have been gastritis, being either an acute or chronic inflammation of the stomach. The plaintiff's evidence tended to show that this condition was created by causes, the direct result of the injury to the knee, the spine and the shock of the accident, while the defendants' evidence tended to dispute this proposition.

Held, that the question of fact as to whether the injury to Mrs. Wooster, which resulted from the defendant's negligence, was the proximate cause of her death, was a question for the jury. The plaintiff having established the injury which might be productive of the result claimed, and shown a state of facts that would naturally produce it, if an intervening cause were established sufficient as a matter of law, to show another cause of the death, the burden of doing so devolved upon the defendant. A careful examination of the whole evidence in the case satisfies us that this was not done, at least so far accomplished as to justify the trial court in taking the question from the jury.

The fact that the deceased survived the accident a year and four or five months is greatly relied upon by the defendants to justify their position, that a presumption has obtained from the lapse of time that some intervening cause not connected with the accident caused the death of Mrs. Wooster, and they refer to the common law presumption that the injury was not the proximate cause of the death, because it did not occur within a year and a day after the injury. This was a rule of the common law in relation to homicide, and does not prevail in this State in criminal cases, and has no application to civil cases. Schlichting *v.* Wintgen, 25 *Hun*, 626 ; Sias *v.* Rochester R. R. Co., 92 *Hun*, 140. But this lapse of time was a circumstance to be submitted to the jury in connection with the other evidence in the case.

The appellants' counsel relies principally upon Scheffer *v.* R. R. Co.,(105 U. S. 249), which was a railway collision case where a passenger was injured and afterwards became disordered in mind and body, and some eight months after the accident committed suicide. In an action by his representatives to recover damages for his death, it was held that the proximate cause of his death was the *suicide* and not the injury received by the deceased. It did not seem susceptible of clear proof that the injury

caused the suicide ; whether it did or not was necessarily
a matter of conjecture. Could it have been fairly shown
that the suicide would not have occurred but for the injury, a different case would have been presented, but the
court, in that case, recognized the rule to be that, ordinarily in such cases, the liability of the defendant is a question for the jury, and cite with approval Milwaukee & St.
P. R. R. Co. *v.* Kellogg (94 *U. S.* 469), which was a fire
case, where the sparks from a steam ferryboat had,
through the negligence of its owners (the defendants), set
fire to an elevator. The sparks from the elevator had set
fire to the plaintiff's sawmill and lumber yards, which
were three or four hundred feet from the elevator. The
court was requested to charge the jury that the injuries
sustained by the plaintiff were too remote from the negligence to afford a ground for a recovery. This the court
refused, but submitted to the jury to find whether the
burning of the mill and lumber was the result reasonably
to be expected from the burning of the elevator ; whether
it was the result which, under the circumstances, would
not naturally follow from the burning of the elevator, and whether it was the result of the continued effect of the sparks from the steamboat, without the aid of
other causes not reasonably to be expected.

In Ehrgott *v.* Mayor, etc., of *N. Y.* (96 *N. Y.* 264), the
plaintiff drove into a ditch in the street, his horses jumped,
the axle of his carriage was broken, and he was dragged
partly over the dashboard. He procured another carriage,
the matter was reported to the police, and the plaintiff
drove several miles to his home, which took several hours,
during which time he was exposed to the cold rain, and
his clothes became saturated with water. The plaintiff's
evidence tended to show that the injuries which resulted
were caused by the strain and shock of the accident, and
the defendant gave evidence tending to show that the diseases were the result of the subsequent exposure to the
cold rain. The trial court charged that, whether his in-

juries resulted from the strain and shock, *or from the exposure after the accident,* the defendant was still responsible for the injuries from which the plaintiff was suffering. Upon appeal, the Court of Appeals sustained this charge, and the opinion of Judge EARL in the case tends to sustain the conclusions here reached.

See also, Pollett *v.* Long, 56 *N. Y.* 200 ; Sauter *v.* N. Y. Central etc., R. R. Co., 66 *Id.* 50 ; Mitchell *v.* Rochester Ry. Co., 4 *Misc.* 575 ; Leonard *v.* N. Y., etc., Telegraph Co., 41 *N. Y.* 544 ; Perley *v.* Eastern R. R. Co., 98 *Mass.* 414 ; Jucker *v.* Chicago, etc., R. R. Co., 52 *Wis.* 150 ; Delie *v.* Chicago, etc., R. R. Co., 51 *Id.* 400 ; Baltimore, etc., R. R. Co. *v.* Kemp, 61 *Md.* 74 ; Williams *v.* Vanderbilt, 28 *N. Y.* 217.

The jury awarded a verdict to the plaintiff of $3,000. The plaintiff, the next of kin, was before them. They could judge from his appearance something as to the years that should be allotted to him in the future. They found a penniless and dependent old man whose span of life might be stretched out a decade. The only child upon whom he could depend for his support in his old age, and who was comfortably supporting him at the time she was injured, had been taken away from him by the negligence of the defendants, as the jury found. We cannot say from this evidence that this verdict was so excessive as to justify us in reversing it for that reason.

Opinion by WARD, J.   All concurred, except GREEN, J., dissenting.

Judgment and order affirmed, with costs.

George F. Yeoman, for the defendants, appellants.

George Raines, for the plaintiff, respondent.

WOODWARD *v.* MUSGRAVE.

*Supreme Court, First Department, Appellate Division;
February,* 1897.

1. *Reference ; on motion to vacate attachment.*] Where a motion to
vacate an attachment was denied, with leave to renew upon
the coming in of the report of a referee appointed to take testimony as to the question of the place of residence of the defendant,—*Held,* that the original motion having been denied
there was nothing before the court upon which to found the
order of reference and it should be vacated.

2. *The same ; general rule.*] An order of reference to aid the court
in determining a motion should not be made except in extreme
cases, where large interests are involved and it is impossible to
reach a conclusion upon the papers before the court.*

Appeal by the plaintiff from an order of the Supreme
Court, New York Special Term, made upon a motion to
vacate and set aside an attachment, excepting that portion
of said order which denies the motion to vacate said attachment.

On July 31, 1896, the plaintiff, Edwin P. Woodward,
applied to one of the justices of the supreme court for an
attachment against the property of the defendant, Fannie
E. Musgrave, upon the ground of non-residence, in an
action brought to recover upon certain promissory notes
mentioned in the complaint. The defendant procured an
order to show cause upon her own affidavit why the warrant of attachment issued in this action against the property of the defendant, on the ground that she was a non-
resident, should not be vacated and set aside because the
defendant was, at such time, and still is, a resident of the

* See Note on Reference of Issues Arising on Motions, at the end
of this case.

Woodward *v*. Musgrave.

city, county and State of New York. Upon said motion coming on to be heard the plaintiff submitted affidavits tending to contradict the affidavit of the defendant, and to sustain the contention that the defendant was a non-resident. The court thereupon made an order that the question of the defendant's residence at the time of the issuing of the attachment be referred to a referee, and such order required the referee to report the proof taken by him, together with his opinion thereon, to the court, with all convenient speed. The parties appeared before the referee and the defendant claimed that the plaintiff had the affirmative, and should commence the proceedings. The referee having so held, the plaintiff declined to proceed with the reference or to produce any witnesses, and took an exception. The referee thereupon reported the foregoing facts, and that, as in his opinion, the plaintiff had failed to establish the defendant's non-residence, the attachment should be vacated. It may be observed in passing that the question of vacating the attachment had never been referred to the referee, and he had no authority to report thereon. The simple question referred to him was the question of the defendant's residence at the time of the issuing of the attachment.

Thereupon, on November 24, 1896, the defendant procured an order to show cause why the attachment should not be vacated and set aside on the ground that the defendant was a resident of the State of New York at the time of the issuance thereof, and for the reason that the plaintiff had failed to make out the non-residence of the defendant, as directed by the referee, which question was referred to said referee, and for such other relief as might be proper. This motion came on to be heard on December 21, 1896, the court having before it all the papers which were used upon the motion of August 5, 1896, together with the proceedings before the referee and the affidavit upon which the order to show cause of November 24 was obtained; and it was ordered that said motion to

vacate the attachment " be at this time, and upon the
papers now presented, denied, with leave, however, to the
defendant to renew said motion upon the coming in of the
referee's report provided for by this order.'" It was further ordered that the affidavits and papers upon which
said attachment was granted, together with those which
were before the court upon the previous motion to vacate
the attachment, and which were recited in the order of
September 17, 1896, be referred back to the same referee,
with the right to either party to examine the affiants, and
to introduce such other proof as to the defendant's residence as they might be advised. The referee was ordered
to take such proof as might be offered and report the
same, with his opinion thereon, and it was ordered that
the affirmative of the question referred to the referee be
with the plaintiff.

The plaintiff thereupon appealed from such order of
December 21, 1896, and from each and every part thereof,
excepting that part of the order which orders that the motion to vacate the attachment be denied.

Held, that that part of the order directing a reference
should be reversed. It will be seen that the order under
consideration does not refer any question of fact to the
referee or direct him to take proof upon any question of
fact. Certain affidavits and papers are referred back to
the referee and he is directed to take such proof as may
be offered and to report the same with his opinion thereon—the proof not being confined to any particular question or subject. It is to be observed that, in references
upon motions the proceedings before the referee do not
supersede the affidavits which are before the court upon
the motion. Such references are only made for the purpose of giving the parties an opportunity to cross-examine
affiants and for the introduction of additional testimony
upon the question involved in the motion. Therefore,
when neither party offered any additional proof, or asked
for the cross-examination of either of the affiants, and the

case came back to the court, the court was bound to decide the motion upon the papers then before it, being the papers which were before the court upon the original motion.   This the court apparently did and denied the motion to vacate the attachment, as it would seem it was its duty to do from the nature of the proof which was then before it.

The order of reference was entirely unnecessary in the first instance and was improper.   Such orders should not be made except in extreme cases where large interests are involved, and it is impossible to reach a conclusion upon the papers before the court.   The expenses of such references are always great—in many instances largely exceeding the value of the real subject-matter in controversy. This expense is necessarily a great hardship which is imposed upon the defeated party and sometimes upon the successful party.

It would seem that the court upon the papers before it should have absolutely denied the motion to vacate the attachment, and that the order of reference was ill-advised and must be reversed.

Opinion by VAN BRUNT, P. J.   WILLIAMS, PATTERSON, INGRAHAM and O'BRIEN JJ., concurred.

Order so far as appealed from reversed, with ten dollars costs and disbursements.

James J. Allen, for the plaintiff, appellant.

Franklin Bien, for the defendant, respondent.

NOTE ON REFERENCE OF ISSUES ARISING ON MOTIONS.

Section 1015 of the Code of Civil Procedure provides that : "The court may . . . upon its own motion, or upon the application of either party, without the consent of the other, direct a reference . . . to determine and report upon a question of fact, arising at any stage of the action, upon a motion, or otherwise, except upon the pleadings."

Under the broad power given by this section there has never been any doubt that the court had power to appoint a referee to take testimony and report as to disputed questions of fact arising in any proceeding incidental to the action. But the courts do not look upon this procedure with favor, and as was said in Martin *v.* Hodges, 45 *Hun*, 38, 40 : "It is not the usual practice to order a reference in such case, and we think the practice should not be followed, except in extraordinary cases, where the court is unable to determine the facts from the papers read upon the motion."

That was a motion to set aside a judgment alleged to have been taken by default, on the ground that there had been no default and the answer had been served in time. The question of fact was as to the exact day upon which the complaint was served. The court also held in that case that there could only be $10 motion costs and disbursements allowed where the court ordered a reference on a motion, and that Rule 30 of the General Rules of Practice, requiring exceptions to be filed to the report of a referee in a reference other than for the trial of the issues in an action or for computing the amount due in foreclosure cases, did not apply to a reference on such a motion.

Without regard to the provisions of the Code the court has a right to order a reference to take proofs upon matters upon which it desires fuller information. Dwight *v.* St. John, 25 *N. Y.* 205 ; People *ex rel.* Delmar *v.* St. Louis & San Francisco Ry. Co., 44 *Hun*, 552.

Such a reference is merely for the purpose of aiding the court in determining the questions involved in the motion. The report of the referee is in no wise binding upon the court, and it has power to disregard it and draw its own conclusions from the evidence. Marshall *v.* Meech, 51 *N. Y.* 140.

Such a reference is proper on a motion to set aside a judgment on the ground that an attorney was not author-

ized to appear for one of the parties.   Vilas *v.* Plattsburgh &
Montreal R. R. Co., 123 *N. Y.* 440.   Or as to the date of
the service of a paper in the action.   Dovale *v.* Ackerman,
7 *Supp.* 833 ; s. c., 27 *St. R.* 895.   Or on a motion to continue an injunction.   Stubbs *v.* Ripley, 39 *Hun*, 620 ; Continental Steamship Co. *v.* Clark, 7 *Civ. Pro. R.* 183.   Or
upon a motion to cancel a judgment entered upon confession without action as having been paid.   Dwight *v.* St.
John, 25 *N. Y.* 203 ; Demelt *v.* Leonard, 19 *How. Pr.* 140 ;
s. c., 11 *Abb. Pr.* 252.   Or to satisfy a judgment, where it
appeared that through a mistake two records had been
made and two judgments were entered upon one claim.
Pendleton *v.* Weed, 17 *N. Y.* 72.   To discharge an order
of arrest.   Stelle *v.* Palmer, 7 *Abb. Pr.* 181.   To vacate an
attachment.   Burnett *v.* Snyder, 41 *Super. Ct.* (*J. & S.*) 342.
On a motion to compel an attorney to pay over moneys
collected.   Gillespie *v.* Mulholland, 12 *Misc.* 44 ; Barber *v.*
Case, 12 *How. Pr.* 351.   Or to punish parties for contempt
for alleged disobedience of an injunction order.   Aldinger
v. Pugh, 57 *Hun*, 181 ; s. c., 19 *Civ. Pro. R.* 91 ; People
ex rel. Alexander *v.* Alexander, 3 *Hun*, 211.   Or upon a
motion where there are conflicting claims to moneys in the
hands of the sheriff.   Patten *v.* Bullard, 3 *St. R.* 735.   Or
upon a motion for a mandamus to compel an inspection of
corporate books.   People *ex rel.* Delmar *v.* St. Louis & San
Francisco Ry. Co., 44 *Hun*, 552.

DRENNAN *v.* BOICE.

*Supreme   Court,   First   Department,   Appellate   Term ;
March,* 1897.

*Election of remedies ; judgment against agent ; undisclosed princi-
pal.*]   Where one party to a contract proceeds to judgment
against another party, after discovery of the fact that the latter
was acting as agent for an undisclosed principal, he thereby
elects to hold the agent alone, and cannot maintain a second
action against the principal.*

---

* The doctrine of this case is similar by analogy to the rule of
law that where one dealing with an agent and knowing him to be
an agent charges the agent personally and depends exclusively upon

Drennan v. Boice.

Appeal from a judgment for the dismissal of the complaint upon the merits, rendered by the District Court in the city of New York for the thirteenth judicial district.

Action by William Drennan against Hewit Boice to recover for services alleged to have been performed at the defendant's instance and request.

During the months of October, November and December, 1894, the plaintiff performed certain services in and about one of the streets of the city of New York, at the

the agent's credit in selling him goods, or in otherwise dealing with him, that this will be such an election as prevents the person so dealing with the agent from holding the principal responsible. Thus, if the vendor of goods takes an agent's note with full knowledge of the agency, and depending upon the credit of the agent, he cannot afterwards recover from the principal. Hyde v. Paige, 9 *Barb.* 150.

But it has been held that taking the agent's note does not discharge the principal, unless the latter shows affirmatively that he has been in some way injured by the creditor thus dealing with the agent. Rathbone v. Tucker, 15 *Wend.* 498.

If the vendor voluntarily selects the agent as his debtor he cannot afterwards resort to the principal. Burdin v. Williamson, 5 *Hun*, 560.

Where a vendor of goods charged them on his books to the agent instead of the principal, this is strong but not conclusive evidence that credit was given exclusively to the agent. Foster v. Persch, 68 *N. Y.* 400.

" Where a broker purchases or sells property without disclosing to the respective principals in the transaction the name of the party for whom he acts, he becomes, on the one side, liable personally for the purchase price of the property bought, and on the other is entitled to collect such price from the principal at whose instance the purchase was made. The vendee in such a case can relieve himself from liability to the broker only by showing payment of the contract price by him to the original vendor, or a release for a good and valuable consideration from the broker." Knapp v. Simon, 96 *N. Y.* 284, 290.

A principal and an agent cannot be sued together in the same action upon a contract made by the agent for his principal. First Nat. Bank of Oxford v. Turner, 24 *Supp.* 793.

Drennan *v.* Boice.

direct request of one William Martin, who had entered into a contract with the municipality whereby he undertook the grading of such street. As a matter of fact Martin had actually assigned all his rights under the municipal contract to the defendant who, with the consent of the municipality, assumed the performance of the work, the assignment having taken place before the plaintiff's relations with Martin commenced, and this action was brought against the defendant, as Martin's undisclosed principal in the transaction, to recover the value of the services performed.

In view of the fact that the defendant was the party who directly benefited by this work, to the exclusion of Martin by reason of the prior assignment of the latter's interest, it may be that the defendant's relation as principal to Martin was made out satisfactorily, and, also, we may assume, that the plaintiff's proof of the performance of the services was sufficient, although it was not as clear as might have been desired. Without objection, proof was given by the defendant which established a complete defense to the action, and, while this defense was not pleaded, the plaintiff's consent to the litigation of it was to be inferred from his failure to oppose the introduction of the evidence as irrelevant to the issues. Frear *v.* Sweet, 118 *N. Y.* 454. Indeed, the main part of this defense was supported by the voluntary stipulation of counsel as to the facts, and this stipulation was quite apart from anything which the plaintiff's proof of the cause of action required. So far, then, there was, in effect, an actual consent to the introduction of the defense.

It was shown that on October 16, 1895, judgment was rendered in an action brought by this plaintiff in the late court of common pleas to foreclose a mechanic's lien for the services now in suit, this defendant together with Martin and the municipality being named as defendants.

From this record it appears that the judgment proceeded in favor of the plaintiff against Martin, personally, for the amount of the claim, but the complaint was dismissed as against the other defendants, the lien not having been established. In that action the answer of this defendant set forth at length the assignment to him by Martin of the municipal contract, and all the facts upon which such defendant's relation to Martin, as principal, are now based were there fully disclosed, yet in the month of January, 1896, the plaintiff brought an action in one of the district courts and obtained a judgment against Martin and his business associates upon this precise claim, notwithstanding that the present defendant's answer as a defendant in the foreclosure action had apprised him of the fact of Martin's agency, such as it was, several months before.

The complaint was properly dismissed on the merits. It is claimed that the plaintiff was ignorant of the facts, but the justice, we must assume, found with the defendant upon that issue, and ample evidence justified the finding. We have, therefore, merely a case of an election by the plaintiff to hold the agent personally for the claim after full disclosure of the principal's identity, since this was the effect of the prosecution of the demand to judgment against the agent after the principal had been disclosed. Tuthill *v.* Wilson, 90 *N. Y.* 423.

While the liability of the agent and of the principal was several it was an alternate liability, and a recovery against both was not open to the plaintiff. See Election of Remedies, 7 *Am. & Eng. Encyc. of Practice*, 360 ; notes, 2 *Silvernail's Ct. App.* 291 ; 4 *Silvernail's Sup. Ct.* 347 ; *Bigelow on Estoppel*, 68 ; note to Wheeler *v.* McGuire, 2 *Lawyers' R. Ann.* 812 ; Carter, Rice & Co. *v.* Howard, 17 *Misc. Rep.* 381, 384. Tuthil *v.* Wilson (*supra*) ; Priestly *v.* Fernie, 3 *H. & C. Exch.* 982, in which case it was said : "Where the agent, having made a contract in his own name, has been sued on it to judgment, there can be no doubt that no second action would be maintainable

Welling *v.* Ivoroyd M'f'g. Co.

against the principal." See, also, Meeker *v.* Claghorn, 44 *N. Y.* 351.

The cases to which our attention is called by counsel for the appellant (Cobb *v.* Knapp, 71 *N. Y.* 348 ; Knapp *v.* Simon, 96 *Id.* 286), hold no more than that the commencement, only, of an action against either principal or agent does not necessarily import an abandonment of the claim against the other, but neither case holds that the pursuit of both principal and agent may be continued after the recovery of a judgment against one.

Opinions by BISCHOFF, J. DALY, P. J., and MCADAM J., concur.

Judgment affirmed, with costs.

J. Baldwin Hands, for plaintiff, appellant.

William H. Reed, for defendant, respondent.

WELLING *v.* IVOROYD M'F'G. CO.

Supreme Court, Second Department, Appellate Division ; March, 1897.

1 *Corporations ; insolvency ; unlawful preferences to officers ; remedy.*] Where an officer of a foreign corporation in contemplation of its insolvency assigned a claim against the corporation to his wife, who procured an attachment against the corporation and thereby secured a preference over other creditors,—*Held,* that as the judgment was for a valid claim it could not be set aside, but the court had power, in a proper action, to vacate the attachment and set aside the execution, to prevent such director from securing an unlawful preference.*

---

* In connection with this case it is important to note the new section (§ 60) of article 3 of the Stock Corporation Law, contained

Welling *v*. Ivoroyd M'f'g. Co.

2 *Costs ; judgment for defendant on one of several causes of action.*]
Where a suit was brought on several causes of action and the
plaintiff succeeded on some, and as to one cause of action there
was a finding in favor of the defendant that "the contract or
contracts with the defendant upon which the said cause of action is based is invalid,"—*Held*, that the defendant was entitled
to costs to be applied in reduction of the plaintiff's judgment.

in *L.* 1897, c. 384, providing: " Except as otherwise provided in this
chapter the officers, directors, and stockholders of a foreign stock
corporation transacting business in this State, except moneyed and
railroad corporations, shall be liable under the provisions of this
chapter, in the same manner and to the same extent as the officers,
directors, and stockholders of a domestic corporation, for :

1. The making of unauthorized dividends ;
2. The creation of unauthorized and excessive indebtedness ;
3. Unlawful loans to stockholders ;
4. Making false certificates, reports, or public notices ;
5. An illegal transfer of the stock and property of such corporation, when it is insolvent or its insolvency is threatened ;
6. The failure to file an annual report.

Such liabilities may be enforced in the courts of this State, in
the same manner as similar liabilities imposed by law upon the officers, directors and stockholders of domestic corporations."

Under this statute and the ruling of the case in the text it
would seem now that the courts of this State have practically the
same power in enforcing claims against foreign corporations and
their officers that they have against those organized under the laws
of New York. Thus they can not only prevent the officers from
gaining any advantage by securing a preference directly or indi-
rectly, or if this is done the creditor has his remedy against the stockholders, etc. For the various provisions of the present law as to the
liability of stockholders, etc., of domestic corporations, see Note on
Primary Liability of Directors and Stockholders, 3 *N. Y. Ann. Cas.*
390. See, also, Note on Statutory Provisions for the Protection and
Enforcement of Claims for Wages, etc., *Id.* 7, and Note on Protection of Minority Stockholders, *Id.* 368.

In Jefferson County National Bank *v.* Townley (92 *Hun*, 172),
an officer of a domestic corporation assigned a claim he held
against the corporation to his wife, who brought suit and secured a
judgment by default after the corporation had failed to pay accounts
which were overdue, and in an action by another judgment creditor
her judgment was set aside.

In Olney *v.* Baird (7 *App. Div.* 95), it was held that a judgment

Welling *v*. Ivoroyd M'f'g. Co.

Appeal by the defendant, from a judgment of the Supreme Court, New York county, in favor of the plaintiff, entered upon the report of a referee, with notice of an intention to bring up for review an order of the New York Special Term, denying the defendant's motion for leave to tax a bill of costs against the plaintiff, for an extra allowance, and to have costs to defendant included in the final judgment, and that said final judgment show the fact that the defendant recovered against the plaintiff on one of the causes of action alleged in the complaint in the action.

This appeal was transferred from the first department to the second department.

The plaintiff, Urania P. Welling, as assignor of her husband, William M. Welling, sued the defendant on three causes of action :   The first for goods sold and delivered, the second for salary of the plaintiff's assignor as president of the defendant, the third for moneys expended for the defendant's benefit.   The referee reported in favor of the plaintiff on the first cause of action and for part of the claim the subject of the third cause of action, and for the defendant on the second cause of action.   The defendant moved for leave to tax a bill of costs on its recovery on the second cause of action.   This application was denied. Judgment was entered in favor of the plaintiff, on the report of the referee, with costs.   From that judgment this appeal is taken, and the defendant gave notice of its intention to review the order denying it a bill of costs.

which a corporation suffered to be taken against it by one who was the practical owner of the corporation was void so far as it created a preference in favor of such judgment creditor.

And where a creditor has obtained a preference forbidden by our laws by a judgment in a foreign State he may be compelled to account to the other creditors. Olney *v*. Baird, 15 *Misc.* 385 ; aff'd 7 *App. Div.* 95.

But a corporation is not obliged to defend a suit for a valid debt merely for the purpose of avoiding the creation of a preference. Ridgway *v*. Symons, 4 *App. Div.* 98.

Held, that the judgment should be affirmed and the order denying costs to the defendant should be reversed. The plaintiff's assignor was a director of the defendant, a foreign corporation organized under the laws of the State of New Jersey. Shortly before the commencement of the action, he transferred to the plaintiff his claims against the defendant. The defendant, in its answer, set forth the relation the plaintiff's assignor bore to the defendant; alleged that at the time of the assignment to the plaintiff defendant was insolvent and unable to pay its debts, and that the assignment was made to the plaintiff for the benefit of the assignor with intent to get a preference in the payment of his claims over those of other creditors of the corporation. The referee disposed of this defense on the ground that the law of this State prohibiting transfers by corporations in contemplation of insolvency did not apply to a New Jersey corporation, and that, by the laws of New Jersey, preferential transfers were not illegal. We are inclined to the opinion that the referee erred in his determination as to the law of the State of New Jersey on this subject. The case of Montgomery *v.* Phillips (53 *N. J. Eq.* 203), a later decision than any cited by the referee, holds that a director of an insolvent corporation cannot obtain, by the action of the board of directors, a preference over other creditors of the corporation. But, however this may be, and also, however the question may be determined, whether the laws of this State affect the disposition of property of insolvent foreign corporations doing business within this State, we think that the question does not properly arise as a defense to the action. In Throop *v.* Hatch Litho. Co. (125 *N. Y.* 530; s. c., 35 *St. R.* 816), the question arose on a motion to vacate an attachment which the plaintiff had obtained in the action. It was there held that the director of a domestic corporation could not, by attachment, obtain a preference in the payment of his claim. But in that case the objection was raised by a motion to vacate the attachment, which was

granted. The only other case on the subject, of importance, is that of Kingsley *v.* First Nat. Bank (31 *Hun*, 329),
the reasoning of which is referred to with approval by
the court of appeals in the Throop case. In the Kingsley
case a director had recovered judgment against the insolvent corporation and, under an execution issued on the
judgment, levied on the property of the corporation. The
action was brought by the receiver of the corporation to
set aside the judgment and execution as creating an illegal
preference. The court held that the director had the right
to bring the action, that there was no statutory restraint
upon it, and that it might be necessary and proper so as
to determine the existence, validity or extent of the claim
of the director against the company. But it was held that
he had no right to obtain a preference by the execution
levy on the assets of the corporation. In accordance with
this determination the judgment was allowed to stand, but
the execution and levy under it were set aside. Therefore, Kingsley *v.* Bank is authority that the facts pleaded
on this subject by the defendant do not constitute a defense to the cause of action, but that relief against an unlawful preference must be obtained in another way. Here
the plaintiff obtained an attachment and, we may assume,
has levied execution on her judgment upon the attached
property. If the proceedings taken by the plaintiff to
obtain satisfaction of her claim have resulted in an unlawful preference in favor of a director or officer of the corporation against other creditors, the defendant may proceed by a motion to vacate her attachment and to set
aside the execution ; or the receiver of the corporation
may maintain an action to set aside such attachment and
execution. But we think that the facts shown do not constitute a defense to the action.

We are of the opinion that the defendant was improperly denied its costs. As to the second cause of action it
obtained, not a nonsuit, but an affirmative finding in its
favor that "judgment should be entered for the defend-

ant upon the second cause of action set forth in the complaint," upon the ground that "the contract or contracts with the defendant upon which the said cause of action is based were invalid." This effectively disposed of that cause of action. No new suit upon it can ever be brought. It is, therefore, precisely such a case as is stated in the opinion of Judge O'BRIEN in Burns *v.* D., L. & W. R. R. Co. (135 *N. Y.* 268 ; S. C., 48 *St. R.* 106), entitles the defendant to his costs within the provisions of the Code. In Moosbrugger *v.* Kaufman (7 *App. Div.* 380 ; S. C., 40 *Supp.* 213), the appellate division in the fourth department, by a vote of three to two, in a case substantially the same as that now before us, held that the defendant was not entitled to costs. We look upon this decision as opposed to the doctrine of the Burns case, and while it may be that the statement of the court of appeals on this question was *obiter* and not necessary to the determination of the question before it, it certainly was related to the subject-matter and fairly proceeded from its discussion. It should, therefore, be regarded as controlling authority. The case of Dougherty *v.* Metropolitan Life Ins. Co. (3 *App. Div.* 317) is not in point. There was not a decision of the second cause of action in favor of the defendant. On the contrary, the plaintiff on that cause of action recovered three dollars.

Judgment appealed from should be affirmed, with costs, except that the order appealed from should be reversed, with ten dollars costs and disbursements, and motion granted, with ten dollars costs, and that such costs and the costs of the action, as they may be taxed by the defendant, be applied upon the judgment hereby affirmed, and such judgment reduced accordingly.

Opinion by CULLEN, J. All concurred.

Judgment accordingly.

J. K. Long, for defendant, appellant.

P. Q. Eckerson, for plaintiff, respondent.

Bliven *v.* Robinson.

BLIVEN *v.* ROBINSON.

Court of Appeals ; March, 1897.

Dismissal of complaint; on the merits.] Where, in an equitable action, after a motion to dismiss the complaint had been granted, at the close of the plaintiff's case, counsel for both parties joined in a request that the court make formal findings and this was done and every question of fact was passed upon by the court,—*Held,* that this amounted to a decision on the merits and was not a mere nonsuit.*

Appeal from a judgment of the General Term of the Supreme Court, Second Department, which affirmed a

---

* The distinction between this case and the case of Place *v.* Hayward (117 *N. Y.* 487) is that there the referee made findings of fact and conclusions of law after dismissing the complaint, but not upon the request of either of the parties. The distinction, is, perhaps, a trifle refined except for the general principle that a nonsuit merely determines that facts constituting a cause of action have not been proved, while in this case the court at the request of both parties considered all the facts presented by the plaintiff's evidence and decided them against the plaintiff, thus going a step farther than was necessary for the purpose of a mere nonsuit.

In Raabe *v.* Squier (148 *N. Y.* 81) the procedure was the same as that in Place *v.* Hayward (*supra*).

The case of McNaughton *v.* Osgood (114 *N. Y.* 574), although not exactly in point, is instructive as to the practice in equity cases in the disposition of questions of fact. There certain questions of fact were ordered to be tried before a jury. After the plaintiff had presented his case on these facts the justice presiding at the trial at circuit dismissed the complaint without allowing the jury to determine the facts and without sending it back to the special term. This, it was held, was error, and that there could not be a nonsuit ordered by the justice presiding at the trial of these issues of fact ; that after the rendering of the jury's verdict as to the facts the case must go back to the special term for final determination, the same as if no jury trial had been ordered.

For a full discussion of the subject see Note on Dismissal of Complaint on the Merits. 2 *N. Y. Ann. Cas.* 249.

Bliven *v.* Robinson.

judgment in favor of defendants, entered upon a decision of the court dismissing the complaint upon the merits, without costs, on trial at special term.

Also, appeal from an order of the same general term, which affirmed an order of special term denying a motion by the plaintiff to correct and modify the judgment of the special term by striking out the words "upon the merits," so that the judgment should read: That the plaintiff's complaint be and the same is hereby dismissed, without costs, instead of reading: That the plaintiff's complaint be and the same is hereby dismissed upon the merits, without costs.

This was an action by Cora E. Bliven against George H. Robinson and others, the principal purpose of which was to set aside three written instruments executed by the plaintiff, upon the ground that her signatures thereto were obtained by fraud. These instruments were, in effect, a consent by the plaintiff to the investment of certain moneys belonging to the estate of her father in the business of a firm of which he was a member at the time of his decease, and which continued the business after his death; a release of the defendants from any liability for making such loan, and a request to them not to file or record the mortgages taken as security therefor. At the close of the plaintiff's case the defendants' counsel moved to dismiss the complaint upon the ground that the facts proved did not constitute a cause of action. That motion was in form granted, and an exception was taken by the plaintiff. Subsequently, and after the cause was summed up by the parties, the court, at their request, made findings of fact and conclusions of law, and thereupon directed a judgment dismissing the plaintiff's complaint without costs. In pursuance of that direction, and upon the findings of the court, a judgment was entered dismissing the complaint upon the merits. Afterwards the plaintiff moved at special term for an order to strike out the words "upon the merits" in both the decision and the judgment, which was denied. An appeal was taken from both the judgment and the order to the general term, where they were affirmed. The order, as well as the judgment, is before us for review upon this appeal.

Held, that the judgment and order should be affirmed. As the decision of the trial court on the issues was justified and has been affirmed by the general term, the remaining question to be determined is as to the correctness of the order.   In Place *v.* Hayward (117 *N. Y.* 487, S. C., 27 *St. R.* 710; *rev'g* 55 *Super. Ct.* 208), where the proceedings upon the trial were somewhat similar to those had in this case, it was held that the decision of the referee dismissing the complaint on the defendant's motion was equivalent to a nonsuit; that he could subsequently make no findings of fact, except such as would justify a nonsuit, and that to maintain the judgment which dismissed the complaint upon the merits, the defendant was bound to show that he was entitled to it upon the undisputed evidence, and that there was no disputed material question of fact which, upon a jury trial, a court would have been required to submit to the jury. The doctrine of that case is reaffirmed in the case of Raabe *v.* Squier, 148 *N. Y.* 81.

It may be that the evidence in this case upon the question of fraud was not such as to justify the court in holding as matter of law that there was no proof thereof, and that it presented a question of fact to be determined upon the proof and circumstances developed by the evidence, so that the question whether the decision of the trial court is to be regarded as a nonsuit or as a decision upon the merits becomes important. If the latter, it was clearly justified ; if the former, it may be otherwise. At the conclusion of the evidence, the court not only made and signed findings of fact and conclusions of law, but the plaintiff requested the court to find upon all the issues of fact in the case, and such requests were duly passed upon and judgment subsequently directed in accordance there-with.

Under these circumstances it seems to me that the principle of the decision in the case of Neuberger *v.* Keim (134 *N. Y.* 35; S. C., 45 *St. R.* 394), should be applied, and that the doctrine of that case requires an affirmance of the judgment and order. In that case, after the plaintiff rested, the defendant moved to dismiss the complaint on the ground that the plaintiff had failed to prove facts sufficient to constitute a cause of action. The court refused, but stated that, upon the evidence as it stood, it would not feel justified in finding for the plaintiff. Thereafter both parties prepared findings and submitted them to the court, when the complaint was dismissed upon the merits and the judgment was affirmed by this court.

In this case, as in the one cited, the facts were to be determined by the court. At the close of the plaintiff's evidence, it was satisfied that the plaintiff ought not to succeed, and subsequently, at the request of the parties, it passed upon every question of fact and considered every question of law involved in the case, or submitted to it for its determination. After the plaintiff had procured the court to pass upon thirty-two questions of fact and eight questions of law, I think she should not be permitted to say that this case was not decided upon its merits.

We are of the opinion that the decision was sustained by the evidence, that the court properly refused to amend the judgment and decision by striking out the words " upon the merits," and that both the judgment and order should be affirmed, with costs.

Opinion by MARTIN, J. All concur.

Judgment and order affirmed.

Alfred B. Cruikshank, for the plaintiff, appellant.

Thomas Darlington, for defendant, Robinson, respondent.

William B. Ellison, for defendant, Colwell, respondent.

ARMSTRONG *v.* COMBS.

Supreme Court, Third Department, Appellate Division; March, 1897.

1. *Mortgage; acknowledgment of assignment; notary; disqualification by interest.*] Where an assignment of a mortgage was acknowledged before one of the grantors, who was a notary public, and such assignment was recorded before a prior assignment of the same mortgage was put on record,—*Held,* in an action by one to whom the mortgage had been transferred by such second assignee to foreclose the mortgage, that the acknowledgment was a nullity and did not entitle the assignment to be recorded, and a payment by a subsequent purchaser of the property to the first assignee operated as a full discharge of the mortgage, notwithstanding that the mortgage was not produced when such payment was made.*

---

* In the cases where a notary has been held to be disqualified from taking an acknowledgment or affidavit, the decisions have invariably been on the ground of the interest in some manner of the notary in the event. As will be seen in the cases cited below, mere relationship of the notary to one of the parties, is not enough to disqualify him.

In Lynch *v.* Livingston (6 *N. Y.* 422), the acknowledgment was taken by a commissioner who was a nephew of the grantee's and it was held to be valid.

In Remington Paper Co. *v.* O'Dougherty (81 *N. Y.* 474), it was held that a justice of the peace was not disqualified to take the acknowledgment of his father to a deed conveying property to his wife.

In Griffin *v.* Borst (4 *Wend.* 195), it was held that the fact that the oath of commissioners appointed to admeasure the dower of a widow was taken before the attorney for the widow, was not a valid objection to a motion to confirm the report of the commissioners.

Appeal by the defendant, from a judgment of the Supreme Court, Warren County, in favor of the plaintiff, entered upon the report of a referee in an action brought for the foreclosure of a mortgage.

The mortgage sought to be foreclosed in this action is dated May 10, 1889, was executed by James M. Tucker to Joseph Wood, and duly recorded, May 10, 1889. On March 1, 1890, Joseph Wood assigned and delivered the mortgage and the bond accompanying the same, to Mary Jane Wood for a good and valu-

---

An affidavit will not be allowed to be read in support of a motion if taken before an attorney in the case. Taylor *v.* Hatch, 12 *Johns.* 340 ; Kuh *v.* Barnett, 6 *Supp.* 881 (application for injunction).

But this applies only to an attorney in a pending suit, and an attorney is not disqualified from taking a preliminary affidavit before the commencement of proceedings. Vary *v.* Godfrey, 6 *Cow.* 587 (affidavit for certiorari).

Nor is a counsel in the cause, not being the attorney of record, disqualified from taking an affidavit to be used in proceedings in the case. Willard *v.* Judd, 15 *Johns.* 531 ; People *v.* Spalding, 2 *Paige*, 326.

An affidavit may also be taken before the law partner of an attorney in the case. Hallenback *v.* Whitaker, 17 *Johns.* 2.

An affidavit cannot be taken in replevin before a sheriff or coroner as to the plaintiff's ownership. Berrien *v.* Westervelt, 12 *Wend.* 194.

The sureties in an undertaking for the discharge of an attachment cannot justify before the defendant's attorney. Bliss *v.* Molter, 58 *How. Pr.* 112.

It is provided in 2 R. S. (9th ed.) p. 1842, § 41, that "the recording of an assignment of a mortgage shall not be deemed, in itself, notice of such assignment to a mortgagor, his heirs or personal representatives, so as to invalidate any payment made by them, or either of them, to the mortgagee."

Under this statute it was held in Brewster *v.* Carnes (103 *N. Y.* 556) and in Larned *v.* Donovan (31 *Abb. N. C.* 308 ; s. c., 29 *Supp.* 825) that the recording of an assignment of a mortgage was notice to the purchaser of an equity of redemption in the mortgaged premises.

Armstrong *v.* Combs.

able consideration, the assignment being recorded on
May 15, 1891. On September 10, 1890, Joseph Wood, as
the referee finds, assigned this same bond and mortgage
to Charles P. Coyle and John H. Cunningham, and delivered to them the same with the assignment, the latter being recorded December 24, 1890. On May 7, 1891, Coyle
& Cunningham executed and delivered to the plaintiff,
Mary Jane Armstrong, an assignment of the said bond and
mortgage. This is expressed to be " for a good and valuable consideration to them in hand paid by the said party
of the second part." The bond and mortgage were delivered with the assignment, and the latter was recorded on
May 12, 1891. On April 28, 1891, Tucker, the mortgagor,
conveyed the premises covered by the mortgage to the
defendant, Edward Combs, the latter assuming and agree-
ing to pay the mortgage. The deed to Combs was recorded September 23, 1891. On September 1, 1891,
Combs paid the mortgage to Mary Jane Wood, and took
from her a discharge, which was recorded June 15, 1892.

The question here is whether the payment by Combs
to Mary Jane Wood is available against the plaintiff.
There is evidence tending to show that Coyle & Cunningham, when they took their assignment, knew of the
assignment to Mrs. Wood. The referee, however, does
not pass on this question, but finds that the plaintiff was a
purchaser in good faith and is entitled to protection, as
the assignments from Joseph Wood to Coyle & Cunningham, and from them to the plaintiff, were recorded before
the assignment to Mary Jane Wood. The finding that
the plaintiff is a purchaser for value, without notice, rests
only on presumptions to be drawn from the recital in the
assignment to her. The acknowledgment by Joseph
Wood of the assignment to Coyle & Cunningham was
taken before Mr. Cunningham, one of the assignees, as
notary public. The defendant claims that such an acknowledgment is a nullity, and that, therefore, the assignment was not properly recorded, and, if not, did not give

to Coyle & Cunningham or the plaintiff, their assignee, any priority over the prior assignment to Mrs. Wood.

Held, that such acknowledgment was a nullity and the judgment should be reversed.   We are not referred to any case in this State where the right of a grantee or assignee to take the acknowledgment of the execution of the instrument has been passed upon.   In Goodhue v. Berrian, (2 *Sandf. Ch.* 630) it is said that if the witness sworn by a commissioner of deeds to identify the grantor in a conveyance is the grantee, the certificate of the officer of its due acknowledgment furnishes no proof of its execution. In Lynch v. Livingston (6 *N. Y.* 422) it was held that relationship to the parties did not disqualify an officer from taking the acknowledgment, it being said that the act of taking and certifying the acknowledgment was a ministerial act.   This case was followed in Remington Paper Co. *v.* O'Dougherty, 81 *N. Y.* 474.

In other States the question has been frequently considered, and quite uniformly it has been held that an acknowledgment by the grantor before the grantee is a nullity.   Groesbeck v. Seeley, 13 *Mich.* 330; Laprad *v.* Sherwood, 79 *Id.* 520; Hammers v. Dole, 61 *Ill.* 307; Wilson *v.* Traer & Co., 20 *Iowa* 231 ; City Bank of Boone *v.* Radtke, 87 *Id.* 363; Hubble v. Wright, 23 *Ind.* 322; Bowden v. Parrish, 86 *Va.* 68 ; Wasson *v.* Connor, 54 *Miss.* 351 ; Hogans v. Carruth, 18 *Fla.* 587; *Tiedeman on Real Prop.* § 810; 3 *Washb. on Real Prop.* (4th ed.) 314; 1 *Am. & Eng. Ency. of Law* (2d ed.) 493, and cases cited.

The object of acknowledgment and record is to make title secure and prevent frauds in conveyancing as well as to furnish proof of the due execution of conveyances.   A history of the practice on that subject in this State will be found in Van Cortlandt v. Tozer, 17 *Wend.* 338.   The early acts will be found in 3 *Revised Statutes* (1st ed.) appendix, 5–46.*   It is very plain that when the right to

---

* The first act providing for the recording of deeds was passed on October 30, 1710, which remained in effect until February 16,

Armstrong *v.* Combs.

acknowledge was provided for, it was not contemplated-that the officer could be one of the parties to the instru-ment.   The object of the act and the manner in which it was required to be done were utterly inconsistent with such an idea.   A good deal of the formality has since dis-appeared, but the object remains and the law should be construed in the light of its original object and scope. The statute does not in terms say that a grantee may or may not be the acknowledging officer.   It should not be deemed to give that right without an express provision to that effect.   "A thing within the letter is not within the statute if contrary to the intention of it."   People *v.* Utica Ins. Co., 15 *Johns.* 358 ; Riggs *v.* Palmer, 115 *N. Y.* 506 ; S. C., 23 *Abb. N. C.* 452 ; 26 *St. R.* 198 ; *Smith's Comm. on State Const. Law,* § 701.   It should be held, I think, that the acknowledgment before one of the assignees was a nullity,   He was a party to the record and, therefore, disqualified.

In some cases it is said that if the defect is not appar-ent on the record it may operate as constructive notice. Bank of Benson *v.* Hove, 45 *Minn.* 40.   If not duly acknowledged, it is not properly on record, and if not properly there, it is not constructive notice.   In 4 *Kent's Commentaries,* *174, it is said : "A deed unduly regis-tered, either from want of a valid acknowledgment or otherwise, is not notice according to the prevailing opinion in this country."   See, also, Doe *v.* Roe, 1 *Johns. Cas.* 402 ; 1 *Story's Eq. Juris.* § 404 ; Lemmer *v.* Morison, 89 *Hun,* 277.

If the assignment to Coyle & Cunningham had been

1771.   The act of 1710 provided that the record of any deed which had been duly acknowledged and recorded could be read in evi-dence with the same effect as the original.   The act of 1771 provided that any deed, etc., which was duly acknowledged or proved by a subscribing witness might be read in evidence, etc.   In Van Cort-landt *v.* Tozer, 17 *Wend.* 338, it was held that due acknowledgment under the act of 1710 included the cases where deeds were proved by a subscribing witness.

properly acknowledged and recorded, its priority of record to the assignment to Mary Jane Wood would have been constructive notice to Combs of a prior right. Brewster *v.* Carnes, 103 *N. Y.* 556 ; s. c., 4 *St. R.* 264. As, however, it was not properly recorded, it would not be such notice, and Combs had a right to pay to Mrs. Wood, although the assignment to plaintiff herself was recorded before Mrs. Wood's. Page *v.* Waring, 76 *N. Y.* 463.

It is, however, claimed on the part of the plaintiff, that Combs, in paying Mrs. Wood, without the production and surrender of the bond and mortgage, was guilty of laches, and, therefore, still liable to plaintiff. The assignment to Mrs. Wood was first in time, and is found by the referee to be valid as between the parties. The subsequent attempted transfer by the mortgagee was, therefore, in fraud of the rights of Mrs. Wood. She continued to be the owner and entitled to payment unless the plaintiff, by virtue of the recording act, acquired a better right. Failing in that, the possession of the bond and mortgage through the fraud of the mortgagee, did not, of itself, give the plaintiff any right to demand payment as against Mrs. Wood, the transfer to whom was on record when the payment was made to her. Mrs. Wood, as against the plaintiff, was entitled to payment. The claim of laches is not, we think, made out. Nor is the evidence sufficient to establish an estoppel against Mrs. Wood from claiming payment, by reason of the fact that she did not have possession of the bond and mortgage.

Opinion by MERWIN, J. All concurred.

Judgment reversed, referee discharged, and a new trial granted, costs to the appellant to abide the event.

J. C. Aldrich, for the defendant, appellant.

Charles P. Coyle, and *A. Armstrong, Jr.,* for the plaint. iff, respondent.

BIDWELL *v.* SULLIVAN.

Supreme Court, First Department, Appellate Division; April, 1897.

1. *Notary public; personal acquaintance with person making acknowledgment.*] Evidence tending to show that the notary who took the mortgagor's acknowledgment of the execution of the mortgage, reviewed, and *held*, in foreclosure, sufficient.

2. *The same; general rule.*] The personal acquaintance which the statute requires that a notary public should have with persons making acknowledgments before him, does not mean an acquaintance acquired upon the instant, by means of an introduction, at the time the acknowledgment is taken, but means an acquaintance of such a character and existing for such a length of time as enables the notary to identify the person as the individual described in the instrument to be recorded.* Per VAN BRUNT, P. J.

---

* The opinion of the presiding justice goes somewhat farther than some of the older cases in requiring a notary to identify a party appearing before him to take an acknowledgment. Thus in Wood *v.* Bach (54 *Barb.* 134) it was held that where persons acknowledging the execution of an instrument, although previously unknown to the officer, are introduced to him by a mutual acquaintance, this, if it satisfies the conscience of the officer as to the identity of the parties, is sufficient to authorize him to take the acknowledgment and give the certificate. And the court there said: " Knowledge of persons and their identity is most frequently acquired by introduction through mutual friends, and when such introduction has taken place the parties certainly know each other. Every day, men, in social life, thus become known to each other, and I never heard that such an introduction was not sufficient, or that any length of time after it must elapse, to justify a statement or certificate that they were acquainted. When an introduction does not proceed from such a source as satisfies the officer's conscience, undoubtedly he should not certify that he knows the party, but should require ' evidence ' which, of course, must be an oath ; but when the character of the introducer—whom the officer knows—conveys knowledge to the officer's conscience, he may well be satisfied and may properly give the certificate."

In Rexford *v.* Rexford (7 *Lans.* 6) it was held that where a wife is introduced to the officer taking her acknowledgment to a deed by

Bidwell *v.* Sullivan.

3. *Costs ; extra allowance ; foreclosure.*] In an action to foreclose a mortgage where the trial court finds that it is unreasonably defended, an extra allowance under Code Civ. Pro. § 3253 to plaintiff cannot exceed $200.

Appeal by the defendant from a judgment of the Supreme Court, New York County, in favor of the plaintiff, in an action to foreclose a mortgage, after a trial at Special Term.

This suit was brought by Clara E. Bidwell for the foreclosure of a mortgage covering premises upon which the defendant Maurice J. Sullivan has a subsequent mortgage. Sullivan by his answer put in issue the allegations of the complaint as to the execution, acknowledgement and record of the mortgage. Upon the trial the plaintiff, as part of her proof, put in evidence the record of her mortgage as contained in the register's office in the city and county of New York. From such record it appears that the notary public's certificate of acknowledg-

---

her husband, in the presence of his brother, both known to the officer, there is sufficient ground for his certificate of knowledge of the grantor. The court cited and approved Wood *v.* Bach (*supra*).

See, however, People *v.* Schooley (89 *Hun*, 391), and cases there cited, holding that mere introduction at the time of taking the acknowledgment is not enough to satisfy the requirements of the statute.

The requisites of an acknowledgment as found in 2 R. S. (Banks & Bro. 9th ed.) 1836, §9, are as follows: "No acknowledgment of any conveyance having been executed, shall be taken by any officer, unless the officer taking the same, shall know, or have satisfactory evidence, that the person making such acknowledgment is the individual described in, and who executed such conveyance."

Section 15 provides: "Every officer who shall take the acknowledgment or proof of any conveyance, shall endorse a certificate thereof, signed by himself, on the conveyance ; and in such certificate, shall set forth the matters herein required to be done, known, or proved on such acknowledgment or proof, together with the names of the witnesses examined before such officer, and their places of residence and the substance of the evidence given by them."

ment and the register's certificate of record are in strict compliance with the statute. Section 935 of the Code provides that " a conveyance acknowledged or proved and certified in the manner prescribed by law, to entitle it to be recorded in the county where it is offered, is evidence, without further proof thereof."

By the introduction of the record, therefore, the plaintiff made out a *prima facie* case as to the due execution, acknowledgment and recording of the mortgage. But section 936 of the Code provides that " the certificate of the acknowledgment, or of the proof of a conveyance, or the record, or the transcript of the record, of such a conveyance is not conclusive ; and it may be rebutted and the effect thereof may be contested by a party affected thereby." Under this section, the defendant was at liberty to introduce evidence in support of the issue which he had tendered by his answer, and he attempted to do so. Testimony was adduced tending to show that Clark, the mortgagor, did not know the notary who took the acknowledgment. But the question was whether the notary knew Clark. The notary's testimony conclusively established that he did know him. This assertion is fully warranted by the personal transactions between the notary and Clark prior to the taking of the acknowledgment, which the notary detailed to support his assertion that he knew him when taking the acknowledgment. Mr. McClelland, a notary public, testified that he was appointed referee to sell in a judgment of foreclosure and sale in an action wherein Francis A. Clark, the maker of the mortgage in suit, was the defendant : that the property was sold by McClelland, as referee, on September 17th, 1890, to Francis A. Clark, who was the highest bidder therefor ; and that Clark signed the terms of sale and paid the ten per cent. of the purchase price required to be paid down by giving to McClelland his check for $700, which check McClelland presented for payment and the same was paid. On October 20th, a little over a month later,

McClelland delivered the referee's deed to Clark, who, at about the same time and in the office of the referee, executed the bond and mortgage in question, receiving therefor a check for $18,000 drawn by Clara E. Bidwell, on the National City Bank of New York and payable to the order of Francis A. Clark. This check Clark endorsed " Payable to the order of Charles B. McClelland, referee, Francis A. Clark," and delivered the same to the referee in payment of the balance of the purchase price of the property. Clark was called for the defendant and at first testified that he did not recollect meeting the notary public until the day when the bond and mortgage was executed, and that he was then introduced to him in his office by Clark's attorney. But his cross-examination showed that he was mistaken, for he testified that he was the purchaser of the property at the referee's sale, and that he signed the terms of sale, which was more than thirty days before the time of the execution of the bond and mortgage in suit ; and he was obliged to admit that the notary public was also the referee at the sale and must have been at the sale as well as Clark.

From this testimony it is apparent that the court was right in holding that the defendant had failed to support by evidence the issue which he tendered by his answer. The trial court was, therefore, right in giving judgment to the plaintiff.

The court determined that the action was unreasonably defended by Sullivan, and that by reason thereof the plaintiff was entitled to recover costs, under Code Civ. Pro. § 423, and granted an extra allowance of $500. We agree with the trial court in this determination, except as to the amount of costs. As the action is one to foreclose a mortgage the amount of the extra allowance is regulated by Code Civ. Pro. § 3253, which provides that " the court may also, in its discretion, award to any party a further sum, as follows : 1. In an action to foreclose a mortgage, a sum not exceeding two and one half per centum upon the sum due or claimed to be due on the mortgage, nor the aggregate sum of two hundred dollars."

The judgment should be modified by deducting from the award of costs against Sullivan the sum of three hundred dollars, and as thus modified the judgment should be affirmed, without costs.

Opinion by PARKER, J. RUMSEY, WILLIAMS and PATTERSON, JJ., concur.

VAN BRUNT, P. J.—I concur in the result reached in the opinion of the court. But it seems to me clear that the notary public who took the acknowledgment of the mortgagor had not that personal acquaintance with the latter which is required by the statute in order that he might take an acknowledgment based upon such personal acquaintance. The statute provides a method by which the identity of a party executing an instrument to be acknowledged, can be proven before the notary who takes the acknowledgment; in which case the notary must set out the substance of the evidence produced before him in his certificate.

In the case at bar the notary nowhere swears that he was personally acquainted with the person who executed the mortgage. The mortgagor swears that the only acquaintance that he had with the notary was the result of the introduction at the time of the execution of the mortgage. It is true that the notary swears that the mortgagor signed the terms of sale at the time of the sale under foreclosure referred to in these proceedings; but he nowhere swears that at the time of the taking of the acknowledgment he had any other acquaintance with or recollection of the person who executed the mortgage than that which was sworn to by the mortgagor, namely, an introduction at the time of the execution. This in my judgment is clearly insufficient to justify the notary in certifying as to personal acquaintance. Personal acquaintance does not mean an acquaintance acquired upon the instant. It means an acquaintance of such a character and existing for such a length of time as enables the notary to indentify the person as the individual described in the instrument to be executed.

The mortgage having been actually executed by Clark, the mortgagor, the objections raised were unavailable, although the notary, as is too often the case in instances of this description, violated his duty in taking the acknowledgment in the manner and under the circumstances disclosed by this record.

Judgment modified and as modified affirmed without costs.

Wilson H. Hoover, for the defendant, appellant.

W. W. Thompson, for the plaintiff, respondent.

CLASON *v.* NASSAU FERRY CO.

Supreme Court, First Department, Appellate Term; April, 1897.

Corporations; inspection of books; damages for refusal; expenses of mandamus proceedings.] Under the Stock Corporation Law (*L.* 1892, c. 688, § 29) providing for a penalty of $50 "and all damages resulting," to a stockholder for the refusal of a corporation, or its officers, to allow a stockholder to inspect, and take extracts from, the corporation stock-book, counsel fees and other expenses of maintaining mandamus proceedings, which are not allowed as costs in such proceedings, cannot be recovered as damages in addition to the $50 allowed by the statute.*

---

* When this case was before the court on the mandamus proceedings it was held that a stockholder of a corporation had the right to inspect the stock-book during business hours, with his attorney, or other person having the requisite knowledge to obtain for him the information to which he was entitled. People *ex rel.* Clason *v.* Nassau Ferry Co., 86 *Hun,* 128.

Clason v. Nassau Ferry Co.

Appeal by defendants from an affirmance by the City Court of New York of a judgment in favor of plaintiff, Augustus Clason, entered upon the verdict of a jury.

The action was to recover a penalty of $50 and damages amounting to $513.22 from the defendant corporation and Jarvis C. Howard, its treasurer, under the Stock Corporation Act (*L.* 1892, c. 688, § 29) for refusal to allow plaintiff, a stockholder in said corporation, to inspect its books and make extracts therefrom. The only question upon this appeal is whether a stockholder suing for damages under the above statute can recover the costs and counsel fees of mandamus proceedings by which he compelled the corporation and its officers to allow an inspection of the

In Fenlon v. Dempsey (50 *Hun*, 131) proceedings were instituted for contempt because of the failure of the corporation to produce its stock-book, among other things, pursuant to an order for the examination of such corporation under Code Civ. Pro. §§ 872, 873. The court in granting the order punishing the officers of the corporations included in the fine imposed the sum of $100 as counsel fee. The general term reversed the order as to that item on the ground, however, that this item had not been proved as an element of damages, and the court says that such an item might be allowed under proper proof.

Where contempt proceedings are instituted for a failure to produce the stock-book pursuant to the command of a mandamus there is a presumption that such books have been kept. Fenlon v. Dempsey, 50 *Hun*, 131.

In Martin v. W. J. Johnston Co. (62 *Hun*, 557; aff'd 133 *N. Y.* 692) the applicant made his demand upon the treasurer of the corporation, and it was shown that by a provision of the by-laws of the corporation the stock-book was in the possession of the secretary. It was held that this was not a defense to an application for a mandamus where the refusal by the treasurer to produce the book was not put on that ground and the stockholder was not referred to any other person by him.

. As to the evidence necessary to support a recovery of the penalty provided by this section, see Kelsey v. Pfandler P. F. Co., 20 *St. R.* 533.

As to sufficiency of complaint, see Levy v. Cohn, 45 *St. R.* 278.

books. The trial court allowed the plaintiff $513.22 for the legal expenses of maintaining those proceedings.

Held, error. The current of authorities is against such a recovery, counsel fees and expenses incurred by the plaintiff in the prosecution of one action not being recoverable in another action against the same party, and the statutory costs and allowance awarded a successful party in an action being deemed in law a sufficient indemnity for the prosecution or defense of his right therein. The case is different where a bond is given, upon obtaining an injunction, attachment and the like, to indemnify a defendant against damage from an unfounded prosecution of such remedies. There may be little ground for the distinction since the injured party is as much forced to resort to law by the refusal of his adversary to accord his rights as he is by being compelled to defend an unjust action ; but the courts have invariably made the distinction for a good reason—to diminish the burdens and uncertainty of litigation; and the law may be regarded as settled. Stewart *v*. Sonneborn, 98 *U. S.*, 187 ; Hicks *v*. Foster, 13 *Barb.*, 663 ; Bishop *v*. Hendrick, 82 *Hun*, 323 ; aff'd on opinion below, 146 *N. Y.* 398.

In the case last cited, damages were claimed under the statute which allows a recovery against an executor *de son tort* of all damages caused by his act to the estate of the deceased (2 *R. S.*, 449, §17). It was sought to recover the legal expenses of certain actions and proceedings against the defendant for wrongfully withholding property, resisting proceedings for contempt and actions of interpleader, but it was held that they could not be recovered.

The case of Mattlage *v*. N. Y. Elevated R. R. Co. (17 *Supp*. 537 ; S. C., 44 *St. R.* 289) was referred to in the above opinion, and the ruling of the general term of the common pleas quoted with approval. "We know of no rule of law by which a party can recover from his opponent a counsel fee paid on the argument of an appeal by way of damages over and above those allowed as costs, except by virtue of an express contract, as when a bond of indemnity has been given on procuring an injunction, attachment, etc. In any other case, if a party chooses to pay more than the amount allowed by law as costs, he must do so at his own expense." In an action against one usurping an office, when the statute allows damages sustained in consequence of this usurpation, it has been held that counsel fees and expenses incurred in ousting the defendant from office cannot be recovered in an action for such damages. Palmer v. Darby, 2 *Ohio N. P.*, 410. The statute which awards damages for refusal to permit inspection of books is not broader nor more comprehensive than that which allows the recovery of damages against an executor *de son tort* or against one usurping an office, and it would seem, therefore, that the allowance of damages by statute does not give as broad a right of recovery as is afforded by contracts of indemnity in injunction and attachment bonds.

Legal expenses are as recoverable as damages when incurred in proceedings taken by the injured party to prevent or reduce the damage which he would incur by the continuance of the wrong which he has abated by resort to such proceedings. Expenses incurred to prevent or lessen damages are recoverable as damages. Sutherland on Damages, § 88; Sedgwick on Damages, §§215, 437 and 948; Hoffman v. U. Ferry Co. 68 *N. Y.* 386; Jewelers' Agency v. Rothschild, 6 *App. Div.* 499. The latter case illustrates the rule and its limitations. In an action to punish defendants for contempt in violating an injunction against a certain publication, the expense of a new injunction which the plaintiff had to sue out against a corporation organized by the original defendants, to prevent the continuance of the publication, was included in the fine inflicted upon defendants for disobeying the original injunction. In that case the legal expenses allowed were incurred in an action brought expressly to restrain a continuance of the damage and for no other purpose. The mandamus proceeding of this plaintiff was not instituted with that object, although it might have directly effected it; yet there is no evidence in the case that any continuing damage was thereby prevented. In a general sense most, if not all, legal proceedings are taken with that object or have that result, but I apprehend it is only where the litigation is for the specific purpose, as in the case of injunction, that the rule above referred to will be applied.

The judgment appealed from should be modified by reducing the recovery to $50 and affirmed for that amount, without costs of this appeal or of the general term of the city court to either party.

Opinion by DALY, P. J. MCADAM and BISCHOFF, JJ., concur.

Judgment accordingly.

S. Handford (Shipman, Larocque & Choate, attorneys) for defendants, appellants.

L. Laflin Kellogg, and Alfred C. Pette (Kellogg, Rose & Smith, attorneys), for plaintiff, respondent.

DISHAW v. WADLEIGH.

Supreme Court, Third Department, Appellate Division; March, 1897.

1. *Action for abuse of process; subpœna; attorneys.*] Where it appeared that an attorney entered into an arrangement to have a person take assignments of claims against debtors residing at some distance from the office of the justice of the peace before whom suits were brought upon such claim, and under this ar-

rangement a subpœna was served upon a debtor, with a summons, requiring him to appear as a witness on behalf of the plaintiff, and upon his failure to appear an affidavit was presented stating that he was a material witness for the plaintiff, and he was arrested and fined for disobeying the subpœna, and while he was in court the case was tried and a judgment rendered for the plaintiff, but the defendant was not called as a witness, and it appeared that this proceeding was taken merely to coerce the defendant to pay the debt rather than appear in court at such a distance from his home,—*Held*, that this was such an abuse of the process of the court as rendered the attorney liable for damages.*

2. *Evidence ; parol proof of contents of letter*.] Parol proof of the contents of a letter is not competent, unless it is shown that an effort has been made to produce such letter, and that it cannot be found.

Appeal by the defendant from a judgment of the Supreme Court, St. Lawrence County, in favor of the plaintiff, entered upon the verdict of a jury, for $500, and also from an order denying the defendant's motion for a new trial, made upon the minutes.

The defendant, L. Ogden Wadleigh, is an attorney at law, residing and practicing his profession at Potsdam, St. Lawrence County. Some time in the year 1895 he entered into an arrangement with one Charles M. Woodward, who resided at Gouverneur, St. Lawrence County, about thirty miles distant from Potsdam, by which the defendant was to procure accounts to be assigned to the said Woodward, and then Woodward was to commence suits thereon in his own name as plaintiff in the justice's court at Gouverneur, and at the time of having the summons issued in such actions he was also to take out and have served subpœnas upon the defendants therein. In return for such services Woodward received five dollars from the defendant, who also rendered some services for Woodward in looking after his personal affairs. Woodward paid nothing for the

---

* See Note on Actions for Abuse of Process, following this case.

claims assigned to him, and upon the trial testified that
the reason given to him by the defendant for such pro-
ceedure was " that a large number of those men, if they
were sued there in the town, they would confess judgment,
and that the judgment was not collectible; men that
were able to pay, and would not pay, and by confessing
judgment confessed they owed their account; and that by
bringing them to Gouverneur they would, as a rule, pay
their accounts." Question by the Court: " That is, they
rather pay than come over to Gouverneur, and be subpœnaed to come there?" Answer: " That, as I understand it, is the gist of it." Under this arrangement a
number of actions were commenced in the justice's court
at Gouverneur by Woodward, and subpœnas for each of
the defendants in such actions were taken out. Among
the parties so sued was the plaintiff, Frank W. Dishaw.
He was indebted to a man named Tucker, who appears to
have resided at Potsdam, in the sum of about $20. This
account was assigned to Woodward. The plaintiff resides
in the town of Brasher, about twenty-four miles from
Potsdam, and nearly sixty miles from Gouverneur; several
towns intervening between plaintiff's residence and Gouverneur; the usual route from plaintiff's residence to
Gouverneur being through the village of Potsdam. A
summons and subpœna were served upon the plaintiff.
Both were issued at the same time at the request of the
defendant, returnable September 28, 1895, at 10 o'clock
a.m. To reach Gouverneur at that time the plaintiff
would have been obliged to start the day before. Upon
the return day the plaintiff did not appear. The defendant thereupon made an affidavit in which he swore that
the testimony of the plaintiff was material to the
plaintiff in that action, and upon such affidavit an attachment was issued against the plaintiff, and the suit in the
justice's court adjourned to a future day. A constable
arrested the plaintiff upon such attachment, and brought
him before the justice upon the adjourned day, when he

was fined $1 for his disobedience to the command of the subpœna, and $15.20, the expenses of the attachment—amounting in all to the sum of $16.20; and an execution against his person was issued to collect such fine and costs. At the same time judgment was taken against him upon the claim sued for, the plaintiff in that action and his assignor, Mr. Tucker, being sworn as witnesses; and the plaintiff in this action, although present under the attachment, was not sworn as a witness. While the execution against his person was still in the hands of the constable, unserved, the plaintiff brought this action against the defendant, which resulted in the judgment appealed from.

Held, that the facts proved constituted a good cause of action, but the judgment must be reversed for error in the admission of evidence. This case is somewhat novel in its character; and, owing to its peculiar features, my associates have thought that while this appeal might perhaps be determined upon some of the rulings made upon the trial, yet it would be well to express our opinion upon the question as to whether such an action is maintainable, and also give expression to our views upon the practice indulged in which led to this litigation, and by such expression perhaps relieve the court from resorting to harsher measures to cause a cessation of such practice in this department.

The appellant, as one of the reasons for asking for a reversal of the judgment against him, contends that the facts proved are insufficient to constitute a cause of action. He asserts that every step taken by him was authorized in law. It is true that Tucker had a legal right to assign his account to Woodward; that Woodward had a legal right to bring an action thereon in his own name in the town where he lived. It is true that a party plaintiff has a right to subpœna the defendant as a witness. It is true also that where a witness does not obey a subpœna it is legal to issue an attachment for him, and all these things can be done or advised to be done by an attorney for his client. Still, proceedings that are authorized by law may be made use of for an improper purpose, and acts which separately are legal may be so combined together for an illegal purpose as to constitute a single act that is obnoxious to the law.

The facts here disclose a disreputable method of practice, degrading to an honorable profession, and well calculated to bring the administration of justice into reproach and contempt, and it cannot be upheld or justified under the plea that each step taken was one authorized by law, for "'the law is just and good,' and entitled to the obedience of all, the strong as well as the weak, and cannot sustain the perversion of its process to shield lawlessness and wrong, or permit it to be made the tool of trickery and cunning." Sneeden *v.* Harris, 109 *N. C.* 349.

Here it was sought by trickery and cunning to pervert the processes of the law from their proper use and design, in order to reach a result which it was thought could not be arrived at by the ordinary and legitimate procedure of the courts. The action here under review is not one for false imprisonment, malicious prosecution, or the special action authorized by Code Civ. Pro. § 1900, although it possesses some of the features of each of those actions; it is one I think for an abuse of process, something rarely brought to the attention of the courts, except in connection with actions for false imprisonment or malicious prosecution, but for which a separate action will lie, and the attorney guilty of it may be suspended from practice. Counsel have not referred to, nor have I, after a somewhat careful examination, been able to find any reported case in this State where an attorney has been held liable in damages for an abuse of process, but if such an action can be maintained against any one, there is no reason why an attorney should not be held liable, and many why he should. Here the acts complained of were the direct personal acts of the attorney, not dependent upon any evidence or representation of his client, or of any third person, as

Dishaw *v.* Wadleigh.

in most cases of malicious prosecution or false imprisonment, but wholly instigated and carried on by the attorney.   The action for abuse of process is one well defined
at common law.   *Cooley on Torts,* 199 ; Grainger *v.* Hill,
4 *Bing. N. C.* 212 ; Johnson *v.* Reed, 136 *Mass.* 421 ; Herman *v.* Brookerhoff, 8 *Watts,* 240 ; Antcliff *v.* June, 81
Mich. 477 ; S. C., 45 *N. W.* 1019 ; Sneeden *v.* Harris, 109
N. C. 349, 13 *S. E.* 920 ; Fortman *v.* Rottier, 8 *Ohio St.*
548 ; Brand *v.* Hinchman, 68 *Mich.* 590 ; S. C., 36 *N. W.*
664.

From the evidence in this case the jury could have
found that the defendant caused the subpœna to be issued
for the plaintiff in the action against him in the justice's
court, and the subsequent attachment to be issued against
him, not for the purpose of procuring his attendance, and
securing him as a witness in the case, but for the purpose
of coercing payment of the claim against him, with the
idea, the claim being small, that, rather than submit to the
discomfort, inconvenience and expense of attending court
at so great a distance, he would pay the claim.   A subpœna is for the purpose of compelling the attendance of a
person whom it is desired to use as a witness ; its use for
any other purpose is a perversion and abuse of the process
of the court ; and it seems to me that, within the principle
and cases I have referred to, the action is well brought ;
and if there is no precedent for it in this State, the facts
in this case demonstrate that it is time that one was
made.

But while the action is well brought, it is incumbent
upon the plaintiff to establish his case by proper evidence.
Upon the trial the plaintiff was allowed to prove orally, by
the witness Woodward, the arrangement between the defendant and the witness Woodward for the assignment of
the claim against the plaintiff, and also of other assignments of claims, and of the reasons for making such assignments to Woodward, and why he desired suits to be
brought upon such claims in the village of Gouverneur ;

these arrangements were made and the reasons therefor given by letter. No sufficient foundation was laid for giving secondary evidence. The witness said: " I can't tell where the letter is; don't know where it is; don't think I could find it. I think it has been destroyed, but I am not sure." And again, " I have not been asked to produce those letters here. I have destroyed some of the letters, and some I have not." This evidence does not show that any effort whatever was made to produce the letters, or ascertain that they could not be found. I think it was error to receive such evidence, and error not to have stricken it out upon the defendant's motion. Kearney *v.* Mayor, 92 *N. Y.* 617.

Opinion by HERRICK, J. All concurred, except PARKER, P. J., not sitting.

Judgment and order reversed and a new trial granted, costs to abide the event.

L. Ogden Wadleigh and *William P. Goodelle* for defendant, appellant.

John A. Smith, for plaintiff, respondent.

NOTE ON ACTIONS FOR ABUSE OF PROCESS.

While there is a distinction to be drawn between actions for malicious prosecution and those for abuse of process, in many cases it seems to be a distinction of form rather than of substance. The case in the text is purely an action for abuse of process. But many of such actions are founded upon the fact that the defendant has used the process of the court in an action in which he had no reasonable or probable ground on which to proceed or to hope eventually to succeed in the action. These, of course, are the essential features of an action for malicious prosecution, and in such cases the form of the action appears to be

optional with the plaintiff. While a remedy is still afforded
for the malicious prosecution of a civil suit the law applicable to such cases has been to a great extent modified by
the statutes allowing costs to a successful litigant, it being
presumed that such costs are an adequate compensation in
most cases for defending an action which has no foundation on which the plaintiff has a reasonable or probable
hope of success. As was said in Closson *v.* Staples, 42 *Vt.*
217 : " The early English cases show very clearly that
before the statutes entitling defendants to costs existed,
they had a remedy at common law for injuries sustained
by reason of suits which were malicious and without
probable cause. It would seem, however, from more
recent decisions, that the present English rule, which
restricts or limits the right of action for maliciously prosecuting civil suits without probable cause, stands mainly
upon the ground that the costs, which the statute provides
that the successful defendant shall recover, are an adequate
compensation for the damages he sustains ; but, under this
rule, it does not appear that the right of action is restricted to those cases when the process is by attachment. . . . The principle of the common law recognized
by the English courts before the statutes, allowing costs to
defendants, and which gave a remedy for injuries sustained
by reason of suits which were malicious and without probable cause, is and ought to be operative still, and we think
it affords a remedy in all such cases where the taxation of
costs is not an adequate compensation for the damages sustained. . . . But where the damages sustained by a defendant, in defending a suit maliciously prosecuted, without
reasonable or probable cause, exceed the costs obtained by
him, he has, and of right should have, a remedy by action
on the case."

Practically the same doctrine is announced in Millard *v.*
Holmes, Booth & Hayden, (142 *N. Y.* 492) where it is
said : " The general rule at common law that an ordinary
action, maliciously brought and without probable cause,
which had terminated in favor of the defendant, gave rise
to a right of action, certainly seems to have disappeared in
England with the enactment of statutes giving costs to successful defendants. . . . In this country the authorities are
not agreed upon the doctrine governing such actions. . . .
But I am prepared to assume that there may be satisfactory
authority for holding that where a party has been subjected
to some special, or added, grievance, as by an interference
with his person, or property, in a civil action, brought without probable cause, he may maintain a subsequent action

to recover any legal damages which he avers, and may be able to show, to have been occasioned to him. . . . The action generally is not to be viewed with any favor ; for, in the theory of the law, the costs awarded by the statute to the successful defendant are an adequate compensation to him for all damages."

That case involved a large amount, was argued by able counsel, was carefully considered and the opinion, by GRAY. J., was concurred in by all the justices of the Court of Appeals. In the original suit an attachment had been issued, but upon the trial a judgment was recovered by the defendant there, who was the plaintiff in the case cited. In the action for malicious prosecution it was admitted that the plaintiff had suffered serious pecuniary damages by reason of the former action, but the Court of Appeals reversed a judgment in his favor, on the ground that it was not shown that the defendant had proceeded in the former action without reasonable or probable cause.

In further considering the grounds for an action for abuse of process, although founded upon the fact that the action in which the process issued was maliciously brought, without reasonable or probable cause, it is to be observed that a prerequisite to the issuance of the ordinary process where the most injury might be done to the defendant, such as arrest, attachment, replevin, injunction, etc., is the giving of an undertaking to indemnify the defendant if it eventually appear that the plaintiff was not entitled to the remedy which he obtained by the process. This is by way of damages in addition to the regular costs provided for by statute to the successful litigant, and doubtless, does away with many actions which might otherwise be brought for abuse of process.

The law seems to have been well settled in this State by the case of People v. Warren, 5 *Hill*, 440, which is still frequently cited as an authority that an action would not lie against an officer for any of the actions growing out of an abuse of process such as false arrest, etc., where the process is regular on its face and appeared to have been issued by a court of competent jurisdiction, although the officer had knowledge of facts which rendered the process void. The same rule of law is applied by the courts of Massachusetts. O'Shaughnessy v. Baxter, 121 *Mass.* 515. The courts of other States have held otherwise. Grace v. Mitchell, 31 *Wis.* 545 ; Leachman v. Dougherty, 81 *Ill.* 324 ; Sumner v. Beeler, 50 *Ind.* 341.

In People v. Warren (*supra*) the defendant was convicted of an assault and battery upon a constable who arrested him on a warrant issued by the inspectors of election of the City of Utica, for interrupting the proceedings of the election, by disorderly conduct, in the presence of the inspectors. The defendant offered to prove that he had not been in the presence or hearing of the inspectors at any time during the election, and that the constable knew it. The court excluded the evidence, on the ground that it was immaterial, and that although the inspectors had no jurisdiction of the subject-matter the warrant was regular on its face and the officer was protected by it.

This case is cited with approval in Woolsey v. Morris (96 *N. Y.* 312, 316), where a warrant was executed for taxes which had already been paid, but it was held that the officer was protected. See also Hart v. Dubois, 20 *Wend.* 236 ; Bullymore v. Cooper, 46 *N. Y.* 236, 243 ; Bovee v. King, 11 *Hun*, 250 ; Arrex v. Brodhead, 19 *Id.* 269 ; Noble v. Holmes, 5 *Hill*, 194 ; Webber v. Gay, 24 *Wend.* 485 ; Clearwater v. Brill, 4 *Hun*, 728 ; Smith v. Warden, *Id.* 787 ; Field v. Parker, *Id.* 342.

In several of the cases cited above it is pointed out that the remedy in such a case is against the one who put the officer in motion by placing the invalid process in his hands for execution.

In Smith v. Smith (20 *Hun*, 555), it was held in an opinion written by BRADY, J., and concurred in by DAVIS, P. J., that a complaint which alleged the malicious filing of a notice of lis pendens stated a cause of action for an unlawful abuse of the process of the court. Upon reargument of the same case, in an opinion written by DANIELS, J., and concurred in by DAVIS, P. J. (26 *Hun*, 573), the former decision was reversed and it was held that statements contained in the notice of lis pendens were absolutely privileged and did not create a right of action, although falsely and maliciously made ; that although in form the action was for abuse of process it could not be maintained without an allegation in the complaint that the action in which the notice of lis pendens was filed was brought without reasonable or probable cause. BRADY. J., dissented from this opinion.

In Hazard v. Harding, 63 *How. Pr.* 326, it was held that an action would lie for the abuse of legal process without proof of want of probable cause.

In Brown v. Feeter (7 *Wend.* 301), it was held that an action could be maintained for taking out an execution on a judgment which had been paid, and placing it in the hands of the proper officer who made a levy and sale under it, and it was not necessary that malice should be alleged or proved ; all that was necessary to be shown was that the act was wrongfully and wilfully done.

In Bebinger *v.* Sweet (1 *Abb. N. C.* 263), it was held that in an action for malicious abuse of process it is not necessary to allege a termination of the suit in which the process was issued.

There are many cases holding that where an officer executes process which is void on its face he is liable for trespass. Westfall *v.* Preston, 49 *N. Y.* 349 ; Brown *v.* Feeter, 7 *Wend.* 301.

In Kerr *v.* Mount (28 *N. Y.* 659), it was held that one who sets in motion void process is *prima facie* a trespasser and liable to the party against whom it is issued for damages done to the property seized by the sheriff while in his possession. See also Newberry *v.* Lee, 3 *Hill,* 523.

The case of Rogers *v.* Brewster (5 *Johns.* 125), illustrates the principle of malicious abuse of process by an officer, even where the process is perfectly regular on its face and is so in fact. In that case a constable received a warrant to collect a military fine. Upon the trial it was proved that when he received the warrant from the president of the court martial he said he would collect it in such a manner that the plaintiff would remember it, and that he would take the property nearest his heart ; that when he called upon the plaintiff he set his eye on a horse, as he thought the taking of it would most touch the plaintiff's feelings ; that when he took the horse the plaintiff showed him six or seven large swine and requested the defendant to take them and leave the horse ; but the defendant replied that he would take that which would most touch the feelings of the plaintiff. Upon this state of facts a verdict for the plaintiff was affirmed and the court remarked : " The constable appears to have executed the warrant in an unreasonable and oppressive manner, and with the avowed and malicious design to vex and oppress the plaintiff below. When the oppression and malice are thus charged as the gist of the action, and are clearly made out, an action on the case will lie."

In Baldwin *v.* Weed (17 *Wend.* 224), it appeared that the defendant caused the arrest of the plaintiff on a charge of defrauding certain persons ; that when the plaintiff was arrested and brought to this State the defendant caused the plaintiff to be fettered and manacled with irons and chains, and thus to be transported from Crown Point to Ballston. It also appeared that the sole object of the proceeding on the part of defendant was to secure two small debts amounting together to less than $100 ; that the plaintiff to obtain his liberation from prison, executed a bond to the defendant for the delivery of property and payment of money to the amount of $700, and the defendant then procured bail for the plaintiff, and promised that he would not appear as a witness against him, and would use his influence to have the prosecution dropped. The court there said that these facts constituted a good cause of action for a malicious abuse of process. See also Cantine *v.* Clark, 41 *Barb.* 629.

In McDonald *v.* Neilson (2 *Cow.* 139), it was held that where a party, whose personal property has been seized under an execution against him, and a sale of it is forced, with great vigor and oppression, and at enormous sacrifice, by the deputy sheriff acting in concert with the creditor, who is the chief bidder at the sale, is induced in order to avoid the sacrifice of the whole property, to yield to the demands of the creditor, and to give him a bond and mortgage for a large sum of money, so as to cover not only the amount of the execution, but also debts due from a son of the debtor who is insolvent, the sale will be declared oppressive and illegal by a court of equity.

In Grunberg *v.* Grant (3 *Misc.* 230), it was held that a sheriff intentionally taking property not authorized to be taken by a warrant of attachment, is liable as a trespasser *ab initio* for all the consequences of his unlawful entry and seizure.

In Hergman *v.* Dettleback (11 *How. Pr.* 46), a deputy sheriff acting under a warrant of attachment seized certain papers to which he had no right, and it was held that it was a gross abuse of power for the deputy to take copies and extracts from them.

In Allen *v.* Crofoot (5 *Wend.* 505), it was held that where authority is given by law to a person to enter a house and the party abuses the license thus obtained he will be considered a trespasser *ab initio*.

In Carnrick *v.* Myers (14 *Barb.* 9), it was held that a sale after sunset of goods seized on execution by a sheriff, was void, and rendered the officer liable for trespass *ab initio*.

KELLOGG *v.* MAYOR, etc., of N. Y.

Supreme Court, First Department, Appellate Division;
March, 1897.

Negligence; what is action for personal injuries; loss of service;
action against city; filing claim.] An action by a husband for
the loss of his wife's services, through the negligence of defendant, is an action for personal injuries within *L.* 1886, c. 572,
providing that such an action shall not be maintained against
a municipal corporation unless commenced within one year,
and notice of intention to sue filed within six months after the
cause of action occurred.*

---

* It would appear from the cases cited below, that where special
laws pertaining to the subject of the giving of notice to a municipal
corporation before bringing an action against it for personal injuries resulting from negligence, unless such laws cover the whole
subject and are inconsistent with the general act on the subject (*L.*
1886, c. 572) both the special and the general laws must be complied
with. Where both laws require the giving of a notice to a certain
officer of the municipality it does not appear to be necessary to give
two notices to him, but the one served must contain all that is required by both the general and special laws. See particularly
Walsh *v.* City of Buffalo, 92 *Hun*, 438 ; Curry *v.* Same, 135 *N. Y.*
366.

Where the charter of the City of Buffalo (*L.* 1891, c. 105) provided for a notice to the city clerk of a claim for injuries resulting
from negligence or a wrong, stating the time and place of the acts
about which complaint was made; that an action could not be
maintained until the expiration of forty days after the presentation
of such notice ; that such an action must be begun within a year
from the time the cause of action occurred, and further that a different notice must be given to the corporation counsel within six
months from the time the cause of action occurred, of an intention
to bring suit thereon, and the charter contained a provision that
" all acts and parts of acts inconsistent with this act are hereby repealed," it was held that this act did not repeal the provisions of the
general law as to municipal corporations, (*L.* 1886, c. 572), but that
the two acts were *in pari materia,* and it was still necessary to
specify in the notice to the corporation counsel the time when and

Kellogg *v.* Mayor, etc. of N. Y.

Motion by the defendant, for a new trial upon a case containing exceptions, ordered to be heard at the Appellate Division in the first instance, pursuant to Code Civ. Pro.

the place where the injury occurred, under the provision of the general law.   Walsh *v.* City of Buffalo, 92 *Hun*, 438.

An action against the City of New York for negligence, or for damages caused by a nuisance suffered to exist through its negligence, cannot be maintained by a compliance with §§ 123, 1104 of the New York City Consolidation Act, requiring the presentment of an account or claim against the city and the commencement of an action within thirty days thereafter, unless there is a compliance also with the provisions of *L.* 1886, c. 572.   Kelly *v.* Mayor, etc., of N. Y., 19 *Misc.* 257.

Where a city charter provided that no action should be brought against the city for a claim founded upon a contract, until a reasonable time had elapsed after the presentation of such claim, and there was another provision to the effect that claims arising from negligence must be presented with a statement of the time and place of the happening of the accident, within three months after it occurred,—*Held*, that the provision as to contracts did not affect the right to sue for personal injuries caused by negligence at any time after the presentation of the proper claim and notice.   Jones *v.* City of Albany, 151 *N. Y.* 223 ; LaFlamme *v.* Same, 91 *Hun*, 65 ; s. c., 36 *Supp.* 686.

In Lewis *v.* City of Syracuse (13 *App. Div.* 587) it was held that *L.* 1886, c. 572, which provides that actions for personal injuries resulting from negligence, against cities having over 50,000 inhabitants, shall be commenced within one year after the cause of action accrues, did not operate to repeal or amend a special act applicable to the City of Syracuse alone (*L.* 1885, c. 26) which provided a different limitation for such actions.   To the same effect is Moriarty *v.* City of Albany, 8 *App. Div.* 118.

Under the act of 1886 (*L.* 1886, c. 572) the commencement of an action cannot be considered such notice as is required by the statute.   Curry *v.* City of Buffalo, 135 *N. Y.* 366.

A claim against a municipal corporation must be made by one who at least claims authority to act for the claimant to authorize the recovery of costs under Code Civ. Pro. § 3245, providing that in an action against a municipal corporation costs cannot be awarded to the plaintiff unless the claim has been duly presented to the city before the commencement of the action.   Spaulding *v.* Village of Waverly, 12 *App. Div.* 594 ; s. c., 44 *Supp.* 112.

§ 1,000, upon the verdict of a jury rendered at a Trial Term of the Supreme Court, New York County.

The action was brought by Edwin C. Kellogg to recover for the loss of the services of his wife, occasioned by injuries received by her, alleged to have been caused by the negligence of the defendant, and also to recover for expenses incurred for medicines, medical attendance, care and nursing of the wife rendered necessary by such injuries so caused. The injuries were received on March 26, 1891. The action was commenced December 11, 1893. There was never any notice of intention to commence the action served upon the counsel to the corporation. The answer set up the one-year statute of limitations and the failure to serve such notice of intention to commence action, and called attention to the provisions of *L.* 1886, c. 572, providing: Section 1. " No action against the mayor, aldermen and commonalty . . . for damages for personal injuries alleged to have been sustained by reason of the negligence of such mayor, aldermen and commonalty . . . shall be maintained unless the same shall be commenced within one year after the cause of action therefor shall have accrued, nor unless notice of the intention to commence such action, and of the time and place at which the injuries were received, shall have been filed with the counsel to the corporation, or other proper law officer thereof, within six months after such cause of action shall have accrued."

Held, that the action is for damages for personal injuries sustained by reason of negligence of the defendant within the provision of this statute, and is not an action to recover for an injury to a property right. Whatever the courts may have written in other cases, the court of appeals in Maxson *v.* Delaware & L. R. R. Co. (112 *N. Y.* 561 ; S. C. 21 *St. R.* 767; rev'g 48 *Hun,* 172) made it quite clear that such an action as this was an action for damages for personal injuries. That was an action. like this for loss of services of the wife, etc., by reason of personal injuries to her caused by the negligence of the defendant. The defense was the three years' statute of limitations, under Code Civ. Pro. § 383, subd. 5, which reads as follows: 5. "An action to recover damages for a personal injury resulting from negligence." It was held that this provision of the Code applied to the case in hand, and to every case where the action was founded on the fact of an injury to a person, accompanied by negligence, whether the person was that of the plaintiff or of any other individual, for whose injury the plaintiff was entitled to bring the action.

The language of the act in question is not materially different from that of the three years' statute in the Code considered in the case above cited. In both, the action is for damages for " a personal injury."

In Curry *v.* City of Buffalo (135 *N. Y.* 366) it was held that a compliance with the provisions of the statute in question, as to the service of the notice, was a condition precedent to the right to bring the action, and the commencement of the action could not be regarded as such notice. It was held in that case that the action could not be maintained in the absence of such notice, and we must decide in the same way here.

Opinion by WILLIAMS, J. VAN BRUNT, P. J., PATTERSON, O'BRIEN, and INGRAHAM, JJ., concurred.

Exceptions sustained, and motion for new trial granted, with costs to defendant to abide event.

L. J. Morrison, for the plaintiff.

Robert C. Beatty and *Francis M. Scott,* for the defendant.

MISSANO *v.* MAYOR, ETC., OF N. Y.

*Supreme Court, Appellate Division, First Department;
May,* 1897.

*Action against city for negligence ; notice of intention to sue, how
filed.*] Under *L.* 1886, C. 572, § 1,—requiring the filing with the
"counsel to the corporation, or other proper law officer" of
certain cities notice of intention to sue for personal injuries
from negligence,—the notice must be filed with the counsel to
the corporation by the plaintiff or on his behalf, and if filed by
him merely with the comptroller, and by the latter of his own
motion sent to the corporation counsel, this is not a compliance
with the statute.[*]

Appeal by the defendant, from a judgment of the
Supreme Court in favor of the plaintiffs, entered upon the
verdict of a jury, and also from an order denying the defendant's motion for a new trial made upon the minutes.

Action by Pasquale Missano and another as administrators, etc., of Rosina Missano, deceased, to recover damages for the death of the plaintiff's intestate, alleged to
have been caused by the negligence of the defendant.

By Section 1 of *L.* 1886, c. 572, it is provided : " No
action against the mayor, aldermen and commonalty of
any city in this State having fifty thousand inhabitants or
over, for damages for personal injuries alleged to have
been sustained by reason of the negligence of such mayor,
aldermen and commonalty . - . shall be maintained
unless . . . notice of the intention to commence such
action, and of the time and place at which the injuries

---

[*] See the preceding case, Kellogg *v.* Mayor, etc., of N. Y., that
an action for loss of services from negligence is an action for personal injuries within this statute.

See Spaulding *v.* Village of Waverly, 12 *App. Div.* 594 ; s. c., 44
Supp. 112.

were received, shall have been filed with the counsel to the corporation, or other proper law officer thereof, within six months after such cause of action shall have accrued." The injuries resulting in death were received September 23, 1894. October 4, 1894, there was delivered to the comptroller of the city of New York by the plaintiffs a notice, signed by the plaintiffs, bearing date October 2, 1894, and addressed to the comptroller, in which they stated that, in compliance with section 1104 of the Consolidation Act (*L.* 1882, c. 410), they served the comptroller with notice of their intention to begin the action, and then stated the time and place at which the injuries were received.

Thereafter, and on October 9, 1894, the comptroller sent this notice to the office of the corporation counsel, accompanied with a letter signed by the comptroller, dated October 8, 1894, addressed to the corporation counsel, in which it was said: " Herewith I enclose for your consideration notice filed here on the 4th inst. by Pasquale Missano, etc., Administrator of the estate of Rosina Missano, of intention to sue." This letter and the notice accompanying it were received by the corporation counsel and marked received in his office October 9, 1894. No other notice of intention to commence the action was filed with the corporation counsel in attempted compliance with the statute above quoted. Thereafter, and on January 16, 1895, the comptroller served a notice upon the plaintiffs, dated that day and signed by him, wherein he quoted from the provision of section 123 of the Consolidation Act, and stated that, in accordance with the power thus conferred upon the comptroller, he thereby required them to appear and be sworn before him, at the office of the corporation counsel, to answer orally as to any facts relative to the justness of the account or claim presented October, 1894, and that the assistant corporation counsel would take the examination. Pursuant to this notice the plaintiffs did appear and were examined by the corporation counsel. Upon these facts appearing the court held that the notice of an intention to commence the action was filed with the corporation counsel, as required by the statute above quoted, and the defendant excepted.

Held, that there has been no sufficient compliance with the act of 1886. It has been held that compliance with the provisions of this statute is a condition precedent to the maintenance of the action (Curry *v.* City of Buffalo, 135 *N. Y.* 366; s. c., 48 *St. R.* 482; Foley *v.* Mayor, 1 *App. Div.* 586; s. c., 73 *St. R.* 187; 37 *Supp.* 465); that notice, under the Consolidation Act, served upon the comptroller cannot be held to be a compliance with this statute (Babcock *v.* Mayor, 56 *Hun*, 196; s. c., 24 *Abb. N. C.* 276; 31 *St. R.* 110; 9 *Supp.* 368); that the commencement of an action is not a compliance with the statute (Curry *v.* City of Buffalo, *supra*), and that the notice cannot be a verbal one, but must be written. Foley *v.* Mayor, *supra*.

In this case, however, although the notice was stated to be pursuant to the provisions of the Consolidation Act, it was sufficient in other respects to comply with the statute in question; and, although it was not filed by plaintiffs with the corporation counsel, but was served upon the comptroller, it, nevertheless, came into the custody of the corporation counsel, and remained there. The comptroller sent it to the corporation counsel. The only question is, whether this was a substantial compliance with the statute. We are not inclined to relax the rule that the statute must be strictly complied with. It in effect required a filing of the notice by the plaintiffs with the corporation counsel. Another notice was required by the provisions of the Consolidation Act to be served upon the comptroller, and compliance with one of these statutes would not excuse plaintiffs from complying with the provisions of the other. The statutes were not inconsistent. The delivery of the notice in question to the comptroller was not a compliance with the act in question. If com-

Missano *v.* Mayor, etc., of New York.

plied with at all, it must have been when, by the act of the comptroller, the notice was sent to the corporation counsel, and was received and retained by him.

It seems to us, however, that in order to comply with the statute the notice must have been filed with the corporation counsel by the plaintiffs themselves, or in their behalf by their duly authorized agent. They never authorized the comptroller to send the notice to the corporation counsel. They never expected or intended he should do so. He did not assume to act as their agent in doing so. The notice was served upon the comptroller, was intended for him, and for no one else. The act of the plaintiffs was completed when they delivered the notice, or caused it to be delivered, to the comptroller. The comptroller, in doing what he did, acted of his own volition, and the act was his, and was not his act as agent for, or in behalf of, the plaintiffs. Finding the notice in his hands, and thinking the corporation counsel should know of it, he sent it to him, as he stated in his letter, for his consideration. The plaintiffs never complied with the provision of the statute by filing a notice of intention to commence the action with the corporation counsel.

Our conclusion is that there was for this reason no right to maintain the action. It should have been dismissed by the trial court, and the refusal so to do was error for which the judgment should be reversed. No new trial is necessary. The complaint should be dismissed, the judgment and order reversed, with costs of this appeal, and complaint dismissed, with costs.

Opinion by WILLIAMS, J. VAN BRUNT, P. J., and RUMSEY, J., concurred ; PATTERSON and PARKER, JJ., dissented.

Judgment and order reversed, with costs of this appeal, and complaint dismissed, with costs.

Theodore Connoly, for the defendant, appellant.

M. P. O'Connor, for the plaintiffs, respondents.

SHARP v. CLAPP.

Supreme Court, First Department, Appellate Division; March, 1897.

Summons ; with notice ; complaint in tort.] Where a summons served contained a notice, under Code Civ. Pro., § 419, that in case of the defendant's default judgment would be taken for $2,800, and upon the defendant's appearance, a complaint was served in an action for conversion,—*Held,* that the notice did not preclude the plaintiff from setting up any cause of action he saw fit, and that it was error to strike out the complaint upon the ground that it did not conform to the summons. *

Appeal by the plaintiffs, from an order of the Supreme Court, New York Special Term, granting the defendants' motion to strike out the complaint herein, upon the

---

* In Cassidy v. Boyland (15 *Civ. Pro. R.* 320 ; S. C., 3 *Supp.* 258) it was held that the court had power to make an order amending a notice on a summons, but only after notice to the defendant.

In Curry v. Wiborn (12 *App. Div.* 1) the plaintiff had previously begun another action by the service of a summons only and nothing further had ever been done in that action. The defendant set up as a defense to the second action the pendency of the former action and offered to prove by the plaintiff and her attorney that the first action was for precisely the same cause of action as the second. The court excluded the evidence on the ground that the plaintiff could set up any cause of action which she pleased in the first action and a complaint not having been served the cause of action could not be proved by parol.

To the same effect are Phelps v. Gee, 29 *Hun,* 202 ; Hoag v. Weston, 10 *Civ. Pro. R.* 92.

In Gardner v. Clark (21 *N. Y.* 399), it was held, under the old practice, that the issuance and service of a *capias* containing what was called an *ac aetiam* clause, that is, a clause stating in general terms the nature and form of the action, but where no declaration had ever been filed, could not be successfully pleaded as a bar to a subsequent action between the parties, as the plaintiff was at liberty to declare in such form and for such cause of action as he saw fit.

Sharp *v.* Clapp.

ground that it did not conform to the summons and notice.

The action was begun by William W. Sharp and another, against Ozro W. Clapp and another, by the service of summons, attached to which was a notice addressed to the defendants, that, upon their default to appear and answer the summons, a judgment would be taken against them for the sum of $2,800, with interest thereon and costs. The defendants did appear and demanded a copy of the complaint, whereupon there was served upon them a complaint setting out a cause for action for conversion, upon which the damages alleged were $2,800, and for which damages judgment in that sum was asked. Thereupon a motion was made by the defendants to set aside the complaint, for the reason that it did not conform to the summons and notice, in that the nature of the action set forth in the summons and the notice was one on contract, and the complaint was one for conversion. That motion was granted by the special term, upon the authority, as is stated in the opinion, of the case of Adams *v.* Arkenburgh, 106 *N. Y.* 615; rev'g 42 *Hun*, 278.

Held, error. We do not think that the case cited is any authority for the order made. In that case an action has been begun by a summons with which a notice had been served in the form prescribed by section 419 of the Code, as was done in this case. The notice was to the effect that in default of an appearance or answer, judgment would be taken against the defendant for a sum of money therein stated. The action was in fact for the dissolution of a partnership between the parties and the taking of an account. The defendants succeeded in the action and, upon motion, an extra allowance of costs was granted to them, based upon the sum of $65,000, which was the amount stated in the notice for which judgment would be taken. The plaintiff objected to the consideration of the notice as proof of the amount involved in the action;

and the only question was, whether or not the notice of the plaintiff thus served upon the defendant, was properly considered as evidence of the amount involved upon which the court was at liberty to act in fixing the extra allowance. It was held that this notice operated as an admission on the part of the plaintiff that the amount involved in the action was the sum stated in it, and that it was sufficient for the court to act upon, and that the plaintiff was not at liberty to say that the notice did not truly state the amount which he would be entitled to recover in case he succeeded in the action. But the principle laid down in that case is not in any way applicable to the case at bar. The form of the summons is prescribed by section 418 of the Code of Civil Procedure. One form is prescribed for use in all actions, and when the defendant has been brought into court by the service of that summons the plaintiff is at liberty to set up against him any cause of action which he may see fit. Curry *v.* Wiborn, 12 *App. Div.* 1. His right in this respect is unlimited except so far as it is controlled by the necessity of bringing the proper parties into court. But unless he has served a complaint with his summons, he cannot take judgment by default without application to the court unless he has complied with the provisions of section 419 of the Code. Those provisions are that he shall not take judgment by default without application to the court if a copy of the complaint is not served, unless the defendant appears, or a notice is served with the summons stating the sum of money for which judgment will be taken, and the case is one embraced in section 420. The only effect of the notice, therefore, is to permit the plaintiff to take judgment for the sum stated in it in a proper case, and to limit the amount of his claim in case the defendant does not appear. The law prescribes no other effect to this notice. If the plaintiff should attempt to take judgment without the appearance of the defendant he is not saved from the necessity of applying to the court unless his action is one

Sharp *v.* Clapp.

of those mentioned in section 420 of the Code.   This is so whether he has served a notice or not.   If the action is brought for any other cause than one of those mentioned in section 420, the notice is entirely useless, except, perhaps, it may be sufficient to limit the amount of the plaintiff's recovery, but if the defendant appears the notice at once is rendered of no importance.   No judgment can be taken against the defendant then until a complaint has been served upon him, and his liability and the rights of the plaintiff are measured entirely by the allegations of the complaint.   Unless he is in some way misled, the fact that a notice has been served with the complaint can be of no possible importance, because he knows that, whatever may be the notice, the cause of action is contained in the complaint which is served upon him.   It is difficult to see how he could be misled in such a case, after he has appeared and received a copy of the complaint.   There is no reason, therefore, why the complaint, even though notice was served with the summons, should set up any particular cause of action.   There is no provision in the Code requiring it, and it is not apparent how any harm could come to the defendant from insisting upon it.   It cannot be said to be in any respect an irregularity to serve such a complaint as this, although a notice was served with the summons.

Opinion by RUMSEY, J.   VAN BRUNT, P. J., PATTERson, O'BRIEN and INGRAHAM, JJ., concurred.

Order reversed, with ten dollars costs and disbursements, and motion denied, with ten dollars costs.

Eugene D. Hawkins, for the plaintiffs, appellants.

B. P. Stratton, for the defendants, respondents.

UHLFELDER *v.* TAMSEN.

Supreme Court, First Department, Appellate Division;
March, 1897.

Parties; right to be made party defendant.] Under Code Civ. Pro.
§ 452, where a person, not a party to an action, has an interest
in the subject thereof, or in real property, the title to which
may in any manner be affected by the judgment, he has an absolute right to be made a party defendant therein on his own
motion without imposing any conditions upon him, and a condition requiring security for costs is properly stricken out on
appeal.*

---

* The case in the text holds, in effect, that, under Code Civ.
Pro. § 452, where a person not a party to an action has an interest in
the subject thereof, he has an absolute right to be made a party
defendant, upon his own motion, without conditions being imposed
upon him. Under this decision the question to be determined,
therefore, upon such applications, is, whether or not the applicant
has such an interest in the subject of the action as comes within the
meaning of the statute.

Where one member of a firm transferred all his property to
another member under an agreement that he should pay the firm
debts and then divide the net proceeds between the parties to the
agreement, according to the terms thereof, and the liquidating partner died before completing the transactions, it was held that one of
the children of the deceased partner should be made a party to an
action brought by the surviving partner against the executors and
trustees of the deceased partner, for an accounting of the partnership property so turned over, to enable such child to protect his interests in the estate. Haas *v.* Craighead, 19 *Hun,* 396.

In Rosenberg *v.* Salomon (144 *N. Y.* 92) a third person claiming
title to property which had been seized by the sheriff on execution
brought an action in replevin against the sheriff, and the judgment
debtor, whose property had been seized was allowed to come in
and defend the replevin suit.

To the same effect is Rosenberg *v.* Flack, 10 *Supp.* 759.

In an action for the foreclosure of a mortgage one who holds a
deed made before the action is begun, but not recorded until after

Uhlfelder *v.* Tamsen.

Appeal by the petitioners, Daniel Lenobel and Jacob Cohen, from an order of the Appellate Term of the Supreme Court, reversing an order of the General Term

the filing of the notice of lis pendens, has an absolute right to be made a party defendant on his own motion.   Johnston *v.* Donvan, 106 *N. Y.* 269.

In Lawton *v.* Lawton, (54 *Hun*, 415), it was held that a party who had a substantial interest in the subject of an action to foreclose a mortgage had an absolute right to be made a party thereto and that it was improper to impose as conditions that the applicant pay the referee appointed to sell the mortgaged premises his fees, file a bond to pay costs, and consent to try the case before a referee on short notice.

In Earl *v.* Hart, (20 *Hun*, 75), it was held that while a person who is interested in real property, the title to which is sought to be affected by a pending action, has an absolute right to be made a party to the action, on his own motion, if he had such interest at the time of the filing of the notice of lis pendens, yet if his interest was acquired after the filing of such notice it rests in the sound discretion of the court whether or not he shall be made a party.

See also Ladd *v.* Stevenson, 112 *N. Y.* 325.

In Strowbridge Lithographic Co. *v.* Crane, (20 *Civ. Pro. R.* 15 ; s. c., 12 *Supp.* 834), in an action to restrain the defendant from working for a third party by reason of a restrictive contract which the defendant was alleged to have made with the plaintiff, it was held that such third party had an interest in the action which entitled it to be made a party defendant in the action upon its own motion.

In People *v.* Albany & Vermont R. R. Co. (77 *N. Y.* 232) it was held that the lessee of a railroad corporation, whose charter was sought to be annulled, was entitled to be made a party defendant.

In Christman *v.* Thatcher, (48 *Hun*, 446) it was held that it was not proper to allow the Town of Amsterdam to be made a party defendant upon its own motion, in an action by a physician for services rendered to a poor person upon the order of the overseer of the poor, against whom the action was brought.

It has been held that this section applies only to actions and not to special proceedings.   People *v.* Board of Commissioners, 18 *St. R.* 797.

In special proceedings the court has power, however, to bring in a party as defendant upon his own application, but this power is discretionary with the lower court, and an order refusing to allow a party to come in and defend mandamus proceedings will not be

Uhlfelder *v.* Tamsen.

of the City Court of New York, in so far as such order modified an order of the Special Term of said court permitting the petitioners to come in as parties defendants, by striking therefrom the provision requiring the petitioners to give an undertaking as security for costs.

The sole question presented in this case is whether the provisions of section 452 of the Code, to the effect that where a person not a party to an action has an interest in the subject thereof or in real property, the title to which

---

reviewed by the court of appeals. Matter of Bohnet, 3 *N. Y. Ann. Cas.* 249; s. c., 150 *N. Y.* 279.

It is to be observed that section 452 applies, in terms, only to actions and the power to bring in on motion in special proceedings is one inherent in the court.

The provisions of this section do not apply to proceedings in surrogates' courts. Estate of Tilden, 5 *Civ. Pro. R.* 449.

In Matter of N. Y. Lackawanna & W. R. R. Co., (26 *Hun,* 194), it was held that where, after proceedings to acquire title to land for railroad purposes had been commenced, persons who showed by affidavits that they had an interest in the land, had an absolute right to be made parties to the proceeding without conditions being imposed upon them not to question the regularity of the proceedings thus far had, etc.

As to when persons whose property interests, or whose reputations would be affected by suits for divorce, will be allowed to be made parties, see Clay *v.* Clay, 21 *Hun,* 609; Quigley *v.* Quigley, 45 *Id.* 23; Tilby *v.* Hayes, 27 *Id.* 253.

It is said in Hornby *v.* Gordon, (9 *Bosw.* 656) that the provision of the Code which allows a party upon his own application to be made a party to the action is confined to cases in which a bill of interpleader would have accomplished the same end.

It is the duty of the party moving to be made a party because of his interest in the subject of the action to establish the fact of such interest on the motion. Palmer *v.* Mutural Life Ins. Co., 55 *Super. Ct. (J. & S.)* 352; s. c., 14 *St. R.* 759.

No supplemental summons need be served where one is made a party to an action on his own petition. Haas *v.* Craighead, 19 *Hun,* 396.

See Note on Bringing in New Parties Defendant, 1 *N. Y. Ann. Cas.* 217.

Uhlfelder *v.* Tamsen.

may in any manner be affected by the judgment, makes application to the court to be made a party, it must direct him to be brought in by the proper amendment, imposes upon the court an absolute duty to require such party to be brought in upon his own application when he presents the proper proof, or whether the duty of the court is so far discretionary that it may impose terms upon the applicant as a condition of his being made a party.

Held, that such party had a right to be brought in without conditions. In the case of Haas *v.* Craighead (19 *Hun,* 396) an application made under this section had been denied by the special term, although there was no question of the interest of the applicant in the subject-matter of the action, and that it would be affected by the judgment. The court at general term reversed the order, saying that the statute was comprehensive and peremptory, and the court directed that no costs should be charged against the applicant as a condition of such amendment. This case was decided long before the case of Wood *v.* Swift (81 *N. Y.* 31), and of course did not refer to that case.

In the case of Earle *v.* Hart (20 *Hun,* 75) the same question was presented to the general term of the first department, and it was held that as to persons having an interest at the time of the commencement of the suit the right was absolute under the section. This case was also decided before Wood *v.* Swift was argued in the court of appeals.

In Lawton *v.* Lawton (54 *Hun,* 415; S. C., 27 *St. R.* 302 ; 7 *Supp.* 556), the same question was presented in such a way that it is decisive of this motion.

The same question has necessarily been decided by the court of appeals as it seems to me in the case of People *v.* Albany & Vermont R. R. Co. (77 *N. Y.* 232), in which an application had been made by the Troy and Boston Railroad Company to be made a defendant under section 452. The court, at special term, had granted the order, but the general term reversed the same and denied the application. An appeal was taken to the court of appeals, which held that the applicant had such an interest as entitled it to be brought in, and that under the provisions of section 452 it was error to deny the application. The court of appeals accordingly reversed the order of the general term and affirmed the order of the special term. If there had been any discretionary power in the supreme court to deny this order, this action of the court of appeals could not have been taken.

The same question was presented again to the court of appeals in the case of Johnston *v.* Donvan (106 *N. Y.* 269; S. C., 8 *St. R.* 676; 12 *Civ. Pro. R.* 315; rev'g 6 *St. R.* 861).

In the case of Ashton *v.* City of Rochester (133 *N. Y.* 187; S. C., 44 *St. R.* 526), Judge O'BRIEN, in delivering the opinion of the court, lays stress upon the right of the applicant under section 452, and emphasizes the word "must," which is used in that section, and cites the case of People *v.* Albany & Vermont R. R. Co. (*supra*) as establishing the absolute right of the applicant. I have been unable to find any case, either in the court of appeals or in the general term, which overrules these authorities or suggests any other construction of the section in question.

In Chapman *v.* Forbes (123 *N. Y.* 532; S. C., 34 *St. R.* 351), the motion to bring in a person as defendant was denied; but that motion was not made by a third party asking to be brought in, but by the defendant asking that the plaintiff be compelled to bring in a third party as defendant, and the court held that the section did not apply to a motion of that kind, and accordingly that it was proper to deny the same.

In Rosenberg *v.* Salomon (144 *N. Y.* 92; S. C., 1 *N. Y. Ann. Cas.* 11), two persons, situated as these applicants are, applied to be brought into an action of replevin

Uhlfelder *v.* Tamsen.

which had been commenced against the sheriff. The order was granted and affirmed by the general term, and on the appeal to the court of appeals the point was made that the order was improper under the decision in Chapman *v.* Forbes (*supra*), because under that decision the court had no power to grant relief. What is said in that case as to the power of the court must be construed in view of the question which the court was examining, that is, whether the case of Chapman *v.* Forbes had decided that there was no power in the court to grant the relief asked for under this section. That was the only question presented in Rosenberg *v.* Salomon, and for that reason it is no authority in regard to the point now under consideration.

In the case of Bohnet *v.* Mayor of N. Y. (150 *N. Y.* 279 ; S. C., 3 *N. Y. Ann. Cas.* 249), a final order had been entered in a mandamus proceeding and the application was to open the case and allow the applicant to come in. Whether or not the final order should be opened to allow a person to come in who had made no application to the court during the pendency of the matter was clearly within the discretion of the court. The court say : "Undoubtedly that court (the supreme court) had the power to open the proceedings and allow the appellant to be brought in as a party ; but whether this power should be exercised rested in its discretion." That case is no authority upon the point in question here.

The question presented in this case is not of itself perhaps of great importance ; but it is of importance, as it seems to me, that any rule of construction of the Code which is established by a long series of decisions should not be overthrown unless it is made to appear that the construction heretofore given to it is unquestionably wrong. If that construction is required by the language of the statute, but nevertheless produces inconvenience, the remedy is not with the courts, but with the legislature.

Opinion by RUMSEY, J.   VAN BRUNT, P. J., PATTER-
SON, O'BRIEN and INGRAHAM, JJ., concurred.

Order of Appellate Term reversed, and order of
General Term of the City Court affirmed, with costs in
this court and in the Appellate Term.

Jacob Barnett, for the appellants.

Arthur Furber, for the respondent.

Burritt S. Stone, for the sheriff.

GILLIN v. CANARY.

*Supreme   Court,   First   Department,   Appellate   Term ;
March,* 1897.

Consolidation of actions ; N. Y. City Court ; monetary jurisdiction.]
   The general power conferred upon the city court of New York
   as a court of record to consolidate actions (Code Civ. Pro. §§ 817.
   3347, subd. 6) is limited by § 316, and that court has no jurisdiction to consolidate actions in that court which involve an aggregate sum exceeding $2,000 ; exclusive of interest and costs ;
   and an order of consolidation of such actions and all the
   proceedings thereon, including the judgment, are void.*

Appeal by the defendant from a judgment of the General Term of the City Court of New York, affirming a
judgment of said court rendered after trial at a trial term.

The plaintiff, Robert F. Gillin, brought two actions in
the city court against the defendant, Thomas Canary, each
to recover the sum of $2,000, on promissory notes.   The
defendant applied for and obtained an order consolidating

* See Note following this case on Consolidation of Actions.

Gillin *v.* Canary.

the actions, and the trial resulted in a judgment in favor of the plaintiff for $4,227.50.

Held, that the order was void.   The power conferred by Code Civ. Pro. § 817 is ancillary only to § 315, which confers jurisdiction upon the city court, and to § 316, which regulates it.   In other words, § 817 merely furnishes one of the means to attain the end in view ; that is, a recovery not exceeding $2,000, with interest, etc.   Section 817 neither in express terms nor by necessary implication warrants a larger recovery in case of consolidation than that limited by § 316.

The question was considered in Epstin *v.* Levenson (79 *Ga.* 718), Gerding *v.* Anderson (64 *Id.* 304), Manufacturers' Bank *v.* Goolsby (35 *Id.* 82), Parrot *v.* Green (1 McCord, 521), where it was held proper to deny applications for consolidation when the aggregate amount carried the demand beyond the monetary limitation under which the court acted, upon the ground that the effect would be to oust it of jurisdiction.   The legal effect of consolidation is to turn two or more actions into one, and the chief ground for the union is that the plaintiff should have brought one instead of two.   Bank of U. S. *v.* Strong, 9 *Wend.* 451.   If it had been intended that in case of consolidation the limitation imposed by § 316 should not apply, there naturally would have been incorporated therein some language excepting actions consolidated from its operation.   Consolidation is a mere prelude to the trial, resulting as it does in uniting two or more actions which thenceforth are one, and as one action only must be tried that it may terminate in a judgment, which in the city court, by force of the prohibition of section 316, "cannot exceed " $2,000, with interest and costs.

The plaintiff's construction separates § 817 from the special provisions regulating the jurisdiction of the city court, on the assumption that it contains within itself everything necessary to its execution as an independent enactment—a position wholly unwarranted.   Lyon *v.*

Manhattan Ry. Co., 142 *N. Y.* at p. 303 ; S. C., 31 *Abb. N. C.* 356; 58 *St. R.* 860; aff'g 7 *Misc.* 401. The obvious intention was that consolidation might be directed when it could be had consistently with sections 315 and 316, that the various provisions might work in harmony, each in aid of the other. It cannot be assumed that the general provision which makes § 817 applicable to the city court was intended to overleap the special provisions so carefully guarded by § 316. McCartee *v.* Orphan Asylum, 9 *Cow.* at p. 507.

The chief purpose of the legislature was the establishment of a local court with a defined and limited jurisdiction, which, in the language of § 316, " cannot exceed two thousand dollars, exclusive of interest, and costs as taxed ;" and in making § 817 applicable it was intended that up to this limit consolidation might in proper cases be ordered. See Const. art. 6, secs. 14, 18. To go further would infringe upon the legislative design, and in effect hold that in all cases to which § 817 could be applied the court might render judgment to an amount restricted only by the pleadings and proofs, and that the limitation so carefully expressed in § 316 was meaningless, or repealed by mere implication. We cannot adopt such a course. Sedg. St. Lim. 2d ed. Pom. Notes, 105, 106. Sections 315 and 316 are special in their character, applying exclusively to the city court, and it is by force only of the general provisions of § 3347, subdivision 6, making §§ 817 and 819 inclusive applicable " to all courts of record," that the city court acquired even the power to consolidate. There is not a word or suggestion in that general provision which warrants even the implication that the monetary jurisdiction of the court was to be enlarged. And it is a rule of general construction that a general statute will not by implication defeat the operation of a special and local statute unless the two are so inconsistent that both cannot stand. McKenna *v.* Edmondstone, 91 *N. Y.* 231 ; Coxe *v.* State, 144 *Id.* 396 ; S. C., 63 *St. R.* 642 ; Reynolds *v.*

Gillin *v.* Canary.

City, 81 *Hun*, 353; S. C., 63 *St. R.* 118; 30 *Supp.* 954;
Boecha *v.* Brown, 9 *App. Div.* 369.

The proceedings of a court of limited jurisdiction must
be within the powers granted to it by law, and if it tran-
scends the jurisdiction conferred its judgment will be void.
12 *Am. & Eng. Enc. of L.* 268, 269, 312; *Cow. Tr.* § 650;
Hill *v.* Fowler, 6 *Hill*, 630; Bellinger *v.* Ford, 14 *Barb.*
250; Van Etten *v.* Van Etten, 69 *Hun*, 499; Ramsey *v.*
Robinson, 86 *Id.* 511. Jurisdiction of the person and subject matter is not alone sufficient; power to render the
particular judgment is also essential, for no court can give
a judgment valid for any purpose which is not authorized
by law. People *v.* Liscomb, 60 *N. Y.* 559; Ex parte
Lange, 18 *Wall.* 163; Mattison *v.* Bancus, *Lalor's Supp.
to Hill. & Den. R.* 321. Transcending jurisdiction in this
instance is as fatal to the judgment as if the court rendering it had been without jurisdiction of the subject matter,
which as applied here means " the object, the thing in dispute " (Hunt *v.* Hunt, 72 *N. Y.* at p. 228); or " the debt "
(Borst *v.* Corey, 15 *N. Y.* at p. 509), which by the consolidation was $4,000, exclusive of interest. See also 2
Waitt's Law & Pr. in Justices' Courts, p. 14 *et seq.*

If the effect of the consolidation allowed here was to
require a judgment of $4,000—one which the court could
not render—then, in the language of SEDGWICK, J., in
Alexander *v.* Bennett (38 *super.* at p. 505), " The exercise
of the power is suicide of jurisdiction, for it puts an action
in a position where the court will have no power to adju-
dicate in it." Judge SEDGWICK'S view was sustained on
appeal. 60 *N. Y.* 204. If notwithstanding the consolidation the court below had awarded judgment within the
statutory limit, a different question would have been presented.

The fact that the consolidation was had on the application of the defendant and that he gained a benefit from
it, however much it may justify unfavorable comment,
does not estop him from raising the question of jurisdic-

tion; for whenever there is a want of authority to hear and determine the subject matter of the controversy or to render the judgment, an adjudication upon the merits is a nullity, and does not estop even an assenting party, and a defeated party may raise the question for the first time upon appeal. Matter of Walker, 136 *N. Y.* 20; Wilmore *v.* Flack, 96 *Id.* 512; Kamp *v.* Kamp, 59 *Id.* 212, 216; Davidsburgh *v.* Ins. Co., 90 *Id.* 526; Craig *v.* Town of Andes, 93 *Id.* 405; McMahon *v.* Rauhr, 47 *Id.* 67; Cunard Co. *v.* Voorhis, 104 *Id.* 525; Robinson *v.* Oceanic S. N. Co., 112 *Id.* 315; Bartlett *v.* Mudgett, 75 *Hun*, at p. 297. Even confessing a judgment does not cure the want of jurisdiction in the court. Coffin *v.* Tracy, 3 *Cai.* 129.

The only method of preserving the rights of all the parties is to decide that the order for consolidation and all the proceedings founded upon it are void and of no effect, leaving the two actions to proceed as if no such order had been made.

Opinion by MCADAM, J. DALY, P. J., and BISCHOFF, JR., J., concur.

Judgment accordingly.

Joseph C. Rosenbaum, for the defendant, appellant.

W. F. Severance, (*Oppenheim & Severance*, attorneys), for the plaintiff, respondent.

NOTE ON CONSOLIDATION OF ACTIONS.

Statutes.] Section 817 of the Code of Civil Procedure provides : "Where two or more actions, in favor of the same plaintiff against the same defendant, for causes of action which may be joined, are pending in the same court, the court may, in its discretion, by order, consolidate any or all of them, into one action."

By section 818 it is provided that where one of the actions is pending in the supreme court and another is pending in another court, the supreme court may, by order, remove to itself the action in the other court, and consolidate it with that in the supreme court.

It is further provided, by section 819, that where separate actions are commenced against two or more joint and several debtors, in the same court, and for the same causes of action, the plaintiff may, in any stage of the proceedings, consolidate them into one action.

By section 3347, subdivision 6, all three of the foregoing sections are made applicable to all courts of record.

Actions in different courts.] The city court of New York may remove to itself and consolidate with an action pending in that court, an action pending in one of the district courts in the city of New York. McKay *v.* Reed, 12 *Abb. N. C.* 58*n.*

The same rule applied to the Court of Common Pleas before it was abolished. Sire *v.* Kneuper, 22 *Abb. N. C.* 62.

Also to the superior court of the city of New York in removing a case from the City Court of New York. Carter *v.* Sulley, 28 *Abb. N. C.* 130 ; s. c., 19 *Supp.* 244.

As to removal to supreme court from another court, see Salomon *v.* Belden, 12 *Abb. N. C.* 58.

Different causes, or parties ; amount.] To justify a consolidation not only must the causes of action be such as might be joined, but the two actions must be brought against the same defendants. Isear *v.* Daynes, 1 *App. Div.* 557.

In that case an action had been begun in a district court in the city of New York, on an insurance policy, against two defendants. Another action was commenced in the supreme court on the same policy of insurance, but naming fifty defendants, including the two in the district court action. It was held under such circumstances, the defendants being different, that the court had no power to bring the district court action to the supreme court and consolidate two actions. The appellate division granted a stay, however, of the district court action, pending the final determination of the action in the supreme court.

See also Gloucester Iron Works *v.* Board of Water Commissioners (10 *Supp.* 168), where a motion for consolidation was denied, because of different defendants in the two actions ; also Mayor *v.* Mayor, 11 *Abb. N. C.* 367.

The primary test on such a motion is whether or not the causes of action set up in the two suits sought to be consolidated are such as might be joined under Code Civ. Pro. § 484, in one complaint. See Rosenberg *v.* Staten Island R. R. Co., 14 *Supp.* 476 ; s. c., 38 *St. R.* 106, where an action for a personal injury and one for injury to property, both resulting simultaneously from the same accident, were consolidated.

See also De Wolfe *v.* Abraham (3 *N. Y. Ann. Cas.* 301), and Note on Joinder of Causes of Action Growing out of the Same Transaction, *Id.* 304 ; Farmers' & Manufacturers' Bank *v.* Tracy, 19 *Wend.* 23.

In Bush *v.* Abrahams (2 *Supp.* 391), the defendant moved to consolidate five actions in the City Court of New York each of which was brought to recover less than $2,000, but the amount claimed in all amounted to $5,500. In his moving papers the defendant stipulated to waive the question of jurisdiction and not to take advantage of the point that the consolidated action would be for a sum greater than the jurisdiction of the court warranted. The motion was denied at special term and the order was reversed by the general term of the city court and the proceedings remitted back to the special term for further action, the special term originally having denied the motion on the ground of want of power to make the order.

Upon appeal to the general term of the court of common pleas the appeal was dismissed on the ground that the order was not appealable and a motion for a reargument was subsequently denied. 4 *Supp.* 833. That case is distinguishable from the one in the text only in the fact of the stipulation by the defendant.

Either equitable or legal actions may be consolidated. Wooster *v.* Case, 12 *Supp.* 769 ; s. c., 34 *St. R.* 577.

In the case last cited two actions were begun to foreclose mortgages on the same premises, but the descriptions in the two mortgages were somewhat different and the court for that reason refused to consolidate them but declared that in a proper case it could be done in an equitable action.

Rent.] In Sire *v.* Kneuper (3 *Supp.* 533), both actions

were for rent under the same instrument ; one action was brought in a district court and the other in the court of common pleas, and the latter court ordered them consolidated.

In Carter *v.* Sulley, (28 *Abb. N. C.* 130 ; s. c., 19 *Supp.* 244), an action was begun for rent, in the Superior Court of New York City against a surety under a lease, and subsequently another action was begun in the City Court for rent for the following month, against the same defendant. The Superior Court removed the City Court action to itself and consolidated the two actions.

Mortgage foreclosure.] Actions to foreclose mortgages on separate lots although the defendants are identical cannot · be consolidated. Selkirk *v.* Wood, 9 *Civ. Pro. R.* 141 ; Bech *v.* Ruggles, 6 *Abb. N. C.* 69 ; Kipp *v.* Delamater, 58 *How. Pr.* 183.

Actions to foreclose mortgages upon separate parcels of land cannot be joined under Code Civ. Pro. § 484, and the court cannot consolidate them under section 817. Selkirk *v.* Wood, 9 *Civ. Pro. R.* 141.

But *it seems* that if both mortgages are on the same land, the parties are identical and the defenses are the same, the actions may be consolidated. *Id.*

Partition.] Actions for partition of separate parcels of land in different counties cannot be consolidated. Mayor *v.* Caffin, 90 *N. Y.* 312.

Libel]. Sixty-two actions for libel, one brought in each county of the State against the same defendant were ordered consolidated in Percy *v.* Seward, 6 *Abb. Pr.* 326.

But where two actions were brought for the same libel, one against the editor and the other against the publisher of a newspaper, the court refused to consolidate them. Cooper *v.* Weed, 2 *How. Pr.* 40.

Penalties.] In Cook *v.* Metropolitan Bank (5 *Sandf.* 665), the court refused to consolidate several actions brought to recover penalties, but ordered all except one to be stayed.

Insurance.] In Camman *v.* N. Y. Insurance Co. (*Col. & Cai.* 188), which was decided in 1803, the court refused to consolidate eleven actions on policies of insurance on one cargo, the defendant being the same in each, and one of the plaintiffs being the same in all of the actions, but associated with him in each policy were other persons who had interests in the separate portions of the cargo insured.

Conditions.] In case the consolidation may prejudice

the plaintiff the court has power to impose such terms as will protect the plaintiff's rights, as a condition of granting the motion. Solomon *v.* Belden, 12 *Abb. N. C.* 58; Carter *v.* Sulley, 28 *Abb. N. C.* 130; s. c., 19 *Supp.* 244; Dunning *v.* Bank of Auburn, 19 *Wend.* 23.

Costs.] The plaintiff will be ordered to pay costs of the motion, where both actions were commenced at the same time or under circumstances which evince a disposition to make the proceedings burdensome to the defendant. Bank of U. S. *v.* Strong, 9 *Wend.* 451.

As to costs after consolidation, see Hiscox *v.* N. Y. Staats Zeitung, 23 *Civ. Pro. R.* 87.

Practice.] As to the practice generally and what the moving papers must show see Campbell Printing Press & M'f'g Co. *v.* Lyddy, 1 *Civ. Pro. R.* 364; Wilkinson *v.* Johnson, 4 *Hill* 46; Dunning *v.* Bank of Auburn, 19 *Wend.* 23; Pierce *v.* Lyon, 3 *Hill* 450; Thompson *v.* Shepard, 9 *Johns.* 262; Bowman *v.* Purtell, 1 *Monthly L. Bull.* 29; Woodward *v.* Frost, 19 *W. Dig.* 125.

The fact that one action was begun before the other cause of action accrued upon which another action has been commenced is not a valid reason for refusing consolidation. Dunning *v.* Bank of Auburn, 19 *Wend.* 23; Carter *v.* Sulley, 28 *Abb. N. C.* 130; 19 *Supp.* 244; Brewster *v.* Stewart, 3 *Wend.* 44.

If the motion is made by the defendant before answer it seems necessary to present an affidavit of merits. Brewster *v.* Stewart, 9 *Wend.* 441; Crane *v.* Kolhler, 6 *Abb. Pr.* 328*n.*, unless the motion is made to save costs and it is stipulated that no defense will be put in. Wilkinson *v.* Johnson, 4 *Hill*, 46; Dunn *v.* Mason, 7 *Id.* 154; Morris *v.* Knox, 6 *Abb. Pr.* 328*n.* Farmers & Manufacturers' Bank *v.* Tracy, 19 *Wend.* 23. And it has been held that a motion to consolidate should not be made until both actions are at issue. Le Roy *v.* Bedell, 1 *Code R.* (*N. S.*) 201; Boyle *v.* Staten Island & S. B. L. Co., 87 *Hun,* 233; s. c., 33 *Supp.* 836; 67 *St. R.* 424.

The motion to consolidate may be made either by the plaintiff or defendant. Briggs *v.* Gaunt, 4 *Duer,* 664; s. c., 2 *Abb. Pr.* 77.

It is too late to move to consolidate when the cases are called for trial. Eleventh Ward Sav. Bank *v.* Hay, 8 *Daly,* 328; aff'd without opinion, 73 *N. Y.* 609.

Where two actions on notes are consolidated it is error to strike out the answer in one of them; the judgment roll should contain both answers. Colt *v.* Davis, 50 *Hun,* 366; s. c., 3 *Supp.* 354; 16 *Civ. Pro. R.* 180; 20 *St. R.* 309.

Reilly *v.* Sicilian Asphalt Paving Co.

As to the question in which district an application for consolidation must be made, where two actions are pending in the Supreme Court, see Dupignac *v.* Van Buskirk, 44 *Hun*, 45.

As to severing after consolidation, see Colt *v.* Davis, 16 *Civ. Pro. R.* 180.

REILLY *v* SICILIAN ASPHALT PAVING CO.

Supreme Court, First Department, Appellate Division; February, 1897.

Former adjudication; successive actions for one act of negligence; injury to property; personal injury.] Where, pending an action for personal injury resulting from the defendant's negligence, the plaintiff recovered a judgment, which was thereafter satisfied, for damages to property resulting from the same act of negligence,—*Held*, that it was error to refuse to allow the defendant to serve a supplemental answer setting up such judgment and satisfaction as a defense. *

Appeal by the defendant from an order of the Supreme Court, New York Special Term, denying its motion for leave to serve a supplemental answer.

This action is brought by John F. Reilly to recover damages for personal injuries alleged to have been sustained through the negligence of the defendant. Issue was joined on August 7, 1895. Thereafter, an amended complaint, increasing the demand for damages, was received, and issue was finally joined by service of an answer on October 3, 1895. Prior to the service of this second answer, the plaintiff brought another action against the defendant in the district court, based upon precisely the

---

* See note following this case on Separate Actions for Injuries to Person and Property from the same Tort.

As to when supplemental pleading should be allowed, see the next case of Pollmann *v.* Livingston, and notes.

Reilly *v.* Sicilian Asphalt Paving Co.

same state of facts alleged in the complaint herein ; but instead of attempting to recover for damages for personal injuries, demanded judgment for damages to the wagon in which he was riding at the time of the accident. In the district court action a judgment was rendered for the plaintiff on October 31, 1895, and was thereafter satisfied. The proposed supplemental answer seeks to set up the recovery and satisfaction of the district court judgment as a plea or defense in bar of a recovery in this action. The motion was denied at special term.

Held, error. The district court judgment was recovered and satisfied subsequent to the service of the answer in this action ; and, unless some good legal reason was shown to the contrary, the motion should have been granted. As appears by the memorandum of the learned judge at special term, questions of *laches* and good faith were eliminated, and his denial was placed upon the case of Perry *v.* Dickerson (85 *N. Y.* 345) which he concluded was an authority against the validity of the defense sought to be interposed by the supplemental answer. In that case the plaintiff brought an action to recover damages for an alleged wrongful dismissal from defendant's employment before the expiration of a stipulated term. It was held that the judgment therein was not a bar to a subsequent action to recover wages earned during the time the plaintiff was actually employed, and due and payable before the wrongful dismissal ; and that the two claims constituted separate and independent causes of action, upon which separate actions were maintainable. It was therein further held that, to sustain a plea of a former judgment in bar, it must appear that the cause of action in both suits was the same, or that some fact essential to the maintenance of the second suit was in issue in the first action.

This, however, is not a case where two causes of action spring out of the same contract, but is one in tort ; and the defendant insists that, though the plaintiff may have separate causes of action for loss of property and for

Reilly *v.* Sicilian Asphalt Paving Co.

injuries to the person, yet, where both come from but one
act of negligence, there can be but one suit to recover the
whole damage. In support of this view, our attention is
called to the case of Nathans *v.* Hope (77 *N. Y.* 420),
wherein the rule is laid down in the following language :
" The principle is well settled that an entire indivisible
demand cannot be split up into several claims so as to
make it a subject of two or more separate actions. . . .
It follows as the result of this rule that where a claim
arises upon a contract, or from a tort, the entire claim
must be prosecuted in a single suit, and several suits cannot be brought for separate parts of such claim. Where
several suits are brought, the pendency of the first may
be pleaded in abatement of the other suit or suits, and a
judgment in either will be a bar to a recovery in any
other suit." See, also, Secor *v.* Sturgis, 16 *N. Y.* 548.

The distinction between the case of Perry *v.* Dickerson
(*supra*) relied upon by the learned judge below, and the
facts appearing in the case at bar, is apparent ; and
enforced as this distinction is by the other cases to
which reference has been made, it is manifest that the
defense sought to be here interposed by way of supplemental answer is by no means a frivolous one, but is
such as should be passed upon in the usual and orderly
way upon a trial. Without, therefore, expressing any
view upon the merits of such defense, we think, under the
decisions, where neither *laches* nor want of good faith, nor
the frivolousness of a pleading can be urged against the
granting of the relief, it was error not to accord to the
defendant the right to serve the proposed supplemental
answer and thus afford him an opportunity to present the
merits of the defense upon the trial.

Opinion by O'BRIEN, J. VAN BRUNT, P. J., BARRETT,
RUMSEY and INGRAHAM, JJ., concurred.

Order reversed, with ten dollars costs and disbursements, and motion granted, with ten dollars costs to abide the event.

Herbert C. Smyth, for the defendant, appellant.

James Kearney, for the plaintiff, respondent.

NOTE ON SEPARATE ACTIONS FOR INJURIES TO PERSON AND PROPERTY FROM THE SAME TORT.

The question involved in the case in the text does not appear as yet to have been definitely settled in this State. In one case entirely parallel to the principal one here a contrary doctrine was announced. See McAndrew *v.* Lake Shore & M. S. R'y Co., 70 *Hun*, 46 (cited below). It is to be observed, however, that in neither of these cases is the proposition of substantive law actually decided as to whether or not a judgment for either injuries to person or property is a bar to another action for either of these causes of action, when both resulted from the same tort. The court in the case here reported goes no farther than to say that such a defense is not frivolous and leaves the trial court to determine the real question of law involved. In the McAndrew case the decision is equally inconclusive on the main question. There the court refused to allow the amendment, and said that that was not the proper remedy, while also declaring that the pendency of the first action might have been pleaded in abatement of the second, or that both actions might have been consolidated. That case apparently holds merely that the court, in the exercise of its discretion, would refuse to allow the defendant to amend its pleading by the service of a supplemental answer, setting up as a bar the judgment already recovered. An appeal was dismissed from that order by the court of appeals (146 *N. Y.* 377) without considering the merits, and merely upon the ground that the order was discretionary.

From the opinion of the court in the case in the text it does not appear that its attention was called to the McAndrew case.

In the leading case of Secor *v.* Sturgis (16 *N. Y.* 548), it is said at page 554: "The principle is settled beyond dispute that a judgment concludes the rights of the parties in respect to the cause of action stated in the pleadings on which it is rendered, whether the suit embraces the whole or only part of the demand constituting the cause of action. It results from this principle, and the rule is fully established, that an entire claim, arising either upon a contract or from a wrong, cannot be divided and made the subject of several suits ; and if several suits be brought for different parts of such a claim the pendency of the first may be pleaded in abatement of the others, and a judgment upon the merits in either will be available as a bar in the other suits." And further, at page 558 : " In the case of torts, each trespass, or conversion, or fraud, gives a right of action and but a single one, however numerous the items of wrong or damage may be."

In Rosenberg *v.* Staten Island Ry. Co. (14 *Supp.* 476), two actions, one for personal injuries and the other for injuries to property, resulting from one accident, were consolidated, under Code Civ. Pro. § 817. Mr. Justice Pryor, upon granting the motion to consolidate said : " Hitherto the argument has proceeded on the hypothesis that the complaints exhibit two several causes of action ; but is it so ? In both cases the cause of action is the negligence of defendant in running its train, and one and the same act of negligence is alleged as the occasion of each injury. In other words by the same tort plaintiff is damaged in person and property. The tort is single, while the effects of it are double ; and the question is, are there two several and separate causes of action ? Or, is there but one cause of action, *i. e.,* defendant's negligent act, attended, however, with injurious consequences both to his person and property? And since, for a wrong, plaintiff must recover all his damages, present and prospective, in a single action, would not a judgment in one of these actions be a bar to the other ? Is not plaintiff here 'splitting up' a single cause of action into two? However this may be, to spare the expense and vexation of two trials when one will suffice for all the purposes of justice, these actions should be consolidated."

In Bendernagle *v.* Cocks (19 *Wend.* 207), it is said : "All damages accruing from a single wrong, though at different times, make but one cause of action, and all debts or demands already due by the same contract make one entire cause of action."

In Townsend *v.* Coon (7 *Civ. Pro. R.* 56), the complaint set forth three causes of action in one court, one for the breach of a contract to employ, one for personal injuries and a third for injuries to personal property. In sustaining a demurrer to the complaint the court said that three distinct causes of action were averred. The second and third appeared to have arisen from the same tort on the part of the defendant, but the question of whether or not these two could have been joined without the first was not discussed by the court.

The trend of these cases seems to be to the effect that, as a general principle, one tort is the foundation for only one action, and that all injuries which result from such tort, whatever their nature, are items of damage merely, all of which are to be recovered in one action, and that a judgment for one item bars an action for any of the other items. But this doctrine is subject to and is probably modified by the case of DeWolfe *v.* Abraham (3 *N. Y. Ann. Cas.* 301 ; rev'g 6 *App. Div.* 172). Where the Court of Appeals held that a cause of action for slander may not be joined with one for false imprisonment in the same complaint, although they both arose at the same time, and that it does not follow, as a matter of law, that two causes of action arising simultaneously from the happening of one event necessarily arise from the same transaction. See note to that case on Joinder of Causes of Action Growing Out of the Same Transaction, 3 *N. Y. Ann. Cas.* 304.

POLLMANN *v.* LIVINGSTON.

Supreme Court, First Department, Appellate Division; May, 1897.

1. *Pleading ; supplemental answer ; when allowed.*] Where, after issue is joined in an action to set aside a general assignment as fraudulent, proceedings then pending for an accounting by the assignee result in a final order adjudging the validity of the transactions complained of by the plaintiff, it is error to refuse to permit the defendant to serve a supplemental answer setting up such final order.*

---

* Compare the preceding case of Reilly *v.* Sicilian Asphalt Paving Co., *ante,* p. 209.

In Bank of the Metropolis *v.* Lissner (6 *App. Div.* 378), an order allowing the defendant to serve a supplemental answer setting up a former judgment between the same parties as a bar to the action, was reversed, on the ground that the fact adjudicated in the former

2. *The same ; laches.*] Leave should not be refused for the laches of defendant in entering such final order, where no harm to plaintiff resulted except the burden of costs, but the order granting leave should require compensation for such injury.

---

action could be introduced in evidence to defeat the plaintiff's claim without pleading the judgment as a bar. The court cited Krekeler *v.* Ritter, 62 *N. Y.* 372, as an authority for the latter proposition.

But see Dempsey *v.* Baldwin, 15 *Misc.* 455 ; s. c., 37 *Supp.* 28 ; (N. Y. City Court) where the court allowed a judgment between the same parties to be set up by way of supplemental answer.

See also Williams *v.* Lindblom (90 *Hun*, 370), where it was held that a foreign judgment could be introduced in evidence by the defendant without setting it up in a supplemental answer.

In Sullivan *v.* N. Y. Elevated R. R. Co. (14 *Misc.* 426), it was held, in an action for injunctive relief, that the cause of action survived the death of a sole plaintiff, and in order to revive the action in the name of the personal representatives or heirs of such plaintiff it was not necessary to serve a supplemental complaint setting up the devolution of title.

Where there are laches, or the granting of leave to serve a supplemental pleading would result in fraud or injustice to the other party the motion will be denied. Haas *v.* Colton, 12 *Misc.* 308 ; s. c., 34 *Supp.* 35 ; 67 *St. R.* 836 ; Abram French Co. *v.* Shapiro, 11 *Misc.* 633 ; s. c., 33 *Supp.* 9 ; 66 *St. R.* 510.

In the last mentioned case the motion was made thirteen months after issue was joined, for leave to set up the fact that the plaintiff, a foreign corporation, had not secured the certificate from the secretary of State, required by law, allowing it to do business in this State, and the motion was denied.

In Purdy *v.* Manhattan Ry. Co. (11 *Misc.* 394), the defendant was allowed to set up by way of supplemental answer, a stipulation entered into between the parties, which might affect the right of the plaintiff to recover.

Where the defense proposed to be set up in a supplemental answer is manifestly frivolous, leave will not be granted to do so. Gerstein *v.* Fisher, 12 *Misc.* 211 ; s. c., 33 *Supp.* 1120 ; 67 *St. R.* 824.

See also Wamsley *v.* H. L. Horton Co., 87 *Hun*, 347 ; s. c., 34 *Supp.* 306 ; 68 *St. R.* 458.

See Fleischmann *v.* Bennett (79 *N. Y.* 579) holding that it is discretionary with the court whether or not to grant an application for leave to serve a supplemental pleading.

Appeal by the defendants, Morris Livingston and another, from an order of the Supreme Court, made at the New York Special Term denying their motion for leave to serve a supplemental answer.

The action was brought by the creditors of the defendant, Morris Livingston, to set aside a general assignment made by Livingston for the benefit of his creditors to the defendant Brenauer. The assignment was claimed to have been fraudulent and void, and as facts to establish that fraudulent intent there was alleged a sale by the assignee to Bella Livingston, the wife of the assignor, of a large quantity of the assets of the estate, for a grossly inadequate sum, the allowance by the assignee of a fraudulent claim made by Bella Livingston against her husband, and a fraudulent preference in the assignment of the estate of one Julia Livingston, a former wife of the assignor.

Some months before this action was begun to set aside the assignment, the assignee, Brenauer, presented to the court of common pleas an account of his proceedings as assignee and obtained a citation for a final settlement of his accounts. Upon the return day of that citation all the plaintiffs except one appeared, and their appearance was noted. The plaintiff Borchers, who was not then a creditor, did not appear, but the Folsom Arms Company, who subsequently assigned their claim to Borchers, did appear on that proceeding. The plaintiffs and the Folsom Arms Company filed objections to the account of the assignee, and especially they attacked the alleged sale to Bella Livingston by the assignee and the claim of the estate of Julia Livingston against the assignor, and the claim of Bella Livingston against the assignor. These

---

Where by mistake a motion is made for leave to serve a supplemental complaint, when an amended complaint was the proper remedy, the motion should not be denied for that reason, but should be granted on proper terms. Frisbie *v.* Averell, 87 *Hun*, 217.

Pollmann *v.* Livingston.

proceedings were pending at the time the action was begun, and the answer set up the pendency of these proceedings.   After the action was at issue it was referred,
and the trial before the referee was entered upon and continued for a considerable time.   On May 1, 1896, the referee's report in the proceedings for an accounting was
prepared and signed.   It was filed in the office of the
clerk of this court on January 12, 1897, and the final order upon it was entered on February 8, 1897, by which
the report was confirmed and the assigned estate distributed in accordance with the report.   In this final order,
as it is claimed, the sale to Bella Livingston and the
claims of Bella Livingston and Julia Livingston against
the assignor's estate were sustained.   The defendants,
after the entry of the final order upon the accounting,
moved for leave to serve a supplemental answer setting
up that order as a bar to the claim of the plaintiffs that
the assignment was fraudulent by reason of the facts indicated above.   This motion was denied, and from the
order denying it this appeal is taken.

Held, error ; that when the proceedings which had been
begun in the Court of Common Pleas for the settlement
of the assignee's accounts, had resulted in a final order, if
they did so before the final determination of this action,
the successful party there would be entitled to use that
order so far as it was a determination of the facts disputed
in this action, either as a bar or as evidence in his behalf.
Krekler *v.* Ritter, 62 *N. Y.* 372.   The final order settling
the assignee's accounts could only be a bar if it were
pleaded, and, as it was entered after the trial of this action had begun, it could only be pleaded in a supplemental answer to be served by leave of the court.   The
courts have construed Code Civ. Pro. § 544, in spite of its
quasi mandatory form, as leaving it discretionary with the
court to permit the service of a supplemental pleading
(Spears *v.* Mayor, 72 *N. Y.* 442), and it is said that the
change in the wording of the statute does not change the

authority of the court which, it had been well settled, had
a discretion whether to permit the service of a supplemental answer or not, but usually did so almost as a matter of course, unless the facts disclosed upon the motion
made it entirely improper. Holyoke *v.* Adams, 59 *N. Y.*
233. If, as alleged by the defendants, the acts insisted
upon as making this assignment fraudulent have been examined upon the assignee's accounting, and it has been
decided there that these acts were all proper and done in
good faith, the final order entered upon that report would
undoubtedly be conclusive in favor of the defendants as
to these facts. No reason is apparent why the defendants,
having succeeded in a litigation upon those facts in one
branch of this court, should not be permitted to have the
benefit of the adjudication in that litigation in another
branch.

The defendants' *laches* in delaying the entry of the
final order upon the report of the referee upon the accounting from May 1, 1896, when the report was signed,
down to the month of February, 1897, and thereby putting the plaintiffs to considerable expense upon the trial
of the action, which would have been entirely avoided had
that order been promptly entered and presented to the
referee at the first opportunity after the trial began, did no
harm to the plaintiffs except the imposition upon them of
unnecessary costs of the reference, and for that they can
be compensated, and they should be compensated as a
condition of granting leave to serve this supplemental
answer, which, if it is in fact what it is alleged to be by
the defendants, will result in a substantial determination
of this suit.

Opinion by RUMSEY J. VAN BRUNT, P. J., WIL-
LIAMS, PATTERSON and PARKER, J.J., concurred.

Order reversed, without costs, and the motion granted
upon condition that the defendants pay all the expenses

of the reference which have accrued since May 1, 1896, and ten dollars costs of the motion.

George Bell and *Benjamin Patterson*, for the defendants, appellants.

Elmer S. White, for the plaintiff, respondent.

HARTFORD NAT. BANK *v.* BEINECKE.

Supreme Court, First Department, Appellate Division; March, 1897.

Pleading ; reply ; when ordered ; action against partners ; special partnership.] Where, in an action against several as partners, two of the defendants, answering separately, alleged a special partnership by way of avoidance,—*Held,* error, to deny a motion to compel a reply under Code Civ. Pro., § 516, setting forth such facts as would be relied upon by the plaintiff at the trial to hold such defendants liable as general and not as special partners.*

---

* Section 516 of the Code of Civil Procedure provides : '' Where an answer contains new matter, constituting a defense by way of avoidance, the court may, in its discretion, on the defendant's application, direct the plaintiff to reply to the new matter. In that case, the reply, and the proceedings upon failure to reply, are subject to the same rules as in the case of a counterclaim.''

· This section applies strictly to defenses by way of avoidance and not to counterclaims. O'Gorman *v.* Arnoux, 63 *How. Pr.* 159 ; Adams *v.* Roberts, 1 *Civ. Pro. R.* 204 ; s. c., 62 *How. Pr.* 253.

It has been held that it is within the discretion of the court to require a reply to a defence of the statute of limitations. Perls *v.* Metropolitan Ins. Co.. 29 *St. R.* 409 ; s. c., 8 *Supp.* 532 ; Hubbell *v.* Fowler, 1 *Abb. Pr.* (*N. S.*) 207.

Where the complaint shows that the period of limitation has

Hartford Nat. Bank *v.* Beinecke.

Appeal by the defendants, Bernhard Beinecke and another, from an order of the Supreme Court, New York

elapsed and shows an avoidance, a reply should not be required to a defence of the statute. Avery *v.* N. Y. Central, etc., R. R. Co. 6 *Supp.* 547 ; S. C., 24 *St, R.* 918.

In Scofield *v.* Demorest, (55 *Hun,* 254), which was an action for libel, the defendant justified the publication of the alleged libel, by alleging the truth of the matter therein contained, and setting forth at considerable length the entire history of a prior legal proceeding. The court held that while this defense was in reality by way of a confession and avoidance the court would not compel the plaintiff to reply to the detailed statements in the answer, as the allegations therein contained could nearly all be proved, if at all, by the introduction of record evidence, and it was not necessary for the defendant to prepare for trial to know how the plaintiff would meet the facts so alleged.

To the same effect is Columbus, Hocking V. & T. R. R. Co. *v.* Ellis, 25 *Abb. N. C.* 150.

As to the power of court to order a reply, which has been made pursuant to a former order, more definite and certain, see Winchester *v.* Brown, 26 *Abb. N. C.* 387.

A reply was ordered in an action against an assessment insurance company, where the defendant alleged non-payment of an assessment. Rogers *v.* Mutual R. F. Assn., 1 *How. Pr.* (*N. S.*) 194. And in an action for negligence causing the death of plaintiff's intestate, where the defense was the statute of limitations. Cavanagh *v.* Oceanic S. S. Co. 9 *Supp.* 198 ; S. C., 30 *St. R.* 532. Where an answer set up a discharge in bankruptcy. Poillon *v.* Lawrence, 43 *Super. Ct.* (*J. & S.*) 385 ; reversed, 77 *N. Y.* 207, on the ground that the demurrer to the reply should not have been sustained.

Also in an action for dower where the answer alleged that the plaintiff and the deceased had been divorced. Brinkerhoff *v.* Brinkerhoff (8 *Abb. N. C.* 207) ; and where a defendant set up false statements in an application for an insurance policy (Schwan *v.* Mutual Trust F. L. Assn. 9 *Civ. Pro. R.* 82) ; and where the defendant alleged a former adjudication as a bar to the action. Mercantile Nat. Bank of N. Y. *v.* Corn Exchange Bank, 25 *Supp.* 1068.

Where the defendant set forth certain facts which, it was alleged constituted a ratification of proceedings which were the foundation of the suit,—*Held*, that the defendant was entitled to know, by a

Hartford Nat. Bank *v.* Beinecke.

Special Term, denying their motion to require the plaintiff to reply to new matter set up in their answer.

The action was brought against Emil Seidenberg, Joseph Seidenberg, Adolph Stiefel, Bernhard Beinecke and Joseph Hesdorfer, and the allegation of the complaint is that the defendants were co-partners in trade under the firm name and style of E. Seidenberg, Stiefel & Co. The defendants Beinecke and Hesdorfer in their answer deny that they were, or either of them was, at any time a partner of the firm of E. Seidenberg, Stiefel & Co. mentioned in said complaint, except as thereafter stated in the answer; and then they proceed to set up that each of them was a member of a limited copartnership duly formed under the laws of the State of New York, wherein the defendants other than themselves were the general partners and they the special partners, and they allege that the obligation sued upon in the complaint was the act and obligation of the limited copartnership. They also allege that they complied with all the provisions of the law of the State of New York relating to limited partnerships. By their motion the appellants sought to compel the plaintiff to set forth in a reply such facts as they may claim would render the appellants liable, notwithstanding the nature of the copartnership as pleaded by them. The special term denied the motion.

Held, error. The allegation of the complaint relating to the copartnership of the defendants is of such a character that the special partners could not interpose a general denial to that allegation. They were copartners with the other defendants under the firm name and style of E. Seidenberg, Stiefel & Co. A limited partnership under the statute is, except as provided by that statute, subject to the rules of the common law. Ames *v.* Downing, 1 *Bradf. Supp.* 326. Such being the relations of the defend-

reply, whether or not the plaintiff denied the truth of the facts as alleged. Steinway *v.* Steinway, 68 *Hun*, 430.

ants Beinecke and Hesdorfer to the firm, they in their answer set up in avoidance of the liability sought to be enforced against them as partners, the special fact of their
relationship to the firm being such as they were authorized
to create by becoming special partners in a limited partnership, for thereby they set up such matter as enables
them to evade or escape from the legal effect of a pleading by alleging new matter in answer to that pleading, and
that is a definition of avoidance. The Code authorizes
the court where an answer contains new matter constituting a defense by way of avoidance to require the plaintiff
on the defendant's application to reply to that new matter. *Code Civ. Pro.* § 516. The question here is, whether
in this case, such a requirement should have been made.
Upon the issue joined as it now is, it is not disputed that
it would be competent for the plaintiff at the trial to
overcome the matter in avoidance by proving such facts
as would make the defendants appellants, liable as general
partners. There are two distinct and separate kinds of
liability of general partners to which a special partner
may be subjected. One relates to irregularities or insuffi-
ciencies in the formation of the limited partnership caused
by a non-compliance with any of the provisions of the law
relating to the organization or the establishment of such
limited partnership. The other is a liability arising from
the commission of any one of the acts prohibited by section 20 and 21 of the Limited Partnership Act (1 *R. S.*
763–767). This distinct liability is pointed out in Van
Ingen *v.* Whitman, 62 *N. Y.* 523.

What the appellants desire in this case is information
as to which class of liability it may be claimed they are
subject to, and it seems but just and reasonable that they
should have such information to be set forth in a reply in
order that they might be prepared at the trial to meet
what is alleged against them. It may be claimed that the
protection of the statute is not available to them because
of their concurrence in or assent to some act prohibited

Wessels *v.* Carr.

by sections 20 and 21 of the limited partnership act, and if that be so, they should not be compelled to proceed to trial without any notification of the particular transaction to be made the subject of inquiry at a time when they would be utterly helpless.   This is in no sense a mere attempt to elicit the plaintiff's evidence before the trial, but it is only an application to be informed as to particular facts (and not evidence of the facts) which it may be claimed would convert their limited partnership relations into those of general partners.   The order below was wrong and should be reversed.

Opinion by PATTERSON, J.   RUMSEY, O'BRIEN and INGRAHAM, JJ., concurred; VAN BRUNT, P. J., dissented.

Order reversed, with ten dollars costs and disbursements, and the motion granted, without costs.

Joseph Fettretch, for the defendants, appellants.

Charles E. Rushmore, for the plaintiff, respondent.

WESSELS *v.* CARR.

Supreme Court, First Department, Appellate Division; March, 1897.

Fraud; procuring release of debtor; false assertion of insolvency.]
A complaint showing that defendant wilfully and falsely represented himself to be a poor man and unable to pay a judgment against him in favor of the plaintiff, and thereby induced the plaintiff to give him a general release and assign the judgment to another upon payment of a small amount, states a cause of action for fraud.

---

* See Note on Actions Without Precedent, *ante*, p. 15.

In Adams *v.* Sage (28 *N. Y.* 103), it is said, at page 108:

Wessels *v.* Carr.

Appeal by the defendant, Alfred Carr, from an interlocutory judgment of the Supreme Court, New York County, in favor of the plaintiff, entered upon the decision of the court rendered after a trial at the New York Special Term overruling the defendant's demurrer to the plaintiff's complaint.

The allegations of the complaint are, in substance, that the plaintiff recovered a judgment against the defendant for $1,237.49, which he endeavored to collect ; that the defendant willfully, intentionally and falsely represented to the plaintiff that he was a poor man and could not pay, but that if plaintiff would accept $250 and give the de-

---

" Where a party to whom representations are made, has the means at hand of determining their truth or falsehood, and resorts to such means, and after investigation, avows his belief that the statements are false, and acts upon such belief, by bringing an action to recover money obtained by him by means of the fraudulent representations, he is not entitled to credit, when he alleges, that upon the reiteration of the truth of the same statements, by the same party, he was induced to enter into an agreement to settle the suit, and was thereby defrauded."

The rule is laid down in 2 *Parsons on Contracts,* 270, that it must appear that the injured party not only did, in fact, rely upon the fraudulent statement, but had a right to rely upon it, in the full belief of its truth, for, otherwise, it was his own fault, or folly, and he cannot ask the law to relieve him.

A mere suspicion that the statements which have induced the plaintiff to compromise a controversy, are false, is not enough to defeat an action to set aside the compromise agreement where such suspicions were alleged by the statement of the party making them, under oath, that they were true. Baker *v.* Spencer, 47 *N. Y.* 562.

A debtor is not compelled to disclose his financial condition when compromising a pending suit and no questions are asked by the creditor concerning such condition. Graham *v.* Meyer, 99 *N. Y.* 611.

In Van Nuys *v.* Titsworth (57 *Hun*, 5), a compromise of a pending suit made by a plaintiff, who was an invalid, to escape further litigation, and which was made against the advice of his counsel, was set aside as having been improvidently made.

Wessels *v.* Carr.

fendant a general release the defendant would procure a party to take an assignment of the judgment for that sum ; that, relying on such statement, the plaintiff gave the defendant a release and made and executed an assignment of the judgment to a clerk in the defendant's employ, who paid nothing for such assignment—the $250 being paid by the defendant ; that the object in having the assignment made to the clerk was to defraud the plaintiff and deceive him into believing that the defendant was a poor man and unable to pay ; that such representations were false and untrue and made with intent to defraud and deceive the plaintiff, that the defendant at that time was a man of means and able to pay, and that, by reason of the premises, the plaintiff has suffered damages in the sum of $1,500.

The defendant demurred to the complaint, on the ground that it did not state facts sufficient to constitute a cause of action. The demurrer was overruled at special term.

Held, no error. Little need be added to the satisfactory opinion delivered by the learned judge below.* The

---

* The opinion of PRYOR, J., at special term, after stating the facts, was as follows: Obviously, here are all the constituents of an action for deceit, namely : " Representations, falsity, *scienter*, deception and injury." CHURCH, CH. J., in Arthur *v.* Griswold, 55 *N. Y.* 400, 410 ; Brackett *v.* Griswold, 112 *Id.* 454 ; s. c., 4 *St. R.* 219 ; Hickey *v.* Morrell, 102 *N. Y.* 454, 463).

"In determining the sufficiency of the pleading demurred to, it must be assumed that the facts stated therein, as well as such as may by reasonable and fair intendment be implied from the allegations made, are true." Milliken *v.* Western Union Tel. Co., 110 *N. Y.* 403 ; s. c., 18 *St. R.* 328 ; rev'g 53 *Super. Ct.* 111. "To sustain a demurrer to a complaint it is not sufficient that the facts are imperfectly or informally averred, or that it lacks definiteness and precision, or that the material facts are argumentatively averred ; it will be deemed to allege what can by reasonable and fair intendment be implied from the allegations." Marie *v.* Garrison, 83 *N. Y.* 14 ; Sanders *v.* Soutter, 126 *Id.* 193 ; s. c., 37 *St. R.* 1 ; rev'g 36 *Id.* 824. While the court may not, by implication, import an absent allega-

essential constituents of an action for fraud are, representations, falsity, *scienter*, deception and injury. The complaint contains all these elements. The only question
that can arise is whether the character of the representations, if proved, is of a sufficiently grave nature to entitle
the plaintiff to relief. In other words, will a false and
fraudulent representation, made with intent to induce a
compromise, that one is poor and unable to pay his debts,
when in fact he is able, justify an action for damages?
Of course, if the fraud is sufficiently grave the release and
assignment present no insuperable barrier to a recovery.

In Gould *v.* Cayuga Co. Nat. Bank (86 *N. Y.* 81) it is
said : " If there had been no dispute as to the amount
due the plaintiff, if the sole defense of the defendants had
been the compromise, and if at least the $25,000 was in-
disputably due the plaintiff, then it would have been un-

---

tion into a complaint (Clark *v.* Dillon, 97 *N. Y.* 370), still " pleadings are to be liberally construed with a view to substantial justice,
or, in other words, with a view to get out the real truth of the case,
when it will not involve surprise or injustice to either party."
PECKHAM, J., in Bowe *v.* Wilkins, 105 *N. Y.* 322, 328 ; S. C., 7 *St. R.*
539.

But why have recourse to rules of construction when the complaint is explicit in the statement of every fact essential to the support of the action ?

Indeed the demurrant does not challenge the right of plaintiff on
the facts pleaded to some relief, but the contention is that his only
remedy is an action for cancellation of the assignment and release
of the judgment. But if the complaint show title to any redress in
any form, it is good against the demurrer. Johnson *v.* Girdwood,
7 *Misc. Rep.* 651 ; aff'd by court of appeals, 143 *N. Y.* 660.

On discovery of the fraud plaintiff had an alternative of remedies;
that is, either to rescind the contract, or to affirm it and sue for damages. Krumm *v.* Beach, 96 *N. Y.* 398, 406 ; Vail *v.* Reynolds, 118
Id. 297, 302 ; *Cooley on Torts,* 503. He adopts the latter expedient;
to the pursuit of which, manifestly, the assignment and release of
the judgment, instead of opposing an obstacle, are indispensable
conditions. Such assignment and release, fraudulently procured, is
the gravamen of the action.

Demurrer overruled, with leave to answer.

necessary for the plaintiff to tender or return to the bank the money paid, because, in any view of the case, so much would have been due the plaintiff by virtue of the compromise, if that was upheld, and, if that was vacated, then in consequence of the original liability.   It was in principle so held in Pierce v. Wood (3 *Fost.* [*N. H.*] 519).   It was there decided that, if a person effect a compromise of his debts by fraudulent representations and procure a discharge of the same by paying a per cent. thereon, and an action be brought to recover the balance on the ground of fraud, it is not necessary, as preliminary to the right of recovery, that the plaintiff repay or offer to repay the per cent. received, and that the doctrine of the rescission of contracts does not apply to such a case.   In that case, ... the plaintiff was entitled to the per cent. paid him, whether he succeeded in the action or not."

While we have been unable to find an authority precisely in point upon the question whether the representations, if false, were of a sufficiently grave nature to vitiate an assignment of judgment or a compromise, we have found cases in which fraudulent representations as to solvency and as to one's assets and liabilities were held sufficient.   We think the fair inference to be drawn from the statement that defendant was unable to pay his debts is that he was insolvent, and that such statement, coupled with the other facts alleged, was intended to induce the plaintiff to believe that the defendant, being without any means whatever, would need the assistance of a third person to furnish him the money to be paid upon the compromise.   If such representations were, as alleged, false and untrue and fraudulently made, we think they are sufficient.

The appellant insists, however, that the form of the action is bad, and that, if it can be maintained, then the plaintiff would be able to succeed in recovering a judgment in addition to the one that he sold and assigned, for the same claim that was merged in the assigned judgment.

As this same question was presented and disposed of in the case of Gould *v.*Cayuga Nat. Bank, from which we have quoted (and also in the same case subsequently reported in 99 *N. Y.* 338), it is unnecessary to discuss it further.

Opinion by O'BRIEN, J. VAN BRUNT, P. J., WILLIAMS, PATTERSON and INGRAHAM, JJ., concurred.

Judgment affirmed, with costs, but with leave to defendant to withdraw the demurrer and answer over on payment of costs in this court and in the court below.

Franklin Bien, for the defendant, appellant.

W. J. Woods, for the plaintiff, respondent.

HEWITT *v.* BALLARD.

Supreme Court, Fourth Department, Appellate Division;
April, 1897.

Judgment ; power of appellate court to modify.] Where the judgment entered upon the decision of a county court, reversing a judgment for the plaintiff in a justice's court does not conform to the decision, but contains a wholly unwarranted clause awarding a recovery to defendant, the appellate division, upon plaintiff's appeal has power, under Code Civ. Pro. § 1317, to modify the judgment by striking out such clause and affirming it as modified ; the plaintiff's remedy is not limited to a motion in the county court to correct the judgment.*

---

* ADAMS, J., in concurring with the majority of the court cited Wood *v.* Baker, 60 *Hun,* 337, as an authority for the decision. He added, however : "It is true that the judgment, as entered by the county clerk of Jefferson county, is not the judgment the defendant was authorized to enter by the decision of the county court, and undoubtedly the better practice would have been for the plaintiff to have moved in the court below for the correction or modification of

Hewitt v. Ballard.

Appeal by the plaintiff from a judgment of the Jefferson County Court in favor of defendant, entered upon an order of that court reversing a judgment in favor of the plaintiff, rendered by a justice of the peace.

Action by Jessie Hewitt against Thomas T. Ballard for $30 damages for the conversion of certain corn which had been seized on execution against the plaintiff's hus-

---

the judgment. But inasmuch as he has appealed to this county, and this court has the power to grant the relief to which he is entitled, I am in favor of a modification of the judgment as appealed from in accordance with the opinion of HARDIN, P. J.

FOLLETT and GREEN, P. J., dissented on the ground that the only proper remedy in such a case was by way of an application to the county court to correct the judgment, as it was manifest that the judgment entered by the county clerk was not authorized by the decision rendered by the county court, and cited Code Civ. Pro. §§ 1282, 1283; Kenney v. Apgar, 93 N. Y. 539; Baylies' N. T. & App. 6, 7; 2 Rumsey s Pr. 610.

In Kenney v. Apgar (supra) the judgment was rendered in an action to foreclose a mechanic's lien. The judgment directed a sale of the right, title and interest which the owner had in the premises on February 12, 1879, or at any time thereafter, whereas the lien of the plaintiff was not filed until April 29. 1879, and the court said, at page 547: "In this respect the judgment departs from the direction contained in the decision of the court, and where a judgment does not conform to the decision the remedy of the party aggrieved is by application to the court to correct the judgment, and not by appeal."

In Stafford v. Van Zandt (2 Johns. Cas. 66), a judgment was entered which was for 99 cents more than was authorized by the report of a referee, and for that reason the judgment was reversed.

In Hanley v. Crowe (19 St. R. 828), it was held that the general term had power, under Code Civ. Pro. § 1317, to modify a judgment when the exact amount of the proper modification appears from an application of the law to the facts.

The general term has power to vacate a judgment entered by the clerk on an order of a former general term, when the judgment does not conform to the order. Caro v. Metropolitan El. R. R. Co., 2 Civ. Pro. R. 371.

See Stilwell v. Stilwell (1 N. Y. Ann. Cas. 31), where it was held that the court had no power to correct a judgment entered upon an offer.

band. The plaintiff recovered before the justice, but upon appeal the judgment was reversed, the county judge writing an opinion on reversal holding that the evidence showed the husband to be the owner of the corn. In the judgment of reversal, there was inserted, whether by the defendant's attorney or by the county clerk does not appear, a clause awarding to the defendant $30 as the value of the property in dispute. Plaintiff appealed.

Held, that this court had power to modify the judgment by striking out the unwarranted clause, and that the plaintiff's remedy was not confined to a motion in the county court to correct the judgment. *Code Civ. Pro.* § 1317; Ludlum v. Couch, 42 *Supp.* 370; s. c., 10 *App. Div.* 603. The county judge only had power to affirm or reverse the judgment. The award of a recovery of thirty dollars in favor of the defendant against the plaintiff has no warrant in the decision or in the evidence, or in the proceedings found in the record before us. Section 1317 of the Code provides that upon an appeal to this court, it "may reverse or affirm, wholly or partly, or may modify the judgment or order appealed from." Power to modify is, therefore, conferred by statute, and it seems orderly that that power should be exercised in respect to the judgment brought before us, which contains, as above stated, improper words and relief beyond the authority of the county court to give, so far as the record discloses any foundation for its action. Schoonmaker v. Bonnie, 16 *Civ. Pro. R.* 66; s. c., 51 *Hun,* 34; 20 *St. R.* 428; 3 *Supp.* 492; Gelston v. Codwise, 1 *Johns. Ch.* 189; Marshall v. Boyer, 23 *St. R.* 302; Hubbard v. Copcutt, 9 *Abb. Pr. N. S.* 289; Sheldon v. Williams, 52 *Barb.* 183; Sheridan v. Andrews, 80 *N. Y.* 648; Decker v. Decker, 108 *Id.* 128; Goodsell v. Western Union Tel. Co. 109 *Id.* 151; Fischer v. Blank, 138 *Id.* 671; s. c., 53 *St. R.* 293; Petrie v. Trustees of Hamilton College, 92 *Hun,* 81; 71 s. c., *St. R.* 804; 36 *Supp.* 1009.

In Kenney v. Apgar, 93 *N. Y.* 539, an action to fore-

Hewitt *v.* Ballard.

close a mechanic's lien was brought before the court for consideration, and incidentally, in the course of the opinion of ANDREWS, J. (at p. 548), he says : " Where a judgment does not conform to the decision, the remedy of the party .aggrieved is by application to the court to correct the judgment, and not by appeal." That remark was made in respect to the direction of sale " of the right, title and interest which the owner had in the premises February 12, 1879," and he followed it with the remark that, inasmuch as there had been no change of title, "the point is wholly immaterial." Doubtless in that case a party might have appropriately sought relief by motion, if he was entitled to any relief. However, near the conclusion of the opinion in that case the learned judge observed : " We think the judgment should be modified by directing payment of the several liens in the order of priority fixed by the judgment to the extent of $1,300 and interest thereon from May 1, 1879, to the time of the sale, after deducting therefrom the amount of Ryan's lien found to be outstanding. . . ." The conclusion reached in the court was that the judgment " as modified " was affirmed.

The judgment of the county court should be modified by striking therefrom the words " and that the said Thomas T. Ballard, appellant, recover of and from the said Jessie Hewitt, respondent, the sum of $30," and as so modified, affirmed, with costs.

Opinion by HARDIN, P. J. All concurred, except FOLLET and GREEN, JJ., dissenting.

Judgment modified, and as modified, affirmed with costs.

John C. Trolan, for the plaintiff, appellant.

C. A. Van Allen, for the defendant, respondent.

Halbert *v.* Gibbs.

HALBERT *v.* GIBBS.

*Supreme Court, Second Department, Appellate Division;
April,* 1897.

*Attorney and client ; refusal of attorney to proceed ; client's right to
substitution.*] Where an attorney refuses to proceed with a
case, or to allow any one else to appear for his client, until his
claim for services thus far performed is paid, unless he shows a
condition of affairs which clearly justifies such action, he
thereby discharges himself, the relation of attorney and client
is terminated, and the attorney loses the lien which is given to
him by *Code Civ. Pro.* § 66.*

---

* A client has a right to change his attorney at his own volition,
whatever may be his motives ; whether a mere caprice or a substantial reason.   Trust *v.* Repoor, 15 *How. Pr.* 570.

But in such a case he must pay his attorney for services already performed.   Board of Supervisors of Ulster Co. *v.* Brodhead,
44 *How. Pr.* 411 ; Hoffman *v.* Van Nostrand, 14 *Abb. Pr.* 336.

In matter of Prospect Avenue (1 *N. Y. Ann. Cas.* 347), it was
held that a client, subject only to the payment of his attorney's
fees, in a proper case, or securing them if they cannot then be
fixed and determined, has the right, without assigning cause, at
any point in a suit or proceeding, to change his attorney ; and
where the attorney has been guilty of misconduct, substitution will
be ordered unconditionally, leaving the attorney to his action for
his fees.

In Pierce *v.* Waters (10 *W. Dig.* 432, head-note), it is said :
"Upon an application by a party for substitution of another attorney in place of his attorney of record, ordinarily the court will see
that the attorney is protected as to his fees ; yet where the attorney's conduct has been improper and neglectful the court will deny
this protection and direct an unconditional substitution, leaving the
attorney to his action for his fees."

See Estate of Hoyt (12 *Civ. Pro. R.* 208), in which Surrogate
Rollins gives a history of attorneys' liens in this State and collates
the various cases on the subject.

See Note on Substitution of Attorneys, 1 *N. Y. Ann. Cas.* 352

See Notes on Attorney's Liens, 18 *Abb. N. C.* 23 ; 23 *Id.* 246.

Halbert *v.* Gibbs.

Appeal by the defendant, from an order of the Supreme Court, Kings County Trial Term, denying the defendant's motion for the substitution of an attorney in the action.

The action out of which the present controversy arose was brought by George Halbert against Albert R. Gibbs to recover a balance of $6,014, claimed to be due to the plaintiff from the defendant for material furnished, and labor and services performed upon private residence premises in the city of New York. The defendant denied liability and set up by way of counterclaim improper work, failure to furnish material, loss of rent, money loaned and other items, amounting in the aggregate to the sum of $20,510.18. The action was begun about April, 1893, and Augustus B. Prentice was retained to defend the action and served notice of appearance therein. He had, prior to this time, performed some service in endeavoring to negotiate a settlement of the matters in dispute. The cause being at issue, the same was, upon December 28, 1893, referred to Levi A. Fuller, as referee, to hear, try and determine. The hearing before the referee began on the day of February 23d, 1893, and has continued down to the day of February 8th, 1897. There have been one hundred and forty-four hearings before the referee, the longest hearing being four hours, and the shortest one hour, the average being a fraction less than two and one-half hours for each hearing. From time to time the defendant has paid to his attorney the sum of

As to the extent of the lien of a defendant's attorney, see Longyear *v.* Carter, 2 *N. Y. Ann. Cas.* 192, and notes.

See also the following cases as to the right of set-off of judgments between principals, where the attorneys' lien is affected, and also as to the enforcement of the attorney's lien as against an assignee of a judgment: Guliano *v.* Whitenack, 1 *N. Y. Ann. Cas.* 75; Hopper *v.* Ersler, *Id.* 192; Winterson *v.* Higgins, *Id.* 193; Delaney *v.* Miller, *Id.* 266.

$1,500; to the referee from time to time $900; to steno-graphers and witnesses, $1,526.53. The referee has been paid in all about $1,700, and the stenographer about $1,900; 4,970 pages of testimony have been taken, and fifty-three witnesses examined. On the day of February 5th, 1897, defendant's attorney wrote the defendant that, in looking up his account, he found that he had only received from the defendant $300 since November 25, 1895, and that he had spent in actual attendance before the referee, one hundred and fifty hours since that date, and further stated : " I must decline to go a step further with the case until you send me a check for $500.00." This demand was not complied with by the defendant. The reference at this time stood adjourned until the 8th day of February, at two P. M. At that time the defendant appeared before the referee, ready to proceed with the hearing. The cross-examination of a witness for the defendant was unfinished ; the witness was present and plaintiff's counsel desired to proceed with the examination. The defendant's attorney refused to proceed or do any act in the matter. At the solicitation of counsel for the plaintiff, the attorney consented to proceed and conclude the examination of the witness, and at the close of the session stated that he would take no further part in the trial unless his bill was paid. The reference was adjourned to February 15, 1897. In the meantime the defendant retained Archibald C. Shenstone to conduct his defense, and requested him to procure an order of substitution of himself as attorney of record, and for that purpose the defendant executed and acknowleged a consent to have said Shenstone substituted as his attorney. Shenstone procured an order of substitution and presented the same to the defendant's attorney, with the consent of defendant. Prentice refused to sign a consent for substitution, and refused to deliver the papers in the action to Shenstone. On the adjourned day the parties, Prentice and Shenstone, appeared before the ref-

Halbert *v.* Gibbs.

eree. The latter again endeavored to have said Prentice execute the consent for substitution ; Prentice refused, stating that he refused to deliver any papers in the case until his bill for services was paid. Shenstone thereupon attempted to appear as counsel for the defendant, to which Prentice objected, stating that he still considered himself the attorney in the case, and requested an adjournment for such time as the referee might think proper ; and further stated that he only refused to proceed on the ground that his client refused to compensate him for his labor and time ; " if his fees were paid he would be glad and willing to proceed with the case." Against the opposition of the counsel for the plaintiff the referee adjourned the case for two weeks. Thereupon this motion was made, resulting in an order of reference to hear, try and determine what amount, if any, is due from the defendant to his said attorney for services and disbursements in the action. On motion to resettle this order an order was made denying the defendant's motion to substitute the said Shenstone as attorney for the defendant in the action, and directing the hearing before the referee appointed by the former order to proceed, and for the referee to file his report as expeditiously as practical.

Held, that an order of substitution should have been made. One proposition stands out before us clear and distinct ; it is that the attorney for the defendant refuses to proceed with the trial of this action, or to permit any one else to represent the defendant unless he be paid, either in whole or in part, his claim for services. He, therefore brings himself squarely within the doctrine laid down in Matter of H——, 93 *N. Y.* 381. By his refusal to proceed, in the language of the above case, " he discharged himself, and, in such a case, it is clear that an attorney cannot leave his client in the middle of a matter because he does not supply him with money, or by reason of any other difficulty, without running the risk of losing the benefit of that relation." The attorney insists, however, that he has a lien upon the counterclaim set up in the answer, and also upon his client's papers, which he may not be deprived of, and which he is entitled to have protected before any order will be made substituting another attorney. *Code Civ. Pro.* § 66; Bowling Green Savings Bank *v.* Todd, 52 *N. Y.* 489; Matter of Knapp, 85 *Id.* 284; Tenny *v.* Berger, 93 *Id.* 524. But in all these cases the lien was upheld and continued upon the ground that the relation of attorney and client continued, and that the business in which the attorney was engaged was finished while the relation continued. But the clear distinction is always made that the attorney, in order to maintain his lien, must show performance upon his part or such a condition as clearly justifies his withdrawal. Sessions *v.* Palmeter, 75 *Hun*, 268; S. C., 58 *St. R.* 289; 26 *Supp.* 1076. When he discharges himself by an absolute refusal to proceed, no lien for service attaches either to judgment, proceeds or papers. Tuck *v.* Manning, 53 *Hun.* 455; S. C., 25 *St R.* 130; 6 *Supp* 140; 17 *Civ. Pro. R.* 175. It will be found, and has been found, within the authorities above cited, quite practicable for the court to protect an attorney in a proper case against a dishonest client. It is equally practicable to protect a client against improper practice and unjust demands of his attorney. So much is left to the general equitable power of the court in this regard that but little real difficulty will be encountered. In the present case we think that nothing appears which justified the attorney in the abandonment of his client in the midst of the trial.

Opinion by HATCH, J. All concurred.

Order reversed, with ten dollars costs and disbursements, and motion to substitute granted, with ten dollars costs.

Archibald Shenstone, for defendant, appellant.

Augustus B. Prentice, for the respondent, in person.

DONNELLY *v.* PANCOAST.

Supreme Court, First Department, Appellate Division ; March, 1897.

1. *Corporations ; de facto directors ; liability.*] Where a person elected a director of a corporation held only one share of stock when he was required by law to hold at least five shares, but continued, notwithstanding, to act as such director,—*Held*, that he was a director *de facto*, and as such estopped from denying his liability to creditors of the corporation in case of a failure to file an annual report of the corporation.*

* The term of office of a director ceases at the end of the time for which he was elected, and it is not necessary for him to resign even though no other director is elected in his place. He does not hold over unless he continues to act as such director or trustee. Van Amburgh *v.* Baker, 81 *N. Y.* 46.

Where a director or trustee resigns before the debt is created by the corporation he relieves himself from liability although the resignation is not acted upon by the board of trustees or entered in the books of the corporation. Blake *v.* Wheeler, 18 *Hun*, 496 ; rev'd on another point *sub nom.* Bonnell *v.* Griswold, 80 *N. Y.* 128 ; Chanler *v.* Hoag, 2 *Hun*, 613 ; aff'd 63 *N. Y.* 624 ; Wilson *v.* Brentwood Hotel Co., 16 *Misc.* 48 ; s. c., 37 *Supp.* 655 ; 73 *St. R.* 274.

It seems where a director resigns before the default is made in filing a report he is not liable. Bruce *v.* Platt, 80 *N. Y.* 379.

As to what is sufficient evidence of *bona fide* transfer of stock so as to avoid liability to creditors of the corporation, see Rochester & Kettle Falls L. Co. *v.* Raymond, 4 *App. Div.* 600 ; Sinclair *v.* Dwight 9 *App. Div.* 297 ; S. C., 41 *Supp.* 193.

One who has acted as a director, although not elected, cannot repudiate his directorship and recover from others with whom he has acted. Easterly *v.* Barber, 65 *N. Y.* 252.

But see Cornell *v.* Roach, 101 *N. Y.* 373, where the assignee of a claim originally held by a director against the corporation, was allowed to recover.

As to individual liability of officers of foreign corporations, see Marshall *v.* Sherman, 148 *N. Y.* 42.

2. *The same ; exhausting remedy against corporation.*] Under section 30 of the Stock Corporation Law a creditor of a corporation can maintain an action against the directors thereof personally to recover his debt, upon the failure of the corporation to file its annual report, without first recovering a judgment against the corporation.

Appeal by the defendants, Archer V. Pancoast and others, from a judgment of the Supreme Court, New York County, entered upon the verdict of a jury rendered by direction of the court, in favor of the plaintiff.

This action was brought by John R. Donnelly against the defendants as directors of the Archer & Pancoast Manufacturing Company, a domestic corporation, for goods sold and delivered to said corporation between March 1, 1893, and May 19, 1893, the said company having failed to file its annual report for that year. The evidence showed that the Archer & Pancoast Manufacturing Company was organized in September, 1868, by the filing of a certificate of incorporation in the offices of the Secretary of State and of the clerk of the city and county of New York. On February 19, 1890, the number of the directors of the company was increased from five to eight. At the time of the original election of the defendants as directors they held a sufficient number of shares of stock in said company to qualify them to act as such directors. On July 21, 1890, all the capital stock of the company was transferred to the defendant Biddle, except the single shares held by the other defendants respectively; and during the years 1892 and 1893 each defendant, against whom a verdict was directed by the court below, held and owned but one share of stock. No annual report was filed in January, 1893. It further appeared that the defendants were duly elected directors of the company on February 16, 1892, for the term expiring on February 16, 1893, and were elected on February 21, 1893, and acted as such directors and managed the business and affairs of the cor-

Donnelly *v.* Pancoast.

poration until the last of May, when receivers of the corporation were appointed, who had possession of the affairs of the corporation until November, 1893. In January, 1894, the corporation filed its annual report, signed by said directors. There is no dispute but that the goods in question were sold to the corporation. Upon this state of facts, the court directed a verdict in favor of the plaintiff, and from the judgment thereupon entered this appeal is taken.

Held, no error. It appears that in July, 1890, all the directors transferred all their shares of stock except one. What the object of this transfer was does not appear, except perhaps to escape the obligations which pertained to the office of director, upon the theory that they were disqualified from being directors, and consequently could not be held liable as such. It has been suggested by the counsel for the respondent that all that was necessary after the organization of the company was that the directors should be stockholders; and that the provisions of section 2 of chapter 691 of the laws of 1892 did not apply, but rather the provisions of section 20 of chapter 688 of the laws of that year. Upon an examination of this section, however, it will appear that the requirement that the directors shall hold five shares of stock does not obtain as to the directors of the first year only, but is a general requirement relating to the office of director. We do not think, however, that the defendants can avail themselves of any such objection for the purpose of escaping the liability attaching to the office which they claimed to have usurped. They were elected directors of the corporation; they accepted the position; they managed the business and affairs of the corporation, assuming all the duties and emoluments attached thereto ; and it is too late now for them to attempt to escape the burden. Their title to the office cannot be attacked collaterally. They were *de facto* directors, and they cannot now claim that they were not directors *de jure*, not because of any estoppel, but simply because the rule of law is well established that he who enters upon an office and exercises all its functions is responsible for his acts therein to the same extent as though he of right occupied the position.

It seems to us that, it having been established that these defendants were elected directors, that they accepted the office and exercised its duties without any one questioning their title, they cannot now denude themselves of the office which they have taken for the purpose of escaping the responsibilities attaching thereto.

The claim made by the appellant, that the plaintiff cannot maintain this action because he was not a judgment creditor of the corporation with an execution returned unsatisfied, has been disposed of by this court in the case of Camp Mf'g Co. *v.* Reamer, 14 *App. Div.* 408.[*]

Opinion by VAN BRUNT, P. J. WILLIAMS, PATTERSON, O'BRIEN and INGRAHAM, JJ., concurred.

Judgment affirmed, with costs.

Julien T. Davies, Byron Traver, George L. Nichols and *Benjamin H. Bayliss,* for the defendants, appellants.

D. M. Porter, for the plaintiff, respondent.

---

[*] To same effect. see Rose *v.* Chadwick, 3 *N. Y. Ann. Cas.* 389, with Note on Primary Liability of Directors and Stockholders.

FURBUSH *v.* NYE.

Supreme Court, First Department, Appellate Division;
May, 1897.

1. *Jurisdiction ; non-residents ; action on contract.*] The courts of
this State will take jurisdiction of an action on contract, although all the parties reside in another State.*
2. *Attachment; doubtful cause of action; merits not considered on
motion to vacate attachment.*] Where, on a motion to vacate
an attachment, it does not clearly appear that the plaintiff has
no cause of action, the merits of the action will not be determined, but that question will be left to the trial court.†

Appeal by the plaintiff, from an order of the Supreme
Court, New York Special Term, setting aside the service
of the summons, dismissing the complaint against the defendant Nye, and vacating a warrant of attachment granted
against him in the action

This was an action by Charles A. Furbush against
Allen T. Nye and another to recover $300,000 as damages
for the breach of an alleged contract by which the defendants agreed to purchase stock and bonds of a corporation
to be formed by the plaintiff. It appeared from the papers that all of the parties to the action are non-residents
of this State, and that the defendant Nye appeared specially in the action for the purpose only of setting aside
the service of the summons and vacating the warrant of
attachment. The motion was granted by the learned
judge at special term for the reason, as appears in his
opinion, that all the parties being non-residents the courts
of this State would not take jurisdiction of their contro-

---

* See Note at the end of this case.
† See Note on Proof of Cause of Action to Sustain Attachment,
2 *N. Y. Ann. Cas.* 359.

versy, but would remit them to the courts of the State where they lived to settle their affairs there.

Held, error. There is no doubt a rule that the courts of this State will not take jurisdiction of actions of tort between parties resident of, and located in, another State. But that rule does not apply, and has never been applied, to actions on contract. Where actions are brought for a breach of a contract, courts of this State will take jurisdiction, although all the parties may reside in another State. Especially is that so where the contract is made in this State. Smith *v.* Crocker, 14 *App. Div.* 245.

The motion to vacate the attachment was put not only upon the ground that the parties were non-residents, and for that reason the court would not take jurisdiction, but upon the further ground that upon all the facts the plaint- iff had no cause of action against the defendants. An ex- amination of the papers shows that it is by no means clear that there is not a cause of action, and that it is not at all certain that the damages may not amount to a con- siderable sum. In such case the court will not consider the merits of the action upon affidavits and vacate the warrants because it determines upon the motion that the plaintiff cannot succeed, but will deny the motion, leaving the merits of the case to be disposed of upon the trial. Johnson *v.* Hardwood Door & Trim Co., 79 *Hun*, 407 ; s. c., 61 *St. R.* 502 ; 29 *Supp.* 797. That course should have been pursued in this case.

Opinion by RUMSEY, J. VAN BRUNT, P. J., WIL- LIAMS, PATTERSON and PARKER, JJ., concurred.

Order reversed, with ten dollars costs and disburse- ments, and motion denied with ten dollars costs.

J. Edward Ackley, for the plaintiff, appellant.

James McNaught, for the defendant, respondent.

NOTE ON JURISDICTION OF NON-RESIDENTS.

In general.] In considering the question discussed in this note, it should be observed that no attempt is made here to draw the line of demarcation between such actions as are local and those which are transitory in their nature. But assuming that the cause of action is transitory, the discussion here relates solely to the effect upon the jurisdiction of the courts of this State in such an action, of the fact that the cause of action arose in a foreign State, or country, and the further fact that all the parties thereto are non-residents of this State or some of them are foreign corporations. And assuming that the court has jurisdiction of the subject matter, the inquiry is then directed to the manner of securing jurisdiction of the person of non-resident defendants.

Natural persons ; contracts.] Where the parties to an action are natural persons, it seems to be well settled by recent as well as by some older decisions, that the courts of this State have jurisdiction of the subject matter of all actions founded upon contract, whether the parties are non-residents or not. This is said to be true, particularly where the contract was made in this State, as remarked in the case in the text, but it would seem from the language of the court, here as well as in other cases cited below, that the question of where the contract was made is of no importance.

In Reed *v.* Chilson (142 *N. Y.* 152), an action was brought by a non-resident against non-residents upon a judgment recovered in the State of Michigan. An attachment was issued, but no property was attached, and the summons was served on the defendants by publication. The defendants appeared generally in the action and interposed an answer setting up the lack of jurisdiction of the court, on the ground that none of the parties were residents of this State, and also that the defendants had no property in this State. It was held that the court had jurisdiction of the subject matter of the action, and that it acquired jurisdiction of the persons of the defendants by the general appearance. It also appeared in that action that a judgment had been recovered by the same plaintiff against the same defendants on the identical cause of action, in this State, but that in the former action there had been no personal service of the summons within this State, that no property had been attached, and no appearance had been entered by the defendants. It was held that such former judgment was void for lack of jurisdiction of the person, and could not be successfully pleaded as a bar to the subsequent action.

A judgment of a foreign State upon which an action is brought is a claim for "damages for the breach of a contract, express or implied, other than a contract to marry," within the meaning of Code Civ. Pro., § 635, (attachment) whether the original claim was founded upon a contract or a tort. Gutta Percha & Rubber Mfg. Co. *v.* Mayor, etc., of Houston, 108 *N. Y.* 276.

The same; torts.] It was clearly settled in Burdick *v.* Freeman (120 *N. Y.* 420), that in actions for torts committed without the State, where all the parties are non-residents, the courts of this State, may, in their discretion, entertain jurisdiction. That was an action for criminal conversation. All of the acts complained of were committed without the State, and all the parties were residents of the State of Pennsylvania when the action was begun. No objection was made by the defendant to the jurisdiction of the court until the close of the trial, when he asked for a dismissal on that ground, it appearing from the evidence that all the parties were non-residents, and that the acts complained of were committed without the State. The motion was denied, and that ruling was upheld by the Court of Appeals on the ground stated above.

The court in that case expressly overruled the cases of Molony *v.* Dowes, 8 *Abb. Pr.* 316 ; and Latourette *v.* Clark, 30 *How. Pr.* 242.

In Gardner *v.* Thomas (14 *Johns.* 134), it was said that the courts of this State had jurisdiction of an action for damages for assault and battery committed on the high seas, brought by a British subject against another subject of the same country, where the act was committed on a foreign vessel. But the court said that whether or not it would take jurisdiction rested in the sound discretion of the court. And it added, at page 137 : " It must be conceded that the law of nations gives complete and entire jurisdiction to the courts of the country to which the vessel belongs, but not exclusively. It is exclusive only as it respects the public injury, but concurrent with the tribunals of other nations as to the private remedy. There may be cases, however, where the refusal to take cognizance of causes for such torts may be justified by the manifest public inconvenience and injury which it would create to the community of both nations ; and the present is such a case. . . .

It is evident, then, that our courts may take cognizance of torts committed on the high seas, on board of a foreign vessel where both parties are foreigners ; but I am inclined to think it must, on principles of policy, often rest in the sound discretion of the court to afford jurisdiction or not, according to the circumstances of the case."

This case is still frequently cited as an authority for the principle that our courts may, in their discretion, take jurisdiction of cases sounding in tort, even where all the parties are non-residents and the acts complained of were committed without the State.

In De Witt *v.* Buchanan (54 *Barb.* 31), the action was for damages for an assault and battery committed in Canada, both parties being residents of that country when the action was brought. The court, while refusing to retain jurisdiction in that case, recognized the principle that in some cases jurisdiction of actions of that nature would be retained, and the court said : " Actions for injuries to the person are transitory and follow the person ; and, therefore, so far as the nature of the action is concerned, one foreigner may sue another foreigner in our courts for a tort committed in another country, the same as on a contract made in another country. . . But as a question of policy there are many reasons why jurisdiction should not be entertained. Unless for special reasons non-resident foreigners should not be permitted to use our courts to redress wrongs or enforce contracts committed or made within their own territory. Our courts are organized and maintained at our own expense for the use, benefit and protection of our citizens. Foreigners should not be invited to bring their matters here for litigation. But if a foreigner flee to this country he may be pursued and prosecuted here. Nothing appears in this case showing why jurisdiction should be entertained. It seems an ordinary case of assault and battery committed in Canada, both parties still residing there, the defendant being casually here when arrested. It is most clearly against the interests of those living on the border for our courts to encourage or entertain jurisdiction of such actions. To do so would establish a practice which might often be attended with serious disadvantages to persons crossing the border. The true policy is to refuse jurisdiction in all such cases unless for special reasons shown."

The same ; when jurisdiction taken.] While it is said in some of the cases that the courts of this State will not take jurisdiction of actions for torts committed without the State, where the parties are non-residents, except under particular circumstances, it is not made entirely clear by the reported cases what these circumstances must be. In Mostyn v. Fabrigas (2 *Smith's Lead. Cas.* [9 *Am. ed.*] 916), it is said that the courts of England would take cognizance of such cases whén it appeared that no other court had jurisdiction, or the circumstances were such that unless jurisdiction was taken the plaintiff would be without redress. In that case the opinion was written by Lord MANSFIELD, and in the course of the opinion it was suggested that the court would take cognizance of a case where the injury had occurred in a far-distant country to which it was improbable that the defendant would ever return, so that the plaintiff would be unable to secure redress, because of his inability to secure jurisdiction of the person of the defendant, unless jurisdiction was retained by the English courts. That case is cited with approval in Burdick v. Freeman (*supra*).

When the case of Burdick v. Freeman (120 *N. Y.* 420) was in the lower court (46 *Hun*, 138), the general term said, at p. 141 : " There are cases in which jurisdiction has been retained, but they are cases in which reasons appear for such retention. In one case a party charged with having committed a fraud, had come into this State and was about embarking for a long voyage upon the high seas. Surely in such a case the courts should retain jurisdiction, for the defrauded party could no longer seek redress in the courts of his own State, the defendant being in the act of leaving the country."

In Johnson v. Dalton (1 *Cowen*, 543), a judgment for the plaintiff was affirmed in an action by a seaman for damages for an assault committed by the master of a foreign vessel on the high seas, where it appeared that both parties were British subjects. It appeared, however, that the master had discharged the plaintiff, and the court held that under such circumstances it would be unjust to compel the plaintiff to return to his own country and take his witnesses with him in order to secure redress for the injury which he had suffered.

The case of Gardner v. Thomas (14 *Johns.* 134) was distinguished and the doctrine of that case approved.

See *Whart. Confl. Laws*, §§ 705, 707, 743 ; *Story Confl. Laws*, § 545 ; 4 *Phil. on Int. Law*, 701.

In Newman v. Goddard (3 *Hun*, 70), it was held that the courts of this State would take jurisdiction of actions for personal injuries committed abroad where one of the parties was a citizen of the United States ; following De

Witt *v.* Buchanan, 54 *Barb.* 31, and disapproving Molony *v.* Dows, 8 *Abb. Pr.* 316.

See also Lister *v.* Wright, (2 *Hill,* 320), where the action was for a slander spoken in Canada.

Foreign corporations]. Tracing the law of jurisdiction of foreign corporations backward from the time of the enactment of section 1780 of the Code of Civil Procedure, it will be found that that section materially limited such jurisdiction as it had existed under section 427 of the Code of Procedure and the Revised Statutes (2 *R. S.* 459, § 15, as amended by *L.* 1849, c. 107) prior to the enactment of the old Code. The Code of Procedure specified certain cases in which the courts of this State had jurisdiction of actions against foreign corporations, but did not limit the jurisdiction to the cases specified, and it was held in McCormick *v.* Pennsylvania R. R. Co. (49 *N. Y.* 303), that the supreme court had jurisdiction of actions against such a corporation in every case where jurisdiction of the corporation could be secured. But the present Code so clearly specifies in what cases jurisdiction will be taken by our courts that it is not profitable to look any farther back, particularly as it has been held that section 1780 specifies absolutely the *only* cases in which such jurisdiction can be secured. Robinson *v.* Oceanic Steam Nav. Co., 112 *N. Y.* 315 ; Ervin *v.* Oregon R. R. & N. Co., 28 *Hun,* 269 ; Adams *v.* Pennsylvania Bank, 35 *Id.* 393. This section provides that an action may be maintained against a foreign corporation by a resident of this State or by a domestic corporation for any cause of action ; by a non-resident or another foreign corporation in one of the following cases only :

1. " Where the action is brought to recover damages for the breach of a contract, made within the State, or relating to property situated within the State, at the time of the making thereof."

2. " When it is brought to recover real property situated within the State, or a chattel, which is replevied within the State."

3. " Where the cause of action arose within the State, except where the object of the action is to affect the title to real property situated without the State."

The disability of a non-resident to sue a foreign corporation cannot be waived in any manner, even by stipulation *it seems,* and the court may *ex mero motu,* when attention is called to the facts, refuse to proceed further and dismiss the action. Robinson *v.* Oceanic Steam Nav. Co., 112 *N. Y.* 315 ; Davidsburg *v.* Knickerbocker Life Ins. Co., 90 *Id.* 526 ; Galt *v.* Provident Savings Bank, 18 *Abb. N. C.* 431, with Note on Jurisdiction of Foreign Corporations, *Id.* 435.

A non-resident does not become a resident by being appointed an administrator by the courts of this State so as to enable him to bring an action against a foreign corporation upon a cause of action arising without the State. Robinson *v.* Oceanic Steam Nav. Co., 112 *N. Y.* 315 ; aff'g 56 *Super. Ct.* (*J. & S.*) 108.

In Seiser Bros. Co. *v.* Potter Produce Co. (23 *Civ. Pro. R.* 348), an attachment was secured by one foreign corporation against another, and after issue was joined in the action the defendant confessed judgment for a certain amount, and an execution was issued therefor and the attached property was taken to satisfy the execution. Subsequently, upon the motion of a junior attaching creditor, who was a resident, the former attachment and judgment were vacated, on the ground that the court was without jurisdiction, inasmuch as it appeared that both plaintiff and defendant were foreign corporations, and it nowhere appeared that the contract in suit was made in this State or that the cause of action arose here.

To the same effect, see Smith *v.* Union Milk Co., 70 *Hun,* 348.

How jurisdiction acquired.] The acquisition of jurisdiction of non-residents and foreign corporations is a highly technical proceeding, unless personal service can be made upon the non-resident, or the proper officer of the foreign corporation. As to service upon a foreign corporation, see *Code Civ. Pro.,* § 432 ; and Note on Service of Summons on Foreign Corporations, 2 *N. Y. Ann. Cas.* 73.

In actions for partition, foreclosure, replevin, etc., where the court has jurisdiction of the property, the various statutes as to service by publication or personally without the State must be strictly complied with. Except in matrimonial actions (*Code Civ. Pro.* § 1774) it was impossible in personal actions to secure jurisdiction of a non-resident defendant, where he could not be personally served within the State and he did not appear, in all actions except those for a breach of contract, where partial jurisdiction could be secured by attaching property here, until the amendment to Code Civ. Pro. § 635, by L. 1895, c. 578, gave the right to an attachment also in cases of conversion, or injury to person or property, when such injury was caused by the negligence of the defendant.

On entering judgment in such cases Code Civ. Pro. § 1217 must be complied with as well as the statutes allowing service by publication or personally without the State.

Palmer *v.* Van Santvoord.

PALMER *v.* VAN SANTVOORD.*

Supreme Court, Third Department, Appellate Division; May, 1897.

Corporations ; insolvency ; preference of wages.] A person in the employ of a machine manufacturing company, having general charge of putting up and taking down the machines at the place of sale, and performing some manual labor in such connection, and also acting as a selling agent of the company, is within the statute (*L.* 1885, c. 376) giving a preference to the wages of the employes, laborers and operatives of an insolvent corporation.†

Appeal by Seymour Van Santvoord and another, as receivers of the Walter A. Wood Mowing and Reaping Machine Company, from an order of the Supreme Court, Rensselaer Special Term, directing them to pay the plaintiff his wages as a preferred claim under the statute.

The respondent, Wilson E. Palmer, was employed by the Machine Company prior to the appointment of the appellants as its receivers, to set up machines, and to take them down, and to fix the same when out of repair; to go

---

* Aff'd by Court of Appeals, N. Y. Law J., Oct. 20, 1897.

† See People *v.* Beveridge Brewing Co. (3 *N. Y. Ann. Cas.* 4) where it was held that a bookkeeper of a corporation was entitled to a preference under this statute; also Note on Statutory Provisions for the Protection and Enforcement of Claims for Wages, etc. *Id.* 7.

In Gurney *v.* Atlantic & Great W. R. R. Co. (58 *N. Y.* 358) the distinction between the word "employe" as compared with "laborer," "servant," "operative," etc., was pointed out, and to the former was given a much broader and more comprehensive meaning than to those composing the latter class. It was there held that an attorney of a corporation was an employee and was entitled to have his claim for compensation for services preferred under the statute.

The general assignment act, (*L.* 1884, c, 328) contains provisions similar to those in the statute referred to in the text.

Palmer *v.* Van Santvoord.

from place to place and fix and set up the machines of said company for farmers to whom the machines had been sold; to unpack the machines and to repack them, and ship the same to company when necessary; also, to sell or solicit sales of the machines of said corporation; and did, in the discharge of his duties as the employe, operative and laborer of said company, sell machines for them, and that, as such operative, employe and laborer, he set up and repaired machines for said company while in their employ as aforesaid, going from place to place so to do; took the machines from the railroad, unpacked same, bolted together and screwed together the same, and did all necessary work to make said machines work, bolting them together and fitting them so they would work, and that he performed manual labor as well as the labor of selling machines, and obeyed and carried out the instructions, orders and directions given to him by said corporation through its officers and servants."

The question submitted is whether he was an "employe, operative or laborer," and his claim for wages against said company entitled to a preference under the provisions of *L.* 1885, c. 376, which enacts that: "Where a receiver of a corporation, created or organized under the laws of this State and doing business therein, other than insurance and moneyed corporations, shall be appointed, the wages of the employes, operatives and laborers thereof shall be preferred to every other debt or claim against such corporation, and shall be paid by the receiver from the moneys of such corporation which shall first come to his hands."

Held, that the respondent was an "employe, operative or laborer," within the meaning of the statute. Brown *v.* A. B. C. Fence Co., 52 *Hun*, 151; S. C., 23 *St. R.* 415; 5 *Supp.* 95; People *v.* Beveridge Brewing Co., 91 *Hun*, 313: S. C., 3 *N. Y. Ann. Cas.* 4.

The conclusion we reach does not, we think, conflict with the doctrine stated in People *v.* Remington (45 *Hun*,

329 ; S. C., 10 *St. R.* 310), where the claims for a preference under the act in question were made by the superintendent and attorney of the corporation. Nor were the
services rendered by the respondent for the Machine
Company similar to those of the applicants whose claims
were disallowed in Matter of Stryker, (73 *Hun*, 327 ; S. C.,
55 *St. R.* 903 ; 26 *Supp.* 209). In that case, those applying for a preference under the act in question were the
bookkeepers, superintendent and foreman, paid by the
month, and the performance of manual labor by whom, if
performed at all, was merely incidental to their general
employment.

Opinion by PUTNAM, J. All concurred, except MER-
WIN, J., dissenting on the authority of People *v.* Remington, 45 *Hun*, 329 ; aff'd without opinion, 109 *N. Y.* 631.

Order affirmed, with ten dollars costs and disbursements.

G. B. Wellington, for the receivers, appellants.

Amasa J. Parker, for Palmer, respondent.

<hr />

KNOX *v.* DUBROFF.

*Supreme Court, First Department, Appellate Division ;
May,* 1897.

*Calendar ; preference by plaintiff ; defendant arrested ; attach-
ment.*] The right to a preference on the calendar, given by
Rule 36, of the General Rules of Practice, where the defendant
is imprisoned under an order of arrest, or the property of the
defendant is held under an attachment, is available to the
plaintiff as well as to the defendant.*

* See Note on Preference on the Calendar, following this case.

Knox *v.* Dubroff.

Appeal by the plaintiff, Joseph A. Knox, from an order of the Supreme Court, New York Trial Term, denying the plaintiff's motion for a preference.

Action by Joseph A. Knox against Solomon Dubroff, in which the plaintiff moved to have the case preferred on the calendar under Rule 36 of the General Rules of Practice which provides: "Whenever in any action an issue shall have been joined, if the defendant be imprisoned under an order of arrest in the action, or if the property of the defendant be held under attachment, the trial of the ac. tion shall be preferred." The motion was denied on the ground that only the defendant could move for the prefer. ence.

Held, error. The plaintiff obtained an order of arrest, on which the defendant was held to bail, and in addition thereto obtained an attachment upon the defendant's prop. erty, and upon this latter ground the action was one in which a preference was proper. This is not seriously dis. puted, but it is urged by the respondent that the rule granting the preference was made for the benefit of the defendant, and that, unless the latter moves, the plaintiff not being injured, has no right to take advantage of the rule. The language employed, however, is not susceptible of any such construction. It defines under what conditions the trial of the action shall be preferred, and when the conditions are present the benefit of the rule is as much avail. able to the plaintiff as it is to the defendant.

Opinion *Per Curiam.* Present—PATTERSON, WIL LIAMS, O'BRIEN, INGRAHAM and PARKER, JJ.

Order reversed, with ten dollars costs and disburse. ments, and motion granted, with ten dollars costs to ap. pellant to abide event.

John M. Bowers, and *Ralph G. Miller,* for the plaintiff, appellant.

Louis Steckler, for the defendant, respondent.

NOTE ON PREFERENCE ON THE CALENDAR.

Statutes and Rules of Court.] Section 791 of the Code of Civil Procedure contains the general provisions for the order of preference on the calendar of various actions. There are ten sub-divisions to the section, and the different classes of actions are preferred in the order in which they are mentioned in the section.

All the provisions of section 791 are qualified, however, and made subject to sections 789, 790. The former of the last two sections provides an absolute preference in all courts in actions by the people in certain cases as therein specified, to recover funds which have been wrongfully detained or converted by a public officer, or other persons, belonging to the State or certain other political divisions of the State. Section 790 provides for the preference of criminal cases over civil actions, except those mentioned in section 789.

The last sub-division of section 791 provides for a preference after all the other classes of cases mentioned in the section, of " a cause entitled to preference, by the general rules of practice, or by the special order of the court in the particular case."

Section 792 provides that in case of a writ of mandamus or prohibition, from the general term to a special term or a Judge of the same court, the court in its discretion may prefer the trial or hearing of the case over any of the actions mentioned in section 791.

Rule 36, of the General Rules of Practice, provides : " Whenever in any action an issue shall have been joined, if the defendant be imprisoned under an order of arrest, in the action, or if the property of the defendant be held under attachment, the trial of the action shall be preferred.

Rule VI., of the Appellate Division rules of the first department of the supreme court, provides : " In an action for goods sold and delivered, or in an action brought to recover upon a promissory note, check, bill of exchange, bond, policy of life insurance, lease, undertaking or other instruments for the payment of money only, where it shall appear by affidavit that the trial of the action will not occupy over two hours, either party may apply to Part 2 of the Trial Term for an order placing the case upon the preferred calendar. Upon such application the court may by order, if satisfied that the trial of the action will not

occupy more than two hours, and if no good reason is
shown why the same should not be promptly tried, place
the same upon the preferred calendar and dispose of the
same in its regular order thereon. If the trial shall occupy
more than two hours, it shall go to the foot of the general
calendar, unless for good cause shown the court shall otherwise order."

Rules XI., of the same department, provides, among
other things, that any party entitled to have a case preferred, may upon two days notice apply to the court at
special term, Part 3, to have the case placed upon such preferred calendar.

Rule XIV., of the special rules of the New York City
Court, provides that in an action on contract, where it
appears that the trial is not likely to occupy more than one
hour (providing the amount claimed is not less than $100
Rule XV), the case may be preferred and tried at the part
of the court specified for the hearing of such causes and
causes preferred by Code Civ. Pro. § 791.

In the Third Department, Rule 3 provides as follows:

" A party who desires to have a cause heard as a preferred cause must in his note of issue state his claim for
preference, as provided in section 793 of the Code, or if an
order giving the cause a preference has been made under
that section, the note of issue must be accompanied with a
copy of such order."

In the Fourth Department, Rule 2 provides as follows :

" A party who desires to have a case heard as a preferred case must in his note of issue state his claim of preference, as provided in section 793 of the Code ; or if an
order giving the case a preference has been made under
that section, the note of issue must be accompanied with a
copy of such order.   The clerk, in making up the calendar,
shall place such preferred cases at the head of the general
calendar, indicating that they are preferred, and the class
to which they belong."

Under the provisions of section 793, as amended by L.
1896, c. 140, it is now necessary, except in the counties of New
York, Kings and Erie, and in the seventh judicial district,
in order to secure a preference provided for in the Code,
to secure an order, upon notice to the adverse party, and
to serve such order with the notice of trial, or before the
notice of trial is served, where the right to preference does
not appear on the face of the pleadings, or other papers to
be used before the court.   Where such right does appear it is only necessary to specify in the note of issue filed

with the clerk that the moving party claims a right to a preference, and to set forth the provision of law under which the claim is made, and it is then the duty of the clerk to place it upon the calendar in its proper position as a preferred cause.   In the counties of New York, Kings, and Erie, and in the seventh judicial district, where the right to a preference appears upon the face of the papers before the court, it is necessary to serve with the notice of trial a notice that an application will be made at the opening of the court, or at such other time and place as may be specified in the general or special rules of practice, for an order preferring the case, and if a preference depends upon facts which do not appear on the face of the papers, it is necessary to serve with such notice an affidavit setting forth the facts upon which the claim for preference is based.

It would seem to follow from the reading of this section that it applies to cases that are entitled to preference under the general rules of practice as well as to those which come within the provisions of the Code.   But the courts have held in several cases that each court has full control and charge over its calendars, independent of the statute, and it is to be presumed that the court will still grant preferences to what are known as short causes when the motion for preference is made according to general or special rules of practice.

General rules ; power of courts.]   The plain reading of section 791 and Rule 36 seems to indicate that (subject to the provisions of section 789, 790) all the classes of actions mentioned in the first nine subdivisions of section 791 shall be preferred on the calendar, and then shall follow all such actions as shall be preferred under the General Rules of Practice or special rules of any court, and there appears to be no case which holds to the contrary.

It has been held, however, that the court has power to appoint terms of court for the hearing of short causes and to make rules for the preference of certain cases, even though they are not such as are mentioned in the Code. The law on this point is stated in Weiss *v.* Morrell (7 *Misc.* 539) at page 540, as follows :

"The appeal is mainly argued on the question as to whether the courts of this State have power to appoint a short cause calendar, and place causes thereon for trial out of their order upon the general calendar.   It is claimed that this is giving a preference to certain causes not enumerated in the statute of preferences.   Code Civ. Pro., Chap. 8, title 6, Art. 2.   The provisions of the Code are not exclusive and do not limit the power of the court over their calendars, nor consequently prohibit the establishing a calendar for short causes, according to the practice of all the courts long before the adoption of the present Code. The general rules of practice under which summary trials are had, are not inconsistent with any provision of the Code; for since the statute recognizes the propriety of granting certain preferences, the granting of a preference in any other special case is entirely consistent with the statutory provision."

It is said in Smith v. Keepers (5 *Civ. Pro. R.* 66), that section 793, does not prohibit the granting of a preference in a particular case, where it is apparent to the court that great hardship might ensue in case such preference was not allowed. The court has an inherent power to control its own calendar and on that ground alone may grant an order preferring the cause.

But the preference will not be allowed where proceedings to place the case on the calendar have been unnecessarily delayed. Manhattan Co. v. Dunn, 13 *Civ. Pro. R.* 166.

In Angle v. Kaufman (4 *Civ. Pro. R.* 201), it was held that section 793 governed preferences under Rule 36 as well as those under the statute, and that where a case was clearly entitled to preference under Rule 36, that having been noticed for trial by both parties the plaintiff had waived his right to a preference.

In Hunnewell v. Shaffer (9 *Supp.* 540), it is said : " Independently of these (the general rules of practice) every court has a power to regulate (within reasonable bounds) its own calendar, and may, independently of the statute, determine what cause shall be tried first. In other words, it may regulate the order of business. It cannot decline to prefer a cause entitled to preference by the statute or general rules of practice. It cannot dispense with the statutory notice of trial, except as a condition of granting a favor, but it may in the exercise of a wise discretion and in an orderly manner do many things not inhibited." And see also Maretzek v. Cauldwell, 4 *Robt.* 666.

In McHugh v. Astrophe, 2 *Misc.* 478 (N. Y. City Ct.), it was held that a cause may be taken from the regular day calendar and made a preferred cause on the short cause calendar if justice requires it.

In Walton v. Ogden (*Col. and Cai.* 419), the court preferred the cause out of its regular order, upon the ground that the peace of a county depended upon a decision.

An order placing a case on a short cause calendar under

a special or general rule of the court is within the discretion of the court, and it is proper to refuse such order where the court is satisfied that the case cannot be tried within an hour. Guerineau *v.* Weil, 8 *Misc.* 94 ; s. c., 60 *St. R.* 158 ; 28 *Supp.* 775.

Evidence of debt for absolute payment of money.] A money judgment rendered in another State is an evidence of debt for the absolute payment of money within section 791, and an action founded thereon is entitled to a preference. McArthur *v.* Commercial Fire Ins. Co., 67 *How. Pr.* 510.

An action against a railroad corporation for the amount of interest coupons due on the bonds of another company, payment of which has been guaranteed by the defendant, is not entitled to a preference under section 791. Polhemus *v.* Fitchburg R. R. Co., 113 *N. Y.* 617 ; 123 *N. Y.* 502.

Life Insurance policy ; lease.] It was held prior to the adoption of any special rules to the contrary, that an action founded upon a life insurance policy could not be preferred. N. Y. Life Ins. Co. *v.* Universal Life Insurance Co., 88 *N. Y.* 424 ; overruling Studwell *v.* Charter Oak Insurance Co., 19 *Hun,* 127. This is probably still the law applicable to courts other than those which have adopted special rules, as in the first department where actions on life insurance policies are placed upon the short cause calendar. Rule VI. The same may be said of actions brought upon a lease. Philadelphia Steamship Dock Co. *v.* Lorillard Steamship Co., 54 *How. Pr.* 508.

Representative capacity.] The right to a preference upon the calendar given by Code Civ. Pro., § 791, subd. 5, when a person in one of the capacities mentioned therein is the sole plaintiff or sole defendant, does not extend to a case where the same person is joined as a party in his individual capacity as well as in the prescribed capacity. Haux *v.* Dry Dock Savings Inst. 150 *N. Y.* 581.

It *seems* that an action by an administratrix to recover damages for negligence, causing the death of plaintiff's intestate, is entitled to a preference on the trial calendar, under section 791 (Court of Appeals). Hays *v.* Consolidated Gas Co., 60 *St. R.* 480.

Action to construe will.] An action for accounting, partition, and other relief is not entitled to a preference on the calendar because the construction of a will is incidentally involved therein. To entitle it to a preference, the action must be brought expressly for the construction of a will. Peyser *v.* Wendt, 84 *N. Y.* 642.

Dower.] Where two or more actions in different counties are pending at the same time, in which a right of dower is in contest, this is no reason why either one of the actions should not be preferred under the statute. Yates *v.* Stiles, 15 *W. Dig.* 113.

Rule 36 ; defendant in custody ; property attached.] Where the defendant is in actual custody under an order of arrest, he is entitled to a preference even though he has served a cross-notice of trial. Reilly *v.* Byrne, 1 *Civ. Pro. R.* 201 ; Smith *v.* Keepers, 5 *Civ. Pro. R.* 66.

The preference is available to the plaintiff as well as to the defendant. Knox *v.* Dubroff (in text).

It has been held that where both parties notice the cause for trial without giving the notice required by section 793, the plaintiff's right to a preference is waived. Robinson *v.* Schellhaas, 62 *How. Pr.* 489. City National Bank *v.* National Park Bank, *Id.* 495.

Notice of trial must be served.] The party cannot secure a preference under Code Civ. Pro., § 791, without having served a notice of trial. Ritchie *v.* Seaboard Nat. Bank, 12 *Misc.* 146.

Waiver.] The waiver of a right to a preference by serving a notice of trial without an order or notice of motion for preference, cannot be cured by the unnecessary serving of a new notice of trial. Fox *v.* Quinn, 12 *Supp.* 725.

See, also, Robinson *v.* Schellhaas, 62 *How. Pr.* 489: City National Bank *v.* National Park Bank, *Id.* 495.

Court of Appeals.] The provision of Code Civ. Pro. § 791 which specifies as one of the causes entitled to a preference, "a cause entitled to a preference under the general rules of practice," (subd. 10) does not apply to the Court of Appeals, and to obtain a preference upon the calendar of that court in a case not designated in the Code, or the rules of the Court of Appeals, the application must be addressed to the discretion of that court, and such facts must be shown that a preference will be deemed proper in the interests of justice. Nichols *v.* Scranton Steel Co., 135 *N. Y.* 634. In that case, the sole facts relied upon were that certain certificates of stock belonging to the applicant had been levied upon under attachment, and it was held that they did not justify the granting of the motion.

A claim for preference on the calendar of the Court of Appeals should be made in the notice of argument stating the ground on which a preference is claimed. Taylor *v.* Wing, 83 *N. Y.* 527.

The preference on the calendar of the court in an action for dower authorized by Code Civ. Pro. § 791, sub-division 6, can be claimed only when the proof, that is, " that plain-

tiff has not sufficient means of support aside from the estate in controversy" was made, and an order allowiug the
preference obtained, as required by § 793, before the notice of argument was served. Bartlett *v.* Musliuer, 92
N. Y. 646.

An appeal cannot be heard out of its order on a calendar on the motion· of the respondent on the ground that
the appeal is frivolous. Rogers *v.* Hosack, 5 *Hill*, 521 ;
Wilder *v.* Lane, 34 *Barb.* 54 ; s. c. 12 *Abb. Pr.* 351.

The party desiring a preference on a calendar of the
Court of Appeals must procure an order therefor from the
court or a judge thereof, upon notice to the adverse party.
Bank of Attica *v.* Metropolitan Nat. Bank, 91 *N. Y.* 239.

MATTER OF WHITNEY.

Court of Appeals ; June, 1897.

Will ; when not subscribed at end within statute.] Where a will
was written upon a printed form covering one page, and the
testator and subscribing witnesses signed it at the foot thereof,
and the testator added the words " see annexed sheet," and on
the separate slip of paper were written two additional subdivisions to the will, and it was attached to the face of the will with
metal staples so that the slip annexed had to be raised up or
turned back, in order to read the first and second clauses, and
it was evident that it was possible to easily remove such annexed sheet after the execution of the will, and to substitute
another without danger of detection,—*Held*, that the will was
not properly subscribed by the testator at the end thereof, as
required by the statute (2 *R. S.* 63, § 40).*

Appeal from a judgment of the General Term of the
Supreme Court, fifth department, which reversed a decree
of the Surrogate's Court of Monroe county, refusing to
admit to probate the alleged will of James R. Whitney,
deceased.

* See Note on Testator's Subscription at End of Will, following
this case.

.This appeal presents the question whether the paper writing alleged to be the last will and testament of James R. Whitney, deceased, was subscribed by the testator at the end thereof, as the statute requires. (2 *R. S.* 63, § 40.) The Surrogate's Court of Monroe county held that it was not, and the learned General Term has reversed the decree. The facts in the case are undisputed. The will is drawn upon a printed blank, covering only one page, and the testator and subscribing witnesses signed at the foot thereof.

The subdivisions of the will, marked respectively "First" and "Second," fill the entire blank space in the printed form, and at the end of the second subdivision are the words, "See annexed sheet." On a separate slip of paper are written two additional subdivisions, marked respectively "Third" and "Fourth," and this is attached to the face of the will immediately over the first and second subdivisions, by metal staples, so that the slip annexed has to be raised up or turned back, in order to read the first two clauses.

Held, that the alleged will was not subscribed at the end thereof, citing Matter of Hewitt, 91 *N. Y.* 261; Matter of O'Neil, 91 *N. Y.* 516; Matter of Conway, 124 *N. Y.* 455; S. C., 36 *St. R.* 486; rev'g 58 *Hun*, 16; Matter of Blair, 84 *N. Y.* 581; aff'd without opinion, 152 *N. Y.* 645. The only reference to the annexed slip is in the will, and the paper attached contains no word or sign to connect it with the main instrument. Furthermore, the separate slip on which two subdivisions of the will are written, is attached to the face of the printed blank by metal staples, and could be, after the execution of the will, removed and another slip substituted without danger of detection. The statute should not be defeated by judicial construction or frittered away by exceptions. Sisters of Charity *v.* Kelly, 67 *N. Y.* 416. While wills are interpreted so as to carry out the intention of the testator, that rule cannot be invoked when construing the statute regulating their execution, as in the latter case courts do not consider the intention of the testator, but that of the legislature. Matter of O'Neil, 91 *N. Y.* 516.

The cases referred to by the learned General Term to the effect that any written testamentary document in existence at the execution of the will may by reference be incorporated into and become a part of the will, provided the reference in the will is distinct and clearly identifies or renders capable of identification by the aid of extrinsic proof the document to which reference is made (Brown *v.* Clark, 77 *N. Y.* 377) have no bearing upon the point we are considering.

Judgment of the General Term reversed, and the decree of the Surrogate's Court of Monroe county affirmed, with costs.

Opinion by BARTLETT, J. All concur.

Charles S. Baker, for appellants.

George E. Warner, and *Henry J. Sullivan,* for respondents.

NOTE ON TESTATOR'S SUBSCRIPTION AT END OF WILL.

The statute (2 *R. S.* [9th ed.], p. 1877, § 40) provides : § 40. "Every last will and testament of real or personal property, or both, shall be executed and attested in the following manner :

" 1. It shall be subscribed by the testator at the end of the will.

*   ~   .   ..

" 4. There shall be at least two attesting witnesses, each of whom shall sign his name as a witness, at the end of the will, at the request of the testator."

The courts have strictly construed this section and invariably required an exact fulfillment of its requirements, for the reason mainly that the statute was intended to make the alteration of wills as nearly impossible as such a thing could be done by statute.

In Matter of Blair (84 *Hun*, 581 ; aff'd without opinion 152 *N. Y.* 645), after the will had been drawn the testator requested the draughtsman to add another clause giving a power of sale to the executors named in the will of one piece of real property, and stated to him at the time, that this provision had nothing to do with the will, except that he wanted the executors to have sufficient cash in hand to pay the various money bequests. The testator then signed the will in two places : First immediately after the testimonium clause, and, second, at the end of the additional clause giving the executor the power of sale. The witnesses signed only once at the end of the attestation clause, and before the clause which was added giving the executor the power of sale. The court reversed the decision of the surrogate in admitting the will to probate, and said at page 585 : " The fact that no harm will be likely to result in this case from the probate of that part of the will which precedes the first signature of Blair should not have much weight with the court for the more important question after all is whether the decision will establish a good or a bad precedent." The court then declares that it would establish a bad precedent on the authority of the case of Sisters of Charity *v.* Kelly (67 *N. Y.* 409), where it is said that the provision is a wholsome one and was adopted to remedy evils, or threatened evils, and that it should not be frittered away by exceptions.

In Matter of O'Neil (91 *N. Y.* 516), the instrument was drawn upon a printed blank, the formal commencement being on the first page and the formal termination at the foot of the third page. The blank space was filled on the first, second and third pages, and the last clause of the will was partly written on the third page and the balance carried over to the blank fourth page. The names of the testator and the witnesses were subscribed near the bottom of the third page, below the formal printed termination of the will, and there only. The written matter on the fourth page was not connected with the main body of the will by reference of any kind, although it was obviously a continuation and completion of the last paragraph of the will, and the court held that the will was not subscribed at the end thereof.

In Matter of Conway (124 *N. Y.* 455 ; s. c., 36 *St. R.* 486 ; rev'g 58 *Hun*, 16), the facts were very similar to those in Matter of O'Neil (*supra*) with the exception that at the end of the provisions in the body of the will were

Note on Testator's Subscription at End of Will.

the words " carried to back of will " and upon the back of
the sheet was the word " continued." Following this
word were various bequests, and then below them were
added the words : " Signature on face of the will." The
second division of the Court of Appeals declared the will
to be invalid, although three judges dissented, mainly upon
the ground that there was a clear and distinct reference in
the body of the will to the provisions on the back of the
paper and that they were thereby properly connected with
the subject matter preceding the signatures.

In Matter of Hewitt (91 *N. Y.* 261), the will was
written on both sides of an irregular shaped piece of paper
about one half of it upon one side, and the other half
upon the other side. The witnesses signed their names at
the bottom of the first side and again at the top of the
second side ; the testator signed his name at the end of the
disposing portion of the instrument near the middle of the
second side, and again at the bottom of the second side,
and it was held that the statute was not complied with,
and that it was necessary that both the testator and the
witnesses should sign at the end of the will. Judge EARL
in writing the opinion of the court, said :

" Wherever the will ends there the signatures must be
be found and one place cannot be the end for the purpose
of subscribing by testator ; and another be the end for the
purpose of subscribing by the witnesses."

In Matter of Sanderson (9 *Misc.* 574), two wills were
offered for probate to the Surrogate of Orleans County.
One of the wills contained a provision for the sale of the
testator's real estate and the disposition of her household
effects. This clause was written between the signature and
the attestation clause, and it was held that it was void. It
was also held that the second paper containing disposing
clauses, could not be made a part of a valid will by being
referred to in such will.

In Matter of Gedney (17 *Misc.* 500), the signature of the
testator was followed by a clause appointing executors and
containing the date of the will ; and it was held that there
was no signing at the end of the will as required by the
statute.

In Matter of Jacobson (19 *St. R.* 262 ; s. c. 6 *Dem.* 298).
The will contained a clause appointing an executor, which
was written below the signatures of the decedent and the
witnesses, and it was held in that case that the validity of
the will depended upon the question of whether or not the
clause in question was written in before or after the will
was signed.

Note on Testator's Subscription at End of Will.

In Tonnelle *v.* Hall (4 *N. Y.* 140), an instrument propounded as a will, consisted of eight unfolded sheets of paper, securely attached together at the end. The writing of the will commenced on the first and was continued on the four succeeding sheets where it was brought to a close by the usual attestation clause, and was subscribed by the testator and the witnesses. On one of the sheets following the signature was a map, not signed by the testator or witnesses. In the body of the will the testator disposed of certain lots of real estate which were designated by numbers with a reference to the map as follows : "Which said lots are designated on a certain map now on file in the office of the register of the City and County of New York, a copy of which on a reduced scale is hereunto annexed, entitled map of the property, etc.," and it was held that the will was subscribed by the testator at the end of the will, within the meaning of the statute. This case was distinguished in Matter of O'Neil (91 *N. Y.* 516), but not disapproved.

It is stated in the head note of Tonnelle *v.* Hall (*supra*) that where a will otherwise properly executed refers to another paper already written, and so describes it as to leave no doubt of its identity, such paper it. seems makes part of the will, and the paper need not be subscribed or even attached, and the argument in the opinion itself seems to sustain that doctrine ; but the later cases cited in this note appear to have materially modified that doctrine.

In Thompson *v.* Quimby (2 *Bradf.* 449), it was held that a will was not invalidated by reference to a schedule which was not annexed.

See also McGuire *v.* Kerr, 2 *Bradf.* 244 ; Matter of Gilman, 38 *Barb.* 364 ; s. c., *Redf.* 354.

In Comboy *v.* Jennings (16 *S. C.* 622), it was held that a direction by the testator, on a separate page, after the attestation clause, formed no part of the will, and did not effect its validity.

In Matter of Cohen (1 *Tuck.* 286), the testator subscribed the will beneath the attestation clause, and it was held to be a sufficient execution. See to the same effect, Hitchcock *v.* Thompson, 6 *Hun*, 279 ; rev'g 15 *Abb. Pr.* (*N. S.*) 211 ; Younger *v.* Duffie, 94 *N. Y.* 535.

If a will be signed after the disposing clause, but in the middle of the clause appointing the executor, it is not a due execution under the statute. Sisters of Charity *v.* Kelly, 67 *N. Y.* 409 ; rev'g 7 *Hun.* 290. See also Brady *v.* McCrosson, 5 *Redf.* 431 ; Dennett *v.* Taylor, *Id.* 561 ; Matter of Nies, 13 *St. R.* 756.

In Matter of Mandelick (6 *Misc.* 71), the paper pro-

pounded as a will was written on a printed form, and on its
first page was a completed instrument with a full attestation clause. On the second page of the paper was a
further provision for the decedent's mother, small bequests to two sisters, and one to two friends, and for the
expenditure of some money for a stone to mark his grave.
At the foot of the second page the decedent signed the will,
but without attestation, and it was held by the surrogate of
New York County (Fitzgerald, S.) that the writing on the
first page, being a completed instrument, should be admitted to probate, and that the writing on the last page should
be disregarded. This case was decided without contest of
any kind, it would appear from the report of the case, and
it does not seem to be entirely in harmony with the other
cases here cited.

MATTER OF HUMFREYVILLE.

*Supreme Court, First Department, Appellate Division;
June, 1897.*

Contempt ; surrogate's court ; order for the payment of costs.] Under Code Civ. Pro., § 2555, a surrogate has power to punish as
for a contempt the failure of a party to obey an order for the
payment of costs, where such order is founded upon a decree of
a surrogate's court.*

---

* Section 2555 reads as follows : " In either of the following cases,
a decree of the surrogate's court, directing the payment of money,
or requiring the performance of any other act, may be enforced, by
serving a certified copy thereof upon the party against whom it is
rendered, or the officer or person who is required thereby, or by law,
to obey it ; and if he refuses or willfully neglects to obey it, by punishing him for a contempt of court :

1. " Where it cannot be enforced by execution as prescribed in
the last section.

2. " Where part of it cannot be enforced by execution ; in which
case the part or parts, which cannot be so enforced may be enforced
as prescribed in this section.

3. " Where an execution issued as prescribed in the last section

Appeal from order of the surrogate, New York County,
adjudging J. Lee Humfreville guilty as of a contempt of
court, and directing that he be committed to the common

to the sheriff of the surrogate's county has been returned by him
wholly or partly unsatisfied.

4. " Where a delinquent is an executor, administrator, guardian
or testamentary trustee, and the decree relates to the fund or estate,
in which case the surrogate may enforce the decree as prescribed in
this section, either without issuing an execution, or after the return
of an execution, as he thinks proper.

" If the delinquent has given an official bond, his imprisonment,
by virtue of the proceedings to punish him for a contempt, as prescribed in this section, or a levy upon his property by virtue of an
execution, issued as prescribed in the last section, does not bar, suspend, or otherwise affect an action against the sureties in his official
bond."

In Matter of Snyder, (103 *N. Y.* 178 ; aff'g 34 *Hun*, 302), it was
held that an order was properly made by the surrogate punishing an
executor for contempt for failure to pay over money as provided in
a surrogate's decree, after an accounting. Such executor appeared
and it was shown to the surrogate that the executor was insolvent at
the time the order was made, and was unable to comply therewith,
and the court says at page 181 : " The general term have affirmed
the order in face of the dissent of one of its members. I do not
understand that the dissenting member of the court doubted the
jurisdiction or power of the surrogate to make the order appealed
from, but in view of the alleged insolvency of the executor and his declaration of inability to pay thought he ought not to be punished for
not paying. The contempt charged was in violating the decree or
order which directed payment, and the investigation before the surrogate might properly have been limited to the matter contained in
it ; *i. e.*, the service of the decree and the facts of the neglect constituting this violation. To those facts there was no answer."

The court further says, that the order was one resting in discretion
which it did not appear had been unfairly exercised.

The fact that an executor alleges that he has no money in his
hands, with which to obey an order requiring him to pay costs, is
not an answer to a motion to punish him for contempt. Gillies *v.*
Kreeder, 1 *Dem.* 349.

Where an executor is indebted to the testator at the time of his
death, and after qualifying, he becomes insolvent, but accounts for
all moneys received by him, he cannot be punished for contempt in

Matter of Humfreyville.

jail and there be detained in close custody until he pay certain moneys.

Held, that the order was properly made. The single question presented on this appeal is whether a decree of the surrogate directing the payment of costs may be enforced by contempt proceedings. As a matter of first impression, we should be inclined to answer this in the negative ; and this impression is strengthened by our recollection that, prior to the adoption of the present Code, and pursuant to the provisions of the Revised Statutes, no person could be arrested or imprisoned for the non-payment of costs awarded in an action or special proceeding ; and by section 15 of the Code of Civil Procedure it is provided : " But a person shall not be arrested or imprisoned for the non-payment of costs awarded otherwise than by a final judgment, or a final order, made in a special proceeding instituted by state writ, except where an attorney, counselor or other officer of the court is ordered to pay costs for misconduct as such, or a witness is ordered to pay costs on an attachment for non-attendance."

The proceedings for the removal of Mr. Humfreyville as executor, cannot be brought within any of the clauses of this section so as to authorize, under it, his imprisonment, because the moneys directed to be paid were the interlocutory costs and disbursements arising upon an appeal from an order of the surrogate in proceedings pending in the

---

failing to pay the debt. Matter of Rugg, 3 *St. R.* 224 ; s. c., 4 *Dem.* 105 ; Baucus *v.* Stover, 14 *W. Dig.* 313.

Where, after a decree of a surrogate's court requiring an administrator to pay a certain sum to a person therein specified, the surety on a bond of the administrator paid the amount, and then took an assignment of the rights of the party to whom such sum was paid, —*held*, that the surety could then enforce the payment of the decree against the administrator by contempt proceedings. Townsend *v.* Whitney, 75 *N. Y.* 425.

See Schreiber *v.* Raymond & Campbell Mfg. Co., *post*, p. 270, and cases there cited.

surrogate's court; and there are many cases which hold
that, under the Revised Statutes and before the enactment
of the second part of the Code, there was no authority to
punish as for a contempt for the non-payment of costs
even though such costs were provided for by an order or
a decree.   By the provisions, however, of the second part
of the Code, enacted in 1880, and under section 2555, the
courts have recognized in every case, so far as we have
had our attention called to it, the power of the surrogate's
court to enforce a decree, including a direction as to
the payment of costs, by a contempt proceeding.   In
Matter of Kurtzman (2 *St. Rep.*, 655), where the question
was presented as to the power of the surrogate to punish
an administrator for contempt for failure to pay an allowance to a special guardian under a decree, the late general
term in this department said : " Whatever doubt there
may have been before the Code as to the power of the surrogate to punish an administrator for contempt in proceedings of this character, there can no longer be any
doubt as to such power and its extent."   And Mr. Red-
field, in his work on surrogates' courts, says (p. 876): " But
payment of the costs awarded against a party by a final
decree, e. g., a decree granting probate, may be enforced
by attachment."   While Matter of Dissosway (91 *N.
Y.* 235) is not an authority, it furnishes a strong argument
for the construction given to the section by the surrogate.
That was a contest between Dissosway, a creditor, and
one Hayward, as to the qualifications of the latter to receive letters testamentary.   The proceeding terminated
in a decree awarding letters to Hayward, and directing
Dissosway to pay $715.60 costs and disbursements.   A
motion was then made to punish him as for a contempt
for his failure to pay such costs, which was granted.   The
matter came before the supreme court on *habeas corpus.*
The Court of Appeals, referring to the various sections of
the Code, intimated no doubt, but, on the contrary, seem-
ingly recognized the power of the surrogate to enforce

such a decree by contempt proceedings, but held that as no proper foundation in that instance for the proceeding had been laid by the issuance of an execution, as provided in section 2555, the order discharging Dissosway from arrest was proper.

Although the power exercised by surrogates is only that conferred by statute, and is limited thereby, we think that the language of the sections relied upon will justify the construction placed upon it by the surrogate in this proceeding. By section 2554 of the Code it is provided that a decree directing the payment of a sum of money into court, or to one or more parties, may be enforced by an execution against the property of the parties directed to make the same. By section 2555 it is provided that a decree of the surrogate's court directing the payment of moneys may be enforced by serving a certified copy upon the party against whom it is rendered, and if he refuses or willfully neglects to pay it, by punishing him for a contempt of court ; first, where it cannot be enforced by execution ; second, where part of it cannot be so enforced by execution ; and third, where an execution issued has been returned wholly or partly unsatisfied.

It is insisted, however, by the appellant that the payment of money as provided by this section of the Code has reference only to moneys belonging to an estate of which the party was either executor or trustee, which moneys he holds in trust for the benefit of some third party, and has no application to a case in which there has been a non-payment of interlocutory costs in a proceeding pending in the surrogates' court. This view is sought to be upheld by the case of Watson v. Nelson, (69 N. Y. 537), and many other cases that might be referred to, relating to the statutory powers of surrogates s they existed under the Revised Statutes, which, as before stated, have been superseded by the enactment of the second part of the Code in 1880, We do not find in the language used any limitation as to the kind or nature of the money to be paid. It is in the broadest terms and would include costs or any sum of money which by a final decree was directed to be paid. We do not understand that there is any contention but that the direction to pay the money was by a final decree. Therefore, it comes expressly within the terms of the sections; and we fail to find any language that could be construed into a limitation of the general power thus conferred, or that would make it applicable only in cases where the decree has reference to moneys belonging to an estate of which the party is either executor or trustee, which moneys he holds in trust for the benefit of third parties; but it is equally applicable to the payment of all sums of money, whether costs or otherwise, included in and directed to be paid by a final decree.

Opinion by O'BRIEN, J. All concur.

Order affirmed with costs.

Abram Kling, (of counsel), for appellant.

Henry H. Whitman, (of counsel), for respondent.

SCHREIBER *v.* RAYMOND & CAMPBELL MFG. CO.

Supreme Court, Second Department, Appellate Division; May, 1897.

Contempt ; false oath of surety on attachment bond to sheriff; who can maintain proceedings.] One whose property has been wrongfully taken by the sheriff under a warrant of attachment against another person, and who was not a party in the attachment suit, cannot maintain contempt proceedings against the surety on the indemnity bond given to the sheriff, because of

Schreiber *v.* Raymond & Campbell Mfg. Co.

his having sworn falsely as such surety concerning his property ; this remedy is only available to one who was a party to the action or proceeding in which the bond was given, under Code Civ. Pro., § 14, subd. 4.*

---

* One who is not a party to a foreclosure suit, cannot be proceeded against by process of contempt, by reason of his collecting the rents of the mortgaged premises. Bowery Savings Bank *v.* Richards, 3 *Hun*, 366.

One who falsely justifies as a surety and procures the discharge of an attachment is guilty of a contempt. People *ex rel.* Wise *v.* Tamsen, 17 *Misc.* 212 ; S. C., 40 *Supp.* 1047.

In McAveney *v.* Brush (1 *N. Y. Ann. Cas.* 414 ; reported on another appeal, 3 *N. Y. Ann. Cas.* 143), the surety on a bond to discharge a mechanics' lien who swore falsely as to his property and the owner who procured the discharge of the lien by giving a bond with sureties known to him to be insufficient were both punished as for contempt. See, also, Cunningham *v.* Hatch, 3 *Misc.* 101 ; S. C., 30 *Abb. N. C.*, 31 ; 22 *Supp.* 707, where a person was punished as for contempt for failing to re-deposit a sum deposited in the office of the county clerk to discharge the mechanics' lien and subsequently wrongfully withdrawn.

In Matter of Hopper (9 *Misc.* 171 ; S. C., 60 *St. R.* 638 ; 29 *Supp.* 715 ; aff'd 145 *N. Y.* 605, without opinion), a surety on an undertaking discharging a mechanics' lien was found to be insolvent after judgment was recovered against him on the undertaking, and he was adjudged guilty of contempt.

The agent who procures a person to put in fictitious sureties on appeal, may be punished for contempt, though not a party to the suit. Hull *v.* L'Eplatinier, 5 *Daly*, 534 ; S. C., 49 *How. Pr.* 500.

In Foley *v.* Stone (30 *St. Rep.* 834 ; S. C., 18 *Civ. Pro. R.* 190 ; aff'g 15 *Civ. Pro. R.* 224 ; S. C., 3 *Supp.* 288), a party and her attorney were punished as for a contempt in procuring and offering irresponsible sureties on an undertaking for an order of arrest.

See, to the same effect, Eagan *v.* Lynch, 49 *Super. Ct. (J. & S.)* 454

It is not a contempt of court for a party to put in a false answer in an action. Fromme *v.* Gray, 14 *Misc.* 592 ; S. C., 2 *N. Y. Ann. Cas.* 266 ; aff'd 148 *N. Y.* 695 ; but it has been held to be a criminal contempt for an attorney to erase a portion of the verification of an answer served on him, and then to return it for insufficiency. Bennard *v.* Leo, 7 *N. Y. Daily Reg.* 1069, 1213.

It is not essential that a surety upon an undertaking on appeal,

Schreiber *v.* Raymond & Campbell Mfg. Co.

Appeal by the defendant from an order of the Supreme Court, Kings County Special Term, adjudging the defendant guilty of a contempt of court.

The appellant has been adjudged guilty of a contempt of court under subdivision 4 of section 14 of the Code of Civil Procedure. That subdivision provides for the punishment of certain specified acts and " any other unlawful interference with the proceedings " in an action. The appellant is charged with misconduct which constituted such unlawful interference, in having sworn falsely as a surety. He was a surety upon a bond given to indemnify the sheriff of Kings County on an attachment granted in an action in which the Raymond and Campbell Manufacturing Company was the plaintiff and Richard J. Bird and Thomas J. Bird were the defendants. In justifying upon said bond, he swore that he was the owner and holder in his own right of a house and lot known as 492 Jefferson avenue in the city of Brooklyn. It now appears that these premises belonged to his wife. The sheriff proceeded under the attachment against the Birds, but levied upon property in fact belonging to Joseph Schreiber, who subsequently instituted the present suit against the sheriff for the conversion of his said property. The indemnitors were made defendants in place of the sheriff, and Schreiber obtained judgment against them all. He then assigned the judgment to Margaret Winston, in whose behalf this contempt proceeding is conducted. The court below made an order adjudging him guilty of contempt and imposing a fine upon him.

Held, error. The fact that the sheriff erroneously took Schreiber's property under the attachment did not make Schreiber in any sense a party to that litigation although it

who swears falsely upon justification with intent to deceive the court as to his responsibiltiy, should be convicted of perjury before he can be punished for the contempt. Lawrence *v.* Harrington, 63 *Hun*, 195; s. c., 43 *St. R.* 413; 17 *Supp.* 649; aff'd 133 *N. Y.* 690.

Schreiber *v.* Raymond & Campbell Mfg. Co.

had the effect of inducing him speedily to become a party plaintiff in this one.   As far as the parties to the Bird suit were concerned, the false statement in the appellant's affidavit of justification occasioned no injury and has given rise to no complaint.   That it was injurious to Schreiber may be assumed ; for, unless indemnified as he was, the sheriff would hardly have levied upon Schreiber's property under the attachment against the Birds.   Upon this state of facts the question presented for our decision is whether the false justification of a surety is a contempt of a court, when it does not injuriously affect the rights or remedies of any party to an action or special proceeding pending at the time of the justification, but merely operates to the injury of a person who subsequently sues for the redress of such injury.

I think the statute itself furnishes the answer to this question.   The acts of neglect or violation of any duty or other misconduct which a court of record is empowered to punish, under section 14 of the Code of Civil Procedure, are only acts " by which a right or remedy of a party to a civil action or special proceeding *pending in the court* may be defeated, impaired, impeded or prejudiced." Language could hardly be clearer than this.   Unlawful interference to the detriment of suitors with the regular and orderly progress of litigated causes in the courts was what the statute was designed to prevent, and the purpose was to provide summary methods to protect litigants against injury by reason of such unlawful interference.   The protection of persons whose grievances were already before the court was the object in view, not the present protection of those who might at some future time become suitors.

I have not been able to find any case in which an act has been punished as a contempt, under section 14 of the Code, unless it injuriously affected the rights or remedies of a party to a civil action or proceeding which was pending at the time of the commission of the act.

Schreiber *v*. Raymond & Campbell Mfg. Co.

In Lawrence *v*. Harrington (63 *Hun*, 195 ; S. C., 43 *St. R.* 413 ; 17 *Supp.* 649), the contempt consisted in swearing falsely in the course of a justification as sureties on appeal. Here the misconduct had a directly injurious effect upon the plaintiffs in the action, whose execution against the defendant was stayed by the undertaking. The original motion to punish for contempt was denied at special term, but the general term held that it should have been granted. The case then went back to special term, where an order was made imposing a fine of $1,110.89 upon the sureties; and this order was affirmed both at the general term and in the Court of Appeals. See 133 *N. Y.* 690; Court of Appeals Cases, Brooklyn Law Library, vol. 1093.

The acts of misconduct, cognizable under section 14 of the Code of Civil Procedure, belong to the class now usually denominated civil contempts, or sometimes private contempts, and arise out of "an injury or wrong done to a party who is a suitor before the court and has established a claim upon its protection." People *ex rel.* Munsell *v.* Court of Oyer & Terminer, 101 *N. Y.* 245. In the case before us the injury or wrong done by the appellant in swearing falsely as to the ownership of the property mentioned in his affidavit was not done to any one who was a suitor before the court or had established a claim upon its protection. However censurable in morals, or punishable under the criminal law, it did not bring him within the purview of the Code provisions concerning contempt of court. These must be construed strictly. Fromme *v.* Gray, 14 *Misc.* 592, 595 ; S. C., 2 *N. Y. Ann. Cas.* 266; aff'd and opinion approved, 148 *N. Y.* 695, 698. To enlarge the operation of the law of contempt in accordance with the views of the respondent would be a radical departure from the rules which have heretofore been observed by the courts in the interpretation and application of the statutes on the subject.

Opinion by BARTLETT, J.   All concurred.

Order reversed, with ten dollar costs and disbursements and motion denied.

Herbert T. Ketcham, for the defendant Sanford, appellant.

J. Newton Williams, for the plaintiff, and for the assignee of the plaintiff's judgment, respondent.

BURTON *v*. LINN.

Supreme Court, N. Y., Special Term; September, 1897.

Contempt; failure to complete purchase.] Where a person failed to obey an order requiring her to complete a purchase of real estate made at a judicial sale, and it appeared probable that such refusal was due to the purchaser's inability to complete,—*Held*, that an order punishing her for a contempt should not be granted, even upon default.*

---

* In Brasher *v*. Cortlandt (2 *Johns. Ch.* 505), an attachment was issued against the purchaser at a judicial sale because of his failure to comply with the order of the court to complete his purchase, and Chancellor KENT, in deciding the motion said : " I do not mean at present to lay down any general rule on the subject of coercing a purchaser by attachment ; but I ought not to hesitate under the circumstances of this case ; and I have no doubt, the court may, in its discretion, do it in every case where the previous conditions of the sale have not given the purchaser an alternative. Here it has become necessary in order to give due effect to the authority and process of the court, and to preserve them from being treated with contempt. The forfeiture of the deposit would not be sufficient, either as a punishment to one party or as a satisfaction to the other. In Savill *v*. Savill (1 *P. Wms.* 745), where the court would not make an order on the purchaser to complete his purchase, but thought the forfeiture of the deposit, which the purchaser elected to lose, sufficient, the deposit was about one-tenth of the purchase money, and the

Motion to punish Nora O'Connell for contempt in not completing the purchase by her of certain plots of land bought at a sale had pursuant to a judgment of foreclosure.

Upon notice to said Nora O'Connell, an order was made requiring her to complete the purchase, and pay the balance of the purchase money over the ten per cent. deposited, within five days after the service of a copy of the

---

learned editor, Mr. Cox, adds a *quere* whether that case be now the law of the court. I shall order that the purchaser pay the purchase money in six days, or that an attachment issue."

In a note to this case (Lawyer's ed.), it is said : "The purchaser by becoming a bidder, submits himself to the jurisdiction of the court, and if he becomes insolvent, the court may rescind the sale and order a resale ; if he be able to pay, the court, at the instance of the party interested, will compel completion of the contract by process of an attachment ; citing among other cases, Browne *v.* Ritter, 26 *N. J. Eq.* 458 ; Cazet *v.* Hubbell, 36 *N. Y.* 680 ; Collier *v.* Whipple, 13 *Wend.* 232.

In the last mentioned case it is said at page 232 : "The court has also power over the purchaser, to which it is considered he submits by becoming a bidder for premises sold by the order of the court. If, after he make a purchase he becomes insolvent or unable to pay, the court have the power of rescinding the sale, and of ordering a resale ; if, however, he be able to pay and will not, the court at the instance of the party interested, will compel the purchaser to a performance, by process of attachment for contempt. Such power is claimed and exercised by the court of chancery, both in England and in this country, and it is meet and proper that it should exist in the court."

The point there discussed, however, was not decided in that case, as the real controversy was upon a motion for resale, upon the ground that the creditor was absent from the sale through a mistake, and wished to have the resale at which he offered to bid more than the amount for which the property had been sold.

The liability of a purchaser of property at a judicial sale, who refuses to complete his purchase, for the loss arising upon a resale, had by direction of the court, is not enforcible by contempt proceedings, as the order may be enforced by execution. Betz *v.* Buckel, 30 *Ab. N. C.* 278 ; s. c., 54 *St. R.* 324 ; 24 *Supp.* 487.

Burton *v.* Linn.

order upon her. She has neglected to comply with that order, probably on account of incapability, but the cause does not appear. On the hearing of this motion to punish, her counsel did not oppose the motion on the merits but requested time. The motion, therefore, is practically unopposed, but orders are not granted, even in such cases without scrutiny, and especially where the liberty of a person is involved. There is no doubt but that the purchaser, by bidding at the sale and allowing the premises to be struck down to her, subjected herself to the jurisdiction of the court as to all matters incidental to such sale. Miller *v.* Collyer, 36 *Barb.* 250; Requa *v.* Rea, 2 *Paige*, 339; Cazet *v.* Hubbell, 36 *N. Y.* 676. In 1808, in a case in the High Court of Chancery, in England, Lord Chancellor Eldon expressed some doubt as to the power of the Court of Chancery to commit in such a case as this, but finally concluded he would not allow the purchaser to baffle the court and disobey the order, and so gave the order for judgment. 14 *Ves.* 912. But that decision was made in the days when the order of the High Court of Chancery was usually punishable in any case for disobedience as for contempt, and when imprisonment for debt upon simple contract was permitted in all cases. The tendency of the courts in more modern days has been to avoid or refuse imprisonment for debt for the nonpayment of money, even in cases where the party required to pay was trustee. Myers *v.* Becker, 95 *N. Y.* 486. Inability to pay is not a crime, and the difficulty and doubt in the way of correctly ascertaining whether that inability exists has led to the general rule that judgments or orders for the payment of money are enforceable only by proceedings against property. It is with this view that our Code of Civil Procedure, section 16, has enacted that, where it is not otherwise specially provided by law, no person shall be arrested or imprisoned for disobedience to a judgment or order requiring the payment of money due upon a contract, express or implied, or as damages for non-performance of a contract. Where the payment of the money is connected with a duty which makes it a matter of obligation to the public, or to persons protected by the obligations of public duty, as in case of the payment of alimony for the support of a wife, imprisonment may well be directed until its nonefficacy has become apparent. Where a person is enjoined to do or refrain from doing an act, as the execution of a conveyance which he can alone execute, or the abstinence from the use of property which does not belong to him, imprisonment for contempt may well follow disobedience. Where fraud or wrong is coupled with the creation of the obligation, arrest may follow a failure to perform duty. But where performance is in execution of a contract simply, the nonpayment of money should not be punished as for a crime. In the case at bar the ten per cent. deposit was undoubtedly required to protect against the necessity of a resale. If that percentage was not large enough, a better foresight should have required a larger percentage. Upon the amount realized upon a resale the deficiency can be readily ascertained, after deducting the added expenses, and the purchaser required to lose up to the amount of the deposit, or an execution issued to collect the amount to be paid. Motion to punish for contempt denied.

Opinion by RUSSELL, J.

Motion denied.

James C. de La Mare, for the motion.

Hunt V. Smith, opposed.

MARTENS-TURNER CO. *v.* MACKINTOSH.

*Supreme Court, First Department, Appellate Division;
May,* 1897.

*Promissory note ; acceptance by creditor for debt ; suspension of right
to sue.*]   The giving and acceptance by the creditor of a note for
an existing indebtedness for goods sold suspends the right of
the creditor to sue on such indebtedness until after the maturity
of the note.*

Appeal by the defendant, from a judgment of the
Supreme Court in favor of the plaintiff, entered upon the
verdict of a jury directed by the court upon the pleadings,
after a trial at the New York Trial Term.

The action was brought against James Mackintosh, to
recover upon two causes of action.   The first was a cause
of action for goods sold and delivered, and the second,
for goods sold and delivered upon a credit, alleging that
the credit was obtained by false representations.   The answer of the defendant admitted the sale and delivery of the
goods set forth in the first cause of action, alleging the
commencement of the action on the 24th day of December, 1894, and that, at the time the said action was commenced, nothing was due from the defendant to the
plaintiff, except the amount due on a note of $323.11, and
further alleging that the defendant had given to the
plaintiff promissory notes for the goods sold and delivered
in the cause of action set up in the complaint ; that the
plaintiff had accepted the said notes, such notes being
given in payment, and not otherwise, of the entire
amount which was due and owing from the defendant to
the plaintiff, and that said notes were not due at the time
of the commencement of the action, except the note for

* See Note following this case.

Martens-Turner Co. *v.* Mackintosh.

$323.11, and denied the allegations of the second cause of
action as to the fraud alleged.

Upon motion judgment was entered in favor of the
plaintiff for the amount of the promissory note admitted
to be due, and upon the trial, the court, on motion of the
plaintiff, directed a judgment for the balance of the
amount claimed to be due, on the ground that the giving
by the defendant and the acceptance by the plaintiff of a
promissory note for the amount of the sale of such goods
was not an extension of the time of payment, but that notwithstanding the giving and acceptance of the notes in
payment of the indebtedness, which notes were not due at
the time of the commencement of the action, the plaintiff
could at any time maintain an action to recover the price
of the goods sold and delivered.

Held, error. The counsel for the respondent refers to
but one authority as justifying the decision of the court
below, viz.: Graham *v.* Negus, 8 *Supp.* 679; S. C., 55 *Hun.*
440; 29 *St. R.* 114. That case is opposed to a long line
of authorities in this State (including decisions of the
Court of Appeals upon the exact point), in England and
many other States. The rule is stated in the American
and English Encyclopædia of Law (Vol. 18, p. 177), as
follows: "The taking of a note for a debt, whether such
note is negotiable or not, operates to suspend the right of
the creditor to sue on the original cause of action until
after the maturity of the note;" and the cases to which
reference is made in the note amply sustain this proposition. It was expressly applied by the Court of Appeals
in this State in the cases of Happy *v.* Mosher, 48 *N. Y.*
313 and Hubbard *v.* Gurney, 64 *Id.* 457. Whether upon
this allegation in the answer the acceptance of the note
was an extinguishment under the original obligation to
pay for the goods sold and delivered, it is not necessary to
determine. At least the acceptance of the notes was a
suspension of the right to sue for the amount due upon
the original cause of action for goods sold and delivered.

Martens-Turner Co. *v.* Mackintosh.

The consideration for this suspension of the right to enforce the obligation is apparent.   By the execution of the promissory note the debtor places in the hands of the creditor an obligation which imposes upon him a much more onerous obligation than that upon the mere agreement to pay money.   By it the creditor has the right to transfer by mere indorsement and delivery the obligation of debtor, which, in the hands of the indorsee for value before maturity, imposes upon the maker of the note an obligation to pay regardless of any equities which exist between himself and his original creditor.   That this right of transfer to such a third party gives to the creditor an important advantage, and imposes upon the debtor an increased liability is apparent, and is certainly an ample consideration for an agreement, implied by the delivery of the note, that at least the right to enforce the original obligation should be suspended until a failure to pay the note when due.   That this must be so is apparent from the fact that such a right to transfer the note by indorsement exists.   Upon such transfer the right to sue upon the original cause of action would be suspended, not only until the note was due, but until the note so delivered had again become the property of the original debtor.   To hold that, notwithstanding the giving and acceptance by the original creditor of a note for the amount of the indebtedness, such original creditor could at once commence an action to collect the original indebtedness, would expose such a debtor to a two-fold liability in case of the transfer of the note, and would be to allow a violation of a clearly implied agreement for which there was ample consideration.   We think it quite clear that both upon principle and authority the giving and acceptance by the creditor of a note for an existing indebtedness at least suspends the right of the creditor to sue on such indebtedness until after the maturity of the note, and that the direction of the verdict was erroneous.

Opinion by INGRAHAM, J. PATTERSON, WILLIAMS, O'BRIEN and PARKER, JJ., concurred.

Judgment reversed, new trial ordered, costs to appellant to abide the event.

George W. Stephens, for the defendant, appellant.

Terry Smith, for the plaintiff, respondent.

NOTE ON SUSPENSION OF RIGHT TO SUE BY ACCEPTANCE OF NOTE, ETC.

The decisions on the point involved in the case in the text are far from uniform. Some of the older cases appear to have held that the giving of a new security or collateral for a debt then due, or shortly to become due, must be construed the same as any other contract, and that there was no extension of the credit by the giving of such collateral or other obligation unless there was an express agreement for such extension at the time it was made. Cary *v.* White, 52 *N. Y.* 138. Many of the cases, including the one last cited, were actions which were not brought by the original creditor, and the defense was not made that the account was not yet due because of the giving of some collateral, such as a note or mortgage. But the question has been tested upon the theory that the giving of such note or mortgage was without consideration, unless such consideration could be found in the agreement by the creditor to postpone the time of payment ; and the legality of the mortgage frequently depended, as between prior and subsequent mortgagees, upon the sufficiency of the consideration. Some of the older cases held that there could be no implied agreement to postpone the payment of the debt by the giving of such collateral security or new obligation, and that unless there was an express agreement for such postponement, the mortgage or other instrument would be void as to subsequent mortgagees. Some later cases seem to cast some doubt upon this doctrine, and hold that where such new obligation or other collateral security was given, providing for a payment at a later date, a consideration would be implied from an agreement which was also implied that the creditor should postpone the time of payment, in conformity with the new obligation or collateral security. It has been quite uniformly held, however, as between the original debtor and creditor, that the giving of a promissory note, or other security, promising to pay at a later date the sum which was then due, acted as between the parties as a suspension of the right of the creditor to enforce payment, unless there was fraud in the transaction. If there was such fraud, then the creditor could rescind the terms of credit at any time and sue upon the original contract. Gwalter v. N. Y. Seal Plush, etc., Co., 46 *St. R.* 137 ; American Exchange Nat. Bank v. Voisin, 44 *Hun,* 85 ; Vietor v. Henlein, 34 *Id.* 562 ; s. c., reported fully, 1 *How. Pr.* (*N. S.*) 160 ; Eppens v. McGrath, 3 *Supp.* 213 ; Wigand v. Sichel, 3 *Keyes,* 120 ; Foerster v. Gallinger, 62 *Hun,* 439

In other cases it has been held, as between the original debtor and creditor, that the acceptance of a negotiable note by the creditor operated to suspend the right to sue until the maturity of the note, but otherwise if the note was not negotiable. Webster v. Bainbridge, 13 *Hun,* 180, and cases there cited.

In Durkee v. National Bank of Fort Edward (36 *Hun,* 566), a mortgage and new notes were given to secure the payment of a debt, which was then past due and it was provided in the mortgage that if the notes given in renewal of the old indebtedness were paid at the time they became due, then the renewal notes and mortgage should become void, and if default should be made in the payment of the renewal notes, then the party could sell the mortgaged property. It was held that the mortgage extended the time of payment of the debt which was due when it was given, and was therefore, founded upon a valuable consideration. The court there distinguished the case of Cary v. White, 52 *N. Y.* 138, and said that the courts have been disposed to limit the authority of that case to the facts appearing there, citing as to the limitation, Hubbard v. Gurney, 64 *N. Y.* 457; Grocer's Bank v. Penfield, 7 *Hun,* 279; aff'd 69 *N. Y.* 504. In the last mentioned cases it was held that a party receiving accommodation notes without parting with any consideration, cannot recover on them, but that an agreement for an extension of a term of credit of an existing debt, was sufficient consideration ; that this might be implied from circumstances, without anything being said concerning the extension, and that an express agreement for a suspension of the remedy was not necessary. There, a bank holding the matured notes of one of its customers insisted upon the execution of new notes, but refused to give up those which were due, and in renewal of which the new

notes were given, and it was held that from these circumstances it might be inferred as matter of law that there
was an agreement to extend the time of the old indebted.
ness without any such express agreement having in fact
been made.

In Hill *v.* Beebe (13 *N. Y.* 556), at page 562, it is
said : " It is extremely well settled in this State that the
taking of a debtor's note does not merge or extinguish the
demand for which it is taken. Gregory *v.* Thomas, 20
Wend. 17 ; Waydell *v.* Luer, 5 *Hill,* 448 ; Cole *v.* Sackett, 1
Hill, 516. In Cole *v.* Sackett it was held that the original
demand is not extinguished, although it was expressly
agreed to take the note in satisfaction ; and the doctrine
was reiterated and approved in Waydel *v.* Luer (*supra*).
See also Hanley *v.* Foot, 19 *Wend.* 516 ; Frisbie *v.* Larned,
21 *Wend.* 450. 452."

In Hughes *v.* Wheeler (8 *Cow.* 77), it was held that a
promissory negotiable note is not an absolute extinguishment of a simple contract debt, but only *sub modo,* and,
therefore, cannot be pleaded in answer to a declaration
upon a simple contract ; it is but evidence under the general issue, which may be answered by producing and can-
celing the note on the trial.

In Raymond *v.* Merchant (3 *Cow.* 147), it was held that
a promissory negotiable note given for an antecedent debt
is not absolutely an extinguishment of that debt ; but an
action may still be maintained for the original consideration, provided the note be lost, or produced and canceled at the trial.

In neither of the last two cases does it appear from the
reports that either of the notes was not due at the time the
action was begun on the original indebtedness, and those
cases seem to go no farther, than to hold that a promissory
note which is not paid at maturity, does not extinguish an
antecedent indebtedness, unless there is a special agreement to that effect.

The acceptance of notes bearing interest in payment of
interest due upon a mortgage is a discharge of the original
claim ; the including of interest in the notes is a sufficient
consideration for the agreement to accept them in payment. Rice *v.* Dewey, 54 *Barb.* 455.

The discounting of a note and the application of the
proceeds to the payment of a former one extinguishes the
whole debt, and creates a new one. Fisher *v.* Marvin, 47
Barb. 159.

In Webster *v.* Bainbridge (13 *Hun,* 180), it is said that
the acceptance of a negotiable note of the debtor operates

to suspend the cause of action, until the maturity of the note, but if the note be not negotiable it is otherwise. Citing Seller *v.* Seixas, 4 *Abb. Pr.* 103 ; Hughes *v.* Wheeler, 8 *Cow.* 77 ; Raymond *v.* Merchant, 3 *Cow.* 147.

In that case the complaint set forth an action for goods sold and delivered, the answer alleged that the plaintiff had accepted the defendant's promissory note for the amount due, whereby the time for the payment of the debt was extended and that such note was not yet due. The plaintiff moved to strike out the answer as frivolous, and the motion was granted. The general term affirmed the order on the ground that it did not appear by the answer that the note given was negotiable.

In Claflin *v.* Ostrom (54 *N. Y.* 581), it was held that by bringing a suit and proceeding to judgment and execution upon a note received as collateral security, the original debt is not extinguished, nor a guarantor of that debt discharged.

In Bank of Albion *v.* Burns (46 *N. Y.* 170, 177), where the mortgage was given as collateral security for the payment of a debt evidenced by a note, it was held that an extension of time of payment of these notes by a renewal or otherwise necessarily suspended all rights or remedies upon the bond and mortgage ; that there could be no default in the condition of the bond or forfeiture of the mortgage, except by a failure to pay principal debt at maturity, and that an action upon the bonds or to foreclose the mortgage could only be maintained upon a default to pay the debt which they were given to secure. Citing Putman *v.* Lewis, 8 *Johns.* 389 ; Myers *v.* Welles, 5 *Hill,* 463 ; Fellows *v.* Prentiss, 3 *Denio,* 512.

In Happy *v.* Mosher (48 *N. Y.* 313), the son of the plaintiff had taken a promissory note from the defendant for lumber sold and delivered, and had kept the note two weeks before delivering it to his father. The plaintiff upon receipt of the note retained it, and subsequently, without returning the note, brought an action to recover the value of the lumber, the note not being due at the time the action was commenced. It was held that the giving and acceptance of the note extended the time of payment of the debt until the note matured, and that consequently the action was prematurely brought.

In Hubbard *v.* Gurney (64 *N. Y.* 457), the case of Cary *v.* White (52 *N. Y.* 138) was limited, and the court said, at page 468 : " Judge Allen criticises the cases which hold that the taking of a collateral security on time is an extension of the time of payment and suspends the right of action until the collateral security becomes due. The remarks made must be referred to the facts of that case and are not controlling in a case where the security was not received as collateral, and the money realized upon the new note was paid to the creditor, and a direct application made of the proceeds for his benefit."

When a creditor takes the note of his debtor, payable at a future day, he thereby suspends his right of action upon the debt until the maturity of the note, and, taking the check of the debtor, so payable, is the same in principle and should be held to produce a like effect. Place *v.* McIlvain, 38 *N. Y.* 96. Citing Putnam *v.* Lewis, 8 *Johns.* 382 ; Myers *v.* Willey, 5 *Hill*, 463 ; Fellows *v.* Prentiss, 3 *Denio*, 518 ; Bangs *v.* Mosher, 23 *Barb.* 478.

In Pratt *v.* Coman (37 *N. Y.* 440), it was held that the giving of a promissory note of a third party by a debtor to his creditor for a debt then due extended the time of payment by the original debtor until the note of such third person became due, and that such extension of time of payment was a good consideration to make the creditor a *bona fide* holder for value of such third party's note.

The acceptance of the note of a third person for a preexisting debt suspends the creditor's right of action until it is matured. Smith *v.* Applegate, 1 *Daly*, 91.

In Cary *v.* White (52 *N. Y.* 138), it was held that a legal title under an unrecorded deed, was good as against a subsequent mortgagee who received his mortgage as security for a past payment of a pre-existing debt, and who surrendered no security, or parted with no value for the mortgage ; and the court said, at page 144: "The judge, on the trial, has found as fact, that the mortgage was taken by the plaintiff, for and in behalf of the creditor firm of which he was a member, for a purpose of securing the past indebtedness of the mortgagor, and from this fact he has deduced as a legal conclusion, that there was a suspension of the right to sue upon the original debt ; in other words, that by accepting collateral security, the creditors did agree to extend the time of payment. If this was so the mortgage would be valid, but such is not the law. That the consideration would be sufficient to support a promise or agreement not to sue is not denied, but the law will not imply such an agreement merely from the existence of a consideration, and in the absence of any proof tending to show such an agreement to have been in fact made. . . . The rights and obligations which result and the effects which follow the mere taking a collateral security are the same in all cases ; that is, the contract must receive the same interpretation, and have the same legal effect, whether third persons are or are not affected by it. If the legal implication is that by taking collateral security payable in the future the creditor agrees to forbear to sue upon the original indebtedness for a time, then in all cases sureties would be discharged, and if such is not the legal implication then the creditor surrenders no right to sue except as he expressly agrees." Citing United States *v.* Hoge, 6 *How.* (*U. S.*) 297. The general principle was there announced that when there is no agreement to extend the time of payment of the original debt, or no substituted agreement made respecting the debt, the mere taking of a mortgage payable at a future time, as collateral security for the original debt does not operate to extend the time for its payment.

In Wheeler *v.* Jones (42 *Hun*, 374), the defendant being indebted to the plaintiff for an amount then due assigned certain accounts against third parties, due in the future, to the plaintiff as security, upon an agreement that when these accounts became due the plaintiff should collect them and apply the proceeds to the indebtedness of the defendant, and it was held, following Cary *v.* White (52 *N. Y.* 139), that this transaction did not extend the time of payment of the original debt until the plaintiff should collect the assigned accounts.

Where a note is taken as the result of compromise and settlement, the anterior matters are merged in it; and an action should be brought upon the note, not upon the prior indebtedness. Leland *v.* Maning, 4 *Hun*, 7.

PERI *v.* N. Y. CENTRAL, ETC., R. R. CO.

Court of Appeals; April, 1897.

1. *Appeal; Court of Appeals; final order; special proceeding.*] A proceeding to vacate a satisfaction of judgment as in fraud of an attorney's lien, is a special proceeding, and not a motion in the action, and an order vacating the satisfaction is, therefore, appealable to the Court of Appeals as an order finally determining a special proceeding, under art. VI. § 9, of the Constitution and Code Civ. Pro., § 190, subd. 1.

2. *Attorney's lien; notice; satisfaction of judgment vacated.* Where a judgment for the plaintiff is satisfied between the parties in disregard of the lien of plaintiff's attorneys, and with full knowledge of its existence on the part of the attorneys having actual charge of the litigation for the defendant, the satisfaction will be set aside upon the application of the plaintiff's attorneys, the plaintiff being insolvent and having left the country, although no written notice of lien was served upon the defendant or his attorney of record.*

---

* The common law does not give the defendant's attorney any lien before judgment, and a settlement between the parties, in the absence of fraud or collusion will not be disturbed. Longyear *v.* Carter, 2 *N. Y. Ann. Cas.* 192.

See Notes on Attorneys' Lien, 23 *Abb. N. C.* 240; 28 *Id.* 23; and Note on Enforcing Attorneys' Lien, 10 *Id.* 391.

Only the attorney of record is entitled to a lien under Code Civ. Pro. § 66. Kennedy *v.* Carrick, 18 *Misc.* 38; S. C., 40 *Supp.* 1127.

The fact that there is an attorneys' lien outstanding does not affect a settlement of a judgment as between the parties. Williams *v.* Wilson, 18 *Misc.* 42; S. C., 40 *Supp.* 1132; rev'g 17 *Misc.* 317; S. C., 40 *Supp.* 350.

The claims of attorneys for services as adjusted by the court upon a contested motion cannot be docketed as judgments against the party liable under Rule 27 of the General Rules of Practice. Myer *v.* Abbett, 20 *App. Div.* 390.

An attorney has a lien upon real estate, the title to which is established in an action to the extent of compensation for his service in that particular action, but not for a general balance due to him

Peri *v.* N. Y. Central, etc., R. R. Co.

Appeal from an order of the Appellate Division of the Supreme Court, Fourth Department, which affirmed an order of the Special Term vacating the satisfaction of a judgment entered herein for the plaintiff and directing the

from his client for services in that action and in other matters. West *v.* Bacon, 13 *App. Div.* 371 ; S, C., 43 *Supp.* 206.

A defendant's attorney has no lien for his service upon a defence set up in an action, unless there is a counterclaim in which affirmative relief is demanded by the defendant. White *v.* Sumner, 16 *App. Div.* 70 ; S. C., 44 *Supp.* 692.

Where an attorney refuses to proceed with the action or to allow any one else to represent his client, unless he is paid the amount he claims to be due for his service, the attorney thereby forfeits his lien and the court will grant an order of substitution without enforcing the attorney's lien. Halbert *v.* Gibbs, 16 *App. Div.* 126 ; S. C., 45 *Supp.* 113.

The assignee of a judgment takes it subject to equities, and the lien of an attorney given by Code Civ. Pro., § 66, attaches to a judgment assigned for value and without notice of the lien, and a satisfaction by the assignee thereof will be vacated on motion of the judgment creditor's attorney, to the extent of his rightful lien. Guliano *v.* Whitenack. 1 *N. Y. Ann. Cas.* 75. And see cases cited in notes.

Where two judgments are both entered in the same action the equities of the parties are superior to the lien of the attorneys, and set-off will be allowed between the parties without regard to the attorney's lien. Hopper *v.* Ersler. 1 *N. Y. Ann. Cas.* 192.

But where judgments are in different actions, the attorney's lien is superior to the equities of the parties, and set-off will not be allowed to the extent of defeating such lien. Winterson *v.* Hitchings, 1 *N. Y. Ann. Cas.* 193, and notes.

In Krone *v.* Klotz (3 *N. Y. Ann. Cas,* 36), it was held, that where an attorney who had collected a sum of money on a judgment for his client, claimed the balance over and above the sum due for his service in that action, for other services for the same client, that he would not be compelled as a third party in supplementary proceedings to pay over said sum to the sheriff at the instance of a judgment creditor of his client, as the ownership by the judgment debtor of the fund was not so clear and conclusive as required by Code Civ. Pro., § 2447.

See Note on Substitution of Attorneys, 1 *N. Y. Ann. Cas.* 352.

sheriff to enforce such judgment to the extent of the lien of the plaintiff's attorneys thereon.

This proceeding was instituted by the attorneys for the plaintiff to enforce their lien upon the judgment. The plaintiff recovered judgment against the defendant for damages sustained by personal injuries, for $5,000 and costs. The jury brought in a verdict for $10,000, and the trial judge reduced it one-half. After the sheriff had levied upon sufficient property to satisfy the claim and the General Term had affirmed, the plaintiff without knowledge of his attorneys, assigned the judgment, and thereafter a settlement was effected for the sum of $4,200, which was paid to the assignee, who was an attorney at law. The plaintiff was an ignorant Italian laborer and unable to speak the English language. The assignee paid to a creditor of the plaintiff the sum of $2,200, of which the plaintiff was to receive $1,200, and the balance of $2,000 was retained by the assignee.

The referee found that the plaintiff was wholly insolvent except as to the amount of money paid him out of the proceeds of the judgment, and that within a few days after receiving the money he left this country and returned to Italy, where he still remains. About the time the action was commenced plaintiff executed, acknowledged and duly delivered an agreement in writing with one of the plaintiff's attorneys, to the effect that he would advance all money for expenses and pay to the attorney one-half of all that he should recover in addition to the costs, disbursements and interest. He further covenanted that he would not settle the action unless his attorney was present. The attorney of record for the defendant resided in the City of New York, and, as the venue was laid in Erie county, all the papers in the action, after issue joined, were sent to a firm of attorneys in Buffalo, who thereafter acted as the representatives of the New York attorney.

More than a year before the settlement the plaintiff's attorney served upon the Buffalo attorneys the following paper: "Please take notice that we have a lien for one-half of any judgment or settlement recovered in the above entitled action, and for the costs and interest." This was in March, 1894, and before the general term had affirmed the judgment.

In this proceeding the special term appointed a referee to take proof of the facts and circumstances of the matters set forth in the papers read in support of and in opposition to the application, with direction to report the testimony, together with his findings of fact and conclusions of law to the court. The referee found the facts in detail and stated his conclusions of law, that the agreement was binding and the plaintiff's attorneys were entitled to the amounts therein provided for, and by virtue of Code Civ. Pro., § 66, had a lien upon the judgment for the sum so found due, and were entitled to an order vacating the satisfaction of the judgment and to enforce it by execution to the extent of their lien. The referee submitted with his report an opinion. The special term also wrote an opinion and confirmed the report of the referee, and the appellate division affirmed the order of confirmation.

Held, that the order was appealable to this court as an order which finally determined a special proceeding under art VI, § 9, of the Constitution and Code Civ. Pro., § 190, subd. 1. We are of the opinion that this is a special proceeding and cannot be regarded in any proper sense as a motion in the action. At the time this proceeding was instituted, the action had been tried, judgment entered against the defendant and the same had been paid and satisfied. We have here a proceeding by third parties against the defendant upon other issues than those framed in the action, and relating to a lien arising out of a state of facts wholly distinct from those passed upon at the trial.

This proceeding, which is invoked by the plaintiff's attorney, is in place of an action to set aside the satisfaction of the judgment. It is conducted as if it were an independent action. In this instance a referee took a large amount of testimony and reported thirty-six findings of fact and four conclusions of law. It would be an anomaly to hold that a proceeding of this nature is a motion in the action. The motion to dismiss the appeal is denied.

Held, further, that the failure of the attorney to give notice to the defendant or to his attorney of record, did not impair his lien and the order was properly made. Prior to 1879, section 66 of the Code of Civil Procedure simply regulated the agreement an attorney might make in relation to his compensation for services ; it read as follows : " The compensation of an attorney and counsellor for his services is governed by agreement, express or implied, which is not restrained by law." The courts in construing this section held that an attorney in order to protect his lien must give notice of his claim. In 1879 the legislature added these words to the section : " From the commencement of an action or the service of an answer containing a counterclaim, the attorney who appears for a party has a lien upon his client's cause of action or counterclaim, which attaches to a verdict, report, decision, or judgment in his client's favor, and the proceeds thereof in whosesoever hands they may come ; and cannot be affected by any settlement between the parties before or after judgment."

This language is very comprehensive and creates a lien in favor of the attorney on his client's cause of action, in whatever form it may assume in the course of the litigation, and enables him to follow the proceeds into the hands of third parties, without regard to any settlement before or after judgment. This is a statutory lien of which all the world must take notice, and anyone settling with a plaintiff without the knowledge of his attorney, does so at his own risk. Coster *v.* Greenpoint Ferry Co. 5 *Civ. Pro. R.* 146 ; affirmed without opinion, 98 *N. Y.* 660.

The lien operates as security, and if the settlement entered into by the parties is in disregard of it and to the

prejudice of plaintiff's attorney, by reason of the insolvency of his client, or for other sufficient cause, the court
will interfere and protect its officer by vacating the satisfaction of judgment and permitting execution to issue for
the enforcement of the judgment to the extent of the lien,
or by following the proceeds in the hands of the third
parties, who received them before or after judgment
impressed with the lien. Poole *v.* Belcha, 131 *N. Y.* 200 ;
S. C., 42 *St. R.* 856 ; 22 *Civ. Pro. R.* 67 ; Bailey *v.* Murphy,
136 *N. Y.* 50 ; S. C., 49 *St. R.* 82 ; Lee *v.* Vacuum Oil Co.,
126 *N. Y.* at page 587 ; S. C., 38 *St. R.* 662. In the case
at bar the undisputed facts show that this settlement was
made in disregard of the lien of plaintiff's attorneys, with
full knowledge of its existence and in reliance upon the
technical point that written notice of the lien should have
been served either on the defendant or its attorney of
record in the city of New York, instead of upon the firm of
Buffalo attorneys who had actual charge of the litigation.
Without regard to the point that no notice was required,
we have the undisputed facts that the attorneys who
actually represented the defendant in settling the judgment had notice in writing of the lien, and that the plaintiff is without financial responsibility and has returned to
Italy, where he still remains.

Opinion by BARTLETT, J. All concur.

Order affirmed, with costs.

James F. Gluck, for the defendant, appellant.

George W. Cothran, for the respondent.

ALLENTOWN FOUNDRY & MACHINE WORKS
v. LORETZ.

Supreme Court, Second Department, Appellate Division;
April, 1897.

1. *Stay ; actions pending in different jurisdictions.*] The rule that where the decision of one of several actions pending in this State will determine the rights set up in the others, the latter will be stayed, applies to the case of actions pending in different jurisdictions, except where the effect of the stay would be to endanger the plaintiff's obtaining satisfaction of his claim in case of success.*

---

* See Note on Defence of Former Action Pending, (3 *N. Y. Ann. Cas.* 215), where it is pointed out in the cases there cited that the pendency of a former action between the same parties, for the same cause of action, in another State, will not abate an action in this State. While the decision in the text does not in any way hold that the pendency of such former action will defeat an action pending in this State ; it does hold that it will suspend the prosecution of such action, until the determination or discontinuance of the suit pending in a foreign jurisdiction.

"At common law the pendency on another suit for the same cause could at most only be pleaded in abatement, but where the former action is in a court of the United States, or a sister State, it is no stay or bar to a suit in the courts of this State." Oneida County Bank *v.* Bonney, 101 *N. Y.* 173, 175.

In Dolbeer *v.* Stout (139 *N. Y.* 486), cited in the text, the court refused to grant a stay of one action pending the decision of another action in the same State, but a different court, on the ground that the parties to both actions were not the same ; but the court remarked at page 489: "Where the decision in one action will determine the right set up in another action and the judgment on one trial will dispose of the controversy in all the actions, a case for a stay is presented." Citing Travis *v.* Myers, 67 *N. Y.* 542 ; Third Ave. R. R. Co. *v.* Mayor, etc., of N. Y., 54 *Id.* 159 ; People *v.* Wasson, 64 *Id.* 167 ; DeGroot *v.* Jay, 30 *Barb.* 483.

See also Smith *v.* Crocker, *ante,* page 77, and cases there cited.

Allentown Foundry and Machine Works *v.* Loretz.

2. *The same ; case stated.*] *So held,* staying actions by a foreign corporation in this State for goods sold and delivered, where two prior actions had been brought in Massachusetts upon the same claims, one in equity, and one at law and to attach moneys due to the defendant, and the defendant had appeared generally in both actions and an order had been made referring the issues for trial.

Appeal by the plaintiff from an order of the Supreme Court, Kings County Special Term, staying the proceedings in several actions until the final determination of certain actions pending in the State of Massachusetts.

These actions are brought to recover the price of certain machinery sold and delivered to the defendant, Arthur L. J. Loretz, and were commenced on May 1, 1896. The plaintiff is a Pennsylvania corporation, having its place of business within that State. Prior to the institution of these actions the plaintiff brought a suit in Massachusetts, in equity, upon these same claims, to attach moneys due to the defendant from the City of Lynn. Subsequently, and about June 1, 1896, an action at law in that State, was brought by the plaintiff against the defendant to recover the amount of those claims. In both of the actions in Massachusetts the defendant has appeared, answering and contesting the demands of the plaintiff, and an order has been made referring the actions for trial. The defendant interposed answers in the actions in this State, and thereupon applied for an order staying proceedings in these actions until the hearing and determination of the Massachusetts suits. From an order granting such application this appeal is taken.

Held, no error. In the case of several actions pending in this State, where the decision of one action will determine the rights set up in the others, unquestionably a stay may be granted. Dolbeer *v.* Stout, 139 *N. Y.* 486; S. C., 54 *St. R.* 801 ; rev'g 61 *Super. Ct.* 172. We do not see why the same rule should not apply to the case of actions pending in different jurisdictions, except where the effect of the stay would be to hazard or put in jeopardy some chance or opportunity of the party obtaining a satisfaction of his claim in case of success. There is no such hazard to the plaintiff in these cases. The defendant having appeared generally in the Massachusetts actions, the plaintiff, if successful, will obtain a judgment for the full amount of its claims, which will be conclusive in every other jurisdiction. The prosecution, therefore, of the suits in both States will subject the defendant to vexatious and unnecessarily expensive litigation.

There can be no question that, if the plaintiff were a resident of this State, and the courts here could obtain jurisdiction of its person, they might restrain it from prosecuting actions or suits in other States. Kittle *v.* Kittle, 8 *Daly*, 72 ; Vail *v.* Knapp, 49 *Barb.* 299 ; Claflin & Co. *v.* Hamlin, 62 *How. Pr.* 284. It is probable that the defendant could not get such relief against the plaintiff, because he could not secure its appearance in an action in equity brought for that purpose. But, if we cannot restrain the plaintiff's conduct in other jurisdictions, we are at least masters of the procedure in our own State. While we may not say to it, "You shall not proceed in the Massachusetts actions," we can say to it, "As long as you continue to prosecute those actions, you shall not proceed in the actions pending in this State." In Hammond *v.* Baker (3 *Sandf.* 704) the complainant brought his suit for an accounting in this State. Afterwards he commenced another suit against the defendant in Rhode Island for the same cause of action and praying for the same relief. It was held that he must suspend his suit there or here. In Nichols *v.* Nichols (12 *Hun*, 428), the plaintiff brought her action for a separation on charges of cruel and inhuman treatment. Subsequently she brought an action in the State of Connecticut for divorce on the same grounds, cruelty and inhuman treatment in that State being sufficient to authorize a dissolution of the marriage contract. It was held that she must resort to one court or

Heerdegen *v.* Loreck.

the other, and all proceedings in the action in this State were stayed until the plaintiff abandoned her Connecticut suit.

Opinion by CULLEN, J.   All concurred.

Order affirmed, with ten dollars costs and disbursements.

Henry Yonge, for the plaintiff, appellant.

William S. Maddox, for the defendant, respondent.

HEERDEGEN *v.* LORECK.

Supreme Court, First Depatment, Appellate Division ; May, 1897.

Reference ; new referee ; evidence taken before former referee.] Where, after certain evidence had been taken by a referee under a compulsory order of reference, the referee became disqualified to act further by being elected a justice of the Supreme Court,—*Held,* that a provision in an order appointing a new referee that the testimony taken before the former referee should stand and be considered in like manner and form as though such testimony had been originally had and taken before the substituted referee, was improper, and not within the power of the court.*

---

* The court cannot compel new parties brought in after the case has been submitted to a referee to accept the reference, and the evidence taken, even with the right of cross-examination.   Wood *v.* Swift, 81 *N. Y.* 30.

In Bloom *v.* National, etc., Loan Co. (1 *N. Y. Ann. Cas.* 26), it was held where a trial was had at Special Term, and the evidence closed, that the court had no power without the consent of the parties to make an order permitting further evidence and send-

Heerdegen *v.* Loreck.

Appeal by the defendant, Rudolph Loreck, as executor, etc., of Alexander E. Schnee, deceased, from so much of an order of the Supreme Court, made at the New York Special Term, which provided that upon a reference the testimony taken before a former referee should stand and be considered in like manner and form as though such testimony had been originally had and taken before the referee appointed in said order.

Held, that it was not within the power of the court, in appointing a new referee to hear and determine the cause, to annex any condition that would compel that referee to

ing the cause to a referee to hear and determine upon additional evidence and upon the stenographer's minutes of the evidence taken before the court ; but if a party proceeds with the trial before the referee, after his objection that the court has no power to make such order has been overruled by the referee, his right to object thereto upon appeal from the final judgment is lost.

The opinion of one judge upon the issues of fact, announced at the end of a trial which does not result in any judgment, is not competent evidence to guide or influence the determination of those issues of facts by another judge upon the second trial. Eckerson *v.* Archer, 10 *App. Div.* 344. See also Reliance Marine Ins. Co. *v.* Herbert, 87 *Hun*, 285.

As a general rule, a stipulation that a party may read from the evidence taken in one action, and have it considered by the court or the jury in subsequent actions against the same defendant, will be enforced. Crow *v.* Gleason, 20 *Supp.* 590 ; S. C., *St. R.* 912 ; Whiting *v.* Edmunds, 94 *N. Y.* 309.

And the stipulation is binding upon successive trials of the same action, unless avoided by the court. Herbst *v.* Vacuum Oil Co., 68 *Hun*, 222 ; S. C., 22 *Supp.* 807.

But under such stipulation only such testimony as is competent and material to the issues of the second trial is admissible. Garwood *v.* N. Y. Cent. R. R. Co. 19 *W. Dig.* 416; aff'd without opinion on this point, 116 *N. Y.* 649.

See Note on Stipulations Affecting Subsequent Trials, 3 *N. Y. Ann. Cas.* 54.

Minutes of the grand jury are not common law evidence of what a witness testified to before them. People *v.* Conroy, 153 *N. Y.* 174.

Heerdegen *v.* Loreck.

decide the issues upon testimony taken before, or rulings made by, another referee. The reference was a compulsory one, and upon the original referee becoming disqualified to act by reason of his election to the supreme court bench, all proceedings upon the trial before him necessarily ended. The substitution of another referee was required, the case in its nature being such as demanded that method of trial. The case stood precisely as if no trial had ever been had. The defendant was entitled to have the judicial officer who was to pass upon his rights hear the testimony of the witnesses and form his determination upon the issues therefrom. The defendant is not to be compelled to have those rights passed upon in segments or divisions; rulings as to one branch of the case made by one judge and as to another branch by a different judge. There can be but one trial before one judicial officer and it is a trial of the whole case. Upon a new trial being granted on appeal for error, a condition that testimony taken upon a former trial be received as evidence cannot be enforced. Bruce *v.* Davenport, 1 *Abb. Ct. App. Dec.* 235.

The case differs essentially from Countryman *v.* Norton (21 *Hun*, 17), in which there was but a temporary disqualification of the referee by reason of his becoming a judge of the supreme court; after his retirement from office, he merely took up the case again at the point at which he left it. It was the same referee. Nor is the case in any way similar to Roberts *v.* White, 73 *N. Y.* 375. That was merely a proceeding to assess damages on an injunction; the court held that it was within the power of the court on a second proceeding to allow the evidence given on a first hearing to be adopted. There was no trial of issues and it was a matter which might have been heard upon *ex parte* affidavits, and the strict procedure of a trial was not required. In the case at bar the defendant was entitled to a trial according to the strict procedure of a trial, and by one judge and not by two acting upon different branches of the case. That hardship may result to the plaintiff by reason of the substitution of a referee is true, but this court has no power to alter the recognized procedure in the trial of issues. The Code of Civil Procedure provides in what cases testimony previously given in a cause may be used on a subsequent trial, and the court cannot legislate upon that subject.

That part of the order appealed from was erroneously made and must be reversed, and the provision stricken from the order so that such order will stand as one substituting a new referee named in the order in the place of the former referee, with ten dollars costs and disbursements.

Opinion PER CURIAM. Present VAN BRUNT, P. J., RUMSEY, WILLIAMS, PATTERSON and PARKER, JJ.

Ordered accordingly.

Louis O. Van Doren, for the defendant, appellant.

William R. Bronk, for the plaintiff, respondent.

TREPAGNIER & BROS. *v.* ROSE.

Supreme Court, Second Department, Appellate Division; June, 1897.

Attachment ; levy ; instrument for the payment of money ; fire insurance policy.] A policy of fire insurance, where a loss has occurred, does not become an instrument for the payment of money within the meaning of Code Civ. Pro., § 649, subd. 2, and a levy may be made thereon under the warrant of attachment the same as upon any other debt, by giving notice and serving the warrant of attachment upon the insurance company, without taking possession of the policy.[*]

------

[*] The case in the text holds that a levy may be made upon a policy of fire insurance under Code Civ. Pro., § 649, subd. 3, which

Trepagnier & Bros. *v.* Rose.

Appeal by the defendants, Arthur S. Rose and others, from so much of an order of the Supreme Court, Kings County Special Term, as denies their motion to vacate

provides that the levy may be made : " Upon other personal property by leaving a certified copy of the warrant and a notice showing the property attached, with the person holding the same ; or, if it consists of a demand other than as specified in the last subdivision, with the person against whom it exists ; or, if it consists of right or share in the stock of an association or corporation, or interest or profits thereon, with the president or other head of the association or corporation, or the secretary, cashier or managing agent thereof."

In a somewhat recent case the Court of Appeals has said that the notice required to be given by the sheriff must be specific and describe the property and the person whose property is attached, so that there can be no reasonable ground for an error on the part of the person to whom the notice is given, and that such person is not compelled to look at the warrant as well as to the notice to discover whose property is made subject to the attachment.   Hayden *v.* National Bank, 130 *N. Y.* 146 .

In that case the plaintiffs had an account against G. H. Loker & Brothers, who were non-residents.   The plaintiffs did not know the Christian names of the defendants, and brought an action against G. H. Loker and ―― Loker, and they were so described in the summons and complaint and warrant of attachment.   The sheriff served the warrant of attachment upon the National Bank of the State of New York, together with a notice endorsed upon the warrant of attachment, to the effect that by it the sheriff was commanded to attach all the property of the defendant, G. H. Loker, within his county, and that having been informed that the said bank had in its possession, certain moneys belonging to said defendant and was indebted to him, he particularly attached and required to be delivered over to him the said money, and any property of said defendant in possession or under control of said bank. The court held that this notice was plainly insufficient to attach money due to G. H. Loker & Brothers, and could not be made the foundation for a proceeding to divest the title of the firm to any funds on deposit with the bank.   The court said that they might assume that the bank knew whose property was attached, but that it had a right to look to the notice irrespective of the warrant, and that, unless the notice was specific enough to accurately describe the person against whom the attachment was issued, it would be

and set aside an alleged levy under an attachment upon
an indebtedness due the defendants from the Mutual Fire
Insurance Company, under a policy of fire insurance issued
by said company to the defendants, a loss having occurred.
The sheriff failed to obtain possession of the written policy.

Held, that a policy of insurance is not an instrument
for the payment of money, under Code Civ. Pro., § 649,
subd. 2. It is not necessary for us in this case to go to
the extent of holding that instruments for the payment of
money, mentioned by the Code, include only negotiable
instruments. We do not decide that proposition. But we
are clear that, to be an instrument for the payment of
money, it must be an instrument which acknowledges an
absolute obligation to pay, not conditional or contingent;
one, the execution of which being admitted, it would be
incumbent on the plaintiff, in an action to enforce it, only
to offer the instrument in evidence to entitle him to a recovery. In other words, an instrument that admits an existing debt. We think that this is the correct line which
divides such instruments from other written contracts
which contain obligations on the part of one party or the
other to pay money, such as agreements of sale, hiring,
leases, building contracts, etc. The exact terms of the insurance policies are not given in the record before us. We
may assume, in the absence of any express statement to
the contrary, that they are of the character generally issued
by companies doing insurance business. If so, the des-
truction of or injury to the property insured, of itself

---

unavailable to divest the title of the attachment debtor in the
property.

The main ground for the decision in that case was that the
money in the hands of the bank, was that of a firm, while the notice
merely referred to the individual property of one member of the
firm, and the court said that if a notice had been in general terms
so as to include the property of the firm and of either member
thereof it might have been sufficient.

Trepagnier & Bros. *v.* Rose.

alone, did not create a liability on the part of the company. It would be necessary to submit proofs of loss, and the company's obligation to pay is conditioned on the presentation of proper proofs. It is, therefore, plain that a policy of insurance does not fall within the definition we have given to the terms employed by the Code of Civil Procedure.

The counsel for the appellants cites certain decisions which he contends are opposed to the views we here express. Some expressions of the opinions in those cases do conflict with our view, but an examination of the cases will show that the point was not necessarily involved. In Hankinson *v.* Page (19 *Abb. N. C.* 274), Judge WALLACE held that an ordinary policy of insurance after loss was an instrument for the payment of money which the sheriff was required to take into his actual custody to constitute a valid levy under an attachment. But as he also held that a certificate of membership in a mutual benefit company was not such an instrument, he reversed the decision of the referee and granted a new trial. In the case of Kratzenstein *v.* Lehman (19 *App. Div.* 228), the defendant held a life insurance policy, payable at his death or at a specific time if he then survived, which had not yet matured. The sheriff did not obtain possession of the policy, but the levy was made by serving the warrant of attachment and notice upon the life insurance company. The appellate division held the levy valid.*

On the other hand, as supporting a contrary view, is to be found the intimation of Justice VAN BRUNT, in Von Hesse *v.* Mackaye (55 *Hun*, 365), that subdivision 2 of section 649 was meant to include only cases of negotiable iustruments. There is very much to be said in favor of this view. It is difficult to understand the policy or reason of a provision which would enable a debtor to put

---

* No authorities were cited in the dissenting opinion by INGRAHAM, J., which was concurred in by PATTERSON, J.

beyond the reach of his creditor a claim evidenced by a non-negotiable instrument, by secreting that instrument. In the case of negotiable instruments the reason is plain. If the debtor on such an instrument could be compelled to pay the debt on the attachment, without the production of the instrument, he would be liable to have to pay it over again.

There is a long line of authorities which, though not on the exact point before us, tends to support our view. By section 4 of chapter 325 of the Laws of 1825 it was enacted that where any incorporated company should be sued "upon any contract, note, or other evidence of debt," judgment should be entered against it, unless it was made to appear to a judge or the court that it had a substantial defense. Under this statute it was held that a policy of insurance by an incorporated insurance company was not a contract, note, or other evidence of debt, within the meaning of the statute. Anonymous, 6 *Cow.* 41 ; Tyler *v.* Ætna Fire Ins. Co., 2 *Wend.* 280. The Revised Statutes continued this provision, with some change of phraseology, and it is now found in section 1778 of the Code. The language of this section is "for the non-payment of a promissory note, or other evidence of debt, for the absolute payment of money upon demand or at a particular time." In N. Y. Life Ins. Co. *v.* Universal Life Ins. Co. (88 *N. Y.* 424, 428), it was held, overruling Studwell *v.* Charter Oak Ins. Co. (19 *Hun*, 127), that a life insurance policy which had matured and become due, was not an evidence of debt for the absolute payment of money, within the meaning of the Code. The true test, whether a contract is an instrument for the payment of money, is whether it acknowledges an existing debt or not.

Opinion by CULLEN, J. All concurred, except GOODRICH, P. J., not sitting.

Order affirmed, with ten dollars costs and disbursements.

Marshall B. Clarke and *Edward F. Dwight*, for the defendants, appellants.

Theodore F. C. Demarest, for the plaintiff, respondent.

SEWELL *v.* BUTLER.

Supreme Court, Second Department, Appellate Division; April, 1897.

1. *Deposition; physical examination before trial; recovery of plaintiff from injuries.*] Where, upon an application to vacate an order for the physical and oral examination of the plaintiff before trial, in an action for negligence causing physical injury to the plaintiff, the plaintiff swears that he has fully recovered from the injury referred to in the complaint, as received by him and from its effect, the order for his examination should not be vacated, unless he stipulates, for use upon the trial, that he has entirely recovered from such injury and its effect.

2. *The same; affidavit; general rule.*] Where an affidavit to secure the examination of the plaintiff before trial, complies with all the requirements of the statute, in a case to which it is applicable, and it appears that the application is made in good faith for the object as provided for in the statute, it requires something quite substantial in its nature and satisfactory to overcome its effect, and to defeat its sufficiency for the purpose sought.*

Appeal by the defendant from an order of the Supreme Court, Westchester Special Term, vacating an order made

---

* See Note on Physical Examination of Plaintiff Before Trial, 1 *N. Y. Ann. Cas.* 178.

Where a physical examination has been had, the allowance of a further examination rests in the discretion of the court. *Lawrence v.* Samuels, 20 *Misc.* 15; S. C., 44 *Supp.* 602.

Neither the attorney nor any male person can be present at the physical examination of a female plaintiff. *Id.* See also same case, 20 *Misc.* 278.

Sewell *v* Butler.

by a justice of the Supreme Court directing the plaintiff to submit to an oral and physical examination before the trial of the action.

The defendant, James Butler, seeking to have an oral and physical examination of the plaintiff, Robert Sewell, obtained an *ex parte* order to that effect, appointing a referee and designating a physician to take and make such examination, pursuant to the provision of the statute. *Code Civ. Pro.* §§ 870–873. The motion to vacate the order was founded upon the affidavits of the plaintiff and his attorney with the other proceedings in the action, the plaintiff by his affidavit stating that he had fully recovered from the injuries received by him, and that a physical examination of him would reveal nothing relating thereto.

Held, as stated in head notes. The statute providing for such examinations is intended to facilitate the promotion of justice, and is entitled to a reasonably liberal application to accomplish the purposes within the contemplation of its provisions. The cases in the courts have not been entirely uniform on this subject. But, on the whole, when the application is brought within the provisions of the statute, a party is deemed entitled to the order, if he seeks it in good faith. The statute provides that : " The judge to whom such an affidavit is presented must grant an order for the examination if an action is pending." *Code Civ. Pro.* § 873. The plaintiff, in his affidavit, asserts his belief that the order was procured by the defendant to annoy and harass him, and for that purpose only, and such is the contention of the plaintiff's counsel. Such belief may be urged in every case where such an order is obtained. To determine the question whether the application is made in good faith, or for purposes other than object to be attained by the proceeding under the stat reference must be had to the affidavit and to the circu stances which go to characterize the purpose in view the party making it. And if the affidavit comes up

Sewell *v*. Butler.

the requirement of the statute in a case to which it is applicable, it requires something quite substantial in its nature and satisfactory to overcome its effect and to defeat its efficiency for the purpose sought. While the examination may furnish some information to the party obtaining the order, it cannot be supposed to prejudice any legal right of the party examined. His deposition is taken to be used on the trial. None of his rights are curtailed for the purposes of the trial. The statute, by its terms, is made peculiarly applicable to actions for the recovery of damages arising from personal injuries of the nature and extent of which the defendant is ignorant. § 872, *subd.* 4. And by the recent amendment of section 873, a physical examination is provided for in such cases, which until the year 1893 could not be had. McQuigan *v.* Delaware, L. & W. R. R. Co., 129 *N. Y.* 50; s. c. 41 *St. R.* 382; 21 *Civ. Pro. R.* 396. The order in the present case did not limit the oral examination of the plaintiff to any particular matters within the issues, nor was there any occasion for it.

The defendant, by his answer, puts in issue the allegations of the complaint. He alleges no affirmative matter as a defense, and none was necessary to permit him to obtain the order for the examination of the plaintiff. Herbage *v.* City of Utica, 109 *N. Y.* 81; 14 *St. R.* 845; 14 *Civ. Pro. R.* 79. In the view taken of the case no reason appears for denial of the order sought for and obtained by the defendant.

The conclusion follows that the order appealed from should be reversed and the motion denied; that the plaintiff submit to an oral examination as directed by the order heretofore made, and that he also submit to a physical examination as thereby directed unless the plaintiff _ulates, for use upon the trial, that he has entirely re-vered from the injuries referred to in the complaint as :eived by him and from their effect; thereupon such ler be so modified as to relieve him from a physical amination.

Opinion by BRADLEY, J.   All concurred.

Ordered accordingly.

Edwin A. Jones and *Herbert C. Smyth*, for the defendant, appellant.

George C. Andrews, for the plaintiff, respondent.

MATTER OF UNITED STATES PIPE LINE CO.

Supreme Court, First Department, Appellate Division;
April, 1897.

Contempt; refusal of witness to answer ; commission from foreign court.] Where a witness is subpœnaed to appear before a commissioner appointed by a foreign court, under Code Civ. Pro.,
§ 915, he may be punished for contempt for a refusal to testify,
under Code Civ. Pro., §§ 855, *et seq.*, by the judge or justice who
issued the subpœna, but not by the court out of which the subpœna issued.*

---

* Sections 855, *et seq.*, of the Code of Civil Procedure, contain
the general provisions for enforcing a witness to appear and testify
in obedience to a subpœna and for punishing him for his failure or
refusal to obey the subpœna.

In Matter of Whitlock (51 *Hun*, 351), the general term of the
first department said, in deciding a motion to compel a witness to
testify before an open commission issued by the High Court of Justice of England, at page 354: "Undoubtedly under section 915 of
the Code of Civil Procedure, the court or judge has power, when it
appears that a witness refuses to answer a proper and material question put to him before the open commission, to require him to do so,
and in case he fails to answer or produce the writings to punish hii
But to that end it must be made to appear that the question whi
he refuses to answer, or the document which he refuses to produc
is material within the issues of that case, and not merely of anothe
case."

In that case the court refused to compel the witness to answe

Matter of United States Pipe Line Co.

Appeal by the United States Pipe Line Co., from an order of the Supreme Court, New York Special Term, denying its motion to compel the witnesses John D. Arch-

---

on the ground that the questions which were asked, were concerning privileged communications of the witness as an attorney with his client; and as to part of the questions, that they were immaterial and incompetent in the case in which the commission was issued. That opinion was written by Mr. Justice MACOMBER, and concurred in by VAN BRUNT, P, J., and BRADY, J.

The case last mentioned does not appear to have been called to the attention of the court, in the case in the text; nor does it appear to have been cited in any of the cases reported since it was decided, in 1889. No authorities are cited by the court for the doctrine there announced.

In Matter of Bushnell (19 *Misc.* 307), Mr. Justice TRUAX, sitting at the Special Term of the Supreme Court, in New York County, decided that the court had no power to compel a witness subpœnaed to testify under a commission from another State to answer questions put to him; but that the officer before whom he was required to appear had power to punish by fine and imprisonment, the same as a justice of the peace. It is remarked in that case that the words quoted above from the opinion in Matter of Whitlock (51 *Hun*, 351), were *obiter*, and the court refused to follow the ruling there made, and denied a motion to punish the witness.

In Whittenbrock *v.* Mabins (57 *Hun*, 146), it was held that a person who had his place of residence in New Jersey, and a place of business in the City of New York, sojourned in the County of New York within the meaning of section 916, specifying the county in which the witness must be ordered to appear.

In Matter of Savin (9 *Civ. Pro. R.* 175), the subpœna was issued upon an affidavit which stated the facts as to the pending suit and the materiality of the testimony of the witness and, further, that the evidence of a person taken before an officer, who was authorized by the laws of this country to take such an affidavit, and whose official character was certified to by a consul of the Republic of France, would be received in evidence in the courts of that Republic. But it was not shown that any commission had issued in the court in which the action was pending, and the subpœna was vacated on the ground that there was no authority of law for issuing it unless a commission had been actually issued by bold and others to answer certain questions put to them, which they refused to answer.

In September, 1896, an action was pending in the court of common pleas of McKane county, Penn., in which the National Transit Company and another were plaintiffs and the United States Pipe Line Company was defendant. The court in which that action was pending appointed a commissioner to take the testimony in the city of New York of certain persons residing therein, as witnesses, to be used in that action. This testimony was to be taken by oral questions. A proper application was made, as required by the code, to a justice of this court, who issued .a subpœna requiring the witnesses to appear before the commissioner at a time therein named. They did so appear, but they declined to answer certain of the questions asked them. An application was made for an order to show cause at a special term of the court why the witnesses should not be required to answer the questions. Upon the hearing of that order to show cause, the motion was denied. From that denial this appeal is taken.

Held, as stated in headnote. It is claimed on behalf of the appellant that no sufficient means is provided by statute for compelling the attendance of witnesses upon the taking of testimony under a commission of this kind, or to require the witnesses who attend to answer material and proper questions, and, therefore, it is said that the court, by virtue of its inherent power to compel obedience

---

But since the last mentioned case was decided, section 917 of the Code has been amended by the provision (subdivision 3), that a subpœna, may be issued when it appears, "that according to the course and practice of the court in which the action, suit, or special proceedings is pending, the deposition of a witness taken as one applied for is required to be taken, is authorized to be recei in evidence on the trial or hearing."

It was held in Eldridge *v.* Chapman, (13 *Abb. Pr.* 68*n,*) that production of books and papers might be required upon the er ination of a witness under such a commission.

to its own mandates, has authority to issue such process as is necessary to compel the attendance of witnesses and to require them when they attend to answer such questions as are proper to be put to them for the execution of the commission.

It was claimed on the other hand by the respondents that the judge who issued the subpœnas to compel attendance of witnesses before the commissioner, pursuant to section 915 of the Code of Civil Procedure, acted solely under a statutory power in the exercise of an authority unknown to the common law, and that his mandate was not the mandate of the court, and that the only remedy for the disobedience to that mandate was such as was given by the statute, and consequently there was no power in the court to make the order asked for here. This view was concurred in by the learned justice below, and he acted upon it and denied the motion. To a certain extent we concur in the conclusion which he reached.

A proceeding to take testimony in this State for use in an action pending in the court of another State before a commissioner appointed by that court, is entirely unknown to the common law. In the absence of any statute upon the subject, the court of chancery in this country assumed jurisdiction to compel the giving of testimony by residents of the State to be used in a suit pending in a foreign country by a bill of discovery filed for that purpose. Mitchell v. Smith, 1 *Paige*, 287 ; Post & Co. v. Toledo, etc., R. R. Co., 144 *Mass.* 341. That the court of chancery had jurisdiction was not admitted in the English courts, and even where that jurisdiction was exercised it was slow and expensive, but yet, until some statute was passed for the taking of such testimony, no ier way was known to procure it. The whole proceed- is statutory in its nature, and the well-settled rule lies that, where a remedy or proceeding is created by tute, it can be exercised in no other way than that pre- ibed in the statute, and if the statute prescribes any particular mode of enforcing the remedy which it gives, that mode is exclusive, and the remedy must be sought in that way and can be pursued in no other way. *Suth. on Stat. Const.* sections 391, 392, 399; Dudley *v.* Mayhew, 3 *N. Y.* 9. Therefore, we must look to the statute which prescribes the mode of enforcing the attendance of witnesses in these proceedings to see if there is any such mode prescribed, and the remedy of the appellant, if it has any, is to be sought within that statute. It is quite clear that by the statute upon that subject no power is given to the court as such, to compel witnesses appearing before the commissioner to answer questions which are put to them, and for that reason the conclusion reached by the learned justice below, that this application could not be granted, was correct, and his order must be affirmed.

But we do not agree with his conclusion that the only remedy for a refusal to obey the subpœna, or to answer questions when the witness has appeared before the commissioner is that given in section 920 of the Code of Civil Procedure. It has always been the policy of the law for the taking of testimony to be used in a foreign State, not only to provide sufficient means to compel the attendance of witnesses before the commissioner, but also to prescribe the way in which the witnesses when they appear could be compelled to give testimony. See 1 Revised Laws, 1813, p. 49; 2 *R. S.* 397, 398, §§ 29, 32; *Id.* 400–402, §§ 42–49; *Code Civ. Pro.* §§ 854, 855, 856, 859, 914–917, 920, 2870, 2974–2977.

Our conclusion upon the whole matter is, that for a refusal to appear before a commissioner appointed under section 915, upon a subpœna duly issued pursuant to the provisions of that section, or for a refusal to testify where the witness has appeared, his attendance or his testimony may be procured by proceedings taken under section 855 and the subsequent sections of the Code of Civil Procedure. But the remedy provided by those sections is exclsive in its nature, and no power is given to the court, acting as such, to enforce that remedy which by those sections is especially devolved upon a judge of the court and not upon the court.

Opinion by RUMSEY, J. VAN BRUNT, P. J., BARTLETT, O'BRIEN and INGRAHAM, JJ., concurred.

Order affirmed, with ten dollars costs and disbursements.

Horace E. Deming, for the appellant.

William V. Rowe and *Joseph H. Choate*, for the respondents.

KNAPP *v.* MURPHY.

Supreme Court, Fourth Department, Appellate Division; July, 1897

Execution; against person of plaintiff; action for conversion.] A judgment for costs upon dismissal of a complaint for conversion may be enforced by an execution against the person of the plaintiff.*

---

* Section 1487 of the Code of Civ. Pro., provides as follows:

" Where a judgment can be enforced by execution as prescribed in § 1240 of this act, an execution against the person of the judgment debtor may be issued thereupon, subject to the exception specified in the next section, in either of the following cases:

1. " Where the plaintiff's right to arrest the defendant depends upon the nature of the action.

2. " In any other case, where the order of arrest has been granted and executed in the action, and if it was executed against the judgment debtor where it has not been vacated."

Where because of the failure of the plaintiff to prove his cause of action, the defendant recovers a judgment for costs in an action in which the defendant is liable to arrest upon a preliminary order,

Knapp v. Murphy.

and the judgment was reversed by the county court, and thereupon a judgment was entered in favor of the defendant for $35.25 costs. An execution was issued against the property of Knapp, the plaintiff, and delivered to the sheriff of the county of Ontario, and by him returned unsatisfied, and an execution against the person of Knapp was thereupon issued to the sheriff of Ontario county, and Knapp was duly arrested and taken into custody thereunder.

Held, that the execution against the person of the plaintiff was properly issued. The gravamen of the plaintiff's complaint seems to be for a conversion of a sum of money, which the plaintiff alleges he had demanded of the defendant, and after such allegation made in the complaint, the plaintiff further alleges, viz: " That the said defendant has unlawfully and wrongfully converted the said sum of $35, the property of this plaintiff to his own use." Upon recovery by the plaintiff under such a complaint, he was entitled to issue a body execution. Indeed, such seems to have been the construction of his complaint by him when he held a judgment against the defendant.

In subdivision 2 of section 2895 of the Code, which provides for an order of arrest, it is specified that where the recovery is for " an injury to property, including the wrongful taking, detention or conversion of personal property," an order of arrest may be granted. Babcock v. Smith, 19 *Supp.* 817. Under a complaint somewhat similar to the one before us, it was held in Farrelly v. Hubbard (148 *N. Y.* 592), that it authorized the issuing of a body execution. In the course of the opinion delivered it was stated : " As already stated, the action in justice's court was for conversion and within the Code Civ. Pro., 2895, subd. 2. if the act of the plaintiff in this action in failing to pay over the money collected by him was, as matter of law, conversion." Carrigan v. Washburn (14 *Civ. Pro. R.* 350), cited by the respondent, is not applicable to the case in hand. That was a case where the plaintiff's right to arrest the defendant did not depend upon the nature of the action, but upon extraneous grounds. Nor does Roeber *v.* Dawson (14 *Civ. Pro. R.* 354), aid the contention of the respondent. In that case it is said: "The plaintiff in this case could not recover without proof beyond the complaint allegations." In Longuemare *v.* Nichols (7 *Supp.* 672), it was held that "where a plaintiff is defeated, and defendant seeks to pursue him on a judgment for costs, plaintiff becomes a defendant," within Code Civ. Pro., § 572.

Whenever a plaintiff brings an action in tort and seeks to recover in tort, if he is defeated and the defendant recovers costs, he is entitled to have a body execution. Philbrook *v.* Kellogg, 21 *Hun*, 238. The doctrine which we have already adverted to was approved in Parker *v.* Spear (62 *How. Pr.* 394), and it was said that the principle aptly illustrates the truth of the old proverb that "those who take the sword should perish by the sword."

Opinion by HARDIN, P. J.   All concurred.

Order reversed with ten dollars costs and disbursements, and motion denied, with ten dollars costs.

Ellis & Griffith, for the defendant, appellant.

Henry M. Field, for the plaintiff, respondent.

CREMORE v. HUBER.

*Supreme Court, Second Department, Appellate Division ;
June*, 1897.

1. *License ; place of amusement; right to eject one holding ticket.*]
Where a person has paid his entrance fee to a place of public
amusement and does not by disorderly conduct or otherwise
forfeit his right to remain in such place, it is not his duty to
leave upon the request of the proprietor, and the proprietor has
no right to use force to remove him therefrom.*

2. *The same; question for jury.*] Upon conflicting evidence as to
the conduct of such person it is a question for the jury to determine as to whether or not his conduct was such as to justify
the proprietor in forcibly removing him.

---

* The English cases have held that the license to enter a place
of public amusement afforded by a ticket may be revoked, and if
the purchaser of the ticket persists in remaining when requested to
leave, that he may be forcibly removed. Wood *v.* Leadbitter, 13
M. & W. 838.

The same rule has been applied in Massachusetts. See McCrea
v. Marsh. 12 *Gray*, 211.

The prior decisions of the courts of this State appear to have followed the English rule that the license evidenced by a ticket to a
theatre is revocable by the proprietor, and that the only remedy of
the person holding a ticket who has been excluded from such
theatre, is to bring an action to recover back the money paid.
Purcell *v.* Daly, 19 *Abb. N. C.* 301. MacGowan *v.* Duff. 14 *Daly*,
315 ; S. C. 12 *St. R.* 680.

In People *v.* King (110 *N. Y.* 418), it was held that the provision
of the Penal Code, §383, that "no citizen of this State can by reason
of race, color or previous condition of servitude be excluded from
the equal enjoyment of any accommodation, facility, or privilege furnished by the owners, managers or lessees of theatres, or other places
of amusement" is not violative of the Constitution. In that case
certain colored people were excluded from a skating rink for the
reason that they were colored people, and the proprietors of the
rink were indicted and convicted of a misdemeaning under the statute.

Cremore *v.* Huber.

there was a large attendance. And the plaintiff's evidence tended to prove that he was entirely sober, conducted himself with propriety and gave no occasion for his expulsion from the place. But the evidence on the part of the defendants was quite different and to the effect that the plaintiff was intoxicated, noisy, using abusive and offensive language in such manner as to justify his forcible expulsion on his refusal to leave the hall, which he did refuse to do; and that thereupon no more force was employed than was necessary to accomplish his removal from there.

From the judgment for the plaintiff rendered upon a verdict in his favor, the defendants appealed.

Held, that upon the conflicting evidence a question of fact on the main issue was presented for the jury, and that the motion for the dismissal of the complaint was, therefore, properly denied.

The court was requested to charge that the defendants were not responsible to the plaintiff for what was done by the patrons preceding the time when the defendants' servants and agents participated therein, and that "the jury, so far as holding defendants responsible pecuniarily therefor, must disregard wholly all evidence thereof." The court charged as thus requested, except the final words, "must disregard wholly all evidence thereof," and added that the jury might regard that evidence in taking into account the circumstances under which it occurred.

Held, that the exception to this modification was not well taken. The transaction was a continuous one, and the circumstances contributing to it, in its preliminary stages, were properly the subject of evidence bearing upon the causes and provocations which may have led to what ,lowed, although the defendants may not have been in ny sense responsible for what took place at the inception the affair to which the plaintiff was a party; but, as e court charged, the defendants could not be held re-
onsible for anything that occurred before their servants

or agents became participants.   These views, that this
evidence was properly in the case as part of the *res gestæ*,
are applicable alike to the exception taken to the denial
of the motion to strike out such evidence.

Held, further, that the court properly declined to charge
that it was the duty of the plaintiff, if he was requested
by the defendants or their agents to leave the place, to do
so at once and without resistance.   This proposition rests
upon the assumption that the plaintiff had no right to remain in the Casino against the will of the defendants.
They had no right to exclude him from the privileges of
the place as one for public amusement by reason of his
race or color.   Penal Code, § 383.   And it is just to the
defendants to add that they disclaim any such right or
purpose.   We must assume, for the purposes of the question arising upon the proposition which the court was requested to charge, that the plaintiff had paid his entrance
fee and was properly there to witness and enjoy the entertainment, provided he behaved himself and did not, by
his conduct, become a trespasser.   If he did not, by his
conduct, forfeit his right to remain, it was not his duty to
leave on the request of the defendants.   It cannot be assumed as matter of law, that he had thus subjected himself to their direction in that respect, and, therefore, such
request to charge was properly declined.

Held, that the exception of defendants to the refusal
of the court to charge that " if the jury believe that the
plaintiff, in his resistance, exceeded the limits of necessary
protection and employed excessive force for such purpose,
he thereby became a trespasser, and the verdict must be
for the defendants," was not well taken.   It is true, as a
legal proposition, that while a person attacked by another
may in self-defense use such force as he is permitted under
the circumstances to deem necessary for the purpose, he,
by going beyond that and making use of unnecessary
force, may become the aggressor, and thus deny to himself a remedy by action for the assault and incur liability

Cremore *v.* Huber.

to his assailant.   Elliott *v.* Brown, 2 *Wend.* 497 ; Scribner
v. Beach, 4 *Den.* 448.   This proposition leads back to the
inquiry, and its disposition is dependent upon the question, whether the defendants had the right to remove the
plaintiff from the place of entertainment ; because there
can be no well-founded claim, upon the evidence, that after
the defendant's servants proceeded to expel the plaintiff
from there any force was used by him other than in resistance of that employed to remove him, and it was insufficient for that purpose.   If the evidence on the part of the
defense was true, the plaintiff had by his conduct forfeited
all right to remain in the hall, had become a trespasser,
and having refused to leave was properly subject to ejec-
tion by force, to which any resistance on his part was not
justified.   But, on the contrary, if the truth was represented by the plaintiff's evidence, the defendants had no
right to require him to leave the place, or to use force to
remove him therefrom.   The proposition which the court
was so requested to charge was unqualified, and not by its
terms made to depend upon the right of the defendants to
require his departure and to use force for his expulsion
from the place.   As, in any other view, the evidence was
not such as to impute to the plaintiff the use of excessive
force in the sense applicable to it, the exception to the request to so charge was not well taken.   Then the import
of that request to charge was the same as the proposition
which the court had charged.   The learned counsel for
the defendants proceeded upon the assumption that it was
the duty of the plaintiff to go out upon the request of the
defendants to do so.   In that view, the court being requested to charge that if no more force was used to remove the plaintiff than was necessary for the purpose, the
defendants were entitled to a verdict, said to the jury ;
" That is true, if they had the right to remove the plaintiff
at all," and that the question of their right to remove him
for disorderly conduct was for the jury.   In this the court
was right.

Opinion by BRADLEY, J. All concurred, except GOODRICH, P. J., not sitting.

Judgment and order affirmed, with costs.

John A. Straley and *Hugo Hirsh*, for the defendants, appellants.

Charles F. Brandt, for the plaintiff, respondent.

LUPEAN *v.* BRAINARD.

Supreme Court, Fourth Department, Appellate Division ; July, 1897.

Pleading ; statute of frauds in defense ; general denial.]   Under a general denial to a complaint upon a contract within the statute of frauds, which does not aver whether or not the contract is in writing, the defense of the statute of frauds is not available.*

Appeal by the plaintiff, Charles Lupean, from a judgment of the County Court of Chautauqua county in favor of the defendant, Cephas L. Brainard, entered upon a nonsuit granted by the court, and also from an order denying the defendant's motion for a new trial, made upon a case containing exceptions.

The complaint in the action set forth that the parties entered into a contract by the terms of which the plaintiff was to work for the defendant for one year from March 21, 1894, on defendant's farm, in the town of Portland, Chautauqua county, for which services of the plaintiff the defendant agreed to pay him $250 in addition to furnishing him with a house and garden, firewood, and pasture for a cow ; that the plaintiff had fully performed his part of the said agreement ; that after the plaintiff had worked

---

* See Note on Pleading Statute of Frauds, following this case.

Lupean v. Brainard.

eight months under this contract the defendant discharged him from his employ without just cause, for which plaintiff had suffered damage and for which he demanded judgment.

The defendant answered, denying each and every allegation in the plaintiff's complaint contained " which is not hereinafter admitted." The answer proceeded to state a payment to the plaintiff and further alleged a contract to employ the plaintiff and his wife to work on the farm in Portland at the rate of $250 per year, and that they continued to work for the defendant as long as the parties could agree, the contract set forth in the answer being substantially the same as that alleged in the complaint, except that the compensation was to be at the rate of $250 per year, and not for that period. The answer further alleged a breach of the contract on the part of the plaintiff, and counterclaim for damages. The statute of frauds was not set up in the answer, or any allegation that the contract was within its provisions. There was no general denial in the answer, except as above stated.

Upon the trial the plaintiff testified, without objection, that some time in the spring of 1895 he engaged with the defendant to work for him for a year for $250, and that the contract was made in a conversation had with the defendant. He proved the verbal contract by other witnesses, the same as alleged in the complaint. No objection was taken to the evidence, or that the contract was within the statute, until the close of the trial, when the defendant moved for a nonsuit upon the ground that the contract as proved was void under the statute of frauds, inasmuch as it was not in writing and was not to be performed within one year from the making thereof. The motion was granted.

Held error. Some of the earlier cases seem to hold that, if the answer contained a general denial of the contract alleged in the complaint, the plaintiff must establish a valid contract, and if he gave evidence showing a con-

tract within the statute of frauds the defendant was at
liberty, under the general denial, to take that objection,
although it had not been affirmatively pleaded in the
answer. It was said by BRADLEY, J., in Smith *v.* Slosson
(89 *Hun*, 568 ; 35 *Supp.* 548), that there had been a conflict in the earlier cases upon this subject, but the doctrine
of the later cases is that it must be pleaded to render the
statute of frauds available as a defense. And such is the
decided trend of the later cases. Hamer *v.* Sidway, 124
N. Y. 538; Wells *v.* Monihan, 129 *Id.* 161 ; Crane *v.*
Powell, 139 *Id.* 379 ; Bannatyne *v.* Florence Milling Co.,
77 *Hun*, 289; Barrett *v.* Johnson, *Id.* 527; Cheever *v.*
Schall, 87 *Id.* 32; Schultz *v.* Cohen, 34 *Supp.* 927 ; Thelberg *v.* National Starch Manuf. Co., 2 *App. Div.* 173;
Simis *v.* Wissel, 10 *Id.* 323. Where the complaint states
a contract, but does not aver whether it is in writing or
not, for the purposes of the complaint it will be presumed
that it was in writing. Marston *v.* Swett, 66 *N. Y.* 209.

It is claimed in the brief of the respondent's counsel
that the plaintiff did not raise the point upon the trial
that the answer did not allege the statute of frauds as a
defense, and, therefore, that the objection that it had not
done so was waived. The record does not disclose how
the fact was, whether plaintiff's counsel upon the trial, in
opposition to the granting of the motion for a nonsuit,
stated this objection. The pleading was before the court,
and it was apparent from it that the defendant was not
in a position to urge the ground upon which the nonsuit
was granted. We do not think that the failure (if such
failure existed) of the plaintiff's counsel to call the court's
attention to this defect in the answer, was a waiver of the
fatal ruling made by the County Court.

Opinion by WARD, J. All concurred, except FOLLET,
J., not sitting.

Judgment of the County Court reversed and a new
trial ordered, with costs to abide the event.

Hooker & Dikeman, for the plaintiff, appellant.

Franz C. Lewis, for the defendant, respondent.

NOTE ON PLEADING STATUTE OF FRAUDS

Complaint.] The law in respect to the requisites of a complaint in a case involving the statute of frauds has undergone considerable modification within the last few years. Some of the older cases held that, where the complaint alleged the making of such a contract as was required by the statute to be in writing without specifying whether or not it was in fact in writing, and the answer was a denial that the contract was made, then it was necessary for the plaintiff upon the trial to prove such a contract as the statute required. Marston *v.* Swett, 66 *N. Y.* 206. In that case it is said at page 209 : " It is claimed by the defendants that the contract sued on is void under the statute of frauds, as it was not to be performed within a year and was not in writing. A contract valid in form, is set out in the complaint, and it does not there appear that it was not in writing. It was not necessary to allege that it was in writing. For the purposes of the complaint that may be presumed. If the contract alleged in the complaint had been denied or the statute of frauds had been set up as a defense, then it would be necessary upon the trial to prove that the contract was in writing if it was one which the statute required to be in writing." In that case the answer did not deny the making of the contract, but alleged that it was made upon the condition that the plaintiff should do something else which he had not done. See also Berrien *v.* Southack, 7 *Supp.* 324 ; Harris *v.* Knickerbacker, 5 *Wend.* 638 ; Gibbs *v.* Nash, 4 *Barb.* 449, 451 ; Cary *v.* Western Union Telegraph Co., 20 *Abb. N. C.* 336, 343 ; Weinhauer *v.* Morrison, 49 *Hun,* 498.

The authority of these decisions as good law is questioned in Crane *v.* Powell (19 *Supp.* 220 ; aff'd 139 *N. Y.* 379), citing Porter *v.* Wormser, 94 *N. Y.* 431, where it is said at page 450 : " The general rule is that the defense of the statute of frauds must be pleaded, except where the complaint on its face discloses a case within the statute. It cannot be doubted, that if the defendants had brought an action to recover a balance claimed to be due on the contract for the purchase of the bonds without disclosing whether the contract was oral or written, the plaintiff would have been bound to plead the statute to avail him-self of its protection. The plaintiff having become an actor and brought an action to impeach the account which implied the existence of a formal contract, is not in a posi-tion to question the validity of the contract under the statute." See, also, Matthews *v*. Matthews, 154 *N. Y.* 228.

In Wells *v*. Monihan (129 *N. Y.* 161), an action was brought upon a promise by a third party in writing to pay the debt of another, and there was no consideration ex-pressed in the written promise. In affirming a judgment for the plaintiff the court said, at page 164: "So far as the defense in this case rests upon the statute of frauds, it must fail for two reasons. No such defense has been pleaded, and it is not raised by the averment of the complaint, and without one or the other of these conditions, the defense if existing cannot be made available."

The later cases all seem to hold that where the complaint avers a contract, which by the statute of frauds is required to be in writing, but the complaint is silent as to whether or not it is in writing, then it is necessary for the defendant to plead the statute to have it available to him upon the trial. But no case seems to have gone so far as to hold that, where the plaintiff avers that the contract is in writ-ing, and it is one that is required to be in writing by the statute of frauds, it is necessary for the defendant to plead the statute in order to take advantage of it, if the plaint-iff fails to prove such a contract.

Demurrer.] It cannot be considered as conclusively set-tled that a demurrer will lie to a complaint which alleges a contract required by the statute to be in writing and it ap-pears on the face of the complaint that it is not in writing. But in the late case of Crane *v*. Powell (139 *N. Y.* 379), the head note reads that, where it appears on the face of the complaint that the contract sued on is one which is re-quired by the statute of frauds to be in writing, and that it is not in fact in writing, the complaint is bad on demurrer. An examination of that case seems to suggest that such a defect may be taken advantage of by demurrer, but the court does not so hold specifically and a decision upon that point was not necessary in that case. The court does hold, however, very distinctly, that in all cases where the defect does not appear on the face of the complaint, the statute of frauds must be specially pleaded or it is waived.

If this *dictum* correctly states the law the rule is different from that which obtains in the case of the statute of lim-itations, as it has been held that a defense based on this

Note on Pleading Statute of Frauds.

statute cannot be raised by demurrer. Ladew *v.* Hart, 8 *App. Div.* 150, 155 ; Sands *v.* St. John, 36 *Barb.* 628.

Answer.] It appears to be well settled by recent authorities that in all cases where the complaint is not defective on demurrer because it appears on the face thereof that the contract in suit does not comply with the requirements of the statute, the defense of the statute must be pleaded in the answer or it is waived.

In Crane *v.* Powell (139 *N. Y.* 379), it was held in an action for services which were not to be performed within one year from the date of the contract, that the defendant could not avail himself of the defense of the statute of frauds unless it was specifically pleaded. And the court added, at page 388 : " The statute of frauds is a shield which a party may use or not for his protection, just as he may use the statute of limitations, the statute against usury, that against betting and gaming and others that may be mentioned. I take it to be a general rule of universal application that the statutes last mentioned are not available to a party unless specifically pleaded, and there is no reason for making the statute of frauds an exception to the rule."

In Hamer *v.* Sidway (124 *N. Y.* 548), the defendant's testator made an oral promise to pay the plaintiff $5,000 if he refrained from drinking, smoking, etc., for more than a year. The court observed that the agreement was within the condemnation of the statute of frauds, because not to be performed within a year, and was not in writing, but that this defense could be waived and was waived by not pleading it.

As has been already pointed out, some of the older cases hold that where the complaint does not disclose whether or not the contract in suit is in writing, when required by the statute to be written, a mere denial in the answer that the contract was executed requires proof on the part of the plaintiff of such a contract as meets the requirements of the statute. But these cases appear to have been overruled by the case of Crane *v.* Powell (*supra*), and in such cases it is now necessary to plead the statute as a defense or it is waived.

Some of the decisions under the statute of limitations seem to apply to the statute of frauds as well, so far as general principles are concerned. Thus, it has been held that where it appears on the face of the complaint that an action is barred by the statute of limitations and the said statute is pleaded in the answer, it is incumbent upon the plaintiff to repel the presumption of the claim being barred by showing matter in avoidance. Mason *v.* Henry, 152 *N. Y.* 529 ; aff'g 83 *Hun*, 546 ; s. c., 31 *Supp.* 1063 ; 65 *St. R.* 45.

Where no order is secured requiring the plaintiff to reply to the defense of the statute of limitations pleaded in the answer such defense will be deemed to be controverted by the plaintiff. Reilley *v.* Sabater, 26 *Civ. Pro. R.* 34 ; s. c., 43 *Supp.* 383.

Upon the trial the plaintiff may prove any facts for the purpose of avoiding new matter set up as a defense which might have been pleaded by way of reply. Keeler *v.* Keeler, 102 *N. Y.* 30, 36 ; citing Mandeville *v.* Reynolds, 68 *Id.* 528 ; Meyer *v.* Lathrop, 73 *Id.* 315.

STERNE *v.* METROPOLITAN TELE-PHONE CO.

Supreme Court, First Department, Appellate Division; June, 1897.

Deposition ; examination before trial ; corporation defendant ; non-resident officers.] In an action by a subscriber of a telephone company to compel the company to furnish telephone service to the plaintiff at a price less than that demanded by it, upon the ground that such company was a common carrier enjoying public privileges and having a practical monopoly, and that the price demanded was unreasonable and exorbitant,—*Held*, that an order for the examination of the officers of the company before trial and an inspection of the books of the company, to discover whether or not the price charged was reasonable, was properly made, especially as it appeared that such officers were non-residents so that it was not certain that their testimony could be secured at the trial, and such an examination appeared necessary to secure evidence to determine whether or not the company could make a reasonable profit by charging less than the amount demanded for telephone service.[*]

---

[*] In Wallace *v.* Baring (3 *N. Y. Ann. Cas.* 16), it was held that under a deposition to secure testimony to use on a motion a wit-

Sterne *v.* Metropolitan Telephone Co.

Appeal by the plaintiff, Simon Sterne, from an order of the Supreme Court, New York Special Term, vacating an order for the examination before trial of the defendant and its officers.

The order vacated by the order appealed from directed the president, secretary and treasurer of the defendant to appear before a referee appointed to take their testimony for use upon the trial of this action, and required them at the same time to produce before such referee for inspection certain of defendant's books.

It is alleged in the complaint, in substance, that plaintiff was a subscriber of the defendant, and of its predecessor, from some time prior to the year 1891, down to about the time of the commencement of the action ; that during such time the plaintiff paid per year for such service sums varying from $120 to $180 per year; that under the pretense of furnishing a new instrument the defendant demanded that the plaintiff pay the sum of $240 per year, and threatened that, unless he would make a new contract for that sum, it would discontinue the service and deprive him entirely of the means of communication by telephone.

The complaint also alleged that the defendant's business is affected by a public use in its nature and essence a monopoly, and in prosecuting the same it uses public highways and public and private buildings, and occupies and uses public streets ; that it is a common carrier for hire of oral and written messages, and as such common carrier is under contract, implied by law, to furnish its service at a

---

ness could not be compelled by a subpœna *duces tecum* to produce books and papers to qualify himself as such witness.

See authorities cited in notes to that case.

See Cook *v.* New Amsterdam Real Estate Assn. (2 *N. Y. Ann. Cas.* 55), as to requisites of an affidavit to secure an order for examination before trial.

See Note on Physical Examination before Trial, 1 *N. Y. Ann. Cas.* 171.

Sterne *v.* Metropolitan Telephone Co.

fair and reasonable price ; that the sum of $150 adequately remunerates the defendant ; the price demanded in excess of such sum, to wit, $90 per year, constituting an extortionate and unreasonable exaction.

The answer puts in issue many of the allegations of the complaint, including the one which charges in effect that the compensation demanded for the use of the telephone is unlawful, unjust and illegal, and alleges that the increased charges made are reasonable, just and legal. Upon the complaint and affidavits a temporary injunction was granted prohibiting the defendant from removing the telephone from the plaintiff's office. Subsequently the motion to continue the injunction was argued upon the moving papers and affidavits submitted in opposition thereto by the defendant, and it resulted in an order continuing the injunction, the court holding that the defendant's business is in itself a public business affected with a public interest to be exercised under public control, and governed by the same rule which obtains in the case of a common carrier which is bound to furnish transportation to the public for a reasonable charge, and that where a proper allegation is made, the court may compel the corporation to furnish transportation upon the payment of the sum which shall be adjudged to constitute reasonable compensation.

Held, that as it must be taken upon this motion as the law of the case that the defendant is bound to furnish telephone service to the plaintiff upon the payment of a reasonable compensation therefor, the testimony is material which the plaintiff insists he expects to obtain from the officers and books of the company, and the order directing the examination should not have been vacated. Evidence which tends to show the extent of the profit resulting annually from defendant's business is certainly material in an action the principal object of which is to determine what constitutes a reasonable compensation for each of the defendant's subscribers. The defendant urges that it does

Sterne *v.* Metropolitan Telephone Co.

not appear that it is necessary that the examination be had
before rather than at the trial, and that such an examination is never held to be necessary after issue joined where
it appears that the examination can be had at the trial,
except in those cases where fraud is alleged, or some relation of trust or confidence between the parties confers a
present right to know the facts to be elicited by the examination.

If the accuracy of defendant's proposition be conceded
—and it may be said in passing that it is challenged by
several decisions, including Presbrey *v.* Public Opinion
Co. (6 *App. Div.* 600; s. c., 39 *Supp.* 957)—still it would
not operate to prevent an examination in this case, for the
reason that it does not appear that an examination of the
officers of defendant can with certainty be had at the trial.
It is shown by the affidavits of the plaintiff that the president of the defendant resides at Morristown, in the State
of New Jersey, and that the treasurer is a resident of
Boston, Mass., while the books of the company are located
at eighteen Cortlandt street, in the city of New York.
These principal officers, whose testimony the plaintiff desires to take, may choose not to be present at the trial
and they will not be subject to subpœna if they stay at
their several homes. Their examination on commission
would not accomplish the plaintiff's purpose, who desires
to take their testimony in connection with the books, which
are in the city of New York.

The plaintiff alleged in his complaint, and attempted to
show by his affidavit, that when the defendant charged him
and its other customers $150 per annum, it received a rea-
sonable compensation for the service, resulting in a fair
and liberal profit to the defendant. To this the defendant
made answer that the expenses of operation increased in
greater proportion than the number of subscribers, and
that the expense of putting the company's wires under-
ground and establishing a metallic circuit had increased the
company's outlay, and, therefore, justified the increase in

the charges. The defendant did not attempt to give the figures showing the actual receipts and disbursements of the company, or the amount of these extraordinary expenses, or whether they were charged to construction account and capital account as distinguished from expense account.

These facts must have an important bearing upon the issues presented by the pleadings, and, therefore, it is but just that the plaintiff should have an opportunity of presenting the whole truth of the matter upon the trial. No method of accomplishing this result with certainty can be discovered except by an examination before trial, and it was for such a situation that the statute was intended to provide.

Opinion by PARKER, J. VAN BRUNT, P. J., RUMSEY, WILLIAMS and INGRAHAM, JJ., concurred.

Order reversed, with ten dollars costs and disbursements, and motion denied, with ten dollars costs.

William B. Hornblower and *John Alexander Beall*, for the plaintiff, appellant.

James C. Carter and *Melville Egleston*, for the defendant, respondent.

COHEN *v.* CLIMAX CYCLE CO.

Supreme Court, First Department, Appellate Division;

June, 1897.

Sheriff's jury; determination as to ownership of property on attachment; review.] Where a sheriff's jury has determined that property taken by the sheriff on attachment belongs to a third party claimant, this is not such a judicial determination as en-

Cohen *v.* Climax Cycle Co.

titles either party to review it, by a motion to vacate the verdict on the ground that it is unsupported by the evidence.*

Appeal by the plaintiff, Eli M. Cohen, from an order of the Supreme Court, New York Special Term, denying his motion to set aside the verdict of a sheriff's jury rendered in proceedings to determine the validity of a claim

---

* By section 1418 of the Code, the question of whether or not the sheriff will empanel a jury to determine the ownership of the property is left entirely to the officer's discretion.

Section 1419 specifies the undertaking which must be given if the jury determines that the claimant is the owner of the property.

In Greenleaf *v.* Brooklyn, Flatbush & C. I. R. R. Co. (102 *N. Y.* 96), in an action of ejectment the defendant did not appear, and an inquest was taken. A motion was made at special term to set aside the judgment on the ground that the evidence given at the inquest was insufficient to sustain the judgment. The motion was denied at special term, and the order entered thereon was affirmed at general term. An appeal to the Court of Appeals was dismissed but the court said, at p. 97: "We think that the motion made at special term to set aside the inquest was properly denied. Motions of this kind are usually made on the ground of irregularity, or for some valid excuse in allowing the default to be taken, and in case there is any evidence whatever to support the findings, the court will not set aside the inquest. The practice is well settled that a party, in order to avail himself of any objection to any proceeding upon the trial, should appear and raise the question before the judge, and upon a decision against him, except to the ruling made."

See, also, Ward *v.* Haight, 3 *Johns. Cas.* 80.

In Mankleton *v.* Lilly (3 *St. R.* 421), an inquisition was set aside because the defendant was allowed to introduce improper evidence in mitigation of damages against the objection and exception of the plaintiff.

An inquisition by the sheriff will be set aside where there is an irregularity in the proceeding. Woods *v.* Hart, *Col. & Caines,* 447 ; Eden *v.* Rathbone, 3 *Cow.* 296 ; Koy *v.* Clough, *Col. & Caines,* 425 ; Butler *v.* Kelsey, 15 *Johns.* 177.

Where the errors do not appear on the record, the only way to set aside an inquest is by motion. Van Waggenen *v.* McDonald, 3 *Wend.* 478.

made to personal property held by the sheriff under an attachment issued against the defendant.

From the facts it appears that the sheriff having levied upon certain property under an attachment against the defendant, the Climax Cycle Company, one Goldfinger made a claim to such property and filed a notice of such claim with the sheriff; that subsequently the sheriff impanneled a jury to try the validity of the claim, and that such jury having found in favor of the claimant, the defendant moved at special term to set aside the verdict on the ground that it was not sustained by the evidence before the sheriff's jury, thus endeavoring by a motion to review the action of the sheriff's jury in trying this claim to the property levied upon by the sheriff.

Held, that there is no authority in the code for such a proceeding. The jury is summoned by the sheriff and presided over by him; and the only effect of the verdict is that in case it is in favor of the claimant, the execution or attachment creditor is compelled to give a bond of indemnity to the sheriff to protect him as against such claimant. Code Civ. Pro. §§ 1418, 1419. By section 1420 it is expressly provided that if the property is found to belong to the defendant, the finding shall not prejudice the right of the claimant to sue the sheriff for a recovery of the property. It is quite evident from a review of these provisions of the Code that this determination by the sheriff's jury is not such a judicial determination as would entitle either party to review it in the absence of an express provision authorizing such a review. The whole policy of the act would be defeated if, upon this summary application, appeals or applications to review the action of the sheriff's jury should be allowed, thus entailing upon the parties the expense of a regular litigation. From the case cited by the counsel for the respondents it would appear that under the practice at common law in England, such a proceeding by a sheriff was authorized, but Lord Kenyon, in the court of King's Bench, deter-

mined that the parties to the action, not being bound by
the verdict, had no right to interfere and have the verdict
set aside. Roberts *v.* Thomas, *Term Rep.* [6 *Durnf. & East*]
88. We think that the same reason for refusing to permit
a party to interfere applies under our code, as neither
party is bound by this verdict of the sheriff's jury, as it is
a mere inquiry by the sheriff to determine whether he
should require the execution or attachment creditor to
give a bond of indemnity to protect him in holding the
goods or property levied upon as property subject to such
levy.

Opinion by INGRAHAM, J. PATTERSON, RUMSEY,
O'BRIEN and PARKER, JJ., concurred.

Order affirmed, with costs.

Henry Hoelljes, for the plaintiff, appellant.

Charles L. Kingsley, for the respondent.

KRATZENSTEIN *v.* LEHMAN.

*Supreme Court, First Department, Appellate Division ;
June,* 1897.

*Attachment ; levy ; instrument for the payment of money ; un-
matured policy of life insurance.*] An unmatured policy of life
insurance, by which the insurer agrees to pay to the insured the
sum of $5,000 in ten years, if he be then alive, or if he should
die before that time to pay that sum to his personal representatives, and which has a present surrender value under section 88
of the Insurance Law (*L.* 1892, c. 690), is not an instrument for
the payment of money only within the meaning of Code Civ.
Pro. § 649, subd. 2, and a levy may be made thereon under
an attachment against the insured under subdivision 3 of §

649, by delivering a notice and a copy of the warrant to the insurance company.*

Appeal by the defendant by permission, from an order of the Appellate Term of the Supreme Court in favor of the plaintiff, affirming an order of the General Term of the City Court of New York, which denied the defendant's motion to vacate a judgment against him.

The defendant, Charles Lehman, moved to vacate a judgment obtained against him in the city court by the plaintiff, Herman Kratzenstein, on the ground that the defendant was a non-resident, that the summons was served by publication and that no property had been attached to give the court jurisdiction. The city court denied the motion, and the appellate term affirmed the order made thereon.

Held, no error. The serious question presented in this case is whether the levy made by the sheriff, by virtue of the warrant of attachment, was sufficient to give him the custody of the property levied upon and thereby give the court jurisdiction to enter judgment in the action. The property levied upon was the interest of the defendant Lehman in a policy of insurance upon his own life, issued by the Manhattan Insurance Co., which was not yet matured, but upon which permiums were to be paid. As appears by the papers, the policy was an agreement on the part of the company to pay the sum of $5,000 in ten years to Lehman, if he should then be alive, or if he should die before that time, to pay that sum to his personal representatives. It was the ordinary insurance policy, and as may be inferred from the papers, premiums were still payable upon it. Section 88 of the insurance law gave a surrender value to it, and that value at the

---

*See Trepagnier & Bros. *v.* Rose, *ante*, p. 300; People *v.* National Mutual Ins. Co., *post*, p. 340, and Note following that case on Levy of Attachment and Execution on Choses in Action.

Kratzenstein *v.* Lehman.

time of the levy, as appears by the affidavits, was $500. The levy was made by serving a copy of the warrant of attachment and notice showing the property attached upon the life insurance company in the manner provided by Code of Civ. Pro. § 649, subd. 3.   It is claimed by the appellant that this levy was not sufficient, but that the sheriff, to complete the levy, should have taken the property into his actual custody as required by subdivision 2 of the section last referred to.   The correctness of this contention depends upon the answer to the question whether an unmatured policy of life insurance is an instrument for the payment of money, within the meaning of this subdivision.   The words of the law are, that a levy under a warrant of attachment must be made upon personal property capable of manual delivery, including a bond, a promissory note or other instrument for the payment of money, by taking the same into the sheriff's actual custody.   The meaning of this term, "instrument for the payment of money," is the thing to be determined. Some light is thrown upon that question by an examination of Code Civ. Pro. § 648, which prescribes upon what property an attachment can be levied, and directs that it may be levied upon a cause of action arising upon a contract, "including a bond, promissory note or other instrument for the payment of money only, negotiable or otherwise, whether past due or yet to become due, executed by a foreign or domestic government, State, county, public officer, association, municipal or other corporation, or by a private person, either within or without the State, which belongs to the defendant and is found within the county." In this case clearly the words "instrument for the payment of money only," refer to the securities which are described thereafter.   These securites are such as are made primarily for the payment of money, and they involve in every case a promise to pay a sum of money stated therein, to the person who is entitled by the terms of the paper to receive it, or who is the owner of it.   The

payment of the sum of money is the primary object for
which they are made. While they do not always pass by
delivery, but sometimes require an indorsement to transfer a complete title, yet they are usually paid or payable
only to the person who has them in his actual possession,
and the possession itself is ordinarily required as satisfactory evidence to the right to receive the money which is to
be paid by their terms. While they are in a technical
sense choses in action, yet practically the paper itself is
property, is regarded as such and is dealt with like other
tangible personal property. These instruments are primarily those intended to be included within the term " instrument for the payment of money." It is not necessary to
say, however, that other instruments which have for their
primary object the payment of a sum of money by one
person to another, upon a past consideration, may not be
included within the meaning of the term " instrument for
the payment of money," under subdivision 2 of section
649. Whenever it shall appear that the primary object of
any instrument was to assure to any person the payment
of a certain sum of money upon a consideration that is no
longer executory as to him, and where the only thing to
be done to complete the contract is to pay the money for
which the paper was primarily made, that, we think, may
be said to be an instrument for the payment of money
under the provisions of this subdivision.

In several sections of the Code, the phrase or its
equivalent is used, and some of these sections have been
the subject of interpretation by the courts. For instance,
section 1778 provides that in an action against a corporation to recover damages for the non-payment of a promissory note or other evidence of debt, for the absolute
payment of money, the issues presented by the pleadings
shall not be tried except by order of the court or a judge.
In an action brought under that section, it has been held
that a policy of life insurance, although it had then matured
and become payable, was not an evidence of debt for the

Kratzenstein *v.* Lehman.

absolute payment of money upon demand. N. Y. Life
Ins. Co. *v.* Universal Life Ins. Co., 88 *N. Y.* 424.

The same thing was held in the case of McKee *v.*
Metropolitan Life Ins. Co. (25 *Hun*, 583).

The connection in which these words stand in the section is also to be considered. The section, by its terms,
applies to bonds, notes and other instruments for the payment of money, and it should be construed as including
within these other instruments that very large class of
securities, many of which are mentioned in section 648,
but all of which are alike in the respect that they provide
for the absolute payment of a certain sum of money upon
a past consideration, and are regarded themselves, substantially, as property.

The case of Hankinson *v.* Page (12 *Civ. Pro. R.* 279 ;
s. c., 19 *Abb. N. C.* 274) holds that a policy of life insurance
which has become mature and payable by the death of the
assured, so that it is substantially a unilateral contract,
providing simply for the payment absolutely of a certain
sum of money, the consideration for which is entirely past,
is within this subdivision. Between a contract of life
insurance in that condition and one situated as is this contract, there is a very considerable difference ; and although
that case may have been well decided, the principles laid
down there do not conflict with the conclusions reached
here, which are, that the levy in this case was a sufficient
one to give the court jurisdiction.

Opinion by RUMSEY, J. PARKER and O'BRIEN, JJ.,
concurred. INGRAHAM and PATTERSON, JJ., dissented.

Order affirmed with costs.

Moses Weinman, for the defendant, appellant.

Abraham Gruber and *T. B. Chancellor*, for the plaintiff,
respondent.

PEOPLE *v*. NATIONAL MUTUAL INS. CO.

*Supreme Court, First Department, Appellate Division;
June, 1897.*

1. *Execution; levy; promissory note; custodian named by plaintiff's attorney.*] Where, under an execution against a corporation, the secretary of the company turned over to the sheriff a promissory note of a third party, with shares of stock held by said corporation as collateral security for the payment of the note, and after such levy the sheriff, by the direction contained in a letter of the plaintiff's attorney, delivered the note and stock to the secretary of said company as custodian, and took a receipt from him,—*Held*, that the lien created by the levy was not lost to the judgment creditor, and that an order should be made requiring a receiver of the corporation, subsequently appointed, who had sold the note and stock, to turn over enough of the proceeds thereof to satisfy the judgment under which the levy was made, together with the sheriff's fees thereon.

2. *The same; promissory note; general rule.*] *It seems* that, as a general rule, a levy cannot be made upon a promissory note under an execution against a natural person.*

Appeal by the claimant, Anna E. Elmore, a judgment creditor of the defendant, from an order of the Supreme Court, N. Y. Special Term, denying her motion to set aside the report of a referee appointed to take proof concerning her claim, and for an order directing Charles H. Daniels, as receiver of the defendant, to satisfy an execution issued upon the claimant's judgment and alleged to have been levied upon the property of the defendant, on May 10, 1896.

Mrs. Elmore was a judgment creditor of the defendant company, and on May 10, 1894, an execution upon her

---

* See Trepagnier & Bros. *v*. Rose, *ante*, page 300: Kratzenstein *v*. Lehman, *ante*, page 335, and Note on Levy of Attachment and Execution on Choses in Action, following this case.

judgment was issued against that company to the sheriff
of N. Y. county.   On that day the deputy sheriff holding
the execution went to the office of the company, where
he saw William G. Lord, the secretary.   He produced his
execution, and Mr. Lord turned out to him certain property of the company that he might levy upon it.   This
property consisted of office furniture in the office of the
company and a promissory note for $2,500 made by one
Rogers, secured by certificates for twenty-five shares of
stock of the corporation of a value considerably greater
than the face of the note.   All this property, including
the certificates of stock, was taken by the sheriff into his
actual possession, and was then delivered to Mr. Lord as
custodian, and a receipt was given by him in the usual
form, reciting that he held the property as custodian for
the sheriff.   On the same day, but at what hour does not
appear, an order was made appointing D. Edgar Anthony
receiver of the property and effects of the corporation.
It is to be assumed from the papers that Mr. Anthony
qualified as receiver, but precisely when this was done
does not appear.   It has not been made to appear whether
the receiver was appointed before the levy was made ;
and in the absence of any proof upon the subject, there is
no reason to say that the lien of the levy was not prior to
the right of the receiver which became perfected by the
filing of his bond, and when perfected related to the date
of his appointment.   After the appointment of the receiver, the property which Lord had received as custodian
from the sheriff was delivered to him with other property
of the corporation, upon an arrangement made between
Anthony and Lord that Anthony would cause the property to be sold and would pay the amount of Mrs. Elmore's lien out of the proceeds of the property, turning
the remainder, if any, into the general funds of the company which he held as receiver.   After the property had
been sold, Anthony was removed as receiver and the present respondent substituted, who received the proceeds of

the sale of the property which had been levied upon. These proceeds were considerably more than sufficient to pay the claimant's judgment and the sheriff's fees. A demand was made of the new receiver to pay the money to the plaintiff, which he refused to do, and thereupon this motion was made to require him to do so. The motion was denied, and Mrs. Elmore takes this appeal.

The conclusion of law of the referee to whom the motion was sent to report the facts with his opinion thereon, that Mrs. Elmore was not entitled to the payment of the amount of her judgment, is based upon the facts that, before the levy was made, the plaintiff's attorney in the execution delivered to the sheriff a letter, which said in effect that the sheriff was authorized, after making a formal levy upon the property of the company, to permit the same to remain in the possession of William G. Lord, as his custodian, taking a receipt from him for the property levied upon under the execution, and to permit the same so to remain until further direction from the plaintiff's attorney, who signed the letter. The referee held that the legal result of this letter was to deprive the levy of any effect to bind the goods of the judgment debtor. This finding was based upon the idea that the duty of the sheriff, after receiving the letter, was to proceed no further with the execution, and that, being bound to follow the instructions of the plaintiff's attorney, he had no power to do anything more than to permit the property to remain in the custody of Mr. Lord, without taking any steps to reduce it to money and devote it to the payment of the execution.

Held, that the order was erroneous. The sheriff had the right to leave the property in the hands of any person whom he might select as custodian. If, because of the fault of the person so selected, the property was lost and the judgment creditor could not realize the value of it, the sheriff would be liable, because the custody of the custodian was his custody, and he was bound to keep the prop-

People *v.* National Mutual Ins. Co.

erty safely so that it might be devoted to the satisfaction of the execution in the legal way. The letter which authorized the sheriff to select a particular person as custodian would probably have had the effect to relieve him from liability, if the property had been lost because of the negligence of that particular custodian. But it would not have any other effect, unless, by a reasonable construction of the letter, it can be said that the sheriff was directed to do nothing more with the property than to leave it in the custody where he had placed it. The letter cannot be said to require the sheriff to sell, or to forbid him from selling, the property according to the directions of his writ. Much less can it be said to show an intention on the part of the judgment creditor that the writ should not be executed. The case is not at all like that of Robertson *v.* Lawton (91 *Hun*, 67), even if that case was well decided, which we are not prepared to admit.

It is suggested that the sheriff acquired no lien by his levy upon the promissory note, because a promissory note is not a subject of levy upon execution. Undoubtedly, a chose in action of that nature cannot be levied upon by virtue of an execution, against the objection of the judgment debtor. Ingalls *v.* Lord, 1 *Cow.* 240. If that were all there was of the case, no lien could be acquired by this act of the deputy sheriff. But while the judgment debtor, holding the promissory note, is undoubtedly at liberty to say that such a note cannot be levied upon by virtue of an execution against his property, yet if, when the execution is presented to him, he turns over to the sheriff the promissory note with the intention that the latter should hold it subject to the execution, there is no reason why he should afterwards be permitted to say that the sheriff did not acquire the right to hold that property precisely as he should hold any other property. There is nothing in the nature of this particular property which renders it improper that it should be taken into the custody of the sheriff with the consent of the judgment debtor. The statute authorizes a levy upon any chose in action made by a corporation, municipal or otherwise, or by a public officer, which is in terms negotiable or payable to the bearer or holder. *Code Civ. Pro.* § 1411. It is quite true that that section does not include promissory notes made by private persons; but there is no real distinction between the two kinds of property, and no reason why, if such a note as this should be turned over to the sheriff, he should not be permitted to hold it and insist upon his lien upon it. But in this case, in addition to the promissory note, the secretary of the company turned out to the sheriff the shares of stock. So far as they belonged to this company, they were clearly leviable, and the sheriff was authorized to sell the interest of the company; and if the actual owner of the stock, who pledged them as security, found no fault with it, we can see no reason why the sheriff might not properly hold them as against anybody else. We conclude, therefore, that the sheriff acquired, by the act of the secretary of the company, a valid lien upon the property which was turned out to him to apply upon this execution.

Opinion by RUMSEY, J. VAN BRUNT, P. J., WILLIAMS, INGRAHAM and PARKER, JJ., concurred.

Order reversed, with ten dollars costs and disbursements, and motion granted, with ten dollars costs and disbursements of the reference.

Charles S. Foote, for the claimant, appellant.

Hamilton R. Squier, for defendant, respondent.

NEW YORK ANNOTATED CASES.   345

Note on Levy of Attachment and Execution on Choses in Action.

NOTE ON LEVY OF ATTACHMENT AND EXECUTION ON
CHOSES IN ACTION.

I. *In General.*
II. *Attachment.*
III. *Execution.*

In general.] The Code of Civil Procedure contains provisions for a levy under an attachment which are much
broader than the provisions for a levy under an execution.
The reason for this is that a complete scheme for relief
under an execution, where difficulties are experienced in
seizing property or choses in action, is found in proceedings supplementary to execution, while in cases of attachment no such remedy would be possible without injustice
to the defendant before the plaintiff had established his
rights by reducing his claim to judgment. It seems to
have been the policy, therefore, of the framers of the Code
to allow a lien to be created by attachment upon property
which could not be seized under an execution if an attachment had not first been issued. And further than this the
remedy by attachment is allowed in cases where there is
danger that the property of the attachment debtor may be
removed from the jurisdiction of the court, which is an
additional and perhaps the main reason why the officer is
allowed to take or create a lien upon property, rights and
things in action which could not otherwise be taken upon
execution.

" In order to constitute a valid levy under an execution
it is not necessary that the sheriff should take actual possession of the property levied upon. *Crocker, on Sheriffs,*
§ 436. And hence a course of procedure which may create
a valid lien by levy under an execution is of no effect
when an attachment is the process under which the procedure is taken." Warner *v.* Fourth National Bank, 12
Civ. Pro. R. 186, 193.

Attachment.] Subdivision 3 of section 649, of the Code
of Civil Procedure, specifies how a levy may be made
under an attachment upon personal property of the attachment debtor which is not capable of manual delivery consisting of demands, etc., against third persons, as follows :
"Upon other personal property, by leaving a certified
copy of the warrant, and a notice showing the property
attached, with the person holding the same ; or, if it con-

sists of a demand, other than as specified in the last subdivision (bond, promissory notes, or other instrument for
the payment of money), with the person against whom it
exists ; or, if it consists of right or share in the stock of an
association or corporation, or interest or proits thereon,
with the president, or other head of the association or corporation or the secretary, cashier, or managing agent
thereof."

Subdivision 2 provides that in the case of a bond, promissory note, or other instrument for the payment of
money the sheriff must take it into his actual custody.

Under this section (subdivision 3), the sheriff can levy
upon a chose in action, strictly speaking, which is not
capable of manual delivery, by leaving with the person
against whom the demand is held by the attachment
debtor of a copy of the warrant and a notice of the particular demand attached. But, except in the cases hereafter noted, a prior assignment of the demand or claim,
although in fraud of creditors, will defeat an action by the
sheriff or the attachment creditor in aid of the attachment.
Anthony *v.* Wood, 96 *N. Y.* 181 ; Throop Grain Cleaner
Co. *v.* Smith, 110 *N. Y.* 83 ; Harding *v.* Elliott, 12 *Misc.* 521.
The sheriff may disprove the *fact* of the assignment,
although he cannot show that it was made with the intent
to defraud creditors. *Id.* See, also, Hamburger *v.* Baker,
35 *Hun*, 455 ; Weller *v.* J. B. Pace Tobacco Co., 2 *Supp.*
292 ; Thurber *v.* Blanck, 50 *N. Y.* 80 ; Bank *v.* Dakin, 51
N. Y. 519 ; Smith *v.* Longmire, 24 *Hun*, 257 ; Conner *v.*
Webber, 12 *Hun*, 580 ; Matter of True, 4 *Abb. N. C.* 90.

But the sheriff may seize tangible personal property
capable of manual delivery which has been disposed of in
fraud of creditors and defend an action against him on
the ground that such disposition was fraudulent. Rinchey
v. Stryker, 28 *N. Y.* 45 ; s. c., 26 *How. Pr.* 75.

The exception spoken of above is where the attachment
is levied against a person upon whom the summons cannot
be served personally, and it is served without the State or
by publication pursuant to an order therefor, and the defendant is in default. Then the sheriff or the creditor can
bring an action to set aside the transfer of a chose in action as made in fraud of creditors before judgment is entered. *Code Civ. Pro.* § 655, as amended by *L.* 1889, c.
504 ; Whitney *v.* Davis, 3 *N. Y. Ann. Cas.* 88 ; Note on
Action in Aid of Attachment, *Id.* 92 ; First National
Bank of Salem *v.* Davis, 88 *Hun*, 169 ; s. c., 35 *Supp.* 532.

The sheriff can levy an attachment upon the interest of one partner in a firm. Atkin *v.* Saxton, 77 *N. Y.* 195 ; Seligman *v.* Falk, 13 *Civ. Pro. R.* 77.

The interest of a vendee in possession of real estate under a contract of purchase upon which he has made payments is subject to attachment. Higgins *v.* McConnell, 130 *N. Y.* 482 ; S. C., 42 *St. R.* 363.

See Note on How Far Rights of Action can be Subjected to Attachment, 28 *Abb. N. C.* 283.

The courts have under special circumstances granted relief in the nature of an injunction to prevent a threatened transfer of property to defeat an attachment, in cases not mentioned in the Code. People *ex rel.* Cauffman *v.* Van Buren, 136 *N. Y.* 252 ; Falconer *v.* Freeman, 4 *Sandf. Ch.* 565 ; Bates *v.* Plansky, 28 *Hun,* 112 ; Keller *v.* Payne, 22 *Abb. N. C.* 352 ; Tannenbaum *v.* Rossenog, *Id.* 346, 354.

As to what are sufficient allegations in a complaint in an action in aid of attachment, see Backus *v.* Kimball, 27 *Abb. N. C.* 361 ; S. C., 62 *Hun,* 122 ; 16 *Supp.* 619 ; 41 *St. R.* 446 ; Note on Creditor's Suit on Attachment Before Judgment, 23 *Abb. N. C.* 9.

A contingent liability cannot be attached as a chose in action. Excelsior Steam Power Co. *v.* Cosmopolitan Publishing Co., 80 *Hun,* 592.

A debt due from a foreign corporation to a non-resident debtor cannot be attached by a resident creditor of such non-resident debtor. Wood *v.* Furtick, 17 *Misc.* 561 ; Douglass *v.* Phenix Ins. Co., 138 *N. Y.* 209.

In the former of the two cases last cited three insurance companies which were incorporated under the laws of Great Britain and which had their principal offices for the transaction of business in this country in the city of New York, were indebted to the attachment debtor upon fire insurance policies upon which there had been a loss, the debtor residing in South Carolina where the losses had occurred and where the amounts specified in the policies were payable. The court held that the *situs* of the debt was the place of residence of the creditor ; that the residence of the corporation was within the domain of the sovereignty which created it, and that where neither the debtor whose property is sought to be attached, nor his debtor, is a resident of the State, the court is without jurisdiction to make any adjudication involving the payment of the debt from the non-resident debtor to his non-resident creditor, in an action by a resident creditor against his non-resident debtor.

The Code (§ 649) has not changed the inherent charac-

348 VOLUME IV.

Note on Levy of Attachment and Execution on Choses in Action.

ter of a bond or promissory note from a chose in action to that of property capable of manual delivery by merely providing that under an attachment it must be taken into the actual custody of the officer. It has only changed the method by which the levy must be made by the officer. Anthony *v.* Wood, 96 *N. Y.* 180 ; s. c., 6 *Civ. Pro. R.* 164.

Where property is sought to be attached under Code Civ. Pro. § 649. subd. 3, by delivering to the person who has the custody of the property or who is indebted to the debtor of a copy of the warrant and a notice specifying the property or debt attached, the person must look to the notice to ascertain what property is attached, as the notice alone controls and fixes the rights of the parties. Hayden *v.* National Bank of State of N. Y. 130 *N. Y.* 146.

Execution.] Sections 1405 *et seq.*, of the Code of Civil Procedure contain the general provisions as to executions against property. While it is true, as a general rule, that choses in action, strictly speaking, are not subject to levy under an execution (Duffy *v.* Dawson, 2 *Misc.* 401, 405, and cases there cited), there are certain rights and equities which are not tangible property subject to manual delivery, and which have the nature of choses in action, that have been allowed to be sold on execution.

Thus, where personal property is sold under an agreement that the vendee shall have possession until he make default in future payments, every right, legal and equitable, of the vendee may be taken under an execution against the vendee if the judgment creditor pay the balance of the purchase price when due ; he may retain the goods and reap any benefit which would accrue to the vendee. Savall *v.* Wauful, 21 *Civ. Pro. R.* 18 ; Frank *v.* Batten, 49 *Hun*, 91.

And the Code of Civil Procedure (§ 1411) allows a chose in action to be sold in certain cases. It provides as follows :

" The officer to whom an execution against property is delivered must levy upon and sell, a bill, or other evidence of debt, belonging to the judgment debtor, which was issued by a moneyed corporation to circulate as money ; or a bond, or other instrument for the payment of money, belonging to the judgment debtor, which was executed and issued by a government, State, county, public officer, or municipal or other corporation, and is in terms negotiable, or payable to the bearer or holder."

Section 1412 of the Code provides that the interest of a judgment debtor in pledged property may be sold on execution.

Note on Levy of Attachment and Execution on Choses in Action.

But see, as to how a levy must be made upon such property. Warner *v.* Fourth National Bank, 12 *Civ. Pro. R.* 186.

Bank shares and other choses in action cannot be taken in execution. Ransom *v.* Miner, 3 *Sandf.* 692 ; Denton *v.* Livingston, 9 *Johns.* 96 ; Ingalls *v.* Lord, 1 *Cow.* 240 ; unless first lawfully seized under an attachment. Pardee *v.* Leith, 6 *Lans.* 303.

Money in bank cannot be taken under an execution as the relation between a bank and its depositor is merely that of debtor and creditor. Carroll *v.* Cone, 40 *Barb.* 220 ; aff'd 41 *N. Y.* 216.

A mere license cannot be taken on execution. Reinmiller *v.* Skidmore, 7 *Lans.* 161.

The resulting interest in the assigned property of an assignor for the benefit of creditors cannot be taken on execution. Wilkes *v.* Ferris, 5 *Johns.* 335.

The interest of a mortgagor of chattels where the right of possession is in him for a definite period, by the terms of the mortgage, may be sold on execution. Bailey *v.* Burton, 8 *Wend.* 339 ; Gelhaar *v.* Ross, 1 *Hilt.* 117 ; Hull *v.* Carnley, 11 *N. Y.* 501 ; rev'g 2 *Duer*, 99 ; overruling Brown *v.* Cook, 3 *E. D. Smith*, 123 ; Manning *v.* Monaghan, 28 *N. Y.* 585 ; rev'g, 10 *Bosw.* 231 ; Hall *v.* Sampson, 35 *N. Y.* 274 ; Hull *v.* Carnley, 17 *Id.* 202 ; Goulet *v.* Asseler, 22 *Id.* 225 ; Hathaway *v.* Brayman, 42 *Id.* 322 ; Hamill *v.* Gillespie, 48 *Id.* 556.

Where the mortgagee of chattels is in possession of the goods the mortgagor's equity cannot be sold on execution by taking the chattels and selling them subject to the mortgagee's interest. Mattison *v.* Baucus, 1 *N. Y.* 295 ; Nichols *v.* Mead, 2 *Lans.* 222 ; aff'd without opinion, 47 *N. Y.* 653 ; Gelhaar *v.* Ross, 1 *Hilt.* 117 ; Galen *v.* Brown, 22 *N. Y.* 37 ; Hall *v.* Sampson, 35 *Id.* 274.

After default in payment of a chattel mortgage the mortgagor no longer has a leviable interest under an execution. Balteo *v.* Ripp, 1 *Abb. Ct. Ap. Dec.* 78 ; s. c., 3 *Keyes*, 210 ; Champlin *v.* Johnson, 39 *Barb.* 606 ; Fairbanks *v.* Bloomfield, 5 *Duer*, 434.

If the mortgage does not specify the time of payment it is due at once and the mortgagor has no interest in the mortgaged property which can be taken on execution. Howland *v.* Willett, 3 *Sandf.* 607.

It has been held that, where the mortgage gives the right to the mortgagee, if he deems himself insecure, to take possession of the property at once, the mortgagor has no leviable interest which may be taken under an exe-

350 **VOLUME IV.**

Note on Levy of Attachment and Execution on Choses in Action.

cution. Farrell *v.* Hildreth, 38 *Barb.* 178; Stewart *v.* Slater, 6 *Duer*, 83. But this doctrine seems to be limited or modified by Hathaway *v.* Brayman, 42 *N. Y* 322. In that case the mortgage contained the clause that should the mortgagee at any time deem himself unsafe it should be lawful for him to take possession, etc. It also gave the right to possession of the property to the mortgagor for a specified time, subject to the provision above mentioned. The mortgagor disposed of the property before there was a default in payment and before the mortgagee had exercised his right to take possession, to a third person, and such third person also disposed of the property before the mortgage was due, and before the mortgagee had exercised his right to take possession In an action by the mortgagee against the person to whom the property was first transferred by the mortgagor, for conversion, a nonsuit was affirmed, and the court said upon the point under discussion, at page 325 : "Under the rule laid down in Hall *v.* Sampson (35 *N. Y.* 277), the rights of the mortgagor and mortgagee are the same as they would have been if the mortgage had contained the express condition that the mortgagor was to continue in possession until default in payment, or until the mortgagee should deem himself unsafe, and should in consequence thereof take possession. And under such a mortgage as that, the rule clearly is that, prior to such default or taking possession, the mortgagor has an interest in the mortgaged property, which may be levied upon by execution against him, and will authorize the sheriff to take the property into his possession and sell it without reference to the mortgage, and the remedy of the mortgagee in such a case is to follow the property into the hands of the purchaser and require its delivery to him or the payment of his mortgage debt." Citing Hall *v.* Sampson (*supra*) ; Hull *v.* Carnley, 11 *N. Y.* 50 ; Same *v.* Same, 17 *Id.* 202 ; Goulet *v.* Asseler, 22 *N. Y.* 228.

Where the mortgage contains a provision that upon levy of a legal process against the mortgaged property the mortgage shall become due at once the mortgagor has no leviable interest which can be taken on execution. Bryan *v.* Smith, 13 *Daly*, 331.

Bonds of a corporation which it has pledged as security for a debt may be taken in execution, but not bonds which have been executed by the company but which have never been issued by delivery. Sickles *v.* Richardson, 23 *Hun*, 559.

A naked equity of redemption in goods cannot be levied upon under an execution. Hale *v.* Sweet, 40 *N. Y.* 97, 103;

Hill *v.* Beebe, 13 *Id.* 556 ; Marsh *v.* Lawrence, 4 *Cow.* 461 ; Burdick *v.* McVanner, 2 *Denio*, 170.

An equity of redemption in lands may be sold under an execution. Waters *v.* Stewart, 1 *Caines Cas.* 47 ; Shottenkirk *v.* Wheeler, 3 *Johns Ch.* 275 ; Trimm *v.* Marsh, 54 *N. Y.* 599. Also a vendee's title held under a parol contract taken out of the statute of frauds by part payment. Richmond *v* Foote, 3 *Lans.* 244. And so may the interest of a debtor in lands held adversely to him. Tuttle *v.* Hills, 6 *Wend.* 213. But not a naked claim to lands of which the debtor is not in possession. Hagaman *v* Jackson, 1 *Wend.* 502 ; Montgomery *v.* Chapin, 5 *Cow.* 485.

The mortgagee's interest in lands cannot be sold on execution against him before foreclosure of the mortgage although the mortgagor is in default. Jackson *v.* Willard, 4 *Johns.* 41 (Chancellor KENT); cited with approval in Purdy *v* Huntington, 42 *N. Y.* 334, 346.

Possession of lands not under a contract to purchase is such an interest as may be taken on execution. Griffin *v.* Spencer, 6 *Hill,* 525; Talbot *v.* Chamberlain, 3 *Paige* 219 ; although a mere easement. Evangelical Lutheran St. John's O. H. *v.* Buffalo Hydraulic Assn., 64 *N. Y.* 561.

"The question whether the interest of a person holding a contract for the purchase of land was bound by a judgment and could be sold upon execution, was, prior to the Revised Statutes, the subject of frequent and conflicting discussion. The court of errors, in 1819, in Bogert *v.* Perry (17 *Johns.* 351) held that it could not be, but the Supreme Court subsequently held that it could be if the holder of the contract was in possession. Jackson *v.* Scott, 18 *Johns.* 94 ; Jackson *v.* Parker, 9 *Cow.* 73." Higgins *v.* McConnell, 130 *N. Y.* 482, at page 486.

The Revised Statutes, subsequently enacted, provided (1 *R. S.* 744, §§ 4, 5) that the interest of a vendee in possession of land under an executory contract of sale could not be reached on execution, and that it was necessary to bring an equitable action in the nature of a judgment creditor's suit, in which adequate relief could be awarded to the judgment creditor by a decree of specific performance or otherwise. See Sage *v.* Cartwright, 9 *N. Y.* 49.

These two sections were repealed by L. 1880, c. 245, and were practically re-enacted in Code Civ. Pro. §§ 1253, 1873–1875. Section 1253 reads as follows : "The interest of a person holding a contract for the purchase of real property is not bound by the docketing of a judgment, and cannot be levied upon and sold, by virtue of an execution issued upon a judgment."

Sections 1873–1875, specify in what manner the interest of one holding land under an executory contract of purchase may be taken in a judgment creditor's action.

WISE *v.* WISE CO.

Court of Appeals; October, 1897.

Taxes ; corporations ; personal property ; priority of lien of execution or attachment.]   Where no warrant or other process has been issued or a levy made thereunder, for the collection of taxes, upon the personal property of a corporation, until after a specific lien has been acquired against such property by a creditor of the corporation, by a levy under an execution or an attachment, no lien is created for such taxes which is superior to that acquired by the creditor, in the absence of any statutory provision.*

Appeal by the Receiver of Taxes of New York City, from an order of the Appellate Division of the Supreme Court, First Department, which reversed an order of the New York Special Term, which ordered the receiver of the defendant company to prefer claims against the personal property of the company for personal taxes over the claims of certain judgment creditors of the corporation.

* In Matter of Columbia Ins. Co. (3 *Abb. Ct. of App. Dec.* 239), the court remarks that there is great force in the claim that "the State has succeeded to all the prerogatives of the British Crown so far as they are essential to the efficient exercise of powers inherent in the nature of civil government, and that there is the same priority of right here, in respect to the payment of taxes, which existed at common law in favor of the public treasury."

In Roraback *v.* Stebbins (4 *Abb. Ct. of App. Dec.* 100) it was held that a sale of personal property under a voidable, but not void, judgment, conferred a title on the purchaser which was superior to that of a person who bought the property at a tax sale, where the levy under the tax warrant was not made until after the sale under the judgment.

Wise *v.* Wise Co.

The question in this case is whether taxes assessed upon the personal property of a corporation, and which became due subsequent to the levy of an attachment and execution thereon at the suit of creditors, are a prior lien upon the assets in the hands of a receiver for distribution under the direction of the court, and which arose from a sale of the property subject to the levy. The defendant was a New Jersey corporation doing business in New York, and, being insolvent, one McMasters was appointed receiver of its property in this State December 7, 1893. Prior to the time of his appointment, attachments had been levied upon the personal property, issued in actions at law, in which judgments were subsequently recovered and executions issued and levies made. The lien under these executions was acquired September 23, 1893, the date of the levy upon the attachments. On December 23, 1893, the sheriff, under an order of the court, delivered all the property held by him under the attachments and executions to the receiver, who received it subject to all liens thereon, and reserving to all creditors their rights against the proceeds in the hands of the receiver and their respective priorities of lien. The proceeds of the property in the hands of the receiver were not sufficient to pay the judgments upon which the sheriff had taken possession of the property. The receiver of taxes for the City of New York presented a claim to the receiver for $556,92, personal taxes for the year 1893, which he claimed was a lien on the fund prior to the judgments. The court, at special term, sustained this claim, and ordered the receiver to pay the taxes in preference to the judgments. The Appellate Division, however, reversed the order, and directed that the entire fund be paid over to the judgment creditor, and from this decision the receiver of taxes has appealed to this court.

Held, that the order should be affirmed. The contention of the learned counsel for the receiver of taxes rests upon a somewhat novel proposition. It is that from the most ancient times the courts of England have recognized the right of the sovereign, representing the State, to priority of payment over all other claims, though they may have been secured by specific liens. That the people of this State have succeeded to all the prerogatives of the British Crown as parts of the common law suitable and applicable to our condition.

In support of his contention he has called our attention to various authorities in England and in this country. Giles *v.* Grover, 9 *Bing.* 130–285 ; 2 *Bac. Abr.* p. 363 ; *Toller on Ex.*, chap. 2. p. 259 ; Matter of Columbian Ins. Co., 3 *Abb. Ct. App. Dec.* 239 ; Central Trust Co. *v.* N. Y. City & N. R, R. Co., 110 *N. Y.* 250; S. C., 18 *St. R.* 30 ; rev'g 47 *Hun,* 587 ; S. C., 15 *St. R.* 17 ; U. S. Trust Co. *v.* R. R. Co., 117 *U. S.* 434 ; U. S. *v.* State Bank North Carolina, 6 *Peters,* 29–34.

The general doctrines contained in these cases would seem, upon a superficial view, to go far in support of the contention upon which this appeal is based, although it should be observed that a very important fact present in this case was absent in the cases cited, and that was the existence of a specific lien at law upon the personal property acquired by a levy under valid legal process in the hands of the sheriff.

On a closer examination, however, it will be found that they do not sustain the broad principle contended for. They undoubtedly go far enough to sustain the principle that when a fund is in the hands of the court or the trustee of an insolvent person or corporation, a claim due to the government upon a debt or for taxes is entitled to a preference in certain cases or under certain circumstances. The prerogatives of the crown with respect to the imposition and collection of taxes was the subject of a long and obstinate dispute in England between the people and the executive. Without attempting to ascertain whether the limits of this prerogative have ever been judicially defined with anything like precision, it is entirely safe to say that many of the utterances of the English courts on the subject to be found in the books cannot be considered law here, or even in that country. The great contest with respect to the right of the sovereign to levy and collect what was called ship money illustrates the extent to which the claim of prerogative was pushed, the nature of the dispute, and the conflicting views of the Judges. 3 *Howell's State Trials* 826–1254.

In this country the right of the government to be preferred in the distribution of such a fund exists, under the authorities, in two cases.

(1). Where the preference is expressly given by statute as was the case in U. S. *v.* State Bank of North Carolina (*supra*).

(2). Where, before the fund has come to the hands of the receiver or trustee, a warrant or some other legal process has been issued for the collection of the tax or debt, and the fund has come to his hands impressed with a lien in favor of the government in consequence of the proceedings for collection, as was the case in Matter of Columbian Ins. Co., 3 *Abb. Ct. App. Dec.* 239.

But where there is no statute giving the preference, and no warrant or process has been issued for the collection of a tax on personal property, there is no controlling authority for preferring such a claim over specific prior liens in favor of creditors obtained by levy under attachments or executions. Roraback *v.* Stebbins, 4 *Abb. Ct. App. Dec.* 100.

The case of Central Trust Co. *v.* N. Y. Central, etc., R. R. Co. (110 *N. Y.* 250), decides nothing contrary to this rule. In that case the receiver of a railroad failed to pay the franchise tax under chap. 361, *L.* of 1881, for several years. He had in his hands moneys derived from the operations of the road and the exercise of the franchise. The attorney general petitioned the court to order the receiver to pay the tax. The motion was opposed on two grounds : (1) That the tax was against the corporation and not the receiver; (2) that the mortgages upon the property, to foreclose which the action had been commenced, resulting in the appointment of a receiver, were a prior lien upon the fund. The court ordered the receiver to pay the taxes, and held that as the fund was derived from the exercise of a franchise granted by the State and subject to the tax the claim of the State was in equity superior to the mortgages.

The question now before us is quite different. It is simply whether a specific lien upon personal property, acquired by attachment in an action at law, can be displaced in favor of a subsequent claim for taxes on the same property, where no specific lien has been acquired by warrant or any legal process whatever. The learned Appellate Division held that it could not, and that the claim of the vigilant creditor who had thus acquired the lien could not be postponed for the payment of public taxes.

Opinion by O'BRIEN, J. All concur, except GRAY, J., absent.

Order affirmed.

Robert G .Monroe, for the Receiver of Taxes, appellant.

Otto Horowitz, for the respondent.

RALLI *v.* WHITE.

*Supreme Court, First Department, Appellate Term;
September,* 1897.

[Affirming 20 *Misc.* 635.]

1. *Insurance ; fire ; Lloyd's policy ; action against individual members.*] Where the attorneys of a Lloyd's insurance association are not underwriters, an action is properly brought, in the first instance, against the individual underwriters, notwithstanding a provision of the policy that no action shall be brought except against the attorneys, in which action the liability of the underwriters shall be determined.*

2. *The same ; pleading ; defense of stipulation to sue attorneys.*] The defense of a stipulation in such a policy that no action shall be brought under it except against the attorneys of the association is not pleaded with sufficient certainty by an allegation "that the policy of insurance as aforesaid contains the express condition that the attorneys and managers shall be sued before any suit shall be brought against any of the underwriters upon said policy," without giving the names of the parties omitted, and showing that they are alive and within the jurisdiction of the court.

3. *The same ; service of proof of loss ; change of agents.*] Where, since the issuance of such a policy, the old attorneys and agents and the underwriters, by their acts, hold out new agents as the representatives of the company, proof of loss is properly served on such new agents, whether or not they have been properly appointed by the association.

Appeal by the defendant from an affirmance by the General Term of the City Court of New York, of a judgment in favor of the plaintiff, rendered after a trial without a jury.

The action is on a Lloyd's policy, issued in the name of the defendant and nineteen other underwriters, doing business as an insurance association under the name and

---

* See note following this case.

Ralli *v.* White.

---

title of the Metropolitan Lloyds. The policy insured the
Kaufman Milling Company in the sum of $4,000 against
loss or damage by fire to certain merchandise of that corporation contained in the store and frame elevator of the
President Mills, situated at Bethalto, Madison County, Illinois. The form of policy was the usual one issued by
Lloyd's companies, and the liability of each of the twenty
underwriters was severally fixed at $200, making the total
amount insured.

Upon the trial the parties admitted (1) the corporate
existence of the insured, (2) the issuing of the policy, (3)
the interest of the insured in the property, (4) that a fire
occurred during the lifetime of the policy whereby the
property insured was damaged to the amount of $2,675.57.
(5) that the proportionate part of the loss for which the
defendant was liable, if at all, amounted to $133,77, and
that the right of action had been duly transferred to the
plaintiffs.

Two questions were reserved for litigation : (1)
Whether the proofs of loss were properly served. This
was to be determined from the evidence. (2) Whether
the action was properly brought against the defendant as
one of the underwriters, or should have been brought
against the attorneys in fact of all the underwriters—a
question which, as presented, is a mixed one of law and
fact.

Held, as stated above. The second question reserved
is in the nature of an objection to the form of the action,
based on that part of the policy which provides that:
" No action shall be brought by the assured to enforce the
provisions of this policy except against the attorneys in
fact, as representing all of the underwriters ; and each of
the underwriters hereby agrees to abide the result of any
suit so brought, as fixing his individual responsibility
thereunder."

This provision has been before the courts in actions on
similar policies, and it has been decided that where the

attorneys in fact are not underwriters, such provision is contrary to public policy and void.   Knorr *v.* Bates, 14 *Misc.* 501, 12 *Id.*, 395 ; Farjeon *v.* Fogg, 16 *Id.* 219 ; but where the attorneys in fact are underwriters, and liable as such on their contractual obligation, the stipulation that only one of their number should be sued, to prevent a multiplicity of suits and an unnecessary accumulation of costs, is valid.   N. J. & Penn. C. W. *v.* Ackermann, 6 *App. Div.* 540 ; Stieglitz *v.* Belding, 20 *Misc.* 297 ; Lawrence *v.* Schaefer, 20 *App. Div.* 80 ; S. C., 46 *Supp.* 719.   Unless there were one or more attorneys in fact who were underwriters, against whom the action should have been instituted, it was properly brought directly against one of the underwriters, for since the contract is several in its terms, each obligor should be separately sued.   *Barb. Parties* 117.

The defendant claims that William C. Beecher and Arthur White are underwriters, as well as attorneys in fact of all the underwriters, and that the suit should therefore have been against them as such attorneys, in which event judgment might have gone against them in the one action for the entire loss, thus binding all the underwriters for their proportionate amount thereof.   Leiter *v.* Beecher, 2 *App. Div.* 577.

William C. Beecher and Arthur White were undoubtedly attorneys in fact at the time of the organization of the association, but Mr. Beecher testifies that they became such for the purpose merely of organizing, and when the organization was complete they appointed Beecher & Co. (a firm composed of H. B. Beecher and V. R. Schenck) assistant attorneys ; and this firm of Beecher & Co. issued the policy in suit August 23, 1894, signing it not as assistants, but as "attorneys for the underwriters."   William C. Beecher and Arthur White never issued any policies, and the practical details of the business were conducted by Beecher & Co., who in fact managed everything concerning it.

It appears that about January 24, 1895, Beecher &

Co., having by the consent of the underwriters, obtained the right to use the name Metropolitan Lloyds, transferred such right to Edwards & Co., and the latter firm reorganized the association chiefly with new underwriters (a few only of the old underwriters, whose names do not clearly appear, remaining), and continued the business of the Metropolitan Lloyds at the offices occupied by that association when it issued the policy in suit, putting up the sign " Henry Edwards & Co., attorneys and managers for the underwriters at the Metropolitan Fire Lloyds and Indemnity Fire Lloyds," and Beecher & Co., the former managers took offices in another part of the building. It also appears that after this transfer of control, William C. Beecher and Arthur White practically ceased to be the attorneys in fact of the underwriters, and were superseded by Edwards & Co., into whose hands the management of the association was placed.

However objectionable the method of changing control and the right to use the business name Metropolitan Lloyds may have been, the underwriters who authorized and permitted the consummation of the scheme cannot now complain as against a policy holder of the natural results that followed, for the consequences should have been foreseen by them, and they probably were. The question whether the State could complain is not before us.

It was further shown that there were twelve or more changes in the membership of the Metropolitan Lloyds, so that those not in the secret could not become informed thereof. It has not been claimed that this change of *personnel* dissolved the association, or that each change gave rise to a new organization, for the Metropolitan Lloyds went on as before, with the old business name, at its old offices or meeting place ; so that, so far at least as the public is concerned, it survived the different changes. Strange complications might follow the withdrawal of members and the substitution of new ones if those liable

Ralli *v*. White.

as underwriters were not after their retirement bound by the action of the management.

The facts established were sufficient to warrant the trial court in holding, as it did, that William C. Beecher and Arthur White were not the attorneys in fact of the Metropolitan Lloyds at the time of the fire, and that the proofs of loss were properly served at the offices of the association on Edwards & Co., who were openly allowed to hold themselves out as legally representing it as the authorized attorneys in fact and managers of the underwriters; and that such service operated as a valid service on the association within the purposes and requirements of the policy. Walker *v*. Beecher, 15 *Misc.* 149. Indeed the policy specially provides that notice of the fire and the proofs of loss shall be served upon the attorneys of the underwriters, which by legal construction means those for the time being, and such service was made in this instance by the insured.

The Trial Court was also right in deciding that William C. Beecher and Arthur White were not necessary parties as attorneys in fact, and that the action as brought was maintainable. The underwriters adopted the style "at Metropolitan Lloyds" that their venture might be distinguished from other Lloyds concerns. See Crawford *v*. Collins, 45 *Barb.* 269; Wright *v*. Hooker, 10 *N. Y.* 51; Meriden Nat. Bank *v*. Gallaudet, 120 *Id.* 298. The association located offices at which its business was to be carried on and its meetings held, and to which its customers were invited to call in case of loss or other business; and if what occurred thereat with the attorneys in fact and managers does not bind the underwriters, simply because of a devolution of interest and representation, we have reached a stage of Lloyd's insurance fully as dangerous to the public as any that has become known.

The various changes of membership were not made known to the insured, who acted toward the representatives of the association, as it had the right to do, upon

Ralli *v.* White.

appearances which the underwriters created, and upon a holding out to the public which they sanctioned and for which they are responsible upon equitable principles of estoppel. Nth. Riv. B'k *v.* Aymar, 3 *Hill*, 262 ; Griswold *v.* Haven, 25 *N. Y.* 595, 601 ; N. Y. & New Haven R. R. Co. *v.* Schuyler, 34 *Id.* 30 ; Westfield B'k *v.* Cornen, 37 *Id.* 320 ; Grosvenor *v.* N. Y. Cent. R. R. Co., 39 *Id.* 34 ; Armour *v.* Michigan Central R. R. Co., 65 *Id.*, 111 ; B'k of Batavia *v.* N. Y. Lake Erie & W. R. R. Co., 106 *Id.* at p. 199 ; Bridenbecker *v.* Lowell, 32 *Barb.* 9 ; Lefler *v.* Field, 50 *Id.* 407 ; Doubleday *v.* Kress, 60 *Id.* 181* ; Talmadge *v.* Nevins, 32 *N. Y. Super. Ct. (J. & S.)* 38 ; *Rich Ins.*, 2d ed. 87. The underwriters knew that what Edwards & Co. did after succeeding to the use of the trade name would naturally follow change of control, and that patrons would in the nature of things continue to deal at the accredited agency with those placed in charge. The underwriters, therefore, cannot set up ignorance to avoid responsibility. *Bigelow Estoppel,* 540, *et seq.*

Upon well-settled principles direct proof of agency may be dispensed with by estoppel. The inquiry always is whether the party against whom an estoppel is alleged has by his actions or his words influenced the conduct of others, so that a wrong would be done to those influenced if a party should be permitted to show a state of facts inconsistent with his actions and words. Carpenter *v.* Stilwell, 11 *N. Y.* at p. 73 ; Hall *v.* Fisher, 9 *Barb.* 17 ; 6 *Wait's Act & Def.* 705 ; 8 *Wait's Act & Def.* 524 ; Dunn *v.* Steubing, 120 *N. Y.* 232 ; Bishop *v.* Agricultural Ins. Co., 130 *Id.*, 488, 496 ; Stout *v.* Jones, 9 *St. R.* 570 ; aff'd without opinion, 120 *N. Y.* 638 ; Porter *v.* Swann, 44 *St. R.* 375 ; Adams *v.* Brown, 16 *Ohio St. R.* 75 ; Manf. & T. B'k *v.* Hazard, 30 *N. Y.* 226 ; Blair *v.* Wait, 69 *Id.* 113 ; Boardman *v.* Lake Shore & Mich. R. R. Co., 84 *Id.* 157.

The rule is applicable to the law of agency "that

---

* Rev'd 50 *N. Y.* 410.

Ralli *v.* White.

where one of two innocent persons must suffer by the misconduct of a third person, that party shall suffer who by his act and conduct has enabled such third person by giving him credit to practice a fraud or imposition on the other party." *Story on Agency,* § 56; Dreher *v.* Connolly, 16 *Daly,* 106; S. C., 30 *St. R.* 674. So if an insurance company holds out to persons insured an officer or agent to represent it in respect to losses, and to speak for it at its office in negotiations for the settlement and appraisement of losses, it cannot afterwards question his power to bind the company. Solomon *v.* Metropolitan Ins. Co., 42 *N. Y. Superior Ct. (J. & S.)* 24; Van Allen *v.* Farmer's Joint Stock Ins. Co., 10 *Hun,* 397; aff'd, 72 *N. Y.* 604. As to innocent third persons the agent's authority is determined by the nature of the business intrusted to him and the situation in which he is placed. If he is put in possession of an office, he is enabled to do whatever business his principal has represented will be done there. 4 *Wait's Act & Def.* 28.

Upon equitable principles, therefore, the notice of loss to and service of the preliminary proofs on Edwards & Co., were properly given and made, and satisfy all the requirements of the policy. The contract is one *uberrimæ fidei,* demanding from the insured a disclosure of all material facts affecting the risk and in case of loss a corresponding obligation respecting payment ought to be imposed upon the insurer, that the rights of each contracting party may to this extent at least be reciprocal.

In the primitive days of insurance, when the underwriters met at Lloyd's coffee house on Lombard street, London, and passed around the proposed policy of the applicant among the members, so that each could underwrite and subscribe his name for such portion of the required amount as he wished to undertake, until by successive subscriptions the entire amount was covered (*Rich. Ins.* 2d ed. 9, 10; 1 *Arn. Ins.,* Perk. ed. 4, 82), it was sufficient to call the contract a Lloyd's policy, because made at Lloyd's. But since these associations of underwriters are now numerous bodies, each independent of the other, some distinctive name and place of meeting are necessary to determine one enterprise from another and prevent confusion. 6 *Waits Act & Def.* 25. The present policy, therefore, recites that it was made "at Metropolitan Lloyds of New York City," meaning at its meeting place at the offices in Cedar street, the same premises in which Edwards & Co. continued the association's business from January 24, 1895.

These associations of underwriters of common law origin became popular in London, and were so favored in this State that those which on October 1, 1892, were lawfully engaged in the business of insurance were granted certain privileges and exempted from supervision by the insurance department, and not required to report thereto, "notwithstanding any change made therein by death, retirement or withdrawal of any such underwriters, or by the admission of others to said association." *L.* 1892, c. 690, p. 1958; *L.* 1894, c. 684. The privileges conferred upon such Lloyd's companies, and not before specially referred to are described as consisting "of an exemption from the conditions and prohibitions prescribed and provided by Section 54 of said Chapter 690, Laws of 1892, whereby they may transact the business of fire insurance and issue policies in the State of New York without being possessed of the capital required of a fire insurance corporation doing business in this State and invested in the same manner, and without a certificate to the effect that they have complied with all the provisions which a fire insurance corporation doing business in this State is required to observe, and that the business of insurance specified therein may be safely intrusted to them." See complaint drawn by attorney general in the People of the State of New York *v.* Edward V. Loew, *et al.*, N. Y. Supreme Court, First Dept., May 6, 1896.* Associations

---

* Reported, 19 *Misc.* 248.

Ralli *v*. White.

possessing such exemptions and privileges should in other respects he held to the same liability that insurance corporations are to the persons with whom they hold contractual relations.

These associations are anomalous institutions—not corporations or joint stock companies, though in some respects resembling both, but a combination of individuals acting concretely as insurers. The members are not partners, for they do not bind themselves jointly, but severally in a specified amount until the sum insured for is made up. In England, where these institutions originated, they have been alternately called clubs, societies, associations and individual underwriters. There the contract has been held legal where the members bound themselves severally for specified amounts, but void as contrary to the insurance laws of that country when the underwriters undertook a joint liability on joint capital. Lees *v*. Smith, 7 *T. R.* 338 ; Strong *v*. Harvey, 3 *Bing.* 104 ; 11 *Moore*, 72 ; Harrison *v*. Miller, 2 *Esp.* 513 ; 7 *T. R.* 340, *note ;* Bromley *v*. Williams, 32 *Beav.* 177 ; 32 *L. J. Ch.* 176.

While the extent of the liability of each underwriter is specifically limited to his individual share of the loss, the rules of law applicable to insurers generally must in other respects determine when a liability under the policy arises, and to this end the principles of estoppel, adopted from motives of public policy, apply, when necessary to prevent fraud and injustice.

Another circumstance requires comment. The answer is defective in not squarely presenting the defense now urged as to parties defendant. It alleges "that the policy of insurance as aforesaid contains the express condition that the attorneys and managers shall be sued before any suit shall be brought against any of the underwriters upon said policy." This is in the nature of a plea in abatement, which "should give the names of the parties omitted and show that they are alive and within the jurisdiction of the court and within reach of its process." . . . "Where the omitted parties are executors, it should show that they qualified and are acting as such." 1 *Enc. Pl. & Pr.*, 17, 18. Tested by this rule, the answer should have given the names of the attorneys in fact against whom the plaintiffs ought to have proceeded, and alleged that they qualified and were acting as such, so that the plaintiffs might have a better writ. The plaintiffs could not tell from this plea whether Beecher & Co., who issued the policy and are therein described as attorneys in fact, or Henry Edwards & Co., were referred to, and safely might, as they did, ignore both, neither being underwriters and being, consequently, unnecessary parties according to the adjudged cases. The plea should be full, clear and specific, to answer legal requirements. It could not have been reasonably suspected in this instance that hidden behind the technical plea in abatement interposed by the defendant were the prominent and responsible names of William C. Beecher and Arthur White as attorneys in fact, and yet this is the use the defendant sought for the first time at the trial, and more particularly on the appeal, to make of this plea, to the prejudice of the plaintiffs—a circumstance emphasizing the necessity of requiring technical precision in pleas of this character—that the adverse party, being fully advised of the objection, may in advance of the trial recant and mend his hold, or, at least, being intelligently forewarned, advisedly determine what course to pursue to overcome the obstacle presented.

In concluding, it is proper to call attention to the rule that in determining the liability of the defendant he is entitled to the benefits of the contract fairly construed, and can stand upon all of its stipulations. But when the liability has become fixed by the capital fact of a loss, within the range of the responsibility assumed in the contract, courts are reluctant to deprive the insured of the benefit of that liability by any narrow or technical construction of the conditions and stipulations which drescribe the formal requisites by means of which this accrued right is to be made liable for his indemnification. A liberal and reason-able construction of the stipulations of the contract which prescribe the formal acts on the part of the insured, neces-sary to the recovery of the loss, is sanctioned and required by the rules of law. McNally v. Phœnix Ins. Co., 137 *N. Y.* at p. 398; Wehle v. U. S. Mut. Accident Association, 11 *Misc.*, p. 36; aff'd, 153 *N. Y.* 116.

Opinion by MCADAM, J. All concur.

Judgment affirmed, with costs.

E. H. Murphy (*W. C. Beecher* of counsel), for the de-fendant, appellant.

Charles Wehle, for the plaintiff, respondent.

NOTE ON ACTIONS ON LLOYDS' POLICIES.

The question involved in this case, as to whether or not a stipulation in a Lloyds' policy that no action shall be brought against the underwriters until the insured has first brought an action against the agents or attorneys of the asso-ciation, is valid and binding on the insured, cannot be said to be satisfactorily settled. Some of the earlier as well as later cases have held that the clause was void where the agents or attorneys were not underwriters, and that the action against the underwriters could be maintained in the first instance. N. Y. Com. Pl. Gen. T., PRYOR, J., Knorr v. Bates, 14 *Misc.* 501 ; aff'g 12 *Misc.* 395 ; N. Y. City Ct. Gen. T., BISCHOFF, J., Biggert v. Hicks, 18 *Misc.* 593 ; Ralli v. White in text, aff'g 20 *Misc.* 635 ; N. Y. Supm. Ct. Special T. TRUAX, J., Farjeon v. Fogg, 3 *N. Y. Ann. Cas.* 120 ; s. c., 16 *Misc.* 219, where on demurrer to the answer it was held that, as it appeared that the attorneys were not underwriters, the clause under discussion was void as against public policy.

See also Ralli v. Hillyer, 15 *Misc.* 692, following Knorr v. Bates (*supra*).

At about the same time that Knorr v. Bates (*supra*), and Farjeon v. Fogg (*supra*), were decided the question came up in the Supreme Court, First Department, on a demurrer to a complaint against the attorneys under a similar policy, except that it is said that in this case the attorneys were also underwriters. The defendants contended that the clause in the policy, requiring an action to be first brought against the attorneys, was void as against public policy and as ousting the courts of jurisdiction. The court there held that the clause was not void when the plaintiff sued the attorneys, as he had in that case under the stipulation in the policy, and the court remarked that if the action had been brought directly against the underwriters then it would be necessary to inquire into the correctness of the ruling in Knorr *v.* Bates (*supra*). See Leiter *v.* Beecher, 3 *N. Y. Ann. Cas.* 116 ; S. C., 2 *App. Div.* 577.

A little later a somewhat similar question, although not exactly the same, was raised in the case of N. J. and Pennsylvania Concentrating Works *v.* Ackermann, 6 *App. Div.* 540. There a policy was executed by all the underwriters with a provision that only one action should be brought against one of the underwriters to test the validity of any claim which an insured had against the association. The Appellate Division of the First Department, in an opinion written by Mr. Justice BARRETT, held that this was a perfectly legitimate method to prevent a multiplicity of suits, and that the stipulation would be enforced by the courts. It is significant, however, that the court distinctly distinguishes the case of Knorr *v.* Bates (*supra*), and says at page 543 : " These views are not antagonistic to those expressed in Knorr *v.* Bates (14 *Misc.* 501). There the agreement was—so said the court—that action should not be brought against any of the underwriters, but only against their attorneys in fact. The learned court held that that provision in the policy amounted to a stipulation that in no event should the underwriters be sued for the enforcement of their obligation. It is true that the underwriters there agreed to abide the result of the action against their attorneys, but the court held that the attorneys were not parties or privies to the underwriters' promise ; that they were strangers to the contract, and that an action could not be maintained against them upon it. We took a different view of the liability of attorneys in fact for certain underwriters in Leiter *v.* Beecher (2 *App. Div.* 577), where the question arose in a direct action against such attorneys."

In Lawrence *v.* Schaefer (19 *Misc.* 239), SPRING, J., at the Erie Trial Term, reviewed the cases already cited and followed the decision of Leiter *v.* Beecher (*supra*), and refused to follow Knorr *v.* Bates (*supra*). In that case the action was brought against an underwriter and it appears from the opinion that the attorney was also one of the underwriters. But the court says, at page 243, it appears to the court that the attorney was the trustee of an express trust under Code Civ. Pro. § 449 This case was affirmed by the Appellate Division Fourth Dep. (20 *App. Div.* 80) practically on the opinion below.

It is to be observed that in none of the cases thus far decided has it been distinctly decided, as one of the ruling questions of the case, where the attorney was not an underwriter, that an action could not be brought against the underwriters in the first instance. In all the cases where a different state of fact has existed an attempt has been made, at least, to distinguish the principle laid down in Knorr *v.* Bates (*supra*). It is also significant that in every case where the facts were the same as they were in that case the decision has been the same, as shown above. It would seem, therefore, so far as present adjudications go, that where the attorney is not an underwriter, actions may be brought against the underwriters individually in the first instance ; but where the attorney is an underwriter then the action must first be brought against such attorney.

The case in the text lays down a rule that in all cases on such policies the defendant must plead the defense contained in the restrictive clause under discussion, if he wishes to take advantage of it at the trial. None of the cases heretofore decided contain this doctrine in reference to these policies.

In People *v.* Loew (19 *Misc.* 248) it was held that the attorney general could maintain an action under Code Civ. Pro. §§ 1948 *et seq.* to prevent Lloyds associations from exercising franchises and privileges which are not allowed by law.

The supreme court, N. Y. Special Term, refused to allow twenty-one actions against a Lloyds' company to be discontinued without costs, when they were commenced after the cases of Leiter *v.* Beecher (2 *App. Div.* 547), and New Jersey, etc., Works *v.* Ackermann (7 *App. Div.* 540) were decided. See N. Y. Law J., April 6, 1897.

MAAS *v.* McENTEGART.

Supreme Court, First Department, Appellate Term;
October, 1897.

1. *Supplementary proceedings ; reference to determine disputed title to fund ; jurisdiction ; stipulation.*] Where there was a dispute as to the title to a fund held by virtue of an order in supplementary proceedings and the claimants stipulated that the question be sent to a referee for determination.—*Held,* that the defeated party could not object to the proceeding on the ground that the court had no jurisdiction to make the order of reference, as the stipulation did not have the effect of conferring jurisdiction on the court where none existed, but was merely an agreement as to the procedure by which a question should be determined in a proceeding which was properly before the court.*

* Jurisdiction of the subject matter of an action cannot be conferred upon a court by the consent of the parties. Coffin *v.* Tracy, *Col. & Cai.* 470 ; s. c., 3 *Cai.* 129 ; McMahon *v.* Rauhr, 47 *N. Y.* 67 ; Heyer *v.* Burger, *Hoffman Ch.* 1.

But if the court has jurisdiction of the subject matter, jurisdiction of the person can be secured by consent. McCormick *v.* Pennsylvania Central R. R. Co., 49 *N. Y.* 303 ; 80 *Id.* 353 ; another appeal, also 99 *Id.* 65.

" If in an action not in its nature referable without the consent of the parties, they should agree upon a referee for the trial of the same, the court could not change the referee without their consent." Matter of N. Y. Lackawanna & W. R. R. Co., 98 *N. Y.* 447, 453.

" Whenever there is want of authority to hear and determine the subject matter of the controversy or to render the judgment, an adjudication upon the merits is a nullity, and does not estop even an assenting party ; and a defeated party may raise the question for the first time upon appeal." Gillin *v.* Canary, 19 *Misc.* 594 ; s. c., *ante,* p. 200.

In Matter of Walker (136 *N. Y.* 20) in proceedings for the probate of a will the various parties consented that the surrogate should determine certain questions raised as to the title to certain property disposed of by the will, and which some of the parties contended

Maas *v.* McEntegart.

2. *Reference; opening to submit further evidence; discretion.*]
After a reference has been once closed, it is discretionary with
the referee whether or not he will open the case to receive
further evidence offered by one of the parties.

Appeal by James Fitz Gerald, a claimant to a fund
held under an order in supplementary proceedings from an
order of the General Term of the N. Y. City Court, which
affirmed an order made at special term confirming a referee's
report and directed a distribution of the fund.

Prior to June 11, 1896, one William M. May recovered
a judgment against the defendant, Christopher Sullivan.
On that day Sullivan had on deposit to his credit in the
West Side Bank $542.60, and the bank was by a third
party order in supplementary proceedings in aid of ex-

---

did not belong to the testator at the time of his death. The Court
of Appeals held that the surrogate had no power to determine this
question and jurisdiction could not be conferred upon him by the
consent of the parties. And the court said, at page 29 : " Wherever
there is a want of authority to hear and determine the subject-matter
of the controversy, an adjudication upon the merits is a nullity and
does not estop even an assenting party." Citing Chemung Canal
Bank *v.* Judson, 8 *N. Y.* 254. And the court adds : " The present
case illustrates the futility of the attempt to obtain jurisdiction of
the subject matter by the voluntary submission of the parties.
The defeated party is not likely to acquiesce in the judgment, and
he may raise the question for the first time on appeal as one of the
parties to this record has done. She had the legal right to adopt
such a course and it would have been the duty of the court to have
directed a reversal of the decree for want of jurisdiction, even if the
point had not been distinctly raised."

The right to appeal to the Court of Appeals cannot be conferred
by the consent of the parties where the right is not given by statute.
Hoes *v.* Edison General Electric Co., 150 *N. Y.* 87 ; s. c., 3 *N. Y.
Ann. Cas.* 247.

See, as to general rule that the right to appeal cannot be conferred by the stipulation of the parties where it is not given by
statute, Shankland *v.* Washington, 5 *Pet.* (*U. S.*) 390 ; Sampson *v.*
Welsh, 24 *How.* (*U. S.*) 207 ; Mills *v.* Brown, 16 *Pet.* (*U. S.*) 525 ;
McMahon *v.* Rauhr, 47 *N. Y.* 67.

ecution issued on the May judgment restrained from paying out said money, and the officers of the bank were required to submit to an examination under said proceedings on June 15.

On June 16, James J. Fitz Gerald received from Sullivan a paper signed by the latter, which read : "Received
from James J. Fitz Gerald, check of P. S. Treacy, dated
June 5, 1896, for four hundred and seventy-five dollars,
which amount may be deducted from my account which is
now at the West Side Bank, held under restraining order
of the city court of New York, by said James J. Fitz
Gerald, his representatives or assigns, when said restraining order is vacated or set aside." The May judgment
referred to, upon which the restraining order was granted,
was reversed on November 6, 1896.

Upon the appeal from the judgment Sullivan gave no
security, and May, the judgment creditor, obtained an
order on July 15, 1896, directing the West Side Bank to
pay the money on deposit to his attorneys. On July 21,
Sullivan procured an order which modified the one last referred to by directing the bank to pay the money to the
clerk of the city court, to be held by him until the decision
of the appeal, and as security for the judgment in case of
its affirmance. The plaintiff herein obtained a judgment
October 26, 1896, in the city court against Sullivan and
one McEntegart for $204.35, and instituted supplemen-
tary proceedings with the view of reaching the fund on
deposit, and the clerk of the city court was, on November
7, served with an order for his examination in aid of execution.

On November 10 (four days after the reversal of the
May judgment) Fitz Gerald obtained an order to show
cause why the third party order last referred to should not
be modified so as to permit the clerk to pay the money to
Fitz Gerald as the owner of the fund under the instrument
signed by Sullivan June 16. On the return day of
the order, November 16, it was stipulated in writing by

Maas *v.* McEntegart.

the plaintiff herein and the claimant " that the question of the ownership of the said fund, and the question of the persons being entitled to or who is entitled to the whole or any part of the same shall be referred to William A. Crowe, Esq., counselor-at-law, to hear the evidence and determine the facts and report back to this court the evidence and the facts with all convenient speed." An order was entered on the same day pursuant to this stipulation.

The referee proceeded with the reference and reported that Fitz Gerald was the owner of $67.60 of the fund on deposit, and that the judgment debtor was, on October 26, 1896, and since that time, the owner of the balance of the fund. The report was confirmed December 19, and an order made in accordance therewith. On appeal the order was affirmed by the general term of the city court, July 9, 1897, and from the affirmance the present appeal is taken by Fitz Gerald, the claimant of the fund.

Held, that the order should be affirmed. The appellant now insists that the city court had no jurisdiction in supplementary proceedings to try or determine the question of title to property alleged to belong to a judgment debtor when said property is claimed by a third party. The appellant fails to distinguish between a case where there is want of power to act, and one where the power to act in a certain proceeding has been expressly conferred, but is erroneously exercised. Irregularities may be committed in a trial without divesting the court of power to act and to pronounce judgment. Illegality differs from error in this; the one denotes a complete failure of the proceedings, the other something that may be waived. *Brown on Jurisd.*, pp. 285, 287.

If the appellant had urged in the court below that it could not determine a disputed claim of title to property on mere motion, but should have appointed a receiver, who might have the question determined by action (Rodman *v.* Henry, 17 *N. Y.* 484; West Side Bank *v.* Pugsley, 47 *Id.* 368; Teller *v.* Randall, 26 *How. Pr.* 155; Krone *v.*

Klotz, 3 *App. Div.* 587), the court below would, no doubt, have held with him. But, instead of requiring this circuitous course to be adopted, the appellant preferred and therefore consented that the question be determined at once, finally and forever, in the proceeding then pending. The stipulation was not one conferring jurisdiction where none existed before ; it merely waived all ground of objection to that which might have otherwise been deemed an erroneous disposition of a matter properly before the court for determination. While consent cannot confer jurisdiction over the subject matter, it may to an extent regulate the manner in which it shall be exercised. Matter of N. Y. Lackawanna & W. R. R. Co., 98 *N. Y.* 447 ; Armstrong *v.* Percy, 5 *Wend.* 536 ; Baird *v.* Mayor, 74 *N. Y.* 382 ; Lee *v.* Thompson, 24 *Wend.* 337.

The maxim applicable is *modus et conventio vincunt legem*, which the late Judge ALLEN liberally translated as follows : "The terms and conditions of a contract have the force of law over those who are parties to it." Lowry *v.* Inman, 46 *N. Y.* at p. 129. The courts do not hold parties to the strict limits of an inquiry, and where a party by not objecting or otherwise consents to litigate questions not technically within the issues, he will not on appeal be heard to complain that the recovery was not upon the cause of action specifically alleged. Kafka *v.* Levensohn, 18 *Misc.* at p. 205 ; Frear *v.* Sweet, 118 *N. Y.* 454.

The only other objection urged is based on the exclusion of the clerk's minutes showing the reversal of the May judgment by order entered November 6, 1896. This evidence was offered after the close of the reference, and on that and other grounds was objected to. It was discretionary with the referee whether he would open the reference to receive the evidence (Fielden *v.* Lahens, 2 *Abb. Ct. App. Dec.* 111 ; Pearson *v.* Fiske, 2 *Hilt.* 146), and it could not have altered the result if he had received it ; so that the appellant was in no manner prejudiced by the ruling.

Forster *v*. Cantoni.

Opinion by McADAM, J.   DALY, P. J., and BISCHOFF, Jr. J., concur.

Order affirmed, with costs.

James J. Fitz Gerald, for the claimant, appellant.

William H. Klinker, for the plaintiff, respondent.

FORSTER *v*. CANTONI.

Supreme Court, First Department, Appellate Division;

June, 1897.

1. *Abatement and revival ; two causes of action, joined where only one survives.*]   Where two causes of action were joined in one complaint only one of which survived the death of the defendant, —*Held*, that upon the death of the defendant the plaintiff was entitled to an order, under Code Civ. Pro. § 757, continuing the action against his representative.*

2. *The same ; conditions upon granting the order of revival.*]   But the court has discretionary power to impose as a condition of granting the order that the cause of action which does not survive shall be stricken from the complaint.†

---

* Section 757 applies, by its terms, to special proceedings as well as to actions.

See Note on Abatement by Death After Verdict, 3 *N. Y. Ann. Cas.* 310.

† By section 755 an action in no case abates by the death of a party, where the cause of action survives, but as an application to the court is necessary to authorize its revival or continuance, the court may, on the ground of inexcusable laches, or, where, otherwise, irreparable injury will be suffered, deny the application. Legal rights are frequently lost by laches where no question of the statute of limitations is involved ; and the right to a continuance of an action on the death of a party, where the cause survives is not of so absolute a character as to preclude the court, in the exercise of a legal discretion,

Forster *v.* Cantoni.

Appeal by the plaintiff, from an order of the Supreme Court, New York Special Term, denying her motion to continue the action against the executor of the defendant.

having regard to all the circumstances, from denying a continuance. Lyon *v.* Park, 111 *N. Y.* 350, at page 357.

In Coit *v.* Campbell (82 *N. Y.* 509 ; aff'g 20 *Hun,* 50), the court said at page 512 : " To hold that the command of the statute is imperative, and that whatever length of time may have elapsed since the death of the party, the order to revive must be granted, would be contrary to established principles of equity and to the policy upon which our statutes of limitation are founded, while to hold that the subject is wholly within the discretion of the court, and that any lapse of time which it may consider unreasonable is a sufficient ground for refusing the order, would not only be contrary to the letter of the statute, but might lead to irremediable injustice. By denying to a party a continuance or revivor of his action, his rights may be entirely lost, and if the order is purely discretionary, he is without remedy by appeal, unless, perhaps, in a gross case of abuse of discretion. There is no reason why the right of a party to continue or revive his action should be less protected by legal rules and by the privilege of appealing from an adverse decision, than his right to bring or maintain it .
We think the true construction is, that where the party has a right to a revivor or continuance of the action the relief must be granted on motion. And we also think that this right is to be determined according to settled rules of procedure in equity so far as they have been established by equity. No practical inconvenience or hardship can result from the adoption of the views here expressed, as the defendant or his representatives can, and always could, compel the adverse party to revive the suit or dismiss it. But where it is suffered to slumber with the tacit acquiescence of both parties, the statute of limitations should, as a general rule, be adopted as a guide in determining the length of time sufficient to bar the right."

In Knock *v.* Funke (28 *Abb. N. C.* 240 ; S. C., 19 *Supp.* 242; 22 *Civ. Pro. R.* 161), (*N. Y. Super. Ct. Spl. T.,* McADAM, J.), it was held that in an equitable action the court had power to require the plaintiff to give security for costs as a condition to making an order reviving an action against the executrix of a deceased defendant. The court adds : " The Code provision (§ 757), that the court must upon motion allow the action to be continued, merely means that

Forster *v.* Cantoni.

Action by Eliza C. Forster against Salvatore Cantoni, deceased, which the plaintiff moves to have continued against the executor of the defendant. The motion was denied at special term.

By Code Civ. Pro. § 757, it is provided that : " In case of the death of a sole plaintiff or a sole defendant, if the cause of action survives or continues, the court must, upon a motion, allow or compel the action to be continued by or against his representative or successor in interest." The original defendant in this action was the sole defendant, and if the cause of action survives or continues, the plaintiff has a right to have the action continued as against the representative of the defendant. It is conceded that in this case the first cause of action did not survive the death of the defendant, but that the second cause of action did.

Held, that under the mandatory provision of the Code the plaintiff was entitled to have the action continued, at any rate, so far as to allow her to try the second cause of action, assuming that, notwithstanding the mandatory provision of this section of the Code, there is still a discretion vested in the court to determine whether or not the plaintiff has lost her right to continue the action by *laches*, or such conduct as would make it inequitable to allow her to take advantage of the provisions of this section. By section 755 of the Code it is provided that an action does not abate by any event if the cause of action survives or continues. I think this applies when one of several causes of action alleged in the complaint which survives, as well as where all of the causes of action survive, and that in

in a proper case the relief shall be granted. It does not mean that the court must unconditionally grant every application to revive that is presented. If that were intended, no motion would be required ; it would be sufficient to file a suggestion and go on as at common law. The very object of requiring a motion is to preserve the inherent power of the court, merely simplifying and facilitating the mode of its exercise."

such a case the court is bound to allow the action to be continued as to the cause of action which does survive. Such an order is not an adjudication that all of the causes of action survive. The order itself can expressly adjudge that as to the cause of action that did not survive the action is not continued ; or exercising the discretionary power vested in the court, which seems to be recognized by the decisions of the Court of Appeals, the motion could be granted upon condition that the plaintiff consents to strike from the complaint the cause or causes of action which do not survive.

An affirmance of this order would defeat the plaintiff's right to any substantial recovery upon this cause of action which does survive, for the statute of limitations has run against the greater portion, if not all, of this second cause of action. I think the plaintiff is entitled to have that cause of action tried by the method provided by law, and that she should not be deprived of that right unless it appears that in some way she has lost it by virtue of some act of hers which would make it inequitable to allow her to proceed.

In the case of Coit *v.* Campbell (82 *N. Y.* 515), in construing section 757 of the Code, the court says: " We think the true construction is, that where a party has the right to a revivor or continuance of the action, the relief must be granted on motion. And we also think that this right is to be determined according to settled rules of procedure in equity so far as they have been established by precedent." And in the case of Holsman *v.* St. John (90 *N. Y.* 464), it was held that where a cause of action survived, it was error on the part of the court below to refuse to revive the action upon motion, and the Court of Appeals in that case reversed the order of the superior court and granted the motion.

Order reversed and the motion granted, upon condition that the plaintiff consent to strike out the first cause of

action. Ten dollars costs of this appeal and the disbursements to abide the event of the action.

Opinion by INGRAHAM, J. PATTERSON, O'BRIEN and
PARKER, JJ., concurred. RUMSEY, J., dissents.

Samuel H. Randall, for the plaintiff, appellant.

William B. Hornblower, for the executor, respondent.

GRAHAM *v.* LAWYERS' TITLE INS. CO.

*Supreme Court, First Department, Appellate Division;
August,* 1897.

*Parties; defendant; designation when sued in representative cap-
acity; effect of appearance.*] Where a receiver in supplementary proceedings, to whom the debtor had conveyed certain
real property, under an order of the court, was designated in
the title of an action to foreclose a mortgage on the same
property, as "John P. Jenkins, receiver," without further description, and he appeared in the action, as receiver, and the
judgment debtor having died, his executor (but not his heirs)
was made a party defendant,—*Held,* that the appearance of the
receiver, as such, cured the defect in his designation in the
summons, and the purchaser at the foreclosure sale took a good
title to the property.*

---

* In Soldiers' Orphan Home *v.* Sage (1 *N. Y. Ann. Cas.* 106), it
was held that where the allegations of a complaint clearly charge a
defendant in his capacity as trustee and in that capacity only, and
a sufficient cause of action against him as trustee is alleged, a demurrer will not lie upon the ground that he is named in the summons and in the caption of the complaint as an individual, and no
cause of action against him individually is stated.

See Notes to that case.

Where an action was brought by a person as guardian *ad litem*
for an infant defendant instead of in the name of the infant by the
guardian *ad litem,* it was held that the defect was merely formal

Submission of a controversy upon an agreed statement of facts pursuant to Code Civ. Pro., § 1279.

The defendant insured the title of the plaintiff, Amelia M. Graham, to certain premises in New York. Subsequently plaintiff's title was rejected upon an examination for a loan for which application had been made to the Harlem Savings Bank. The loss which the plaintiff claims to have sustained up to the present time is the sum of seventy-four dollars, paid for counsel fees in the examination of the title. The plaintiff claims that the title is not good and marketable, while the defendant insists that it is and nothing is due under the policy.

On March 31, 1858, Benjamin M. Whitlock was the owner in fee of the premises in question. On that day he executed a mortgage thereon to Gouverneur Morris to secure the sum of $4,000. Subsequently three judgments were recovered against Whitlock, and docketed in the county of Westchester, in which the premises were situated. Executions thereon were subsequently issued to the sheriff, who returned them unsatisfied, and thereafter supplementary proceedings were instituted, which resulted in the

and could be cured by amendment. Proweeder *v.* Lewis, 11 *Misc.* 109 ; S. C., 31 *Supp.* 996 ; 24 *Civ. Pro. R.* 299.

A judgment against a party sued as an individual is not an estoppel in a subsequent action in which he sues or is sued in a representative capacity. Rathbone *v.* Hooney, 58 *N. Y.* 463, 467 ; Bumpus *v.* Bumpus, 79 *Hun,* 526.

"The rule is that a former judgment concludes the party only in the character in which he was sued and, therefore, a judgment for or against an executor, administrator, assignee or trustee as such presumptively does not preclude him, in a different cause of action affecting him personally from disputing the findings or judgment though the same questions are involved." Collins *v.* Hydorn, 135 *N. Y.* 320, 324.

See, also, Douglass *v.* Ireland, 73 *N. Y.* 100 ; Hall *v.* Richardson, 22 *Hun,* 444 ; Weston *v.* Turner, 8 *St. R.* 296.

See Munzinger *v.* Courier Co., 1 *N. Y. Ann.Cas.* 32, and Note on Amendment of Summons as to Designation of Parties, *Id.* 34.

Graham *v.* Lawyers' Title Ins. Co.

appointment of one John P. Jenkins as receiver of all the property of the said Benjamin M. Whitlock, who was ordered to assign and transfer all his property to the said receiver. In obedience to said order, Whitlock thereafter executed and delivered to the said receiver a deed conveying all of his property, including the premises in question, and the deed was duly recorded. A little later Whitlock died, and shortly thereafter a suit was commenced to foreclose the mortgage hereinbefore referred to. To this suit, John P. Jenkins, receiver, was made a party defendant, being named and described in the title and caption of the said action as follows, and not otherwise, viz: '' John P. Jenkins, Receiver.'' Subsequently he appeared generally in the action by attorney, the notice of appearance stating that he appeared for John P. Jenkins, receiver. Whitlock's heirs and devisees were not all made parties to the suit, but his executors were and appeared by attorney.

Held as stated in headnote. The plaintiff's first contention is that the title of the debtor Whitlock did not unqualifiedly vest in Jenkins as receiver; that such title as this officer of the court acquired was so qualified and limited as not to exhaust the title of the judgment debtor which descended to his heirs at law upon his death, and as they were not made parties defendant in the foreclosure action, they have not been divested of that title. The plaintiff claims that her position is fully supported by Moore *v.* Duffy (74 *Hun*, 78 ; S. C., 57 *St. R.* 746 ; 26 *Supp.* 340), but a careful examination of the case discloses that this claim is not well founded. In that case the debtor did not convey his real estate to the receiver. An order appointing a receiver was made, and from the time of its filing the real property became vested in the receiver. *Code Civ. Pro.* § 2468. Subsequently the judgment debtor conveyed his right, title and interest to a third party, and it was held that, subject to the right of the receiver to resort to the land for the payment of the judgment, the title remained in the judgment debtor, and by his convey-ance to Costello, became invested in him.

In the case at bar, if the court, after making the order appointing the receiver, had omitted to take further ac-tion, Moore's case and this one would have been alike in so far as the question now under consideration is con-cerned. But Whitlock, instead of conveying whatever in-terest he had in the premises to a third party, as in Moore's case, conveyed it to the receiver. If it be as-sumed, therefore, that by the order appointing Jenkins receiver he only acquired the right to resort to the land to pay the judgment, the title remaining in Whitlock, still that title subsequently became vested in the receiver by the deed from Whitlock. It matters not whether the conveyance was made voluntarily or in pursuance of an order of the court, for in either case the legal effect was to divest the grantor of title and vest it in the grantee. Thereafter the right remained in the judgment debtor to call upon the receiver to account, which right was a chose in action, and passed to the executor who was made a party defendant in the foreclosure suit. Porter *v.* Wil-liams, 9 *N. Y.* 150; Banks *v.* Potter, 21 *How. Pr.* 473.

The title having been vested in the receiver by a deed duly executed and recorded, it was not necessary that his grantor or any of his predecessors in title should have been made parties to the foreclosure suit, but it was es-sential, in order to divest the receiver of title, that he should be made a party. "John P. Jenkins, receiver," was made a party; but it is said that this was not a suffi-cient compliance with the rule which requires that a rea-sonably definite description of a party appearing in a re-presentative capacity must be contained in the title of the action, or, in default thereof, that the allegations in the body of the complaint must clearly indicate the precise character in which the party is sued. In Landon *v.* Townshend (112 *N. Y.* 93; s. c., 20 *St. R.* 223; 16 *Civ. Pro. R.* 161; rev'g 44 *Hun,* 561), Mr. Waddell, general as-

Graham *v.* Lawyers' Title Ins. Co.

signee in bankruptcy, was made a defendant without any addition whatever to his individual name, and he appeared by an attorney, the notice being in the general form specifying an appearance " for the defendants in the action." So far as the record of the case on appeal shows, there was no reference either in the summons and complaint or in the proceedings at any stage of the nature of his title or interest in the premises. In form, therefore, the action was against him as an individual, and his appearance was in his individual, and not in his representative character. It was held that the foreclosure was insufficient to bar the equity of redemption of the defendant as assignee in bankruptcy. In Beers *v.* Shannon (73 *N. Y.* 297), the court said: " But it has been held on the other hand that, though there be naught in the title of the process or the complaint to give a representative character to the plaintiff, the frame and averments and scope of the complaint may be such as to affix to him such character and standing in the litigation." It is true that there was nothing in the complaint, aside from a description of the premises, to apprise him that he was made a defendant in his representative capacity, and if he had refrained from taking a part in the litigation he might have urged that he did not have notice that he was made a party in his official character. He did not take this course, however, but appeared generally in the suit by attorney, who described him in the notice of appearance as receiver. His voluntary appearance not only indicated that he was in fact apprised that the suit was brought against him in his representative capacity, but, considered in connection with the contents of the summons, it operated to affix to him as a defendant his representative capacity in the suit, and the judgment of foreclosure divested him as receiver of all title to the premises.

Opinion by PARKER, J. VAN BRUNT, P. J., RUMSEY, PATTERSON and O'BRIEN, JJ., concurred.

Judgment ordered for defendant, with costs.

Albert E. Siebert, for the plaintiff.

David B. Ogden, for the defendant.

PEOPLE *v.* DURANTE.

Supreme Court, First Department, Appellate Division; June, 1897.

Excise law ; mortgage of tax certificate.] Under the Liquor Tax Law (*L.* 1896, c. 112) a tax certificate issued to a licensee is personal property, and capable of being mortgaged, within Penal Code, § 571, against fraudulent disposition of mortgaged property.*

---

* As a general principle a license to sell liquor is not property which can be assigned. Alger *v.* Weston, 14 *Johns.* 231 ; Lynch *v.* Dowling, 1 *Robt. C. C.* 163 ; Rubenstein *v.* Kahn, 5 *Misc.* 408 ; Koehler *v.* Olsen, 68 *Hun*, 63.

But see David Mayer Brewing Co. *v.* Rizzo, 13 *Misc.* 336, where it was held that a judgment debtor would not be required to assign to a receiver a liquor license held by him where it appeared he had previously made a valid assignment of a mortgage upon it to another person.

And under *L.* 1892, c. 401, § 26, as amended by *L.* 1893, c. 480, a liquor license could be assigned by permission of the board of excise. See Koehler *v.* Olsen (*supra*), and Rubenstein *v.* Kahn (*supra*).

Where a person was convicted under § 571 of the Penal Code, after a trial before a court of special sessions, it was held that the maximum punishment which could be imposed was that allowed by Code Civ. Pro. § 717, that is a fine of $50 or imprisonment not exceeding six months. People *ex rel.* Stokes *v.* Riseley, 38 *Hun*, 280.

And where the defendant had been sentenced to pay a fine of $250 it was said that he could secure his release by *habeas corpus* proceedings because the judgment was invalid. *Id.*

See Millicant *v.* People, 14 *W. Dig.* 252 ; Vans *v.* Middlebrook, 3 *St. R.* 277.

People *v.* Durante.

Appeal by the defendants from a judgment of the Court of General Sessions of the Peace in and for the City of New York, convicting the defendants of a misdemeanor.

The appellants, Michael Durante and another, were convicted, in the court of general sessions of the peace of the city and county of New York, of a misdemeanor, for the violation of section 571 of the Penal Code, by which it is enacted that a person "who having theretofore executed a mortgage of personal property, or any instrument intended to operate as such, sells, assigns, exchanges, secretes or otherwise disposes of any part of the property upon which the mortgage or other instrument is at the time a lien, with intent thereby to defraud the mortgagee or a purchaser thereof, is guilty of a misdemeanor." On the trial of the indictment upon which the conviction was had the following facts were admitted by the defendants, viz: That on July 1, 1896, a liquor tax certificate, mentioned in the indictment, was lawfully and duly issued to Giovanni Durante, one of the defendants, to conduct a saloon at 61 James street, New York City, for the term of one year; that on July 7, 1896, the defendants executed a chattel mortgage, mentioned and set out in the indictment, to one Giovanni Lombardi, in which mortgage was included the liquor tax certificate; that the mortgage was given to secure the payment of a loan of $400; that on July 30, 1896, the defendants surrendered the liquor tax certificate to the excise department and received a rebate therefrom, which they appropriated to their own use; that prior to the surrender of the certificate, a demand for the payment of the $400 was made by the mortgagee upon the mortgagors and not complied with, and that the amount remained unpaid up to the filing of the indictment. The defendants moved the court, after these admissions were made, that it advise the jury to acquit on the ground that the evidence as contained in the admission was of the sale and surrender of a liquor tax certificate, which was not personal property within the meaning of section 571 of the Penal Code. The motion was denied, and the defense thereupon resting, the case was submitted to the jury who returned a verdict of guilty.

Held that a liquor tax certificate was property which might be the subject of a chattel mortgage within the meaning of Penal Code, § 571. That section relates specifically to property upon which a mortgage or instrument intended to operate as such is a lien, and, in order to bring the case within that section, that which is the subject of the lien must be something answering the description of property and capable of being mortgaged. By the Statutory Construction Act of 1892 (Chap. 677, § 4), personal property is defined as including "everything, except real property, which may be the subject of ownership." It is a well-recognized rule that anything that may be sold or assigned may be mortgaged. Judge STORY says, in his Equity Jurisprudence (§ 1021): "As to the kind of property which may be mortgaged, it may be stated that, in equity, whatever property, personal or real, is capable of an absolute sale may be the subject of a mortgage." And in Neligh *v.* Michenor (3 Stockt. Ch. 542) Chancellor WILLIAMSON held that everything which is the subject of a contract, or which may be assigned, is capable of being mortgaged. By the inclusion of the liquor tax certificate in the articles mortgaged by these defendants to Lombardi, it was manifestly intended that, as between the parties to the instrument, that certificate should constitute part of the security for the money loaned. It may be true that, prior to the year 1893, a mere license to sell liquor did not, under the law of the State of New York, constitute property in such a sense as to make it the subject of traffic by way of sale, or that could be mortgaged—but by the provisions of the Liquor Tax Law of 1896 (Chap. 112) a different status is given, and additional qualities are annexed, to a certificate granted under that act, from those which theretofore attached to simple licenses to sell liquor. The certificate is given the characteristics and some essential elements of property, limited and restricted in some respects, but, nevertheless, constituting a thing of value, over and beyond a mere personal permission to one holding it to conduct or carry on a certain business. Any one may now engage in the traffic (with certain exceptions) who shall pay the license tax and give a bond. People *ex rel.* Einsfeld *v.* Murray, 149 *N. Y.* 367.

A person to whom a liquor tax certificate is issued may sell, assign and transfer such certificate during the time for which it was granted under certain conditions, limitations and qualifications provided for in the act. If a person holding a liquor tax certificate dies during the term for which that certificate was given, the administrator or executor of the person so dying may surrender the certificate and have refunded the *pro rata* amount of the tax paid for the unexpired term of the certificate. The same may be done by a receiver or assignee of a corporation or copartnership, and it is also provided that if any person holding a liquor tax certificate, and authorized to sell liquors, shall cease to traffic in them, under certain circumstances, he may surrender that certificate and have refunded the *pro rata* amount of the tax paid. These provisions of the statute, therefore, recognize that a liquor tax certificate may be assets for administration ; may be sold to a person not disqualified ; may be surrendered, and that it has a surrender money value. These incidents of property being attached by law to such certificates, constitute them property in a legal as well as a popular sense ; and, as they are salable and assignable, they are properly the subject of a mortgage. The mortgagee would acquire an absolute right, as between the parties to the instrument, to the certificate on default in the payment of the debt secured ; for the chattel mortgage mentioned in this indictment was payable on demand, and on failure to comply with the demand the instrument would operate as a bill of sale.

Opinion by PATTERSON, J. RUMSEY, WILLIAMS, INGRAHAM and PARKER, JJ., concurred.

Judgment affirmed.

John Mitchell, for the defendants, appellants.

John D. Lindsay, for the plaintiffs, respondents.

BOWMAN *v*. McCLENAHAN.

Supreme Court, First Department, Appellate Division; August, 1897.

Auctions; sale of real estate; employment of puffers.] The employment, by an owner of real estate, of puffers, to run up the price,
at an auction sale of the property, without notice to prospective bidders that the owner reserves the right to bid on the
property, invalidates the sale, without regard to the question
of whether or not the purchaser has been prejudiced by such action; and the purchaser who was the highest bidder will not be
compelled, by a decree of specific performance, to take the property.[*]

---

[*] In Fisher *v*. Hersey (17 *Hun*, 370), the sale was made in a partition suit of property in which the defendant had a five-eighths interest. Each of the two plaintiffs owned an undivided one-eighth
of the property and they bid it in for $32,500 at a sale held pursuant
to the judgment in partition. The plaintiffs then moved to set aside
the sale, on the ground that the defendant had employed a puffer
to enhance the price, and they were thereby induced to bid a larger
sum for the property than they would otherwise have bid. The
general term made an order setting aside the sale and ordering a
resale unless the defendant would stipulate to reduce the purchase

Bowman *v.* McClenahan.

Appeal by the plaintiff from a judgment of the Supreme Court, New York county, in favor of the defendant, entered upon the decision of the court rendered after a trial at Special Term.

The action was brought by Julius Bowman for the specific performance of an alleged contract for the pur-

---

price to $30,000. Upon appeal from this order the Court of Appeals dismissed the appeal upon the ground that it was within the discretion of the general term to order a resale. 78 *N. Y.* 387. The court further said that an order *refusing* a resale had been held appealable, where the conceded or established facts constituted a fraud in law (citing Howell *v.* Mills, 53 *N. Y.* 332), but said it did not follow that where a resale had been granted on allegations of fraud the order was necessarily reviewable.

In Dennerlein *v.* Dennerlein (111 *N. Y.* 518), an order of resale was refused by the court below (not on the ground that puffers had been employed, however), and the Court of Appeals again dismissed the appeal on the ground that the order was discretionary and there was nothing in the case making it an exception to the general rule which leaves each court to control the mode of executing its own judgment.

The rule as to the sale of goods is the same as that in reference to real property, and if the owner thereof bids at the sale and thus enhances the price the purchaser is not bound to take the goods. Trust *v.* Delaplaine, 3 *E. D. Smith*, 219.

See *L.* 1896, c. 376, §§50–54, regulating sales at auction of goods, etc. See, also, *L.* 1897, c. 682, regulating bonds of such auctioneers.

In Doolin *v.* Ward (6 *Johns.* 194), it was held that an agreement between two persons not to bid against each other at a public auction of goods, and that one should purchase the goods and divide them, was against public policy and void. To the same effect, see Wilson *v.* How, 8 *Johns.* 444.

" Arrangements and combinations among those prepared and expecting to become bidders at auctions to prevent competition, and bring about a sale at a price below the fair market value of the article sold, are condemned as immoral and against public policy, and tending to defraud the seller and all interested in the sale. Arrangements and agreements of this character will not be enforced between the bargainers, as directly opposed to the policy of encouraging bids, especially at public judicial sales, and tending to

chase of land made by the defendant, James McClenahan.
The property consists of a house and lot in West Forty-
first street belonging to the plaintiff.   On May 6, 1896,
with other lands belonging to the plaintiff, it was put up
to be sold at auction.   There were three pieces of land in
all, and the one in question was the last of the three to be
sold.   The first two were bid in for the plaintiff, but the
fact that they were so bid in was not made public at the
time of the sale.   After those two pieces had been struck
off, the third piece was put up for sale by the auctioneer.
It was started at $12,000 and was bid up to $27,000, at
which sum it was struck off to the defendant.   How many
bidders there were does not precisely appear, nor is it certain who made the last bid before the one at which it was
struck off, to the defendant.   It does appear, however,
without contradiction, that one of the sons of the plaintiff,
who was present at the sale, bid for the plaintiff upon the
property, and that he bid up at least as high as $20,000.

---

defraud the creditor at whose instance the sale is had, as well as
the debtor whose property is sold.   The same principle is applied to
the like bargains and arrangements to prevent competition at any
sale by public auction and for similar reasons.   Neither will courts
permit judicial sales to be consummated, nor enforce sales made as
between private individuals by auction, when by reason of such arrangements or combinations bidding has been prevented or property has been struck off at a price below its actual value, and the
sum for which it would or might have brought but for such illegal
interference with the bidding.   The general rule is, that a purchaser
at auction who uses unfair means to prevent competition cannot
hold the property." People *v.* Stephens, 71 *N. Y.* 527, 545.

"But . . . it is now settled that agreements between two
or more persons that all but one shall refrain from bidding, and permitting that one to become the purchaser are not necessarily and
under all circumstances void.   They may be entered into from hon-
est motives, and in such cases will be upheld and they will not vitiate the purchase or necessarily destroy the completed contracts to
which they refer and in respect to which they are made." Hopkins
v. Ensign, 122 *N. Y.* 144, 149.

Bowman *v.* McClenahan.

As to whether he bid any higher there was a dispute. It was stated by some of the witnesses, and, among others, by the auctioneer, that the last bid before the one at which the property was struck off to the defendant was made by some one who represented the plaintiff, and in this the auctioneer was corroborated by the defendant, who identified the person making the last bid before the one at which the property was struck off as the son of the plaintiff. This son, however, testified that he did not bid over $20,000. However the fact may be in that regard, it is not to be disputed that bids were made upon this property by which it was run up to a very substantial extent in behalf of the plaintiff, and that this was done privately and without notifying those present at the sale that puffers were to be employed or that anybody was to bid to represent the owner at the sale. The learned justice before whom this case was tried refused specific performance upon the ground, among others, that a puffer having been privately employed by the owner to bid upon the property in his behalf, it was a fraud upon real bidders, and that for that reason the purchaser would not be compelled to perform his contract.

Held, that the judgment should be affirmed. There is no doubt that it is competent for the owner of property who puts it up at auction to use some means to protect his interests and to see that his property is not sacrificed. It is conceded that he may do this either by fixing a price below which the property shall not be sold, and announcing that at the sale, or by publicly reserving to himself the right to make one or more bids if his interests shall require it. For the owner to protect his interests in this way, giving public notice of the fact that he has done so, certainly does not operate as a fraud upon anybody, for any one who begins to bid with the knowledge that these precautions have been taken upon the part of the owner, does so with notice of precisely what he has to meet. But that is a very different thing from giving private instructions to the auctioneer, or from privately procuring one to bid upon the sale in the interest of the owner, who is not to buy the property if he should be the highest bidder. The essence of a sale at auction is that the property offered shall go to the highest real bidder. Whenever it is put up that act constitutes an offer on the part of the owner, through the auctioneer as his agent, to sell to the person who shall bid the highest price for it, and every bid constitutes an offer on the part of the would-be purchaser to take it at the amount of the bid if it shall be struck off to him at that sum. It is well known that bidders at auction sales are influenced to a considerable extent by the number of other bidders, the amounts offered by them, and the apparent anxiety they show to become the owners of the property ; and if these conditions are affected by a private arrangement between the auctioneer and the owner, as the result of which persons who were not in reality intending to buy are allowed to appear as genuine competitors, it holds out to those who are real bidders false inducements, and makes false representations to them as to the desirability of the property and the demand for it, which in fact operate as a fraud upon them. For this reason it would seem, upon principle, that the private employment of a puffer by an owner at an auction sale rendered the sale void, and relieved the person to whom the property was struck off from the necessity of performing his contract.

Upon authority this question is not entirely free from doubt, although the preponderance, both of the cases and of the text writers, is in favor of the conclusion reached by the court below. In this country, while the courts are not unanimous, yet the great weight of authority is in favor of the doctrine announced in the court below. The leading case upon the subject, and one which should be deemed to be conclusive, is the case of Veazie *v.* Williams (8 *How.* 134) in the Supreme Court of the United States. That was an action brought in equity to rescind a sale at auction for the reason that the purchaser had been defrauded by the employment of a puffer at the sale, and thereby induced to bid much more than the value of the property. The serious question in the case was whether the employment of a puffer invalidated the sale, or entitled the purchaser to relief by having refunded to him the amount of his bid above the value of the property. The majority of the court held that the employment of a puffer operated as a fraud upon the real bidders, and that the plaintiff was entitled to be relieved by a repayment to him of the amount of the money which he had bid over the highest real bid.

In many of the States the same rule has been adopted. In the State of Pennsylvania there was some fluctuation in the cases, the supreme court at first holding that the employment of a puffer did not invalidate the sale if it was done solely with the intent of protecting the interest of the owner. Steele *v.* Ellmaker, 11 *S. & R.* 86. This case, however, was subsequently overruled, and it was held by the supreme court of that State that the employment even of a single puffer vitiates the sale (Pennock's Appeal, 14 *Penn. St.* 446; Staines *v.* Shore, 16 *Id.* 200), and that must be now regarded as the settled law of that State. The following cases may also be cited as establishing the same rule: Towle *v.* Leavitt, 23 *N. H.* 360; National Bank *v.* Sprague, 20 *N. J. Eq.* 159; Baham *v.* Bach, 13 *La. Ann.* 287; Smith *v.* Greenlee, 2 *Dev.* 126; Moncrieff *v.* Goldsborough, 4 *H. & McH.* 281; Curtis *v.* Aspinwall, 114 *Mass.* 187; Hartwell *v.* Gurney, 16 *R. I.* 78; Peck *v.* List, 23 *W. Va.* 338. The opinion of the text writers seems to agree with the majority of the authorities. 1 *Kent's Com.* p. *537; *Story on Sales,* § 482; *Sugden on Vendors,* c. 1, § 2; Judge STORY on *Eq. Jurisprudence,* § 293; *Pomeroy's Eq. Jurs.,* § 934.

In this State there is no authoritative decision upon the subject. In the case of Hazul *v.* Dunham (1 *Hall,* 655), Recorder Jay, sitting in the Mayor's court of New York, discusses the question, but it was not presented in that case, and the case itself is not authority. The question was presented in the case of Fisher *v.* Hersey (17 *Hun*, 370), and the general term of the fourth department held that, it appearing that the plaintiffs were induced by the action of the puffer to bid a higher price than they otherwise would have given, they were entitled to have the sale set aside absolutely. The general question was not discussed, and the court did not attempt to investigate the full extent of the doctrine. The limited doctrine announced in that case was more than enough upon the facts of the case to warrant the setting aside of the sale.

It is essential in sales of this kind that there should be the utmost good faith, and the employment by the owner of underhand means to enhance the apparent value of his property is not warranted by any principle of sound morality. When it appears that any such steps have been taken by him it is not necessary for the person insisting upon the invalidity of the sale to show that any harm resulted to him from the improper act. If the fact that no harm resulted is material at all, and we cannot see how it is so, the burden of proving it should be upon the person who has employed the puffers to bid up the price of his property. But the sounder rule, as we think, and the only safe rule to be applied in this transaction, is that a sale at auction must be actually in all cases what it is nominally, an offer by the owner to sell the property to the highest bidder, without any qualification, unless he shall reserve to himself openly at the time of the sale the right to bid upon the property, or shall openly announce a price below which the property shall not be sold.

Opinion by RUMSEY, J. VAN BRUNT, P. J., PATTERSON, O'BRIEN and PARKER, JJ., concurred.

Judgment affirmed, with costs.

Edward W. S. Johnston, for the plaintiff, appellant.

John Hardy, for the defendant, respondent.

BLACKMER *v.* GREENE.

*Supreme Court, Third Department, Appellate Division;
September,* 1897.

1. *Judgment ; by confession ; insufficient statement.*] The statement in a judgment by confession that it is for a debt due to
the plaintiffs " for a balance due for goods, wares and merchandise, sold and delivered to me, the defendant, by the plaintiff, and remaining unpaid and unsecured," is insufficient, within
Code Civ. Pro. § 1274.*

2. *The same ; amendment.*] As against a subsequent judgment
creditor who applies to vacate the judgment an amendment of
the statement should not be allowed.†

*Compare Harrison *v.* Gibbons (71 *N. Y.* 58), where the following
statement was held sufficient : " The following is a statement of
facts upon which said confession of judgment is founded ; that said
Gibbons was for a long time absent from the State of New York
and engaged in the occupation of mining in the State of California
and territory thereto adjoining ; that during his said business and
prior to his leaving said Brockport for said California, he has and
had obtained groceries, provisions, crockery, money, flour, etc., to
the amount of $1,109.41, including interest, of John Owens who has
duly assigned the same to said Harrison ; that since his return to
said Brockport, he has incurred a debt to said Harrison amounting
to the sum of $92.28, being for groceries, provisions furnished by
said Harrison for the use of his family ; that there is now justly
due and owing said Harrison, over and above all off-sets and payments, the sum of $1,207.69."

As to what is generally a sufficient statement for a confession of
judgment, see Read *v.* French, 28 *N. Y.* 285 ; Clements *v.* Gerow, 1
Keyes, 297 ; Delaware *v.* Ensign, 21 *Barb.* 85 ; Kellogg *v.* Cowing, 33
N. Y. 408.

For a confession on promissory notes, see Bonnell *v.* Henry, 13
How. Pr. 142; Dunham *v.* Waterman, 17 *Id.* 9 ; Murray *v.* Judson,
9 *Id.* 73 ; Chappel *v.* Chappel, 12 *Id.* 215 ; Freligh *v.* Brink, 22 *Id.*
418.

† The supreme court has power in its discretion to allow the
amendment of a statement contained in a confession of judgment.

Blackmer *v.* Greene.

Appeal by John. H. Robinson from an order of the Supreme Court, Saratoga Special Term, denying his motion to set aside the judgment in favor of the plaintiff, entered by confession.

This is an appeal by John H. Robinson, a judgment creditor, subsequent to the judgment of the plaintiff, from an order denying his motion to set aside the judgment obtained by the plaintiff, William W. Blackmer, on the confession of the defendant, Fred C. Greene. The statement on which said judgment was entered recites the facts out of which the debt arose as follows : " This confession of judgment is for a debt and liability justly due to the said plaintiff, arising upon the following facts, viz : being for a balance due for goods, wares and merchandise sold and delivered to me, Fred. C. Greene, by the plaintiff, William W. Blackmer, and remaining unpaid and unsecured."

Held, that this statement was insufficient to meet the requirements of Code of Civ. Pro. § 1274. See Wood *v.* Mitchell, 117 *N. Y.* 439; s. c., 27 *St* R. 704; rev'g 53 *Hun*, 451 ; s. c., 25 *St. R.* 147 ; 6 *Supp.* 232; 17 *Civ. Pro.* 346. In that case the statement on which the judgment was obtained was as follows : " The said sum of $5,000 is a balance due to said plaintiff of various sums of money loaned and advanced by him to me, the said defendant, during a period from July 1, 1886, to date, and includes interest upon such loans and advances to this date." It was held to be too indefinite and deficient to meet the requirements of the Code of Civil Procedure, and that the denial of a motion on the part of a subsequent judgment creditor to set aside the judgment was error.

The case of Critten *v.* Vredenburgh (4 *App. Div.* 216 ; aff'd 151 *N. Y.* 536) does not lay down any different doctrine from that stated in Wood *v.* Mitchell (*supra*). In

Union Bank of Sullivan Co. *v.* Bush, 36 *N. Y.* 631 ; Mitchell *v.* Van Buren, 27 *Id.* 300: National Park Bank *v.* Salomon, 17 *Civ. Pro. R.* 8.

Blackmer *v.* Greene.

Critten *v.* Vredenburgh the statement on which the judgment was entered was as follows: That between March 1, 1893, and October 1, 1895, the plaintiffs, as copartners, loaned and advanced to the defendant divers and sundry sums of money, which he agreed to repay with interest, did and performed work, labor and services for the defendant in selling merchandise upon commission and guaranteeing the accounts for the same, and that on October 1, 1895, there was an adjustment of the accounts between the plaintiffs and defendant concerning the said matters, and that the sum of $19,879.02 was found due the plaintiffs, which the defendant agreed to pay with interest. The statement was held sufficient because it set forth an account stated, on the authority of Broisted *v.* Breslin (5 *St. Rep.* 67 ; aff'd, without opinion, 105 *N. Y.* 682), the court assuming that, without the averment of an account stated, the statement, which was similar to that under consideration, would have been insufficient.

As against the appellant, we are of opinion that it would not be proper to allow an amendment of the statement on which the judgment was granted. See Bradley *v.* Glass, 20 *App. Div.* 200.

Opinion PER CURIAM.   All concurred.

Order reversed, with ten dollars costs and disbursements, and motion to set aside judgment granted, with ten dollars costs.

Edgar T. Brackett, for the defendant, appellant.

William J. Miner, and *Charles H. Sturges,* for the plaintiff, respondent.

SEVENTY-THIRD STREET BUILDING CO. *v.* JENCKS.

Supreme Court, First Department, Appellate Division; June, 1897.

1. *Covenants against incumbrances; mortgage; damages.*] Where a deed contained a covenant against incumbrances, and there was an unsatisfied mortgage against six inches of the property, which was not specified in the deed, and the grantee subsequently conveyed the property to another party, who immediately brought action against the original grantor, without removing the incumbrance and before any action had been taken to eject him,—*Held,* that the plaintiff was entitled to nominal damages only.*

2. *The same; does not run with the land.*] *It seems,* that a covenant against incumbrances does not run with the land, and where a covenant contained in such a deed has been broken, if at all, immediately upon the delivery of the deed, a subsequent grantee has no right of action against the original grantor, as there is no privity between the parties.†

---

* In Utica, Chenango & S. V. R. R. Co. *v.* Gates (3 *N. Y. Ann. Cas.* 242), it was held that where a grantee in a deed of premises containing a covenant against incumbrances has been compelled, in order to protect his possession, to pay off the incumbrances, the measure of damages in an action upon such covenant was the amount so paid with interest, not to exceed the true value of the premises; the recovery is not limited to the purchase price of the premises. In that case the decisions which have held that the damages could not exceed the purchase price, are reviewed, and the court reaches the conclusion that such measure of damages is not the true one in all cases. See also cases there cited in the footnotes.

For a breach of a covenant against incumbrances, only the amount actually paid to relieve the premises therefrom can be recovered, and in no event can the recovery exceed the amount of the consideration for which the deed was given. Andrews *v.* Appel, 22 *Hun,* 429.

† " In the United States the local habit and usage varies more or less widely between the different States, and occasionally between different parts of the same State; but in general, what are here

Seventy-third Street Building Co. *v.* Jencks.

Appeal by the plaintiff from a judgment of the Supreme Court in favor of the defendant for costs, entered upon the decision of the court, rendered after a trial at the New York Special Term, adjudging that the plaintiff was only entitled to nominal damages for the breach of a covenant against incumbrances.

often called ' full covenants ' are the covenants for seisin, for right to convey, against incumbrances, for quiet enjoyment, sometimes for further assurance, and almost always of warranty, the last often taking the place of the covenant for quiet enjoyment. Rawle on Covenants for Title, 27. The first three mentioned are personal covenants, not running with the land, or passing to the assignee ; for if not true, there is a breach of them as soon as the deed is executed, and they become choses in action which are not technically assignable." 2 *Wait's Actions and Defenses,* 372 ; Greenby *v.* Wilcocks, 2 *Johns* 1 ; Withy *v.* Mumford, 5 *Cow.* 137.

" The weight of American authority undoubtedly is that the covenant against incumbrances, as generally expressed, standing by itself as a separate and independent covenant, is a covenant *in praesenti.* Being broken, if at all, at the instant of its creation, it is thereby turned into a mere right of action which is not assignable at law, which can be taken advantage of only by the covenantee, or his personal representatives, and can neither pass to an heir, a devisee, nor a subsequent purchaser ; in other words, it does not run with the land. But it has been generally considered, both in England and in this country, that when the covenant against incumbrances is coupled with that for quiet enjoyment, it depends, for its construction, upon the latter, of which it thus forms a part, and is to all intents and for all purposes a covenant *in futuro,* and until breach it runs with the land." Hall *v.* Dean, 13 *Johns.* 105.

In Andrews *v.* Appel (22 *Hun,* 429), it is said at page 432 : " The plaintiff is the grantee and assignee of the covenants contained in the deed of the defendants, and after becoming such, paid off the taxes laid by assessments upon the lands, and thus redeemed the lands from the sale made to enforce the taxes. The taxes were liens upon the land when the covenant of defendants was made. Under such circumstances the plaintiff was the real party in interest who sustained actual damage, having acquired the right to enforce the covenant by an equitable and incidental assignment against incumbrances given by the defendant. Such a rule avoids a circuity and

Seventy-third Street Building Co. *v.* Jencks.

The incumbrance complained of was a mortgage which was a lien upon six inches of a plot of land conveyed by the defendant, Francis W. Jencks, to the plaintiff's grantor, by a deed which contained a covenant against incumbrances, and did not specify the mortgage in question. The deed under which the plaintiff derived title contained a similar covenant, but also omitted to specify the mortgage.

The plaintiff did not pay the incumbrance, but brought this action to recover the damages which it claimed to

---

multiplicity of actions. The objection existing at common law that a covenant or a chose in action, was not assignable has been obviated by modern legislation." In that case the covenant upon which the suit was brought ran to "the assigns" of the first grantee, and the court there held that it ran with the land so that a subsequent grantee could sue the original covenantors.

An assignee may recover when the covenant is with the grantee, "his heirs or assigns." Colby *v.* Osgood, 29 *Barb.* 339.

In Mc Guckin *v.* Milbank (152 *N. Y.* 297), a deed to the plaintiff of a number of lots of land contained a covenant against incumbrances. The plaintiff subsequently sold all of the lots except one, and it then appearing that there was an incumbrance upon all the lots, he brought an action against his grantee to recover damages because of a breach of the covenant as to all of the land. The court there said, as it did not appear that the plaintiff had given deeds containing covenants against incumbrances to his grantees, he could not in any event recover damages for a breach of the covenant, except as to a lot which he owned when the action was begun, unless he had previously suffered damages because of the incumbrance, and the court further remarks, at page 303: "The plaintiff, upon the proofs, was not bound to indemnify his grantees, and the benefit of the covenant did not pass to them by the conveyances from the plaintiff." This language seems to suggest that the covenant of the original grantor would not pass to a subsequent grantee.

Where a grantor covenanted to pay a judgment of record against him and which was a lien upon the land conveyed,—*Held*, that this was not merely a covenant against incumbrances, and that the grantee could recover against the grantor the amount of the judgment whether he had paid it or not. Bristor *v.* McBean, 1 *App. Div.* 217 ; s. c., 72 *St. R.* 658 ; 37 *Supp.* 181.

have sustained because of the fact that a person to whom it had contracted to sell the premises refused to take title because of the incumbrance, and it was thereafter compelled to dispose of the premises at a lower price than that fixed in the contract of sale.

Held, that, assuming that the decision overruling the demurrer was conclusive upon the right of the plaintiff to recover in this action, and that upon this appeal the court could not determine the question of the right of the plaintiff as a grantee of the property which was conveyed to its grantor by the deed which contained the covenant, the court below was clearly right in holding' that the plaintiff was entitled to nominal damages only. The covenant in question was a covenant against incumbrances, and there can be no doubt but that there was a breach of that covenant. That covenant, however, is of such a nature that, if there was a breach, such breach must have existed immediately upon the execution and delivery of the deed. When the deed was delivered, there was either an incumbrance upon the land in violation of such covenant or there was not. If there was, then there was a breach of the covenant, and a cause of action immediately rose in favor of the grantee in the deed. It is not apparent to me upon what principle a person who was a subsequent grantee of the property to which the covenant related, which was broken when the original deed was delivered, can sue to enforce the covenant. Immediately upon the covenant being broken, a right of action vested in the grantee in the deed which contained the covenant, and that right of action could be enforced against the defendant. When the grantee in that deed came to sell the property, if it appeared that, in consequence of this incumbrance, he received a less price than he would have received if the incumbrance had not existed, he could have recovered as damages the difference between the price that he actually realized and what he would have realized if there had been no incumbrance upon the property. McGuckin *v.* Milbank, 152 *N. Y.* 302.

How, then, can the purchaser from such a grantee also sue to recover for the damages that he has sustained because of an incumbrance upon the property which a former owner had covenanted with some one else was not on the property? There was certainly no privity of contract between the parties, and a covenant against incumbrances has never been held to run with the land.

Assuming, however, that the plaintiff in this case stood in the shoes of his grantor as entitled to enforce this covenant, still the measure of damages for a violation of such covenant would not justify a recovery for any of the items of damage claimed by the plaintiff. He has not paid any incumbrance upon this land. He was not disturbed in *its* possession, and, therefore, he was not entitled to recover more than nominal damages. McGuckin *v.* Milbank (*supra*).

Opinion by INGRAHAM, J. VAN BRUNT, P. J., RUMSEY, WILLIAMS and PARKER, JJ., concurred.

Judgment affirmed, with costs.

Allen G. N. Vermilya, for the plaintiff, appellant.

Ernest Hall, for the defendant, respondent.

INDEX.

A.

ABATEMENT AND REVIVAL—Two causes of action joined where only one survives ; terms on granting order, 375.

ABUSE OF PROCESS—Subpœna of defendant at distance ; attorney's liability, 170.

Note on actions for abuse of process, 176.

ACKNOWLEDGMENT—Notary's personal acquaintance with party ; general rule, 161.

Of assignment of mortgage before grantee, void, 155.

ACTIONS—For damages for causing non-payment of alimony ; novelty, 1.

Note on actions without precedent, 15.

To vacate a judgment for non-service of process ; prior denial of motion, 25.

Note on consolidation of actions, 205.

Note on separate actions for injuries to person and property from the same tort, 212.

Stay ; action in another jurisdiction, 294.

Suspension of right to sue ; acceptance of note, 279.

Note on suspension of right to sue by acceptance of note, etc., 282.

Note on actions on Lloyds' policies, 307.

AFFIDAVIT—Attachment ; assignee ; mere averment of positive knowledge, insufficient, 86.

Attachment ; positive averments upon undisclosed sources of information, 82.

To procure physical examination before trial, 305.

APPEAL—Error considered in charge, though no exception
        taken, 7.

    Evidence not in record, 124.

    Judicial notice; evidence, 114.

    Note on introduction of evidence on appeal, 127.

    Court of Appeals; final order; special proceeding;
        motion to vacate satisfaction of judgment in fraud
        of attorney's lien, 288.

    From order denying motion to set aside verdict of
        sheriff's jury, 332.

    Power of appellate court to modify judgment to con-
        form to decision below, 228.

APPEARANCE—By defendant designated in representative
        capacity; effect, 379.

ASSIGNMENT FOR CREDITORS—Assignee's liability for
        rent, 114.

ATTACHMENT—Affidavit; assignee; mere averment of positive
        knowledge, insufficient, 86.

    Affidavit; positive averments upon undisclosed
        sources of information, 82.

    Merits of cause of action not considered on
        motion to vacate, 241.

    Undertaking; amount; increase; unliquidated
        damages, 65.

    Motion to vacate; reference, 136.

    Levy; instrument for payment of money; fire
        insurance policy, 300.

    False oath of surety on bond; contempt; who
        can maintain proceedings, 270.

    Priority of lien over claim for taxes, 352.

    Trial of title to property by sheriff's jury;
        appeal, 332.

    Levy; instrument for payment of money only;
        unmatured life policy, 335.

    *Note on levy of attachment and execution on
        choses in action,* 345.

ATTORNEY AND CLIENT—Attorney's lien; notice; when sat-
        isfaction of judgment will be
        vacated, 288.

    Loss of attorney's lien by refusal
        to proceed; substitution, 232.

    Attorney's liability; abuse of pro-
        cess; subpœna, 170.

AUCTIONS—Employment of puffers; sale of real estate, 388.

B.

BAILMENT—Liability of officer for public money lost by failure of bank, 50.

BILLS, NOTES AND CHECKS—Acceptance of note for debt; suspension of right to sue, 279.

BLASTING—Negligence; injury to property ; injunction ; liability of contractor and principal, 70.

C.

CALENDAR—Preference by plaintiff; defendant arrested; attachment, 251.

Note on preference on the calendar, 253.

CAUSE OF ACTION—Novelty of claim ; action for causing non-payment of alimony, 1.

Action for slander of plaintiff's deceased child, 7.

Action for damages for fraud inducing marriage, 11.

Note on actions without precedent, 15.

CODE CIV. PRO.—§ 14, subd. 4. (Contempt.) 270.

§ 66. (Attorney's lien.) 232, 288.

§ 190, subd. 1. (Appeal to Court of Appeals.) 288.

§ 315. (N. Y. City Court.) 201, 202.

§ 316. (N. Y. City Court.) 200, 201, 202.

§ 325. (Referee's fees.) 48, *n.*

§ 383, subd. 5. (Limitation of Action.) 185.

§ 418. (Summons.) 192.

§ 419. (Summons.) 190, 192.

§ 420. (Judgment by Default.) 192.

§ 423. (Costs.) 164.

§ 432. (Service of Summons.) 248.

§ 449. (Parties.) 369.

§ 452. (Parties.) 194, 196.

§ 516. (Pleading.) 219, 222.

§ 572. (Execution.) 316.

§ 635. (Attachment.) 244.

§ 648. (Attachment.) 337.

§ 649. (Attachment.) 300, 335, 337, 345, 347, 348.

CODE CIV. PRO.—§ 655. (Attachment.) 346.

§ 635, as am'd *L.* 1895, c. 578. (Attachment.) 248.

§ 682. (Attachment.) 65.

§ 687–690. (Attachment.) 66, *n.*

§ 717. (Crimes.) 384.

§ 755. (Abatement.) 375, *n.*, 377.

§ 757. (Abatement.) 375, 376, *n.*, 377, 378.

§ 764. (Abatement and Revival.) 56, *n.*

§ 790, *et seq.* (Preference on Calendar.) 253.

§ 812. (Undertaking.) 66, *n.*

§ 817. (Consolidation of Actions.) 200, 201, 205.

§ 818. (Consolidation of Actions.) 205.

§ 855, *et seq.* (Contempt.) 308.

§§ 870, 873. (Depositions.) 306.

§ 872. (Depositions.) 167.

§ 873. (Physical Examination.) 24, 167.

§ 915. (Commission.) 308.

§§ 935, 936. (Acknowledgments.) 163.

§ 1000. (Exceptions.) 183.

§ 1015. (Reference.) 140, *n.*

§ 1217. (Entering judgment.) 248.

§ 1240. (Execution.) 313.

§ 1253. (Execution.) 351.

§ 1274. (Confession of judgment.) 395.

§ 1317. (Appeal.) 228.

§ 1380. (Execution.) 122.

§ 1393. (Exemption.) 124, *n.*

§ 1405, *et seq.* (Execution.) 348.

§ 1411. (Attachment.) 344, 348.

§ 1412. (Execution.) 348.

§§ 1418, 1419. (Attachment.) 333, *n.*, 334.

§§ 1421, 1427. (Sheriff.) 62, *n.*, 64.

§ 1434. (Publication.) 96, 98.

§ 1487. (Execution.) 313.

§ 1659. (Jury's View.) 23.

§ 1678. (Nature of Sale.) 98.

§§ 1709–1711. (Sheriff.) 60.

§ 1710. (Sheriff.) 59.

§ 1774. (Service of Summons.) 248.

§ 1778. (Trial.) 338.

§ 1780. (Foreign Corporations.) 78, *n.*, 79, *n.*, 247.

§ 1873–5. (Execution.) 351, 352.

CODE CIV. PRO.—§ 1900. (Vexatious Action.) 174.

§ 1902. (Death.) 9.

§ 1948, *et seq.* (Corporations.) 369.

§ 2447. (Supplementary Proceedings.) 289.

§ 2468. (Receiver.) 381.

§ 2554. (Enforcement of Surrogate's Decree.) 269.

§ 2555. (Contempt.) 265.

§ 2695. (Executors.) 56, *n.*

§ 2870. (Contempt.) 312.

§ 2895. (Arrest.) 315.

§§ 2974, 2977. (Contempt.) 312.

§ 3245. (Municipal Corporation.) 183, *n.*

§ 3253. (Additional Allowance.) 164.

§ 3296. (Referee's Fees.) 48, *n.*

§ 3347, subd. 6. (Application of Code). 200, 202, 205.

CODE CRIM. PRO.—§ 411. (Jury's View.) 23.

CODE. PRO.—§ 427. (Jurisdiction.) 247.

CONFESSION OF JUDGMENT—For goods sold; insufficient statement; amendment, 395.

CONSOLIDATION OF ACTIONS—In N. Y. City Court; monetary jurisdiction, 200.

Note on consolidation of actions, 205.

CONSTITUTION—Art. VI. § 9. (Appeal to Court of Appeals,) 288.

CONTEMPT—Non-payment of alimony; remedy by action for damages, 1.

Surrogate's Court; order for payment of costs, 265.

Supplementary proceedings; after-acquired property; rents from lease, 40.

Failure to complete purchase; judicial sale, 275.

False oath of surety on attachment bond to sheriff; who can maintain proceedings, 270.

Refusal of witness to answer; commission from foreign court, 308.

CONTRACTS—Sale of real estate at auction; employment of puffers; validity, 388.

Time, when essence of; building; waiver, 102.

Note on when time is of the essence of a contract, 106.

CONVERSION—Sheriff; substitution of indemnitors, 59.

Note on substitution of sheriff's indemnitors, 62.

CORPORATIONS—Inspection of books by stockholder ; damages
for refusal ; expenses of mandamus proceedings, 166.

      De facto directors ; liability, 237.

      Insolvency ; preference of wages, 249.

      Priority of lien of attachment or execution on
corporate property over claim for taxes,
352.

COSTS—Extra allowance to defendant in foreclosure ; amount,
161.

      Action for conversion ; execution against person of
plaintiff, 313.

      Order for payment of, in Surrogate's Court ; contempt,
265.

COVENANT—Against incumbrances ; does not run with land ;
mortgage ; damages, 398.

CREDITOR'S SUIT—Judgment ; when appointment of receiver
unnecessary, 120.

D.

DAMAGES—Measure of ; for causing death by negligence, 129.

      Breach of covenant against incumbrances ; mortgage ;
nominal only, 398.

      Persons holding ticket ejected from place of amuse-
ment ; insults by other patrons of the place, 317.

DEATH—Mother's action against physician for negligence causing child's death, 7.

      Proximate cause ; common law rule ; question for jury ;
measure of damages, 129.

      Of defendant ; revival of action ; joinder of causes, 375.

DEBTOR AND CREDITOR—Promissory note; acceptance for
debt; suspension of right to
sue, 279.

      *Note on suspension of right to sue by
acceptance of note, etc.,* 282.

DEEDS—Covenant against incumbrances, when broken; personal;
damages, 398.

DEFENSE—Former adjudication ; judgment for goods sold and
delivered ; subsequent action for fraud, 90.

      Note on remedy for fraud after suit on contract, 93.

      Former action pending ; different State; action on
contract ; non-resident parties, 77.

DEPOSITION—Examination before trial; non-resident officers of corporation defendant, 328.

    Commission from foreign court; refusal of witness to answer; contempt. 308.

    Physical examination before trial; recovery of plaintiff from injuries, 305.

DISMISSAL OF COMPLAINT—When on the merits, 151.

DIVORCE—Alimony; action for damages for causing non-payment, 1.

E.

ELECTION OF REMEDIES—Judgment against agent; undisclosed principal, 141.

EVIDENCE—Physical exhibits; foot cut off in accident preserved in alcohol, 19.

    Note on physical exhibits at the trial, 23.

    Judicial notice; Sunday; appeal, 114.

    Parol proof of contents of letter, 170.

    Action for *res gestae;* expulsion from place of amusement; insults from other parties, 317.

    Appeal; supplying defects in record, 124.

    Note on introduction of evidence on appeal, 127.

    Value; *quantum meruit;* special contract, 102.

EXCISE LAW—Mortgage of tax certificate; validity; wrongful sale; misdemeanor, 384.

EXECUTION—Levy on promissory note; possession; custodian named by plaintiff's attorney, 340.

    Note on levy of attachment and execution on choses in action, 345.

EXECUTION—Priority of lien over claim for taxes, 352.

    Against person of plaintiff; action for conversion; costs, 313.

EXECUTORS AND ADMINISTRATORS—Foreign; capacity to sue; substitution on defendant's death, 56.

EXEMPTION—Taxes; house bought with pension money, 124.

F.

FEES—Of referee; overpayment; order of repayment, 47.

FOREIGN CORPORATIONS—Insolvency; unlawful preference to officer; remedy, 145.

FORMER ACTION PENDING—Defense ; different State, 77.

FORMER ADJUDICATION—Order denying motion to vacate judgment: effect on subsequent action to vacate, 25.

Successive actions for same negligence: injuries to person and property, 209.

Set up by supplemental answer, 214.

Judgment for goods sold and delivered ; subsequent action for fraud, 90.

Note on remedy for fraud after suit on contract, 93.

FRAUD—Of third party inducing marriage ; action for damages, 11.

Procuring satisfaction of debt on false plea of poverty, 233

Action for, after judgment for goods sold and delivered, 90.

Note on remedy for fraud after suit on contract, 93.

H.

HUSBAND AND WIFE—Action for damages for causing non-payment of alimony, 1.

marriage induced by fraud of third party ; action for damages, 11.

I.

INJUNCTION—Negligence ; blasting ; injury to property ; adequate remedy at law ; liability of contractor and principal, 70.

INSURANCE—Fire, Lloyds' policy; action against individual members ; defense of stipulation to sue attorneys ; service of proofs of loss ; change of agent, 357.

Note on actions on Lloyds' policies, 367.

J.

JOINDER OF CAUSES—Death of defendant ; revival of action where one only of two causes joined survives, 375.

JUDGMENT—Non-service of process ; remedy by action to vacate; prior order denying motion to vacate; effect, 25.

Power of appellate court to modify to conform to decision below, 228.

By confession; insufficient statement ; claim for goods sold ; amendment, 395.

JUDICIAL SALE—Contempt ; failure to complete purchase, 275.

What is a newspaper, 96.

JURISDICTION—Action on contract ; non-resident parties, 77.

Non-residents ; action on contract, 241.

Note on jurisdiction of non-residents, 243.

Stipulation of parties ; supplementary proceedings, 370.

L.

LAWS—*L.* 1710. (Recording deeds.) 158.

1771. (Recording deeds.) 159.

1880, c. 245. (Execution.) 351.

1881, c. 361. (Taxes.) 350.

1882, c. 410, § 1104. (N. Y. City Consolidation Act.) 187.

1884, c. 328. (Preference of wages.) 249.

1885, c. 26. (Syracuse.) 183, *n.*

1885, c. 376. (Preference of wages.) 249.

1886, c. 572. (Municipal corporations.) 182, 183, *n.* 184, 186.

1887, c. 182. (Sheriff.) 61, 62, *n.,* 64.

1887, c. 453. (Sheriff.) 62, *n.,* 64, *n.*

1892, c. 401, § 26, as amended *L.* 1893, c. 480. (Excise.) 384, *n.*

1892, c. 677. (Personal property.) 386.

1892, c. 688, § 20. (Stock corporations.) 239.

1892, c. 688, § 29. (Stock corporations.) 166, 167.

1892, c. 690. (Insurance.) 335, 364.

1892, c. 691, § 2. (Stock corporations.) 239.

1894, c. 684. (Insurance.) 364.

1896, c. 90. Referee's fees.) 48, *n.*

1896, c. 112. (Liquor tax law.) 384, 386.

1896, c. 140. (Preference on calendar. 254.

1896, c. 376, §§ 50-54. (Auctions.) 389, *n.*

1897, c. 348. (Exemption.) 124, *n.*

1897, c. 384. (Foreign corporations.) 146.

1897, c. 682. (Auctions.) 389, *n.*

LICENSE—Place of amusement; right to eject one holding ticket, 317.

M.

MALICIOUS PROSECUTION—Abuse of process; attorney's liability, 170.
　　　　　Note on actions for abuse of process, 176.
MARRIAGE—Action against third party for fraud in inducing, 11.
MORTGAGE—Acknowledgment of assignment before grantee, void, 155.
　　　　　Of liquor tax certificate; validity; wrongful sale, 384.
MOTIONS AND ORDERS—Order as *res adjudicata*; motion to vacate judgment; subsequent action, 25.
　　　　　Renewal of motion; different grounds; leave, 32.
　　　　　Note on renewal of motion, 35.
　　　　　Reference on motion to vacate attachment, 140.
　　　　　Note on reference of issues arising on motions, 140.
MUNICIPAL CORPORATIONS—Action for loss of service; filing claim before suit, 182.
　　　　　Action for negligence; notice of intention to sue, how filed, 186.

N.

NEGLIGENCE—Of physician; mother's action for child's death, 7.
　　　　　Blasting; injury to property; injunction; liability of contractor and principal, 70.
　　　　　What is action for personal injuries; action for loss of service against city; filing claim, 182.
　　　　　Action against city; notice of intention to sue, how filed, 186.
　　　　　Death; proximate cause; question for jury; common law rule, 129.

NEGLIGENCE—Successive actions for injuries to person and property from same tort, 209.

Note on separate actions for injuries to person and property from the same tort, 212.

NEWSPAPER—What is ; judicial sale, 96.

N. Y. CITY COURT—Consolidation of actions ; monetary jurisdiction, 200.

NON-RESIDENTS—When courts take jurisdiction of actions by, 241.

Note on jurisdiction of non-residents, 243.

NOTARY PUBLIC—When disqualified by interest, 155.

Personal acquaintance with person acknowledging execution ; general rule, 161.

O.

OFFICERS—Liability for public money lost by failure of bank, 50.

P.

PARTIES—Substitution of sheriff's indemnitors, 59.

Note on substitution of sheriff's indemnitors, 62.

Foreign executor ; capacity to sue ; substitution, 56.

Non-residents ; action on contract, 77.

Defendant ; designation when sued in representative capacity ; effect of appearance, 379.

Right to be made defendant without terms, 194.

PEN. CODE—§ 383. (Place of amusement,) 317.

§ 571. (Mortgaged property,) 384.

PLEADING—Complaint in tort after summons with notice, 190.

Statute of frauds in defense ; general denial, 322.

Note on pleading statute of frauds, 325.

Defense of stipulation as to suit on Lloyds' policy, 357.

Supplemental answer, when should be allowed ; adjudication after answer, 214.

Reply, when ordered ; action against partners ; answer of special partnership, 219.

R.

RECEIVERS—When appointment of, unnecessary in creditor's suit, 120.

Manner of designation as defendant in summons ; effect of appearance, 379.

REFERENCE—New referee; evidence taken before former referee not considered, 297.

Motion to vacate attachment; general rule on motions, 136.

Note on reference of issues arising on motions, 136.

Opening to submit further evidence; referee's discretion, 370.

Referee's fees; taxation; overpayment; order for repayment, 47.

REVISED LAWS—L. 1813, page 49; (Contempt,) 312.

REVISED STATUTES—1 R. S. 744, § 45 (Execution,) 351.

2 R. S. 63, § 40; (Subscription to will,) 259.

2 R. S. 397, 398, §§ 29, 32; (Contempt,) 312.

2 R. S. 400, § 42, 49 (Contempt,) 312.

2 R. S. 459, § 15, am'd L. 1849, c. 107, (Foreign corporations,) 247.

2 R. S. 499, § 17, (Executor de son tort,) 168.

2 R. S. 1283, § 6 (8th ed.) (Supervisors,) 54.

2 R. S. (9th ed.) 1836, §§ 9, 15 (Acknowledgments,) 162, *n.*

2 R. S. (9th ed.) 1842, § 41, (Recording mortgages,) 156.

2 R. S. (9th ed.) 1877, § 40; (Subscription to will,) 261.

RULES OF COURT—Rule 1, Fourth Department; preference on calendar, 254.

Rule 3, Third Department; preference on calendar, 254.

Rule 4, undertaking on attachment, 65 *n.*

Rule 6, App. Div. First Department; preference on calendar, 253.

Rule 11, First Department; preference on calendar, 254.

Rule 14, New York City Court; preference on calendar, 254.

Rule 36; preference on calendar, 251.

S.

SERVICE OF SUMMONS—Action to vacate judgment for non-service, 25.

SHERIFF—Conversion ; substitution of indemnitors, 59.
Note on substitution of sheriff's indemnitors, 62.
Review by appeal from determination of sheriff's jury as to ownership of attached property, 332.

SLANDER—Action by mother for slander of deceased child, 7.

STAY OF PROCEEDINGS—Actions pending in different jurisdictions, 294.

STATUTE OF FRAUDS—Pleading, in defense ; general denial, 322.
Note on pleading statute of frauds, 325.

STOCK CORPORATION LAW—Art. 3, § 60. (Liability of officers,) 145.

SUMMONS—With notice ; complaint framed for tort, 190.

SUPPLEMENTARY PROCEEDINGS—What property reached ; contempt ; after acquired property ; rents from lease, 40.
Reference to determine disputed title to fund ; jurisdiction ; stipulation, 370.

SURROGATE'S COURT—Contempt ; order for payment of costs, 265.

T.

TAXES—Exemption ; house bought with pension money, 124.
Against corporations ; priority of lien of execution or attachment, 352.

THEATRE—Right to eject ticket-holder, 317.

TIME--When of essence of contract ; waiver, 102.
Note on when time is of the essence of a contract, 106.

TRIAL—Preference on calendar ; defendant under arrest ; plaintiff's motion, 251.
Note on preference on the calendar, 253.
Physical exhibits ; foot cut off in accident, preserved in alcohol, 19.
Note on physical exhibits at the trial, 23.
Proximate cause of death from negligence ; question for jury, 129.

TRIAL—Physical examination; affidavit; general rule; recovery
of plaintiff from injuries, 305.

New referee; evidence taken before former referee not
considered, 297.

Requests to charge, when to be made, 43.

Determination of sheriff's jury as to title to attached property; review by appeal, 332.

U.

UNDERTAKING—On attachment; interest on amount; unliquidated damages, 65.

W.

WAIVER—Of time as essence of contract, 102.

WILL—When not subscribed at end, within statute, 259.

Note on testator's subscription at end of will, 261.

WITNESS—Refusal to answer; contempt; commission from foreign court, 308.

Lightning Source UK Ltd.
Milton Keynes UK
UKHW022011090119
335262UK00010B/872/P